EU CRIMINAL LAW AFTER LISBON

This monograph is the first comprehensive analysis of the impact of the entry into force of the Treaty of Lisbon on EU criminal law. By focusing on key areas of criminal law and procedure, the book assesses the extent to which the entry into force of the Lisbon Treaty has transformed European criminal justice, and evaluates the impact of post-Lisbon legislation on national criminal justice systems. The monograph examines the constitutionalisation of EU criminal law after Lisbon, by focusing on the impact of institutional and constitutional developments in the field including the influence of the EU Charter of Fundamental Rights on EU criminal law. The analysis covers aspects of criminal justice ranging from criminalisation to judicial co-operation to prosecution to the enforcement of sanctions. The book contains a detailed analysis and evaluation of the powers of the Union to harmonise substantive criminal law and the influence of European Union law on national substantive criminal law; of the evolution of the Europeanisation of prosecution from horizontal co-operation between national criminal justice to forms of vertical integration in the field of prosecution as embodied in the evolution of Eurojust and the establishment of a European Public Prosecutor's Office; of the operation of the principle of mutual recognition (by focusing in particular on the European Arrest Warrant system) and its impact on the relationship between mutual trust and fundamental rights; of EU legislation in the field on criminal procedure, including legislation on the rights of the defendant and the victim; of the relationship between EU criminal law and citizenship of the Union; and of the evolution of an EU model of preventive justice, as exemplified by the proliferation of measures on terrorist sanctions. Throughout the book, the questions of the UK's participation in Europe's area of criminal justice and the feasibility of a Europe 'à-la-carte' in EU criminal law are examined. The book concludes by highlighting the possibilities that the Lisbon Treaty opens for the development of a new paradigm of European criminal justice, which places the individual (and not the state), and the protection of fundamental rights (and not security) at its core.

Volume 1 in the series Hart Studies in European Criminal Law

Hart Studies in European Criminal Law

Series Editors: Professor Katalin Ligeti, University of Luxembourg;
Professor Valsamis Mitsilegas, Queen Mary University of London;
Professor Anne Weyembergh, Brussels Free University

Since the Lisbon Treaty, European criminal law has become an increasingly important field of research and debate. Working with the European Criminal Law Academic Network (ECLAN), the series will publish works of the highest intellectual rigour and cutting edge scholarship which will be required reading for all European criminal lawyers.

The series is happy to consider both edited and single authored titles. The series defines 'European' and 'criminal law' in the broadest sense, so books on European criminal law, justice and policy will be considered. The series also welcomes books which offer different methodological approaches.

Volume 1: *EU Criminal Law after Lisbon: Rights, Trust and the Transformation of Justice in Europe* by Valsamis Mitsilegas

EU Criminal Law After Lisbon

Rights, Trust and the Transformation of Justice in Europe

Valsamis Mitsilegas

·HART·

OXFORD · LONDON · NEW YORK · NEW DELHI · SYDNEY

HART PUBLISHING

Bloomsbury Publishing Plc

Kemp House, Chawley Park, Cumnor Hill, Oxford, OX2 9PH, UK

HART PUBLISHING, the Hart/Stag logo, BLOOMSBURY and the Diana logo are
trademarks of Bloomsbury Publishing Plc

First published in Great Britain 2016

First published in hardback, 2016
Paperback edition, 2018

A catalogue record for this book is available from the British Library.

Library of Congress Cataloging-in-Publication Data

Names: Mitsilegas, Valsamis, 1971– author.

Title: EU criminal law after Lisbon : rights, trust and the transformation of justice in Europe / Valsamis Mitsilegas.

Other titles: European Union criminal law after Lisbon

Description: Oxford ; Portland, Oregon, USA : Hart Publishing, Ltd., 2016. | Series: Hart studies in European
criminal law ; volume 1 | Includes bibliographical references and index.

Identifiers: LCCN 2016005231 (print) | LCCN 2016006632 (ebook) | ISBN 9781849466486
(hardback : alk. paper) | ISBN 9781782259886 (Epub)

Subjects: LCSH: Criminal justice, Administration of—European Union countries. | International and
municipal law—European Union countries. | Treaty on European Union (1992 February 7).
Protocols, etc. (2007 December 13)

Classification: LCC KJE9430 .M58 2016 (print) | LCC KJE9430 (ebook) | DDC 345.24—dc23

LC record available at http://lccn.loc.gov/2016005231

Series: Hart Studies in European Criminal Law, volume 1

ISBN: PB: 978-1-50992-476-9
HB: 978-1-84946-648-6
ePDF: 978-1-78225-987-9
ePub: 978-1-78225-988-6

Typeset by Compuscript Ltd, Shannon

To find out more about our authors and books visit www.hartpublishing.co.uk. Here you will find extracts, author
information, details of forthcoming events and the option to sign up for our newsletters.

ACKNOWLEDGEMENTS

This monograph is the first volume in the new series on Studies in EU Criminal Law launched by Hart/Bloomsbury and supported by the European Criminal Law Academic Network (ECLAN). In my capacity as the author of this book and as Co-ordinator of ECLAN, I am delighted by the launch of this exciting series, which we hope will help raise the profile of EU criminal law even further and reach a truly pan-European and global audience. I would like to thank my colleagues at Hart/Bloomsbury, and in particular Sinead Moloney, for their enthusiasm, dedication and commitment to this series.

In the course of researching and writing this book, I have benefited enormously from the comments and insights of friends and colleagues. I would like to thank first of all Pedro Caeiro and Richard Myers for taking the time to read draft chapters—your input and advice have been invaluable. My conversations with Roger Cotterrell, Daniel Halberstam, Emilio de Capitani and colleagues in the ECLAN Management Committee and in the European Commission's Expert Group on EU Criminal Policy, where I have been a member since 2012, have generated new ideas and provided valuable insights. I would like to thank these colleagues, as well as the audiences in a number of conferences and seminars where for the past seven years I had the opportunity to test ideas and arguments while developing this book. These include events organised by the Université Libre de Bruxelles, King's College London, the European University Institute, Université Paris 1, the Irish Centre for European Law, Cambridge University, the University of Oxford, the London School of Economics, the University of Reading, Hong Kong University, Osgoode Hall, the University of Uppsala, the University of Oslo, the University of Helsinki, the University of Strasbourg, the Polish European Law Research Association, and a series of events organised by the Italian and the Latvian Presidencies of the Council of the European Union in 2014 and 2015. I also had the opportunity to exchange ideas with academic colleagues, researchers and students attending my guest seminars at the Universities of Michigan, Lund, Catania, Geneva, Bonn, A Coruña, Bologna, Naples II and at the University of Ferrara, where I had the honour of being appointed as Copernicus Visiting Scientist for 2015. I am grateful to all these audiences for their attention and interaction.

In this fast-moving field of law, there needs to be a cut-off point with regard to the legal developments analysed in the manuscript. In this case, this point is the end of September 2015. A number of chapters develop further ideas and arguments which first appeared as articles or chapters in edited volumes. Part of Chapter three is based on V Mitsilegas, 'EU Criminal Law Competence After

Lisbon: From Securitised to Functional Criminalisation' in D Acosta Arcarazo and C Murphy (eds), *EU Security and Justice Law* (Oxford, Hart Publishing, 2014) 110–29; part of Chapter four develops arguments which first appeared in V Mitsilegas, 'The European Public Prosecutor Before the Court of Justice. The Challenge of Effective Judicial Protection' in G Giudicelli-Delage, S Manacorda and J Tricot (eds), *Le Contrôle Judiciaire du Parquet Européen. Nécessité, Modèles, Enjeux*, Collection de l'UMR de Droit Comparé de Paris (Université Paris 1) (Société de Législation Comparée, vol 37, 2015) 67–87; elements of Chapters four and five are based on V Mitsilegas, 'The Symbiotic Relationship between Mutual Trust and Fundamental Rights in Europe's Area of Criminal Justice' in (2015) 6 *New Journal of European Criminal Law*; Chapter seven has appeared as V Mitsilegas, 'The Place of the Victim in Europe's Area of Criminal Justice' in F Ippolito and S Iglesias Sanchez (eds), *Protecting Vulnerable Groups* (Oxford, Hart Publishing, 2015) 313–38; and Chapter nine draws upon V Mitsilegas, 'The European Union and the Global Governance of Crime' in V Mitsilegas, P Alldridge and L Cheliotis (eds), *Globalisation, Criminal Law and Criminal Justice. Theoretical, Comparative and Transnational Perspectives* (Oxford, Hart Publishing, 2015) 153–98.

As always, I have been inspired by working with my taught and doctoral students at Queen Mary and would like to dedicate this book to them. The Queen Mary LLM students in the EU Criminal Law class have been consistently impressive, while I have been fortunate to supervise a group of stellar doctoral students working on a number of areas of European and transnational criminal law as well as on various aspects of the relationship between security and human rights. I would like to thank in particular Niovi Vavoula, now Research Assistant in the Queen Mary Law Department, who has provided outstanding research assistance in the preparation of this manuscript.

CONTENTS

TABLE OF CASES

National Cases

Belgium

Germany

Greece

United Kingdom

TABLE OF LEGISLATION

UN Resolutions

National Legislation

Germany

Italy

Poland

United Kingdom

1

Introduction

The entry into force of the Treaty of Lisbon has had a transformative effect on the evolution of European Union criminal law. Not only has the Treaty introduced fundamental institutional and constitutional changes underpinning the development of European Union law in the field, but it has also empowered the European Union to legislate in new areas of criminal law and justice. The aim of this book is to analyse and evaluate the impact of the entry into force of the Lisbon Treaty on the reconfiguration of the legal landscape in Europe's area of criminal justice. The book is not a second edition of my monograph on *EU Criminal Law* published by Hart in 2009. The manuscript of *EU Criminal Law* was completed in 2008, more than a year before the entry into force of the Lisbon Treaty. While *EU Criminal Law* was forward looking in opening up the discussion on the potential impact of the Lisbon Treaty on European Union criminal law, it did not aim to—and could not in the light of its timing—provide a detailed, ex post, analysis of the actual impact of the entry into force of the Lisbon Treaty on criminal justice. The monograph you have in your hands is the culmination of seven years of research on the evolution of European Union criminal law in relation to the entry into force of the Lisbon Treaty. Both its content and focus are different from *EU Criminal Law*. Rather than attempting to systematise European Union criminal law as a distinct academic and policy field, as was the case with *EU Criminal Law*, the present monograph moves on the research agenda to take into account new developments resulting in a growing maturity of EU criminal law as an academic and policy field. By containing exclusively new text, the present book focuses expressly on the impact of post-Lisbon European Union law on the criminal justice process, conceived as including the stages of criminalisation, investigation, prosecution, trial and enforcement of sentences. The examination of the transformative impact of the Lisbon Treaty on criminal justice will be viewed from two primary perspectives: from the perspective of the impact of EU criminal law on the Member States, including state sovereignty and national legal diversity; and from the perspective of the impact of Europeanisation on the relationship between the individual and the state, evaluated in the light of its conformity with upholding the rule of law and protecting fundamental rights. Based on these parameters, this monograph will aim to cast light on the impact of the entry into force of the Lisbon Treaty on the reconfiguration of criminal justice at the national level, while at the same time assessing the effect of this development on the transformation of justice in Europe more broadly.

The monograph will begin by evaluating the impact of the constitutionalisation of European Union criminal law after Lisbon. Chapter two will thus analyse the main contours of such constitutionalisation, focusing in particular on institutional and competence developments as well as on the constitutionalisation of the EU Charter of Fundamental Rights and its impact on EU criminal law. The chapter will also focus on remaining areas of controversy regarding the constitutionalisation of EU criminal law, exploring in particular the tension between supranationalism on the one hand and state sovereignty and national-level diversity on the other. Having set out the constitutional parameters, the book will continue by examining the impact of the entry into force of the Lisbon Treaty on distinct areas of criminal justice. Chapter three will examine the impact of the Lisbon Treaty on criminalisation, by focusing in particular on the impact of Article 83 TFEU on the powers of the Union to harmonise substantive criminal law and on the influence of European Union law on domestic criminal justice systems. Chapter four will focus on prosecution. It will examine the trajectory leading from a system of horizontal co-operation between national criminal justice systems (in particular in cases of conflicts of jurisdiction and the application of *ne bis in idem*) to forms of vertical integration in the field of prosecution as embodied in the evolution of Eurojust and the establishment of a European Public Prosecutor's Office. Chapter five will examine the interaction between national criminal justice systems under the application of the principle of mutual recognition, and will focus in particular on the evolving relationship between mutual trust and fundamental rights after Lisbon. Chapters six and seven will focus on the new possibilities granted by Article 82(2) TFEU for the European Union to harmonise national legislation in the field of criminal procedure. Chapter six will focus on the first major paradigm of Union secondary legislation on human rights in criminal justice, namely the adoption of a series of Directives on the rights of suspects and accused persons in criminal proceedings. Chapter seven will focus on EU legislation on the rights of victims. The impact of the adoption of these measures on the internal balance of power in criminal justice systems will be evaluated, and the transformative effect of EU defence rights legislation will be highlighted. Chapters eight and nine will highlight further areas where EU criminal law after Lisbon has reconfigured concepts of justice. Chapter eight will examine what this book calls the uneasy relationship between EU criminal law and citizenship of the Union, casting light on the misuses of EU criminal law and their detrimental effect on EU citizenship rights. By focusing on terrorist sanctions, Chapter nine examines the growing trend for the European Union to adopt and impose a paradigm of preventive justice, where the focus is not on punishing existing crime, but on preventing future crime.

The impact of EU law as analysed in all these chapters on criminal justice—and on shaping answers to the fundamental questions of 'what kind of justice?' and 'whose justice?'—will be crystallised in the Conclusion. It will be demonstrated that the entry into force of the Treaty of Lisbon has had mixed results in addressing the adverse consequences of the uncritical securitisation which marked the evolution of EU criminal law before the entry into force of the Lisbon Treaty in the old 'third-pillar' days, with considerable deference to Member State security choices and the uncritical acceptance of the existence and importance of mutual trust between EU Member States remaining features of EU criminal law in the post-Lisbon era. However, the conclusion will also highlight the fundamental change that Lisbon has brought about, which is what this book calls 'the promise of rights'. The entry into force of the Lisbon Treaty enables the realisation of a paradigm of European Union criminal justice which places the individual (and not the state) at the heart of its construction. This is achieved in particular by the empowering of the Union by the Lisbon Treaty to legislate for human rights, by adopting in particular secondary EU law on defence rights, and by the transformative potential of the constitutionalisation of the Charter of Fundamental Rights, which has already had a significant impact on the development of EU criminal law after Lisbon. By focusing increasingly and prominently on the impact of EU criminal law on the individual, the Treaty of Lisbon will have a transformative effect on justice in the European Union by changing fundamentally the way in which European Union and national authorities perceive the development of criminal law.

2

The Constitutionalisation of EU Criminal Law After Lisbon

I. Introduction

The entry into force of the Lisbon Treaty has introduced fundamental constitutional changes in the field of EU criminal law. It signified the end of the Treaty three pillar structure and the abolition of the third pillar. In principle, but with some exceptions, this meant the supranationalisation—or 'communautarisation'—of EU criminal law, an area of EU law whose development has been fraught with controversy in the light of the perceived adverse impact of European integration in the field on national sovereignty and on the diversity of national criminal justice systems. The aim of this chapter is to analyse in detail the extent and impact of these constitutional changes. It will be argued that the impact of the entry into force of the Lisbon Treaty is not limited to the normalisation of EU criminal law from an institutional perspective, but has rather led to the constitutionalisation of EU criminal law, which is now located firmly within the EU constitutional framework and principles. The chapter will begin by analysing in detail this constitutionalisation, highlighting in particular the application of EU constitutional principles, including fundamental rights, to EU criminal law and emphasising the importance of implementation and interdependence in the evolution of such constitutionalisation. The chapter will then continue by casting light on potential controversies and limits to constitutionalisation. It will look at how concerns related to national diversity interact with the development of European integration in the field of criminal justice. It will then examine in detail from a variety of angles the ongoing debate over the existence, extent and exercise of EU competence in criminal matters, which remain contested. The chapter will further examine the impact of subsidiarity on the evolution of EU criminal law after Lisbon and continue by analysing the relationship between constitutionalisation based on interdependence, on the one hand, and differentiation based on enhanced cooperation, on the other. The chapter will conclude by highlighting the main features of constitutionalisation which are prominent today and which underpin the content and evolution of EU criminal law post-Lisbon.

II. The Constitutionalisation of EU Criminal Law

It is submitted that the entry into force of the Lisbon Treaty constitutes a major step towards the constitutionalisation of EU criminal law. The term 'constitutionalisation' is understood here within the meaning put forward by Loughlin as the attempt to subject all governmental action within a designated field to the structures, processes, principles and values of a 'constitution'.[1] In the field of European Union law, the constitutionalisation of EU criminal law must be viewed from a number of different perspectives which will be outlined below: from the perspective of the institutional normalisation of decision-making which the post-Lisbon abolition of the third pillar entails; from the perspective of the full application in the field of EU criminal law of the constitutional principles of EU law; and from the perspective of underpinning EU criminal law with a constitutional framework of fundamental rights protection, most notably via the constitutionalisation of the EU Charter of Fundamental Rights in the Lisbon Treaty. The examination of the constitutionalisation of EU criminal law from these perspectives will be accompanied by an analysis of two factors embedding further EU action in the field within the broader EU constitutional framework: the growing emphasis on the correct implementation of EU criminal law by Member States and the enhanced mechanisms for scrutiny and monitoring such implementation at EU level; and the increased interdependence of various areas of criminal law leading to the emergence of a coherent legal framework on EU criminal justice. As will be seen below, such interdependence appears at the level of interconnection between various EU strands of action, but also—and importantly—at the level of the relationship between European Union law and national law, including national constitutional law.

A. Constitutionalisation at EU Level: Institutions, Principles, Rights

The legacy of the third pillar has been the adoption of EU criminal law under a largely intergovernmental method (via unanimity in the Council and the mere consultation of the European Parliament), with limited scrutiny powers entrusted to supranational institutions such as the Court of Justice and the European Commission, and resulting in the adoption of weaker instruments compared to the supranational first pillar (the main EU criminal law instrument post-Amsterdam has been the Framework Decision, which, while similar to a Directive, does not entail direct effect).[2] The entry into force of the Lisbon Treaty has changed radically

---

[1] M Loughlin, 'What is Constitutionalisation?' in P Dobner and M Loughlin (eds), *The Twilight of Constitutionalism?* (Oxford, Oxford University Press, 2010) 47–72.
[2] V Mitsilegas, *EU Criminal Law* (Oxford, Hart Publishing, 2009) chapter 1.

the institutional framework underpinning EU criminal law by granting—with few exceptions—EU institutions their full powers in the field and moving to a system of supranational decision-making. The full powers of EU institutions apply from the entry into force of the Lisbon Treaty vis-à-vis legislation adopted after Lisbon, and from 1 December 2014 (the end of the transitional period provided in the Treaty Protocol on Transitional Provisions)[3] for pre-Lisbon third pillar law remaining in force. The first major institutional change involves *decision-making*, which, for the vast majority of Title V measures will take place under the 'ordinary' legislative procedure,[4] ie, co-decision between the Council (which will decide by majority voting) and the European Parliament.[5] This change is accompanied by a normalisation of the legal instruments of EU criminal law post-Lisbon, which take the form now of Regulations, Directives, and Decisions.[6] The second major institutional change involves the role of the Court of Justice, and the 'communautarisation' of judicial control. The Court has now full jurisdiction to rule on infringement proceedings in criminal matters.[7] The full jurisdiction of the Court in the field of preliminary rulings now applies.[8] The Court also assumes full jurisdiction to hear actions for compensation for damages[9] and the review of legality;[10] to review the compliance of legislative acts with the principle of subsidiarity;[11] and review the legality of acts of the European Council and bodies, offices or agencies of the Union intended to produce legal effects vis-à-vis third parties.[12] The third major change involves the role of the European Commission, which emerges having stronger powers of initiative (albeit still shared with Member States)[13] and full powers as 'guardian of the Treaties' to monitor the implementation of EU criminal law by Member States.[14] The full involvement of EU institutions will have a significant impact on the

---

[3] Protocol No 36. For an analysis see section VI on enhanced cooperation below.

[4] Exceptions include the adoption of legislation establishing a European Public Prosecutor's Office under Article 86(1) TFEU, which requires unanimity in the Council and the consent of the European Parliament; the adoption of measures on operational cooperation in the field of policing under Article 87(3) TFEU, which requires unanimity in the Council and the mere consultation of the European Parliament; the adoption of rules on the operation of national authorities in another Member State in cases of cross-border police and judicial cooperation in criminal matters, which requires unanimity in the Council and consultation of the European Parliament (Article 89 TFEU); and the adoption of minimum EU rules in areas of criminal procedure not mentioned in the Treaty which requires unanimity in the Council and the consent of the European Parliament (Article 82(2)(d)). In Articles 86(1) and 87(3) TFEU, lack of unanimity does not preclude the adoption of legislation under enhanced cooperation.

[5] On the 'ordinary' legislative procedure see Articles 289(1) and 294 TFEU.

[6] Article 288(1) TFEU.

[7] Articles 258–260 TFEU.

[8] On the preliminary ruling jurisdiction under Lisbon, see Art 267 TEU. The last paragraph states that such rulings must be given with a minimum of delay in cases involving individuals in custody.

[9] Article 268 TFEU.

[10] Article 263(4) TFEU.

[11] Article 8, Protocol No 2 on the Application of the Principles of Subsidiarity and Proportionality. For further analysis, see below.

[12] Article 263(1) TFEU. See also Art 277 TFEU.

[13] See Article 76 TFEU. For further analysis see section III on national diversity below.

[14] In particular under Article 258 TFEU.

content, enforcement and development of EU criminal law. The stronger role of the European Parliament in the decision-making process serves to address democratic deficit concerns and may serve to enhance the protection of fundamental rights in the content of secondary EU criminal law adopted post-Lisbon.[15] The full involvement of the Commission as guardian of the treaties and the possibility of instituting infringement proceedings will lead to a greater focus on the correct and timely implementation of EU criminal law including third pillar law—in particular the plethora of Framework Decisions on various aspects of mutual recognition which remain largely unimplemented across the European Union—by Member States.[16] On the other hand, allowing courts of all Member States to send questions on the interpretation of EU law to the Court of Justice in Luxembourg on third pillar measures will have a beneficial effect upon the development and interpretation of the EU third pillar *acquis*, especially in cases where national courts seek recourse to the Court of Justice in order to assist with the interpretation of key third pillar law concepts.[17]

The constitutionalisation of EU criminal law is also inextricably linked with the full application of the constitutional principles of EU law in the field. A major development post-Lisbon has been the change in the legislative instruments of EU criminal law, with the Directive being the main instrument of EU legislative intervention in the field. The use of Directives post-Lisbon means that the principle of direct effect (whose application was expressly excluded by the Treaty in the case of Framework Decisions pre-Lisbon) is now applicable to EU criminal law Directives if the conditions of its application are fulfilled. Despite the limits set out by the Court of Justice regarding the application of direct effect in cases involving substantive criminal law,[18] the Court has found that a Treaty provision related to criminal law—Article 325 TFEU—does have direct effect.[19] Moreover, the application of the principle of direct effect may increasingly come into force in view of the change in the content of EU criminal law post-Lisbon, with the Treaty providing now an express legal basis, Article 82(2) TFEU), which has led to the adoption of EU secondary law conferring rights to individuals in criminal procedure. It is submitted that key provisions in these instruments—including the provision of key rights on access to a lawyer, to a translator and to an interpreter—do entail direct effect, enabling individuals to claim these rights before national courts and ensuring thus the decentralised enforcement of EU criminal law.[20] A key question

---

[15] For an assessment, see V Mitsilegas and N Vavoula, 'Criminal Law: Institutional Rebalancing and Judicialisation as Drivers of Policy Change' in F Trauner and A Ripoll Servent (eds), *Policy Change in the Area of Freedom, Security and Justice: How EU Institutions Matter* (Abingdon/New York, Routledge, 2015) 133–51.

[16] See sub-section II.B on implementation below.

[17] For further details see section VI on enhanced cooperation below.

[18] See Cases C-387/02, C-391/02 and C-403/02, *Berlusconi*, [2005] ECR I-3565.

[19] Case C-105/14, *Taricco and Others*, EU:C:2015:555, judgment of 8 September 2015, paragraph 51. For an analysis of the judgment see Chapter 3 of this volume.

[20] For further details, see Chapter 6 of this volume on defence rights.

in this context concerns the application of constitutional principles of EU law on third pillar law post-Lisbon. In its seminal ruling in *Pupino*, the Court of Justice confirmed already pre-Lisbon the applicability of the principle of indirect effect to Framework Decisions in an attempt to boost the enforceability and binding character of third pillar law.[21] After Lisbon, the Court of Justice has confirmed the applicability of another key constitutional EU law principle to third pillar law, namely the principle of primacy of EU law over national law. In the case of *Melloni*,[22] the Court of Justice confirmed the application of the principle of primacy of EU law in relation to third pillar law, namely the Framework Decision on the European Arrest Warrant as amended by the 2009 Framework Decision of *in absentia* rulings over national constitutional law. Giving priority to national law

> would undermine the principle of the primacy of EU law inasmuch as it would allow a Member State to disapply EU legal rules which are fully in compliance with the Charter where they infringe the fundamental rights guaranteed by that State's constitution.[23]

The Court's ruling in *Melloni* is a clear message that constitutional principles of Union law apply fully to third pillar law. The sole exception appears to be the principle of direct effect, the application of which to Framework Decisions was explicitly excluded by the third pillar legal basis of Article 34(2)(b) TEU. The Protocol on Transitional Provisions states that the legal effects of acts adopted before Lisbon will be preserved until those acts are repealed, annulled or amended.[24] The wording of the Protocol implies that the legal effects of the third pillar Framework Decisions which have not been 'Lisbonised' in this manner remain unchanged. However, this may be of little practical significance as there may be very few provisions in the third pillar *acquis*—focused largely on law enforcement—which would meet the requirements of direct effect.

Another factor of constitutionalisation of EU criminal law after Lisbon has been the central place of the protection of fundamental rights in the Treaty. A key development in this context has been the constitutionalisation of the Charter of Fundamental Rights, which has the same legal value as the Treaties[25] and has been seen as contributing to reinforcing the centrality of fundamental rights in the EU legal order.[26] The Charter contains a whole Title, Title VI, on Justice. Title VI enshrines key rights and principles for the development of EU criminal law

---

[21] Case C-105/03, *Pupino*, [2005] ECR I-5285. For an analysis see V Mitsilegas, 'Constitutional Principles of the European Community and European Criminal Law' (2006) 8 *European Journal of Law Reform* 301–24.

[22] Case C-399/11, *Melloni v Ministerio Fiscal*, judgment of 26.2.2013.

[23] ibid paragraph 58.

[24] Protocol No 36, Article 9.

[25] Article 6(1) TEU. See P Craig, *The Lisbon Treaty. Law, Politics, and Treaty Reform* (Oxford, Oxford University Press, 2010) 200.

[26] See S Iglesias Sanchez, 'The Court and the Charter: The Impact of the Entry into Force of the Lisbon Treaty on the ECJ's Approach to Fundamental Rights' in (2012) 49 *Common Market Law Review* 1565–612, 1582.

including the right to an effective remedy and to a fair trial,[27] the presumption of innocence and right of defence,[28] the principles of legality and proportionality of criminal offences and penalties[29] and the right not to be tried or punished twice in criminal proceedings for the same criminal offence.[30] Further Charter rights which are relevant to EU criminal law include rights and principles enshrined: in Title I of the Charter on dignity (including the provisions on human dignity,[31] the right to life,[32] the right to the integrity of the person[33] and the prohibition of torture and inhuman or degrading treatment or punishment);[34] in Title II on freedoms (including the provisions on the right to liberty and security,[35] respect for private and family life[36] and the protection of personal data[37] as well as the provisions on freedom of expression and information,[38] freedom of assembly and association,[39] right to property[40] and protection in the event of removal, expulsion or extradition);[41] in Title III on Equality (most notably the provisions on equality before the law,[42] non-discrimination[43] and the rights of the child);[44] and in Title V on citizens' rights (including the right to good administration,[45] the right of access to documents[46] and freedom of movement and of residence).[47] A whole raft of Articles—thus the majority of the Charter provisions—are relevant and applicable in the implementation of EU criminal law. The impact of the Charter in this context will be analysed in detail throughout this volume. Linked to the protection by the Charter is the emphasis of the Lisbon Treaty on other sources of rights. Fundamental rights, as guaranteed by European Convention of Human Rights (ECHR) and as they result from the constitutional traditions common to the Member States, constitute general principles of the Union's law.[48] The Treaty also calls for the Union's accession to the ECHR.[49] Throughout this volume it will be demonstrated that, notwithstanding the

---

[27] Article 47.
[28] Article 48.
[29] Article 49.
[30] Article 50.
[31] Article 1.
[32] Article 2.
[33] Article 3.
[34] Article 4.
[35] Article 6.
[36] Article 7.
[37] Article 8.
[38] Article 11.
[39] Article 12.
[40] Article 17.
[41] Article 18.
[42] Article 20.
[43] Article 23.
[44] Article 24.
[45] Article 41.
[46] Article 42.
[47] Article 45.
[48] Article 6(3) TEU.
[49] Article 6(2) TEU.

methodological difficulties regarding the accession of the Union to the ECHR that the Court of Justice is currently facing,[50] the Court has also been using Strasbourg case-law in detail in order to evaluate human rights compliance of EU law.[51]

The influence of the Charter in the development of EU criminal law after Lisbon is not limited to the interpretation of the content of EU criminal law in conformity with the Charter. It is also crucial when determining the scope of application and interpretation of rights and the level of protection provided by the Charter—aspects which are addressed in the final, horizontal provisions of the Charter.[52] These provisions aim to regulate the relationship between the Charter and national law on the one hand, and the relationship between the Charter and other sources of human rights protection (including the ECHR) on the other. The Court of Justice has thus far intervened on both aspects. In the seminal ruling in *Melloni*, the Court found that EU law which is found to be in compliance with the Charter has primacy over national constitutional law which provides a higher level of protection.[53] While this ruling may be seen as lowering the protection of fundamental rights in certain jurisdictions, the Court has compensated for this potential outcome (which was explained by the need to ensure the primacy, unity and effectiveness of Union law) by adopting a broad interpretation of what con-stitutes the implementation of Union law which triggers the application of the Charter under Article 51(1) of the Charter. In the case of *Fransson*,[54] the Court of Justice adopted a broad interpretation of the application of the Charter, including in cases where national legislation does not implement expressly or directly an EU criminal law instrument. The Court found that domestic law on VAT fraud does fall within EU law since there is a direct link between the collection of VAT revenue in compliance with the European Union law applicable and the avail-ability to the European Union budget of the corresponding VAT resources.[55] This reasoning has become influential in the development of the Court's case-law on the relationship between EU law and national law on criminal procedure.[56] At the

---

[50] See the discussion on the impact of Opinion 2/13 in Chapter 5 of this volume on mutual recognition.

[51] See in particular references to the ECHR in the Court's case-law on substantive criminal law on fraud (Chapter 3), *ne bis in idem* (Chapter 4) and mutual recognition and the European Arrest Warrant (Chapter 5).

[52] See in particular Articles 51–53 of the Charter. For commentaries see inter alia K Lenaerts, 'Exploring the Limits of the EU Charter of Fundamental Rights' (2012) 8 *European Constitutional Law Review* 375–403; D Sarmiento, 'Who's Afraid of the Charter? The Court of Justice, National Courts and the New Framework of Fundamental Rights Protection in Europe' (2013) 50 *Common Market Law Review* 1267–304; and F Fontanelli, 'Implementation of EU Law through Domestic Measures after Fransson: the Court of Justice Buys Time and 'Non-Preclusion' Troubles Loom Large' (2014) 39 *European Law Review* 682–700.

[53] Case C-399/11, *Melloni*, judgment of 26.2.2013. For an analysis see Chapter 5 of this volume on mutual recognition.

[54] Case C-617/10, *Åklagaren v Hans Åkerberg Fransson*, judgment of 26 February 2013.

[55] ibid paragraph 26.

[56] See in particular the case of *Taricco*, n 19 above, analysed in Chapter 3 of this volume on the harmonisation of substantive criminal law.

same time, it has caused concern in Member States, fearing that the Court's expansive approach would lead to the extension of the competence of the European Union.[57] The Court of Justice developed its approach on the applicability of the Charter in *Siragusa*,[58] where it ruled that the concept of 'implementing Union law', as referred to in Article 51 of the Charter, requires a certain degree of connection above and beyond the matters covered being closely related or one of those matters having an indirect impact on the other.[59] As will be seen in the section on implementation below, the Court's approach has the effect of including a wide range of national legislation and measures related to national criminal justice systems within the scope of the Charter. This view is reinforced by the Court's finding in *Siragusa* that it is important to consider the objective of protecting fundamental rights in EU law, which is to ensure that those rights are not infringed in areas of EU activity, whether through action at EU level or through the implementation of EU law by the Member States.[60]

B. Constitutionalisation and the Member States: Focusing on Transposition and Implementation

A central feature of the development of EU criminal law after Lisbon is the emphasis on monitoring the implementation of Member States' commitments in the field. On a political level, this emphasis can be explained on the one hand by the need to achieve the smooth transition from the intergovernmental third pillar to the largely supranational Lisbon reality by ensuring in particular the full implementation of pre-Lisbon third pillar law, while on the other hand it may mask the reluctance of Member States to proceed to the adoption of a new raft of EU legislation in EU criminal law. This approach has been reflected in the European Council Conclusions which followed upon the end of the Stockholm Programme, according to which building on the past programmes, the overall priority now is to consistently transpose, effectively implement and consolidate the legal instruments and policy measures in place.[61] Irrespective of whether this approach will have the effect of stifling the Union's legislative ambition in the field, the emphasis on

---

[57] See in this context the judgment of the Bundesverfassungsgericht in the anti-terrorism databases case—1 BvR 1215/07, judgment of 24 April 2013, where the Court adopted a restrictive interpretation of *Fransson* finding that Article 51(1) of the Charter cannot operate when the domestic measure relates to the purely abstract scope of EU law or when it has a merely de facto effect upon it (paragraph 91). See F Fontanelli, '*Hic Sunt Nationes*: The Elusive Limits of the EU Charter and the German Constitutional Watchdog' (2013) 9 *European Constitutional Law Review* 315–34. On the broader concerns of the Bundesverfassungsgericht with regard to the potential impact of the Lisbon Treaty on national sovereignty and competence in criminal law see the commentary on the Lisbon judgment below.

[58] Case C-206/13, *Siragusa v Regione Sicilia*, judgment of 6 March 2014.

[59] ibid paragraph 24.

[60] Paragraph 31.

[61] European Council Conclusions, 26–27 June 2014, Brussels, EUCO 79/14, paragraph 3.

implementation and transposition is key in ensuring the effectiveness of EU law in the field and may have far-reaching consequences for national criminal justice systems which will have to be increasingly scrutinised to ensure their conformity with EU law, including the Charter. As seen above, the Commission has assumed, post-Lisbon, its full powers as guardian of the treaties to monitor implementation of Title V law (and, from 1 December 2014, also third pillar law) and introduce infringement proceedings in cases where national implementation is deemed to be defective. These supranational powers of the Commission are coupled in the Lisbon Treaty with a more intergovernmental level of evaluation established by Article 70 TFEU. The latter establishes a legal basis for the adoption of a system whereby, without prejudice to the infringement powers of the Commission and the Court of Justice, Member States, in collaboration with the Commission, conduct objective and impartial evaluation of the implementation of the Union policies referred to in Title V by Member States' authorities, in particular in order to facilitate full application of the principle of mutual recognition. The European Parliament and national Parliaments will be informed of the content and results of the evaluation. The Treaty provides thus two parallel mechanisms of monitoring the implementation of EU criminal law by Member States, although Article 70 TFEU has not been used extensively since the entry into force of the Lisbon Treaty.[62] What is key in this context is also *what* is going to be evaluated. It is submitted that the Court's case-law on the applicability of the Charter, combined with the EU law requirement for Member States to ensure the effectiveness of EU law, generate the requirement that the scrutiny of implementation of EU criminal law by Member States is not limited to the scrutiny of the implementation of specific provisions set out in Directives and Framework Decisions, but also includes a holistic scrutiny of domestic criminal justice systems to the extent that elements of the latter have a degree of connection with the implementation of EU criminal law along the lines of the Court's approach in *Siragusa*. To give two concrete examples of where such degree of connection may exist, in the case of mutual recognition, the monitoring of the implementation of measures such as the Framework Decisions on the European Arrest Warrant or on the Transfer of Sentenced Persons cannot be complete without monitoring of prison conditions at EU level. Similarly, in the case of the European Arrest Warrant scrutiny of implementation must include scrutiny of pre-trial detention length and conditions in Member States, as well as scrutiny of the duration of pre-trial periods. The second example involves the implementation of the rights of the defendant in criminal proceedings. It is submitted that effective implementation of the relevant Directives will only be ensured if national criminal justice systems are scrutinised holistically from the police station to trial and if scrutiny also covers the levels of resources Member

---

[62] Article 70 TFEU has been used as a legal basis for the establishment of an evaluation and monitoring mechanism of the application of the Schengen *acquis*—Council Regulation No 1053/2013, [2013] OJ L295/27, 6 November 2013.

States commit towards the effective implementation of EU law. The emphasis on implementation in this manner has the potential to have—along with the content of EU law—a transformative effect on national criminal justice systems.[63]

C. Constitutionalisation as Interdependence. Towards a More Coherent EU Criminal Policy

The final element which must be considered in order to assess fully the constitutionalisation of EU criminal law after Lisbon is the growing interdependence between the constitutive elements of Europe's area of criminal justice. This interdependence can be found at two levels: at the level of the interaction and interconnections between various areas of EU law; and at the level of the relationship between EU law and national law. When one examines the first of these levels, namely the level of interconnections between various areas of EU law, it is noteworthy that the Treaty of Lisbon puts forward a considerably integrated model of EU criminal justice in developing the Union's competence to act in the field. Key examples of such interdependence are as follows: the Lisbon Treaty has granted expressly for the first time competence to the European Union to introduce minimum rules in the field of criminal procedure in Article 82(2) TFEU. These rules include procedural rights, victims' rights and rules on the admissibility of evidence—however, competence exists only if these rules are necessary to facilitate the operation of the principle of mutual recognition as enshrined in Article 82(1) TFEU.[64] The express 'functional criminalisation' competence in Article 83(2) TFEU exists only if the adoption of rules on the definition of criminal offences and the imposition of criminal sanctions are essential to ensure the effective implementation of a Union policy in an area where harmonisation has taken place.[65] And there is no parthenogenesis of new EU criminal justice bodies and agencies: another key innovation of the Lisbon Treaty, the provision providing the legal basis for the establishment of a European Public Prosecutor's Office, explicitly states that such Office will be established 'from Eurojust'.[66] On the other hand, the entry into force of the Lisbon Treaty has confirmed the impact of EU law on national criminal justice systems. The impact of the application of the constitutional principles of Union law, including the protection of fundamental rights, has been analysed earlier in this chapter. Here it is also worth noting the effect on the interdependence between national and EU law which compliance with EU law principles, including effectiveness and loyal co-operation, entails. This impact will

---

[63] On the transformative effect of EU defence rights law see Chapter 6 of this volume.
[64] For further details, see Chapter 6 of this volume on defence rights.
[65] For further details, see Chapter 3 of this volume on substantive criminal law.
[66] Article 86(1) TFEU. For further details, see Chapter 4 of this volume on the Europeanisation of prosecution.

be highlighted in the analysis of the case-law of the Court of Justice throughout this book, but it is worth emphasising here the effect of judgments like *Taricco*, where the Court demonstrated clearly the interdependence between national and EU law on the basis of the need for Member States to uphold objectives deriving directly from Treaty provisions, in this case Article 325 TFEU. Both these levels of interdependence demonstrate that EU criminal justice policy is becoming increasingly integrated and that this integration places considerable limits on Member States' choices not to comply with EU criminal law or not to be bound by EU criminal law in the first place.[67]

III. The Persistence of National Diversity

A key concern of Member States accompanying the entry into force of the Lisbon Treaty has been the perceived adverse impact that 'communautarisation' of EU criminal law would have on the diversity of their domestic criminal justice systems. In order to address these concerns, the Treaty of Lisbon introduced a number of mechanisms aiming to safeguard national legal diversity in the field of criminal justice. These mechanisms reflect what I have called resistance to the 'communautarisation' of EU criminal law[68] and have resulted in the shadow of the third pillar 'looming large' post-Lisbon.[69] These mechanisms can be grouped into three categories: provisions highlighting the need to respect national legal diversity; provisions aiming to mirror national legal diversity considerations in the form and instruments of EU criminal law post-Lisbon; and provisions aiming to safeguard Member States' prerogatives and diversity concerns in the decision-making process. These diversity mechanisms appear prima facie to challenge supranational integration, and in the early days after the entry into force of the Lisbon Treaty have been used by Member States to challenge the role of EU institutions, and in particular the European Commission. More than five years after the entry into force of the Treaty, however, it seems that these tensions have somewhat subsided.

In terms of the first mechanism outlined above, respect for national diversity occupies a central place from the very outset in Title V TFEU on the Area of Freedom, Security and Justice (AFSJ). Its opening provision, Article 67(1), states that the Union will constitute an area of freedom, security and justice 'with

---

[67] On the impact of interdependence on differentiation and enhanced cooperation see section VI below.

[68] V Mitsilegas, 'European Criminal Law and Resistance to Communautarisation Post-Lisbon' (2010) 1 *New Journal of European Criminal Law* 458–80.

[69] J Monar, 'The Institutional Framework of the AFSJ: Specific Challenges and Dynamics for Change' in J Monar (ed), *The Institutional Dimension of the European Union's Area of Freedom, Security and Justice* (Brussels, Peter Lang, 2010) 21–52, 47.

respect for fundamental rights and the different legal systems and traditions of Member States'. The emphasis on maintaining the diversity of national legal systems is further reflected in a number of choices made in the Treaty with regard to the method of law-making in EU criminal law. The Lisbon Treaty places great emphasis on mutual recognition as a method of European integration in criminal matters, and, as will be seen further in this chapter, extends Union competence in criminal procedure only by subordinating harmonisation in the field to mutual recognition[70]—this choice is significant, as mutual recognition does not involve in principle the adoption of harmonised EU standards and is perceived, at least prima facie, by Governments as less threatening to state sovereignty, as they will not have to change their law.[71] The need to respect national diversity is also reflected in the choice of the form of EU legislative action concerning harmonisation of substantive criminal law and criminal procedure: in both cases, harmonisation will take place by means of Directives.[72] This choice is significant as Directives leave Member States a considerable margin of manoeuvre as to how to implement EU law, being binding as to the result to be achieved but leaving to the national authorities the choice of form and methods.[73] This discretion left to Member States may serve to take into account the particularities of their domestic criminal justice systems when called on to implement EU measures on matters such as rules on the admissibility of evidence or the rights of the defendant in criminal proceedings.[74] It is clear that Member States opted for such discretion rather than for top-down uniform standards across the EU.

Concerns with regard to the respect of national diversity and the challenges to state sovereignty posed by the introduction of supranational decision-making in EU criminal law have been articulated perhaps in the clearest manner in the introduction of provisions establishing a so-called 'emergency brake' on the adoption of Directives in the fields of criminal procedure and substantive criminal law. Under the 'emergency brake' procedure, where a Member State considers that a draft directive in the field 'would affect fundamental aspects of its criminal justice system', it may request that the draft directive be referred to the European Council—leading to the suspension of the ordinary legislative procedure. After discussions in the European Council, in case of consensus, within four months of this suspension the proposal is sent back to the Council of Ministers for the resumption of negotiations. In case of disagreement, within the same timeframe, authorisation for Member States who wish to proceed with the proposal under enhanced co-operation referred to in Articles 20(2) TEU and 329(1) TFEU is

---

[70] Section III below.

[71] I have developed this point further in V Mitsilegas, 'The Constitutional Implications of Mutual Recognition in Criminal Matters in the EU' (2006) 43 *Common Market Law Review* 1277–311.

[72] Articles 82(2), 83(1) and (2) TFEU respectively.

[73] Article 288(3) TFEU.

[74] For legal bases for such measures see Article 82(2)(a) and (b) TFEU respectively.

deemed to be granted.[75] In this manner, reluctant Member States which may be in the minority may ensure that they do not take part in the measure, while allowing those in favour of the measure to proceed with its adoption. As witnessed by the inclusion of the European Council in the legislative process, the emergency brake is a primarily political mechanism of dispute resolution which places national governments at the centre stage of law-making at EU level.[76] It has not been used widely thus far but its existence remains important for national authorities.[77] The European Council assumes here the role of a mediator in cases where Member States express concerns with the development of EU criminal law and press the emergency brake. A similar procedure is envisaged in case of disagreement on legislation establishing a European Public Prosecutor, and legislation establishing operational co-operation between national law enforcement authorities (in both cases, however, unanimity is in principle required in the Council).[78]

In terms of maintaining national influence at an institutional level by controlling the initiative on future strategic priorities, an important institutional development in the Lisbon Treaty is the express recognition of the European Council as one of the EU institutions.[79] According to the Treaty, the European Council—the most intergovernmental of the Union institutions—will provide the Union with the necessary impetus for its development and define the general political directions and priorities thereof—but will not exercise legislative functions.[80] This is an example of what has been characterised as the 'high politics' nature of the European Council decisions.[81] This role of the European Council is further confirmed in the specific context of EU Justice and Home Affairs, with Title V TFEU stating that the European Council will define 'the strategic guidelines for legislative and operational planning within the area of freedom, security and justice'.[82] It is thus Member States' leaders who will continue to set out, post-Lisbon, (as in the cases of Tampere Conclusions, the Hague and most recently the Stockholm Programme) the general guidelines for the development of EU Justice and Home Affairs law.

---

[75] Article 82(3) TFEU on criminal procedure; Article 83(3) TFEU on substantive criminal law.

[76] For a discussion of the 'emergency brake' provisions, see House of Lords European Union Committee, *The Treaty of Lisbon: An Impact Assessment*, 10th Report, session 2007–08, HL Papers 62-I and 62-II, paragraphs 6.44–6.66.

[77] See the Lisbon judgment of the German Constitutional Court in section IV below.

[78] Articles 86(1) TFEU and 87(3) TFEU respectively.

[79] See Article 13(1) TEU. Under Lisbon, the European Council will consist of the Heads of State or Government of the Member States, together with its President and the President of the Commission—with the High Representative of the Union for Foreign Affairs and Security Policy also taking part in its work—Article 15(2) TEU.

[80] Article 15(1) TEU. Note though that the Treaty does not preclude acts of the European Council from having effects on third parties and thus establishing ECJ jurisdiction—see Article 263(1) TFEU. On the role and procedures of the European Council see Article 15 TEU and Articles 235 and 236 TFEU.

[81] See M Dougan, 'The Treaty of Lisbon 2007: Winning Minds, Not Hearts' (2008) 45 *Common Market Law Review* 617 at 627.

[82] Article 68 TFEU.

This emphasis on the role of the European Council in drawing up the strategy for the Union action in the area of freedom, security and justice creates inevitable tensions in the general framework of supranationalisation of EU criminal law post-Lisbon. The prominent role of the European Council seems potentially at odds with the central role of the Commission as a generator of initiative and policy. These tensions between Member States and the Commission became public in the context of the implementation of the Stockholm Programme and the publication of the Commission's Action Plan to that effect. Member States took the striking step of criticising the Commission's priorities, with the June 2010 Justice and Home Affairs Council emphasising 'strongly that the Stockholm Programme is the only guiding frame of reference for the political and operational agenda of the European Union in the Area of Freedom, Security and Justice', noting that 'some of the actions proposed by the Commission are not in line with the Stockholm Programme and that others, being included in the Stockholm Programme, are not reflected in the Communication of the Commission', urging the Commission 'to take only those initiatives that are in full conformity with the Stockholm Programme in order to ensure its complete and timely implementation' and finally calling on 'all parties concerned to ensure due implementation of all necessary measures and actions stemming from the Stockholm Programme, including those not present in the above Commission proposal'.[83] These are far-reaching conclusions, aiming to assert the exclusivity of the Member States' strategic initiative in the Area of Freedom, Security and Justice, and to push through the totality of Member States' priorities under Stockholm, disregarding the Commission's views. Competition as to who has the final say, rather than co-operation, sits uneasily with the principle of mutual sincere cooperation between the EU institutions.[84] In its post-Stockholm follow-up, the European Council has again departed from the positions of the other institutions[85] and demonstrated a marked lack of ambition with regard to the adoption of new EU legislation in the field of criminal law and a strong emphasis on consolidation and implementation.[86]

Initiative remains with Member States not only at the stage of the initiation of policy and strategy, but also at the stage of the initiation of *legislation*: individual Member States (and not the European Council as such) retain the right of initiative after Lisbon, sharing the right with the Commission—proposals for EU legislation on police co-operation and judicial co-operation in criminal

---

[83] Council conclusions on the Commission Communication 'Delivering an area of freedom, security and justice for Europe's citizens—Action Plan Implementing the Stockholm Programme'—3018th Justice and Home Affairs Council meeting, Luxembourg, 3 June 2010, points 1, 3, 4 and 6 respectively.

[84] Article 13(2) TEU.

[85] On the Commission's views, see Communication from the Commission to the European Parliament, the Council, the European Economic and Social Committee and the Committee of the Regions: An open and secure Europe: making it happen, Brussels, 11.3.2014 COM(2014) 154 final; European Parliament, Motion for a Resolution on the mid-term review of the Stockholm Programme, 2013/2024 (INI), 4 March 2014.

[86] European Council Conclusions, 26–27 June 2014, Brussels, EUCO 79/14, paragraph 3.

matters can be tabled either by the Commission or on the initiative of a quarter of the Member States.[87] In this manner, Member States retain some control of the legislative agenda. Pre-Lisbon, Member States—at times involved in consecutive EU Presidencies/Troikas—have used the right of initiative to table proposals on matters perceived as quite close to state sovereignty and thus rather 'intergovernmental'—examples in this context include a series of Member States' sole or joint initiatives promoting mutual recognition in criminal matters,[88] as well as initiatives than can be seen times as a pre-emptive response to more integrationist proposals due by the Commission.[89] These tendencies have continued to some extent in the early days after the entry into force of the Lisbon Treaty. Key examples are the Directives on the European Protection Order[90] and on the European Investigation Order,[91] which were adopted as Member State initiatives. The rationale behind Member State intervention has been different in these two cases: in the European Investigation Order Member States clearly wanted to control the agenda, while the European Protection Order was an instrument which was essentially promoted by a Member State (Spain) and not by the Commission. Another example of a showdown between the Commission and Member States is the adoption of the first EU instrument on defence rights, namely the Directive on the right to translation and interpretation in criminal proceedings, with Member States tabling a draft Directive in the field shortly after the entry into force of the Treaty (as early as 11 December 2009).[92] The Commission's response

---

[87] Article 76 TFEU.

[88] These include proposals for the adopted Framework Decisions on the mutual recognition of: financial penalties (France, Sweden and the UK, Council doc 19710/01, Brussels, 12 July 2001, and accompanying Explanatory Memorandum (EM) ADD 1, Brussels, 16 July 2001); confiscation orders (Denmark, Council doc 9955/02, Brussels, 14 June 2002, and EM in ADD 1, Brussels, 2 July 2002); and freezing orders (France, Sweden and Belgium, Council doc 13986/00, Brussels, 30 November 2000 and EM in ADD 1, Brussels, 22 December 2000). They also include more recent proposals such as the proposal on the recognition and supervision of suspended sentences and alternative sanctions (Germany and France, Council doc 5325/07, Brussels, 15 January 2007 and EM in ADD 1, Brussels, 1 February 2007); and the proposal on a common approach on judgments *in absentia* for mutual recognition purposes (Slovenia, France, the Czech Republic, Sweden, Slovakia, the UK and Germany, Council doc 5213/08, Brussels, 14 January 2008 and EM in ADD 1, Brussels, 30 January 2008).

[89] The example of the evolution of Eurojust is characteristic in this context—see V Mitsilegas, 'The Third Wave of Third Pillar Law: Which Direction for EU Criminal Justice?' (2009) 34 *European Law Review* 523–60.

[90] Directive 2014/41/EU of the European Parliament and of the Council of 3 April 2014 regarding the European Investigation Order in criminal matters, [2004] OJ L130/1 1.5.2014, was an initiative of the Kingdom of Belgium, the Republic of Bulgaria, the Republic of Estonia, the Kingdom of Spain, the Republic of Austria, the Republic of Slovenia and the Kingdom of Sweden.

[91] Directive of 13 December 2011 on the European protection order, [2011] OJ L338/2, 21.12.2011, was an initiative of the Kingdom of Belgium, the Republic of Bulgaria, the Republic of Estonia, the Kingdom of Spain, the French Republic, the Italian Republic, the Republic of Hungary, the Republic of Poland, the Portuguese Republic, Romania, the Republic of Finland and the Kingdom of Sweden.

[92] Initiative for a Directive on the rights to interpretation and translation in criminal proceedings, tabled by Belgium, Germany, Estonia, Spain, France, Italy, Luxembourg, Hungary, Austria, Portugal, Romania, Finland and Sweden, Council doc 16801/09, Brussels, 11 December 2009.

was to propose its own initiative for a Directive on the right to interpretation and translation in criminal proceedings, tabled in March 2010.[93] The Commission's proposal can be seen as an attempt to defend its own right of initiative in the field after Lisbon. The Directive on the right to interpretation and translation was eventually deemed to be agreed as a Member State initiative[94] but the subsequently adopted measures on procedural rights have been adopted as Commission initiatives, with the decision-making process in the field being now fully normalised.

IV. The Competence Debate—Contested Competence

A key testing ground for the constitutionalisation of EU criminal law is the application of the principle of conferral and the existence, extent and exercise of EU competence in the field of criminal justice. The entry into force of the Lisbon Treaty has demonstrated two at first sight conflicting tendencies in the field: on the one hand, the drafters of the Treaty have been ambitious enough to include in Title V for the first time new, express legal bases which would extend the powers of the Union to new areas of criminal justice including criminal procedure (Article 82(2) TFEU), 'functional' substantive criminal law (Article 83(2) TFEU) and the establishment of a European Public Prosecutor's Office (Article 86 TFEU). On the other hand, and in accordance with the general spirit of the Treaty,[95] the drafters have been careful to articulate and determine as precisely as possible the extent of EU competence in criminal law and to ensure that the Union acts within the limits of conferral. However, the care of the Treaty drafters has not stopped controversy over the existence, extent and exercise of EU competence in criminal matters. There has already been extensive litigation at three levels: at the level of the relationship between national and EU powers in criminal matters; at the level of inter-institutional balance in the adoption of internal EU law; and at the level of inter-institutional balance concerning choice of legal basis in external relations. These three aspects of competence and legal basis litigation will be examined in this section.

A. Contested Competence: Member States v The EU—The *Lissabon-Urteil*

The care taken by the drafters of the Lisbon Treaty to circumscribe the extent of EU competence in the field of criminal law has not addressed fully national

---

[93] COM(2010) 82 final, Brussels, 9.3.2010.

[94] Preamble, recital 2.

[95] See in particular Articles 4(1) and 5(2) TEU and 51(2) of the Charter—for an analysis, see L Azoulai, 'Introduction: The Question of Competence' in L Azoulai (ed), *The Question of Competence in the European Union* (Oxford, Oxford University Press, 2014) 1–18, 10–11.

concerns regarding the potential overreach of the European Union in the field. These concerns have been most vividly reflected in the judgment of the German Constitutional Court on the Treaty of Lisbon.[96] Throughout the judgment, the German Constitutional Court advocated a restrictive interpretation of the Union's competence in criminal matters.[97] Underlying this approach is the attempted link that the Bundesverfassungsgericht has made between criminal law, democracy, community and identity at the national level, and safeguarding of what the Court has deemed 'democratic self-determination'. The German Constitutional Court has emphasised the fact that criminalisation stems essentially from national values and moral choices and only partially from European values.[98] Criminal law harmonisation must extend only to specific cross-border situations on restrictive conditions; in principle, substantial freedom of action must remain reserved to the Member States.[99] The Court applies this reasoning in particular with regard to the Union's criminalisation competence under Article 83(1) TFEU. According to the Court, democratic self-determination is affected in a particularly sensitive manner where a legal community is prevented from deciding on the punishability of conduct, or even the imposition of prison sentences, according to their own values. This applies all the more the closer these values are connected with historical experience, traditions of faith and other factors essential to the self-esteem of the people and their society.[100] The main reference point for the democratic legitimacy of criminal law for the German Constitutional Court thus seems to remain the nation state. Common values, public perception of these values and public opinion are shaped at the national and not at the EU level.[101] This emphasis on democratic legitimacy based on national communities can be seen as addressing the perceived problem of 'moral distance', defined as the frequent remoteness or separation of law's normative expectations from many of those current and familiar in the fields of social interaction that it purports to regulate.[102] Yet the exclusive focus by the Bundesverfassungsgericht on the state as the sole source of democratic legitimacy—which permeates the judgment—has rightly been criticised as unduly German-centric.[103] In the field of criminal law, the ruling appears to disregard the constitutionalisation of EU criminal law outlined above, the prominent role played by democratic institutions such as the European Parliament in this

---

[96] Decision of 30 June 2009 (2 BvE 2/08, 5/08, 2 BvR 1010/08, 1022/08, 1259/08, 182/09).

[97] See in particular paragraphs 358 and 363.

[98] ibid, paragraph 253.

[99] ibid.

[100] Paragraph 363.

[101] See also A Steinbach, 'The Lisbon Judgment of the German Federal Constitutional Court—New Guidance on the Limits of European Integration?' (2010) 11 *German Law Journal* 367–90, in particular 377–79.

[102] R Cotterrell, *Law's Community. Legal Theory in Sociological Perspective* (Oxford, Clarendon Press, 1995) 304–5. See further on this argument in Chapter 5 of this volume on mutual recognition.

[103] For a persuasive critique see D Halberstam and C Möllers, 'The German Constitutional Court says "*Ja zu Deutschland!*"' (2009) 10 *German Law Journal* 1241–57.

context and the thorough attempts by the drafters of the Lisbon Treaty to clarify as far as possible the extent of Union competence in the field and the balance of powers between the Union and Member States.[104] The ruling further does not take into account the safeguards built in the Lisbon Treaty with regard to the exercise of EU competence in criminal matters, and in particular the use of Directives (which leave leeway as regards the means of implementation to Member States) as the exclusive instrument of EU law-making under Articles 82 and 83 TFEU. While the German Constitutional Court has not declared the Treaty unconstitutional (but rather placed emphasis on national control of the operation of a series of Lisbon safeguards such as the emergency brake), its approach leaves the possibility for further constitutional tension between the national and the Union levels on the Union's powers in the field of criminal law open.

B. Contested Competence and Inter-institutional Balance: The Road Traffic Offences Directive Case

The entry into force of the Treaty of Lisbon included an attempt to address the pre-Lisbon inter-institutional battles over the existence and extent of Union competence in criminal matters. As will be analysed in the following chapter, Article 83(2) TFEU establishes a paradigm of functional criminalisation by attempting to translate into Treaty terms the seminal rulings of the Court of Justice in litigation concerning the delimitation of criminal law competence on environmental crime and pollution at sea.[105] The precise scope and contours of EU competence under Article 83(2) TFEU remain contested, and the wording of the provision may still raise questions to be resolved by the Court of Justice. However, competence questions are not limited to substantive criminalisation. The entry into force of the Lisbon Treaty has already triggered litigation regarding the correct legal basis on a measure introducing a cooperation mechanism on the investigation of road traffic offences. Directive 2011/82/EU facilitating the cross-border exchange of information on road safety related traffic offences was adopted on 25 October 2011.[106] Its legal basis was Article 87(2) TFEU, which is a police cooperation legal basis under Title V TFEU.[107] Its stated objective was

---

[104] For a critique of the Court's arguments on the lack of the Union's democratic legitimacy, see D Grimm, 'Comments on the German Constitutional Court's Decision on the Lisbon Treaty. Defending Sovereign Statehood against Transforming the European Union into a State' in (2009) 5 *European Constitutional Law Review* 353–73, 367–68.

[105] Case C-176/03 *Commission v Council* [2005] ECR I-7879; Case C-440/05 *Commission v Council* [2007] ECR I-9097. For an analysis see V Mitsilegas, *EU Criminal Law* (Oxford, Hart Publishing, 2009) chapter 2.

[106] Directive 2011/82/EU of the European Parliament and of the Council of 25 October 2011 facilitating the cross-border exchange of information on road safety related traffic offences, [2011] OJ L288/1, 5.11.2011.

[107] According to Article 87(1) TFEU, the Union will 'establish police cooperation involving all the Member States' competent authorities, including police, customs and other specialised law

to ensure a high level of protection for all road users in the Union by facilitating the cross-border exchange of information on road safety related traffic offences and thereby the enforcement of sanctions, where those offences are committed with a vehicle registered in a Member State other than the Member State where the offence took place.[108] The key measures it introduced were a procedure for the exchange of information between Member States[109] and the issuing of an information letter on the road safety related traffic offences.[110] The Commission challenged the validity of the Directive on the grounds of the incorrect use of legal basis.[111] The Commission argued that Article 87(2) TFEU could be the legal basis only of measures specifically related to the prevention or detection of criminal offences. The Commission further argued that 'it cannot be inferred simply because an "offence" is punitive in nature or seeks to achieve deterrence, that it can automatically be regarded as a "criminal" offence within the meaning of Article 87 TFEU'.[112] According to the Commission, both the goal and the content of the Directive fell within the field of transport policy and in particular Article 91 TFEU which should have been used as the legal basis of the Directive.[113] The aim of the Directive, argued the Commission, was to improve road safety and its content confined itself to 'organising the exchange of information with regard to … conduct bearing upon road safety, without adopting harmonising measures in relation to that conduct and … without obliging the Member States to criminalise such conduct'.[114]

The Commission's arguments were rebutted by the European Parliament and the Council supported by seven Member States (Belgium, Ireland, Hungary, Poland, the Slovak Republic, Sweden and the United Kingdom). The European Parliament, supported by the majority of the intervening Member States, considered that the Directive pursued principally the objective of establishing a system of exchange of information and only indirectly objectives related to road safety—for that reason, the Directive could not have been based on Article 91 TFEU.[115] The Council further pointed out that the Directive provided for rules related to the enforcement of sanctions concerning road safety related traffic offences. While these offences may be of an administrative or criminal nature, the means for enforcing them must be regarded as falling, in all cases, within the category of rules of criminal procedure,

enforcement services in relation to the prevention, detection and investigation of criminal offences'. According to Article 87(2)(a) TFEU, the European Parliament and the Council may establish for the purposes of Article 87(1) measures concerning 'the collection, storage, processing, analysis and exchange of relevant information'.

[108] Directive 2011/82/EU, Article 1.
[109] ibid, Article 4.
[110] Article 5.
[111] Judgment of the CJEU (Grand Chamber) in C-43/12, *European Commission v European Parliament and Council* (6 May 2014) EU:C:2014:298.
[112] ibid, paragraph 17.
[113] Paragraph 19.
[114] Paragraph 20.
[115] Paragraph 24.

with the question of what is a 'criminal matter' to be interpreted autonomously under EU law.[116] The Council argued that

> provisions such as those in [the Directive], the aim of which is to improve road safety by deterring certain types of behaviour regarded as dangerous, are necessarily 'criminal' matters and cannot be classified as road safety related norms within the meaning of Article 91 TFEU.[117]

The Council argued that the Directive fell entirely within the objectives of Article 87(2) TFEU, as the measures sought to facilitate the detection of persons who have committed cross-border road safety related offences and the aim of the Directive was to collect information concerning offences, in order to help deter them, which are measures for which the European Union has competence under Article 87 TFEU. According to the Council, the reference to 'all the ... competent authorities' in Article 87(1) TFEU confirms that it is immaterial, for the purposes of determining the applicability of that provision, whether the services at issue were in each Member State concerned, administrative or criminal in nature.[118]

The Court found in favour of the Commission. It began its reasoning by reiterating that in assessing the appropriate use of the legal basis both the aim and the content of the measure must be examined[119] and that

> if examination of the measure concerned reveals that it pursues a twofold purpose or that it has a twofold component and if one of those is identifiable as the main or predominant purpose or component, whereas the other is merely incidental, that measure must be based on a single legal basis, namely that required by the main or predominant purpose or component.[120]

Examining the Directive in question, the Court found that its main aim was to improve road safety which is a prime objective of the European transport policy.[121] The aim of the establishment of the system of cross-border information exchange set out in the Directive was to enable the Union to pursue the goal of improving road safety.[122] With regard to the content of the Directive, and following an examination of the key provisions of that measure,[123] the Court found again that the system for the exchange of information set up by the Directive provides the means of pursuing the objective of improving road safety and enables the Union to attain that aim.[124] The Directive was thus a measure to improve transport safety within

---

[116] Paragraph 25.
[117] Paragraph 26. On the deterrent effect of the Directive, see also the Opinion of Advocate General Bot, delivered on 10 September 2013, paragraph 33.
[118] Paragraph 27.
[119] Paragraph 29.
[120] Paragraph 30.
[121] Paragraph 36.
[122] Paragraph 37.
[123] Paragraphs 38–41.
[124] Paragraph 42.

the meaning of Article 91(1)(c) TFEU and it should have been adopted under that legal basis.[125] The Directive was not directly linked to the area of freedom, security and justice objectives enshrined in Article 67(2) TFEU.[126] The Court thus annulled the Directive but decided to maintain its effects until the entry into force within a reasonable period of time and not exceeding 12 months as from the date of the delivery of the judgment of a new Directive based on the correct legal basis of Article 91(1)(c) TFEU.[127] A new Directive based on Article 91(1)(c) was indeed adopted and published in the Official Journal 10 months after the date of the delivery of the judgment in the road traffic offences case.[128]

The Court's ruling has far-reaching implications for the delimitation of EU powers to act in criminal matters. First of all, the change in the legal basis of the road traffic offences Directive has had a profound impact on the position of Member States which did not participate (Denmark) or had a right not to opt into (Ireland and the United Kingdom) Title V legislation. All these states are now bound by the new 'transport' road traffic offences Directive (as there is no possibility of an opt-out from Article 91 TFEU), although they were not (Denmark) or chose not to be (Ireland and the United Kingdom) subject to the original Directive adopted under a Title V legal basis. The new Directive recognises this change by granting these Member States additional time to implement a Directive the substance of which is identical to the measure which they were not subject to.[129] The Court's ruling is also significant in that it reiterates the functional criminalisation approach adopted in the earlier rulings on environmental crime and ship-source pollution rulings, and extends this approach beyond the field of substantive criminal law to the field of cooperation in criminal matters. As with its earlier rulings, the Court here views criminal law as merely a means to an end for the achievement of Union objectives, in this case transport. In order to reach this conclusion, the Court has privileged in its analysis the objective of the road traffic offences Directive, while it essentially subordinated the content of the measure (which was—and still is—essentially related to law enforcement cooperation) to the rather general and broad aim of transport policy. In this manner, law enforcement cooperation becomes the means to the end of the achievement of transport policy objectives. This reasoning is not convincing in disregarding the cooperation essence of the measure. It has a profound effect in that it seems to enable the adoption of functional criminal law measures outside the field of substantive criminal law under legal bases outside the scope of Title V TFEU. There is thus a functional criminal law spill-over from Title V to other parts of the Treaty, with the road traffic

---

[125] Paragraph 44.

[126] Paragraphs 47–49.

[127] Paragraph 56.

[128] Directive (EU) 2015/413 of the European Parliament and of the Council of 11 March 2015 facilitating cross-border exchange of information on road-safety-related traffic offences, [2015] OJ L68/9, 13.3.2015.

[129] Recital 29.

offences ruling leaving open the possibility of EU legislation in criminal matters being adopted outside Title V.[130] This approach may challenge significantly the position of Member States which have, as seen in this chapter, inserted a number of sovereignty and legal diversity safeguards into Title V TFEU, which could thus be circumvented.

C. Contested Competence and Inter-institutional Balance: The Internal/External Dimension—The Case of Terrorist Sanctions

Persistent questions with regard to the legality of EU action against terrorism have arisen in the context of the adoption by the European Union of sanctions amounting to the freezing of assets of terrorist suspects, implementing in the EU legal order UN Security Council Resolutions 1267 and 1373. One of the key legality hurdles that the EU legislator had to overcome pre-Lisbon was the absence in the Treaties of an express legal basis conferring on the Community or the Union competence to legislate on sanctions against individuals.[131] In order to overcome this hurdle, and in particular to implement Resolution 1267, the Council adopted a Common Position under Article 15 TEU[132] and in parallel a first pillar Regulation on the basis of Articles 60, 301 and 308 TEC.[133] The addition of Article 308 to the legal basis of Regulation 881/2002 has been attributed to the need to take account of political developments taking place at the time. By January 2002 the Taliban regime in Afghanistan had fallen and so at the time the Regulation was adopted, the persons and entities listed did not have a direct connection with the territory or governing regime of a third country. The initial choice of legal bases of Articles 60 and 301 TEC, which was based on the principle that the individuals and entities listed were in effective control of the territory of a third country, or were associated with those in effective control and provided them with financial support, was thus deemed no longer adequate to address the situation in Afghanistan.[134] Under this technique, sanctions against individuals not linked with the government or the control of a country thus were included within the scope of Community law, with Regulation 881/2002 consolidating and expanding

---

[130] For further detail on this debate, see Chapter 3 of this volume.

[131] V Mitsilegas, 'The European Union and the Globalisation of Criminal Law' (2010) 12 *Cambridge Yearbook of European Legal Studies* 337–407.

[132] Council Common Position of 27 May 2002 concerning restrictive measures against Usama bin Laden, members of the Al-Qaida organisation and the Taliban and other individuals, groups, undertakings and entities associated with them and repealing Common Positions 96/746/CFSP, 1999/727/CFSP, 2001/154/CFSP and 2001/771/CFSP (2002/402/CFSP), [2002] OJ L139/4.

[133] Council Regulation (EC) No 881/2002 of 27 May 2002 imposing certain specific restrictive measures directed against certain persons and entities associated with Usama bin Laden, the Al-Qaida network and the Taliban, and repealing Council Regulation (EC) No 467/2001, [2002] OJ L139/9.

[134] See M Cremona, 'EC Competence, 'Smart Sanctions' and the *Kadi* Case' 28 *Yearbook of European Law 2009* 559, 569.

the sanctions regime in the light of developments in the Security Council.[135] Although the legality of the adoption of Regulation 881/2002 is questionable, it was affirmed by the Court of Justice in its ruling in *Kadi I*. The Court found that

> inasmuch as they provide for Community powers to impose restrictive measures of an economic nature in order to implement actions decided on under the CFSP, Articles 60 and 301 EC are the expression of an implicit underlying objective, namely, that of making it possible to adopt such measures through the efficient use of a Community instrument,[136]

adding that that objective may be regarded as constituting an objective of the Community for the purpose of Article 308.[137] The Court then found a link between the Regulation and the operation of the common market, stating that if sanctions were imposed unilaterally by Member States, the multiplication of those national measures 'might well affect the operation of the common market', adding that such measures could have a particular effect on trade between Member States, especially with regard to the movement of capital and payments, and on the exercise by economic operators of their right of establishment and that they could create distortions of competition, 'because any differences between the measures unilaterally taken by the Member States could operate to the advantage or disadvantage of the competitive position of certain economic operators although there were no economic reasons for that advantage or disadvantage'.[138] The Court has thus attempted to accommodate the transposition of the UNSC sanctions system within the EU legal order, by accepting the legality of the use of Community legal bases targeting states and related to the operation of the common market, for the adoption of EU internal security law introducing sanctions against individuals.[139]

The Lisbon Treaty has addressed the gaps with regard to the legal basis for terrorist sanctions which the Court attempted to fill in *Kadi I* by the introduction of specific provisions in the field. Not one, but two Treaty provisions are potentially applicable in this context. Article 75 TFEU, located in the Treaty part on the Union as an Area of Freedom, Security and Justice, states that

> where necessary to achieve the objectives set out in Article 67, as regards preventing and combating terrorism and related activities, the European Parliament and the Council, acting by means of regulations in accordance with the ordinary legislative procedure, [must] define a framework for administrative measures with regard to capital movements and payments, such as the freezing of funds, financial assets or economic gains belonging to, or owned or held by, natural or legal persons, groups or non-State entities.

---

[135] See in particular Articles 2, 4 and 6 of the Regulation.

[136] Joined Cases C-402/05 P and C-415/05 *Kadi and Al Barakaat International Foundation v Council and Commission* [2008] ECR I-6351. paragraph 226.

[137] ibid, paragraph 227.

[138] Paragraph 230.

[139] For a critical analysis, see Mitsilegas, 'The European Union and the Globalisation of Criminal Law', n 131 above.

Article 215(2) TFEU states that

> where a decision adopted in accordance with Chapter 2 of Title V of the Treaty on European Union so provides, the Council may adopt restrictive measures under the procedure referred to in paragraph 1 against natural or legal persons and groups or non-State entities.

We have thus moved from the pre-Lisbon constitutional landscape, when arguably the EU Treaties did not include a legal basis for the adoption by the EU of sanctions against individuals, to a post-Lisbon proliferation of legal bases in the field. The post-Lisbon developments have thus not stopped legal basis litigation before the Court of Justice, as Article 75 and 215(2) TFEU contain differences in the legislative procedure they set out for the adoption of sanctions, and the proliferation of legal bases leads to a lack of clarity as regards the role, scope and extent of each of these legal bases.

After the entry into force of the Lisbon Treaty, the Council has elected to continue the amendments to Regulation 881/2002 on the basis of Article 215(2) TFEU and not 75 TFEU. Article 215(2) TFEU was the legal basis for Regulation 1286/2009 of 22 December 2009 amending Regulation 881/2002.[140] The validity of Article 215(2) as the legal basis for Regulation 1286/2009 was contested by the European Parliament, which sought the annulment of the measure by the Court of Justice.[141] The Parliament based its plea on two main arguments, related to the aim and content of the contested Regulation and its position in the general scheme of the Treaties. With regard to the aim and content of the Regulation, the Parliament argued that the objective of the contested regulation is, as corroborated by the Court's ruling in *Kadi I*, and like that of Regulation No 881/2002, 'to combat terrorism and the financing of terrorism, which is consistent with the objectives of Article 75 TFEU'.[142] 'Given that it is not the purpose of Regulation No 881/2002 to achieve CFSP objectives, it is difficult to see how the contested regulation, adopted to ensure the application of the former regulation, could do so': according to the Parliament, 'the Council may have recourse to Article 215 TFEU only for measures that pursue CFSP objectives, more particularly when a decision intended to achieve the objectives of that policy makes provision for such recourse'.[143] The Parliament further challenged the Council's distinction between 'internal' and 'external' terrorism, noting that 'the only distinction that can be made in this context is between national measures to combat terrorism, and international anti-terrorism measures' and that 'it is not always possible to say with any

---

[140] Council Regulation (EU) No 1286/2009 of 22 December 2009 amending Regulation (EC) No 881/2002 imposing certain specific restrictive measures directed against certain persons and entities associated with Usama bin Laden, the Al-Qaeda network and the Taliban ([2009] OJ L346/42.

[141] Case C-130/10, *European Parliament v Council*, judgment of 19 July 2012.

[142] ibid, paragraph 14.

[143] Paragraph 15.

certainty whether terrorist and related activities carried out within the European Union will create a threat within or without the European Union'.[144]

The Council on the other hand argued that, 'in the light of its objectives and its content, the contested regulation falls within the scope of the provisions of the Treaties relating to the European Union's external action, and more specifically within the sphere of the CFSP' and that 'Article 215 TFEU constitutes the appropriate legal basis for that measure'.[145] According to the Council, '[t]he purpose of that regulation, like that of Regulation No 881/2002, is to combat international terrorism and its financing *in order to maintain international peace and security*' (emphasis added).[146] Moreover, the Council argued that

> the content of the contested regulation [No 1286/2009] was consistent with that objective. Articles 7a and 7c, which that regulation inserts into Regulation No 881/2002, confirm that those regulations directly implement the listing decisions adopted by the Sanctions Committee and establish a system of interaction between the Sanctions Committee, the European Union and the individuals and entities listed.[147]

> In the Council's view, Regulation No 881/2002 and the contested regulation do not in any way fall within the scope of the provisions intended to create an area of freedom, security and justice within the European Union.[148]

'Article 75 TFEU now provides a legal basis for adopting measures to freeze the funds of "internal" terrorists'; 'conversely, if the threat relates primarily to one or more third States or to the international community in general, Article 215 TFEU is the appropriate legal basis'.[149] The Council was supported by the Commission which, following a different line of argument, challenged

> the Parliament's claim that an act based on Article 308 EC cannot pursue a CFSP objective. According to the Commission, the Court did not in that judgment deny that Articles 60 EC and 301 EC were legal bases permitting the adoption of Community measures pursuing a CFSP objective. As regards Regulation No 881/2002, the Court identified a second, underlying Community objective linked to the functioning of the common market to justify the inclusion of Article 308 EC as a third legal basis. Moreover, it confirmed that the EC Treaty required recourse to that provision for the imposition of restrictive measures in respect of natural or legal persons in cases where there is no link with the governing regime of a non-member State.[150]

---

[144] Paragraph 16.
[145] Paragraph 17.
[146] Paragraph 18.
[147] Paragraph 19.
[148] Paragraph 20.
[149] Paragraph 22. '23. Furthermore, the Council, supported in substance by the Kingdom of Sweden, submits that the Parliament's proposition fails to take account of those cases where, in the context of the fight against terrorism, the European Union seeks to adopt or impose restrictive measures other than the freezing of assets, such as a travel ban, in respect of persons or entities associated with "external" terrorism'.
[150] Paragraph 26.

Moreover, the Commission considered

> that Articles 215 TFEU and 75 TFEU cannot be used jointly as legal bases for the con-
> tested regulation. It is not possible to base an act on those two articles at the same time,
> for they lay down different procedural and decision-making conditions.

The Commission further emphasised that

> one of the crucial differences between Articles 215 TFEU and 75 TFEU is to be found in
> the need of a link to decisions in the sphere of the CFSP, taken in the interests of interna-
> tional peace and security, whatever the precise geographical location or the scope of the
> terrorist threat at issue. When restrictive measures relating to terrorism must be adopted
> under the FEU Treaty following a CFSP decision further to a Security Council Resolu-
> tion, Article 215 TFEU is [according to the Commission] the only possible legal basis.[151]

With regard to the position of the contested Regulation in the general scheme
of the Treaties, the Parliament argued that 'the general scheme and spirit of the
Treaties justify the use of Article 75 TFEU as the legal basis of the contested
regulation'.[152] 'The contested regulation is linked to the protection of individuals
and groups' and '[s]ince the entry into force of the Treaty of Lisbon, however, the
European Union may adopt measures concerning fundamental rights only under
the ordinary legislative procedure or with the consent of the Parliament'. This link
with fundamental rights according to the Parliament means that 'Article 215(2)
TFEU is applicable only in respect of measures that do not raise issues of fundamental rights to the same extent'.[153] The contested Regulation involves 'measures with regard to capital movements and payments, thus recognising that such
measures may affect the proper functioning of the internal capital market and the
provision of financial services' which fall within Article 75 TFEU and 'is linked to
the establishment of an area of freedom, security and justice'.[154] Finally, according
to the Parliament,

> there is no link between the contested regulation and the CFSP. Under Article 24(1) TEU,
> the CFSP is subject to specific rules and procedures. To give effect to those rules and
> procedures outside their ambit would run counter to the objectives set out in the second
> paragraph of Article 1 TEU and have the effect of depriving national parliaments of the
> application of the protocols on their role and on the application of the principles of
> subsidiarity and proportionality, and of denying the Parliament the application of the
> ordinary legislative procedure.[155]

> … [i]t would be contrary to European Union law for it to be possible to adopt meas-
> ures having a direct impact on the fundamental rights of individuals and groups, on the
> internal market and on the fight against crime by means of a procedure which excludes
> the participation of the European Parliament, when the ordinary legislative procedure

---

[151] Paragraph 27.
[152] Paragraph 28.
[153] Paragraph 29.
[154] Paragraphs 30 and 31 respectively.
[155] Paragraph 32.

applies for the adoption of measures in those areas ... Recognising Article 215(2) TFEU as the correct legal basis for measures such as the contested regulation would, in practice, deprive Article 75 TFEU of much of its effectiveness. The Parliament also points out that Article 75 TFEU constitutes a more specific legal basis than Article 215 TFEU.[156]

The Council on the other hand submitted 'that the arguments put forward by the European Parliament with respect to the general scheme of the Treaties do not constitute relevant criteria for determining the correct legal basis of the contested regulation' as 'the Parliament's proposition amounts to a claim that procedures determine the choice of legal basis rather than the other way round'.[157] According to the Council,

> the Parliament's argument to the effect that the European Union can adopt measures concerning respect for human rights only with the Parliament's involvement is contradicted by Article 215(3) TFEU, which provides that '[t]he acts referred to in this Article shall include necessary provisions on legal safeguards'.[158]

The Council submitted too that the purpose of Article 215 TFEU was 'to enable the Council to adopt measures which are directly applicable to economic operators' helping thus 'to ensure the proper functioning of the common market'.[159]

As regards the relationship of the contested regulation to the CFSP ... [the] regulation constitutes the framework within which the European Union performs its obligations under the Charter of the United Nations' and 'it is not unreasonable to take account of the objective of the resolutions adopted by the Security Council in determining the appropriate legal basis'.[160]

> Lastly, the Council points out that the Treaty of Lisbon has not affected the distinction between the CFSP and the area of freedom, security and justice. On the contrary, the importance of a line clearly delimiting those two fields was emphasised in the second paragraph of Article 40 TEU. In consequence, if the Court were to take the view that the contested regulation pursues an objective falling under the CFSP, Article 215(2) TFEU would be the only possible legal basis for its adoption.[161]

The Court dismissed the action brought by the European Parliament, ruling that Article 215(2) was the correct legal basis for the contested legislation. In order to reach this conclusion, the Court proceeded on the basis of three steps: the examination of the relationship between Articles 75 and 215(2) TFEU and the pre-Lisbon legal bases of Articles 60, 301 and 308 TEC; the examination of the ambit of Article 251(2); and the purpose and tenor of the contested Regulation. This

---

[156] Paragraph 34.
[157] Paragraphs 35 and 36.
[158] Paragraph 38.
[159] Paragraph 39.
[160] Paragraph 40.
[161] Paragraph 41.

three-step analysis, however, was preceded by the Court's acceptance of the Commission's argument that,

> even if the contested regulation does pursue several objectives at the same time or have several components indissociably linked, without one's being secondary to the other, the differences in the procedures applicable under Articles 75 TFEU and 215(2) TFEU mean that it is not possible for the two provisions to be cumulated, one with the other, in order to serve as a twofold legal basis for a measure such as the contested regulation.[162]

The Court based this finding in its earlier case-law in *Titanium Dioxide*[163] where it found that recourse to a dual legal basis is not possible where the procedures laid down for each legal basis are incompatible with each other.[164] The Court found that the *Titanium Dioxide* approach 'is still valid, after the entry into force of the Treaty of Lisbon, in the context of the ordinary legislative procedure'.[165]

> In this instance, while Article 75 TFEU provides for application of the ordinary legislative procedure, which entails qualified majority voting in the Council and the Parliament's full participation in the procedure, Article 215(2) TFEU, for its part, entails merely informing the Parliament. In addition, recourse to Article 215(2) TFEU, unlike recourse to Article 75 TFEU, requires a previous decision in the sphere of the CFSP, namely, a decision adopted in accordance with Chapter 2 of Title V of the EU Treaty, providing for the adoption of restrictive measures such as those referred to in that provision. As a general rule, adoption of such a decision calls for unanimous voting in the Council acting alone.[166]

According to the Court, 'differences of that kind are such as to render those procedures incompatible'.[167]

Having established that the procedures laid down under Article 75 and Article 215(2) TFEU are incompatible, the Court went on to assess *the relationship of these provisions in the light of their relationship with the pre-Lisbon legal bases for the Regulation which the contested Regulation sought to amend.* The Court found

> that as a result of the amendments made to primary law after the Treaty of Lisbon entered into force, the content of Articles 60 EC, relating to restrictive measures with regard to capital movements and payments, and 301 EC on the interruption or reduction, in part or completely, of economic relations with one or more third countries, is mirrored in Article 215 TFEU.[168]

Furthermore,

> Article 215(2) TFEU allows the Council to adopt restrictive measures against natural or legal persons and groups or non-State entities, namely, measures that, before the Treaty

---

[162] Paragraph 49.
[163] Case C-300/89 *Commission v Council (Titanium Dioxide)* [1991] ECR I-2867, paragraphs 17–21.
[164] Case C-130/10, *European Parliament v Council*, judgment of 19 July 2012, paragraph 45.
[165] Paragraph 46.
[166] Paragraph 47.
[167] Paragraph 48.
[168] Paragraphs 51 and 52.

of Lisbon entered into force, required Article 308 EC too to be included in their legal basis if their addressees were not linked to the governing regime of a third country.[169]

The 'context and tenor' of Article 75 TFEU differ according to the Court from those of Articles 60 EC and 301 EC as 'Article 75 TFEU does not, in fact, refer to the interruption or reduction, in part or completely, of economic relations with one or more third countries'.[170] However, it is difficult to see how this finding is relevant in the field of terrorist sanctions, which are targeting individuals and not third states.

As its next step, the Court analysed in detail the ambit of Article 215 TFEU (and mentioned only in passing the ambit of Article 75 TFEU). The Court noted in particular the link between restrictive measures and the CFSP. The Court referred to the wording of Article 215(1) and (2), and the fact that the latter

> concerns the adoption by the Council of 'restrictive measures [...] against natural or legal persons and groups or non-State entities', without specifically referring to the combating of terrorism and without limiting those measures to those measures alone that concern capital movements and payments.[171]

Moreover, the Court noted that 'Article 215(2) TFEU, unlike Article 75 TFEU, provides ... that it may not be used until a decision under the CFSP has provided for the adoption of restrictive measures against natural or legal persons, groups or non-State entities' while 'Article 75 TFEU states that it may be used where necessary to achieve the objectives set out in Article 67 TFEU, that is to say, in connection with creating an area of freedom, security and justice'.[172] Referring to *Kadi I*, which established a bridge between the Community legal bases of Articles 60 and 301 and external relations including CFSP, the Court noted that post-Lisbon, 'Article 215 TFEU expressly provides such a bridge, but this is not the case with Article 75 TFEU, which creates no link with decisions taken under the CFSP'.[173] The Court found that as regards combating terrorism and its funding, 'there is nothing in Article 215 TFEU to indicate that measures designed to combat them, taken against natural or legal persons, groups or non-State entities, could not constitute restrictive measures provided for in subparagraph 2 of that article'.[174] The Court noted that while

> admittedly the combating of terrorism and its financing may well be among the objectives of the area of freedom, security and justice, as they appear in Article 3(2) TEU, the objective of combating international terrorism and its financing *in order to preserve*

---

[169] Paragraph 53.
[170] Paragraph 54.
[171] Paragraph 57.
[172] Paragraph 58.
[173] Paragraph 59.
[174] Paragraph 60.

international peace and security corresponds, nevertheless, to the objectives of the Treaty provisions on external action by the Union' (emphasis added).[175]

The Court mentioned in this context the references to the preservation of peace and international security in Article 21(2)(c) TEU the broad reference to 'the Union's security' in the CFSP provision of Article 24(1) TFEU,[176] and the wording of Article 43(1) TFEU according to which the common security and defence policy may contribute to the fight against terrorism.[177] On the basis of this very broad conceptualisation of security, the emphasis on international peace and security, and the establishment of a general link between security and EU foreign and defence policy, the Court asserted that

> given that terrorism constitutes a threat to peace and international security, the object of actions undertaken by the Union in the sphere of the CFSP, and the measures taken in order to give effect to that policy in the Union's external actions, in particular, restrictive measures for the purpose of Article 215(2) TFEU, can be to combat terrorism.[178]

As regards the purpose and tenor of the contested Regulation, the Court stated, quoting again *Kadi I*, that 'the essential purpose and object' of the latter 'is to combat *international terrorism*' (emphasis added).[179] 'In the light of its objectives and of its content, the contested regulation relates to a decision taken by the Union under the CFSP'.[180] The Parliament's argument

> that it is impossible to distinguish the combating of 'internal' terrorism, on the one hand, from the combating of 'external' terrorism, on the other, does not appear capable of calling in question the choice of Article 215(2) TFEU as a legal basis of the contested regulation.[181]

> ... Article 215(2) TFEU provides a sufficient legal basis for adopting, in response to a decision taken under the CFSP, restrictive measures taken in order to apply that policy to natural or legal persons, groups or non-State entities involved in acts of terrorism.[182]

> In the present case ... the contested regulation amends Regulation No 881/2002 which ... constitutes one of the instruments by which the European Union put into effect an action decided upon within the Security Council and intended to preserve international peace and security.[183]

The Parliament

> has not called in question whether it was possible for that Common Position, having enabled adoption of Regulation No 881/2002 in accordance with Articles 60 EC and 301

---

[175] Paragraph 61.
[176] Paragraph 62.
[177] Paragraph 64.
[178] Paragraph 63.
[179] Paragraph 68.
[180] Paragraph 72.
[181] Paragraph 74.
[182] Paragraph 75.
[183] Paragraph 76.

EC, to be validly based on Title V of the EU Treaty, as it stood before the Treaty of Lisbon, that is to say, the title of that treaty concerning the CFSP.[184]

Having regard to those factors, it suffices to find that Article 215(2) TFEU constitutes the appropriate legal basis for measures, such as those at issue in the present case, directed to addressees implicated in acts of terrorism who, having regard to their activities globally and to the international dimension of the threat they pose, affect fundamentally the Union's external activity.[185]

The Court further considered the consequences of this finding for the Parliament's prerogatives. It accepted the Council's assertion that 'it is not procedures that define the legal basis of a measure but the legal basis of a measure that determines the procedures to be followed in adopting that measure'.[186] The Court accepted that 'participation by the Parliament in the legislative process is the reflection, at Union level, of the fundamental democratic principle that the people should participate in the exercise of power through the intermediary of a representative assembly'[187] but stated that

the difference between Article 75 TFEU and Article 215 TFEU, so far as the Parliament's involvement is concerned, is the result of the choice made by the framers of the Treaty of Lisbon conferring a more limited role on the Parliament with regard to the Union's action under the CFSP.[188]

The Court added that

so far as concerns the Parliament's argument that it would be contrary to Union law for it to be possible for measures to be adopted that impinge directly on the fundamental rights of individuals and groups by means of a procedure excluding the Parliament's participation, the duty to respect fundamental rights is imposed, in accordance with Article 51(1) of the Charter of Fundamental Rights of the European Union, on all the institutions and bodies of the Union. In addition, under both Article 75 TFEU and Article 215(3) TFEU, the acts referred to in those articles are to include necessary provisions on legal safeguards.[189]

The Court added that the Parliament's argument 'that such a measure may be adopted only on the basis of Article 75 TFEU, would … render Article 215(2) largely redundant, whereas the duty to respect fundamental rights bears also on Union measures giving effect to resolutions of the Security Council'.[190]

The attempt by the Court of Justice to justify the legality of Article 215(2) TFEU with regard to the adoption of terrorist sanctions by the EU implementing UN

---

[184] Paragraph 77.
[185] Paragraph 78.
[186] Paragraph 80.
[187] Paragraph 81.
[188] Paragraph 82.
[189] Paragraph 83.
[190] Paragraph 84.

Security Council Resolution 1267—at the expense of the Area of Freedom, Security and Justice legal basis of Article 75 TFEU—is premised on a number of contradictions. The Court accepted the Council's statement that it is not procedures that define the legal basis of a measure but the legal basis of a measure that determines the procedures to be followed in adopting that measure, yet its reasoning on the preference of Article 215(2) TFEU over Article 75 TFEU is based essentially on procedural arguments. In the first place, the Court chose to exclude the possibility of Articles 75 and 215(2) acting as joint legal bases for the contested Regulation by ruling that these legal bases are incompatible with each other. This declaration of incompatibility was by no means a one-way street for the Court, which in earlier case-law accepted the adoption of a dual legal basis consisting of Treaty provisions which prescribed different legislative procedures. In these cases, procedural differences were reconciled, with the Court opting for the adoption of the procedure which respects more fully the Parliament's prerogatives.[191] The Court could have certainly followed this reasoning in the present case, where the content and objective of the two legal bases were very similar. Secondly, the Court's emphasis on procedure is evident in its attempt to justify the legality of Article 215(2) on the basis of the existence of a bridge between terrorist sanctions and the CFSP. In order to establish this bridge, the Court adopted a historical approach aiming to interpret the relationship between the post-Lisbon legal bases on terrorist sanctions in the light of the articulation of the relationship between the pre-Lisbon legal bases for the Regulation which the contested measure seeks to amend, as put forward by the Court of Justice in *Kadi I*. Yet this approach disregards the fundamental procedural and constitutional differences between the pre- and the post-Lisbon legal bases for terrorist sanctions. Pre-Lisbon, the Treaties did not include an express legal basis allowing the European Community or the European Union to adopt sanctions against individuals. In *Kadi I*, the Court of Justice went out of its way to find a way to uphold the legality of EU action in the field by establishing a bridge between the first pillar legal bases and the CFSP.[192] Yet the situation is radically different after the entry into force of the Lisbon Treaty. The EU legislator in Lisbon attempted to address the legality gaps in the pre-Lisbon constitutional framework by including express legal bases for the adoption of terrorist sanctions against individuals, including Article 75 TFEU. To establish a continuum between the pre-Lisbon and the post-Lisbon legal bases is to disregard the new legal situation brought about by the Lisbon Treaty. In establishing the constitutional link between Article 75 and 215(2) TFEU, the pre-Lisbon constitutional arrangements should not be decisive.

---

[191] G De Baere, 'From "Don't Mention the *Titanium Dioxide* Judgment" to "I Mentioned it Once, But I Think I Got Away with it All Right": Reflections on the Choice of Legal Basis in EU External Relations after the *Legal Basis for Restrictive Measures* Judgment' (2013) 15 *Cambridge Yearbook of European Legal Studies* 537–62, 541–42.

[192] Mitsilegas, 'The European Union and the Globalisation of Criminal Law', n 131 above.

The Court's approach has profound implications for the conceptualisation of security in EU law, for the relationship between internal and external security in the context of counter-terrorism law, as well as for the configuration of the relationship between CFSP and other areas of Union law and policy after Lisbon. The Court rightly did not attach weight to the artificial distinction made by the Council between 'internal' and 'external' terrorists. Yet at the same time the Court seemed to treat the imposition of terrorist sanctions on individuals under EU law as a matter of 'international terrorism' which was justified in order to achieve the professed CFSP objectives of maintaining peace and security. The reference to international peace and security echoes UN law, and a system which was initially designed to govern inter-state relations. Moreover, references to international terrorism and international peace and security disregard the internal security dimension of counter-terrorism law as well as the impact of these measures on the fundamental rights of affected individuals. By giving security such a broad meaning in order to be able to justify the legality of an external relations legal basis, and at the same time finding that the use of this legal basis is incompatible with the use of an AFSJ legal basis for measures imposing terrorist sanctions, the Court reconfigured radically the relationship between the CFSP and other areas of EU law and policy.[193] Article 40 TEU[194] post-Lisbon has been seen as abolishing the pre-Lisbon hierarchy whereby CFSP should not affect EC policies by establishing an equal relationship between the CFSP and other fields of EU law and policy.[195] Yet the Court's ruling in the terrorist sanctions legal basis case effectively grants primacy to CFSP over other policies, including the AFSJ. Any aspect which may fall under the very broad scope of security for the purposes of CFSP would potentially negate the application of other legal bases located elsewhere in the Treaties. In this manner, EU policies related to security (including internal security and AFSJ policies) are effectively subordinated to CFSP objectives.[196] There is very little room

---

[193] On a broad concept of security see Eeckhout. P Eeckhout, *EU External Relations Law*, 2nd edn, (Oxford, Oxford University Press, 2011) 181–83.

[194] Article 40 reads as follows:

'The implementation of the common foreign and security policy shall not affect the application of the procedures and the extent of the powers of the institutions laid down by the Treaties for the exercise of the Union competences referred to in Articles 3 to 6 of the Treaty on the Functioning of the European Union.

Similarly, the implementation of the policies listed in those Articles shall not affect the application of the procedures and the extent of the powers of the institutions laid down by the Treaties for the exercise of the Union competences under this Chapter'.

[195] On different views on the relationship between CFSP and other areas of EU policy post-Lisbon see Eeckhout (n 193 above); P Van Elsuwege, 'The Adoption of "Targeted Sanctions" and the Potential for Inter-institutional Litigation after Lisbon' (2011) 7 *Journal of Contemporary European Research* 488–99, 494, arguing for a non-hierarchical relationship.

[196] E Neframi, 'L'aspect externe de l'espace de liberté, de sécurité et de justice: quel respect des principes et objectifs de l'action extérieure de l'Union?' in C Flaesch-Mougin and LS Rossi, *La Dimension Extérieure de l'Espace de Liberté, de Sécurité et de Justice de l'Union Européenne après le Traité de Lisbonne* (Brussels, Bruylant, 2013) 509–32. Neframi argues that counter-terrorism measures fall under the external aspect of the AFSJ only to the extent that they do not relate to the CFSP (p 524).

for 'internal security' in a landscape where a large part of counter-terrorism law can be seen as related to external security. In the case in question, the Court's ruling has led to the paradox whereby terrorist sanctions—which are clearly related to internal security—were adopted pre-Lisbon under first pillar legal bases, whereas post-Lisbon, in an era where the old third pillar has collapsed and the AFSJ part of the Treaty contains a specific legal basis on terrorist sanctions, measures on such sanctions are adopted exclusively under an external relations legal basis.

The key issue which the Court's ruling fails to take into account is the content of the contested Regulation and the impact of its provisions on the affected individuals. As confirmed by the Court of Justice in its case-law, including the *Kadi* litigation, terrorist sanctions have profound consequences for the daily lives and fundamental rights of affected individuals. The implementation of the UN sanctions regime by the EU reflects a change of paradigm, in that international law (and EU sanctions law) targets not states, but individuals. The impact of terrorist sanctions on fundamental rights clearly places them within the ambit of the part of the TFEU on the Area of Freedom, Security and Justice, which focuses on law enforcement, contains a specific provision on terrorist sanctions, and whose title and provisions confirm the focus on developing policies on security and justice while respecting free movement and fundamental rights. The impact of terrorist sanctions imposed by EU law on fundamental rights not only justifies their treatment as an internal security measure falling within the Area of Freedom, Security and Justice, but also necessitates a high intensity of scrutiny by the European Parliament. In its ruling the Court seems to accept that fundamental rights will be observed anyway, especially post-adoption (by referring to the *Kadi* litigation). Yet this is not a convincing argument to exclude the European Parliament (which is a co-legislator post-Lisbon in the vast majority of EU internal security law) from having a decisive say on the content of EU measures which have a far-reaching impact on the daily lives and human rights of individuals affected by EU law.

The Court's willingness to prioritise CFSP at the expense of AFSJ objectives in the context of security is confirmed in its recent ruling concerning piracy.[197] The European Parliament sought the annulment of Council Decision 2011/640/CFSP of 12 July 2011 on the signing and conclusion of the Agreement between the EU and the Republic of Mauritius on the conditions of transfer of suspected pirates and associated seized property from the EU-led naval force to the Republic of Mauritius and on the holding conditions of suspected pirates after transfer.[198] The Parliament alleged infringement of Articles 218(6) and 218(0) TFEU. With regard to Article 218(6), the Parliament argued that the Council was wrong to consider that the contested decision concerned an agreement relating exclusively to the CFSP within the meaning of the first part of the second subparagraph of Article 218(6)

---

[197] Case C-658/11, *European Parliament v Council*, judgment of 24 June 2014.
[198] [2011] OJ L254/1.

TFEU.[199] Article 218(6) TFEU envisages the involvement of the European Parliament in the adoption of such decisions via consent[200] or consultation[201] 'except where agreements relate exclusively to the CFSP'. The Council treated the contested Decision as involving an agreement relating exclusively to the CFSP. This is notwithstanding the fact that the agreement contains a number of provisions on judicial and police cooperation[202] and its stated aims include the transfer of persons suspected of attempting to commit, committing or having committed acts of piracy and the treatment of transferred persons.[203] The Joint Action to which the contested Decision and subsequent agreement constitute a follow-up,[204] and which calls for the conduct of an EU military operation (operation 'Atalanta') in support of UN Security Council Resolutions 1814(2008), 1816(2008) and 1838 (2008), includes in its mandate the arrest, detention and transfer of persons suspected of intending to commit acts of piracy or armed robbery[205] and includes a specific provision on the transfer of persons arrested and detained with a view to their prosecution.[206] In spite of the inclusion of specific provisions dealing with judicial cooperation in criminal matters in both the agreement and its underlying Joint Action, the Court of Justice did not accept the Parliament's argument that the contested decision and agreement do not pursue exclusively CFSP objectives.[207] In order to reach this conclusion, the Court employed once again criteria of form rather than substance, focusing on procedure rather than content. According to the Court, Article 218(6) TFEU reflects a symmetry between EU internal and external action, with the substantive legal basis of a measure determining the procedures to be followed in adopting that measure.[208] '[I]n the context of the procedure for concluding an international agreement in accordance with Article 218 TFEU, it must be held that it is the substantive legal basis of the decision concluding the agreement which determines the type of procedure applicable under paragraph 6 of that provision'.[209] The Court's reasoning means in practice that the unilateral decision by the EU legislator (on this occasion the Council) to label a decision concluding an international agreement as a CFSP Decision suffices to exclude the European Parliament from any involvement in the

---

[199] Paragraph 23.

[200] Article 218(6)(a), including cases involving agreements covering fields to which the ordinary legislative procedure applies (Article 218((6)(a)(v)).

[201] Article 218(6)(b).

[202] See in particular Articles 3–6 of the Agreement.

[203] Article 1(a) and (c).

[204] Council Joint Action 2008/851/CFSP of 10 November 2008 on a European Union military operation to contribute to the deterrence, prevention and repression of acts of piracy and armed robbery off the Somali coast ([2008] OJ L3010/33) as amended by Council Decision 2010/766/CFSP of 7 December 2010 ([2010] OJ L327/49).

[205] Article 2(e).

[206] Article 12.

[207] Case C-658/11, *European Parliament v Council*, n 197 above, paragraph 47.

[208] ibid paragraph 57.

[209] Paragraph 58.

adoption of the decision, even in cases where the agreement following the adoption of the decision in question clearly includes elements related to non-CFSP EU policies, including judicial cooperation in criminal matters. This reasoning is even more noteworthy bearing in mind that the Parliament here did not challenge the legality of the use of the CFSP as a legal basis, but argued merely—and correctly—that the contested decision did not relate *exclusively* to the CFSP.

The Court attempted to compensate for the exclusion of the Parliament from the procedure regarding the adoption of the contested decision by affirming its right to be informed immediately and fully under Article 218(10) TFEU. According to the Court, the procedural rule laid down in Article 218(10) 'constitutes an essential procedural requirement within the meaning of the second paragraph of Article 263 TFEU and its infringement leads to the nullity of the measure thereby vitiated'.[210] 'That rule is the expression of the democratic principles on which the European Union is founded'[211] and the Lisbon Treaty has enhanced its importance in the treaty system 'by inserting it as a separate provision that is applicable to all types of procedures envisaged in Article 218 TFEU'.[212] According to the Court,

> it cannot be inferred ... that despite its exclusion from the procedure for negotiating and concluding an agreement relating exclusively to the CFSP, the Parliament has no right of scrutiny in respect of that EU policy.[213]

> On the contrary, it is precisely for that purpose that the information requirement laid down in Article 218(10) TFEU applies to *any procedure for concluding an international agreement including agreements relating exclusively to the CFSP* (emphasis added).[214]

> If the Parliament is not immediately and fully informed at all stages of the procedure in accordance with Article 218(10) TFEU, including that preceding the conclusion of the agreement, it is not in a position to exercise the right of scrutiny which the Treaties have conferred on it in relation to the CFSP or, where appropriate, to make known its views as regards, in particular, the correct legal basis for the act concerned. The infringement of that information requirement impinges, in those circumstances, on the Parliament's performance of its duties in relation to the CFSP, and therefore constitutes an infringement of an essential procedural requirement.[215]

While the Court is thus not ready to grant to the European Parliament a full legislative scrutiny role in cases of measures involving the CFSP and other EU policies, it has attempted to address this democratic deficit not via the route of legality but via the route of transparency: Parliament should be fully and immediately informed in negotiations of international agreements under Article 218, even if

---

[210] Paragraph 80.
[211] Paragraph 81.
[212] Paragraph 82.
[213] Paragraph 84.
[214] Paragraph 85.
[215] Paragraph 86.

the latter relate exclusively to the CFSP. In this manner, the Court has, as will be seen below, prioritised to some extent transparency as a rule of law safeguard for internal security.

V. The Limits of Subsidiarity

A central theme in the discussions on the reform of the EU constitutional frame-work, including the negotiations on the Lisbon Treaty, has been the issue of 'bringing Europe closer to its citizens'—with the principle of subsidiarity, used to best allocate the level of desired action in Europe, playing a central part in this context.[216] The principle of subsidiarity has been enshrined post-Lisbon in Article 5 TEU starting that in areas which do not fall within its exclusive compe-tence, the Union must act only if and in so far as the objectives of the proposed action cannot be sufficiently achieved by the Member States, either at central level or at regional and local level, but can rather, by reason of the scale or effects of the proposed action, be better achieved at Union level. In the field of criminal law, respect for the principle of subsidiarity and its monitoring can be seen as a safeguard for respecting national legal diversity, which as seen above is one of the aims of the evolution of the EU as an Area of Freedom, Security and Justice under Article 67 TFEU. The move towards a greater focus on subsidiarity as a constitu-tional principle of EU law—as a means of better justifying action at EU level and of connecting citizens with the EU—has been inextricably linked with calls to provide national parliaments with a greater role in the scrutiny and development of EU legislation. The view that national parliaments can address the democratic deficit in the EU by providing a useful intermediate link between the Union and citizens in the various Member States, and can provide extra checks on proposed EU action in particular by monitoring subsidiarity, justifies and underpins the expansion of the relevant provisions in the Lisbon Treaty.[217]

The Lisbon Treaty brings national parliaments more prominently into the Union legal framework. According to Article 12 TEU, national parliaments con-tribute actively to the good functioning of the Union in a number of ways, includ-ing being informed by EU institutions of draft legislation[218] and seeing that the

---

[216] See T Tridimas, *The General Principles of EU Law*, 2nd edn (Oxford, OUP, 2006) chapter 4; and, for a post-Lisbon analysis, P Craig, *EU Administrative Law*, 2nd edn (Oxford, OUP, 2012) 390–98.

[217] For an early analysis of the link between national parliaments, subsidiarity and monitoring EU powers in the context of the Convention on the Future of Europe, see A Vergés Bausili, *Rethinking the Methods of Dividing and Exercising Powers in the EU: Reforming Subsidiarity and National Parliaments*, Jean Monnet Working Paper 9/02, NYU School of Law, www.jeanmonnetprogram.org.; see also House of Lords European Union Committee (then Select Committee on the European Union), *The Future of Europe: National Parliaments and Subsidiarity—the Proposed Protocols*, 11th Report, session 2002–03, HL Paper 70.

[218] Article 12(a) TEU.

principle of subsidiarity is respected[219]—with more detailed provisions on both roles included in separate Protocols annexed to the Treaty.[220] A specific provision on national parliaments and subsidiarity is also included in Title V TFEU, stating that national parliaments ensure that proposals and legislative initiatives in the field of police co-operation and judicial co-operation in criminal matters comply with the principle of subsidiarity in accordance with the relevant Protocol.[221] The subsidiarity Protocol establishes a so-called 'early warning mechanism' leading to a 'yellow card': any national parliament or any chamber of a national parliament can send to EU institutions, within eight weeks from the transmission of draft legislative acts (and their amended drafts), 'a reasoned opinion stating why it considers that the draft in question does not comply with the principle of subsidiarity';[222] where such reasoned opinions for EU criminal law proposals represent at least one quarter of the votes allocated to national parliaments, the draft must be reviewed.[223] Protocol No 2 contains a further, 'orange card' mechanism: under the ordinary legislative procedure, where reasoned opinions represent at least a simple majority of the votes allocated to national parliaments, the proposal must be reviewed, and if the Commission chooses to maintain the proposal, a special procedure is triggered in the Council and the European Parliament examining whether negotiations should go ahead.[224] The Protocol also contains a provision on the ex post control of subsidiarity, granting jurisdiction to the Court of Justice in actions on grounds of infringement of the principle of subsidiarity by a legislative act, brought in accordance with the rules laid down in Article 263 TFEU by Member States, or notified by them in accordance with their legal order on behalf of their national Parliament or a chamber thereof.[225] However, it is clear that national parliaments cannot block the adoption of EU law. As Schütze notes, the Lisbon mechanism will leave the political decision on subsidiarity ultimately to the European legislator while allowing national parliaments to channel their scrutiny to where it can be most useful and effective, namely on their respective national governments.[226]

In the field of EU criminal law, it was the Commission's proposal for a Regulation on the establishment of a European Public Prosecutor's Office which has provided national parliaments with the opportunity to issue a 'yellow card', reflecting

---

[219] Article 12(b) TEU. See also Article 5(1) and (3) TEU on the principle of subsidiarity.

[220] Protocol No 1 on the Role of National Parliaments in the European Union and Protocol No 2 on the Application of the Principles of Subsidiarity and Proportionality respectively.

[221] Article 69 TFEU.

[222] Articles 4 and 6 of Protocol No 2.

[223] Protocol No 2, Article 7(2). For all other proposals the threshold is one third of the votes.

[224] ibid, Article 7(3).

[225] Article 8. For an analysis, see J-C Piris, *The Lisbon Treaty. A Legal and Political Analysis* (Cambridge, Cambridge University Press, 2010) 130; and X Groussot and S Bogojevic, 'Subsidiarity as a Procedural Safeguard of Federalism' in Azoulai, n 95 above, 234–52.

[226] R Schütze, *From Dual to Cooperative Federalism. The Changing Structure of European Law* (Oxford, Oxford University Press, 2009) 260–61.

concerns in a number of EU Member States about the content of the proposal and the added value of the European Public Prosecutor's Office. The process and content of the opinions of national parliaments was summarised by the European Commission in its response containing a review of national parliaments' subsidiarity concerns.[227] No fewer than 14 chambers of national parliaments had sent reasoned opinions to the Commission thus triggering the subsidiarity control mechanism provided for in Article 7(2) of the Protocol.[228]

The Commission summarised and responded to the main subsidiarity concerns as follows. The first concern involved the view that the Commission did not sufficiently explain the reasons justifying the proposal. Reference was made to the—quite laconic—subsidiarity assessment put forward by the Commission in the foreword to the text of the draft Regulation. The Commission on the other hand rebuked this claim by referring to the detailed justifications provided in the impact assessment preceding the proposal.[229] While it is true that the Commission did not refer expressly to the impact assessment in the text or the foreword to the draft Regulation,[230] it must be recognised that the impact assessment itself has been extremely detailed and followed detailed external and internal consultation on the proposal. The second principal subsidiarity argument put forward by national parliaments was that investigation and prosecution action by Member State and EU coordination mechanisms are sufficient to tackle fraud against the EU budget. The Commission responded by referring to the statistics from the European Anti-Fraud Office (OLAF), showing that the Treaty objective of an effective, deterrent and equivalent level of protection is not achieved in general[231] and by pointing out the limitations of OLAF, Europol and Eurojust in particular regarding issues of admissibility of cross-border evidence and establishing cross-border links.[232] The latter point can arguably be addressed by reforming existing EU criminal justice bodies, while on the evidence of the scale of the phenomenon, detailed OLAF statistics should be accompanied by external independent studies.[233] The third doubt

---

[227] European Commission, Communication from the Commission to the European Parliament, the Council and the National Parliaments on the review of the proposal for a Council Regulation on the establishment of the European Public Prosecutor's Office with regard to the principle of subsidiarity, in accordance with Protocol No 2, COM(2013) 851 final, Brussels, 27.11.2013.

[228] ibid, p 3.

[229] European Commission, Commission Working Document: Impact Assessment accompanying the proposal for a Council Regulation on the establishment of the European Public Prosecutor's Office, SWD(2013) 274 final, Brussels, 17 July 2013.

[230] H Bang Fugslang Madsen and T Elholm, 'EPPO and the Principle of Subsidiarity' in P Asp (ed), *The European Public Prosecutor's Office—Legal and Criminal Policy Perspectives* (Stifelsen Skrifter utgivna av Juridiska fakulteten vid Stockholms universitet, 2015) 31–50, 40.

[231] ibid, p 5.

[232] ibid, pp 7–8.

[233] Note in this context the criticism by the House of Lords European Union Committee pointing out that the Commission treats VAT fraud as a fraud affecting the financial interests of the Union when the UK, along with other Member States, do not consider that it is. House of Lords European Union Committee, *Subsidiarity Assessment: the European Public Prosecutor's Office*, 3rd Report, session 2013–14, HL Paper 65, pp 6–7.

by national parliaments concerned the added value of the EPPO, to which the Commission responded by stressing the need for a common Union-level prosecution policy and the contribution of the EPPO towards the simplification of action in cross-border cases[234] (although the latter does not seem to be the focal point of the Commission's draft). The fourth subsidiarity concern by national parliaments involved the centralised structure of the EPPO, to which the Commission responded that while a collegiate structure is not necessarily less centralised that that of the proposal, it can hamper efficiency, rendering its decision-making less efficient.[235] The fifth concern involved the extension of the powers of the EPPO via the attribution of exclusive and ancillary competence by the Regulation, to which the Commission responded that exclusive competence arises out of the nature of the crimes in question which have an intrinsic Union dimension (putting thus forward a federal, 'Eurocrimes' argument), while pointing out that the attribution of ancillary competence may work in both directions.[236]

In the light of the above, the Commission concluded that its proposal complied with the principle of subsidiarity enshrined in Article 5(3) TEU and that a 'withdrawal or an amendment of the proposal was not required. The Commission decided to maintain the proposal but reassured the recipients of its report that it would take due account of the reasoned opinions of the national parliaments during the legislative process.[237] The Commission's approach met with adverse reactions at the national level, with the Dutch parliament in particular criticising the lack of willingness by the Commission to engage in a dialogue with national parliaments.[238] Regarding the procedure followed, one can indeed view the glass as half full or half empty depending on one's perspective: from a supranational position, subsidiarity review has played a significant role in forcing the Commission to revisit its proposal and to provide a detailed explanation of its reasoning and justification of the proposal; from a national perspective however, the lack of a detailed follow-up may come as a disappointment, demonstrating a lack of substantive engagement with national parliamentary concerns. Regarding the substance of the Commission's subsidiarity assessment, one may agree or disagree with the content and rigour of its reasoning. However, what has been made clear is the temporal limitation of the 'yellow card' mechanism in that it does not take into account subsequent developments in negotiations in the Council. Indeed, the move from a centralised to a collegiate model may temper the Commission's efficiency argument. Moreover, the possible exclusion of VAT fraud from the scope of the mandate of the EPPO would raise further questions with regard to the evidential basis and added value of the establishment of a new EU prosecutorial

---

[234] ibid, p 9.
[235] ibid, p 10.
[236] ibid, pp 11–12.
[237] ibid, p 11.
[238] Bang Fugslang Madsen and Elholm, n 230 above, pp 45–46.

body. These are questions which can be further addressed before the Court of Justice if an action for annulment of the eventually adopted EPPO Regulation is brought under Article 8 of Protocol No 2.

VI. The Limits of Justice À-la-Carte: Variable Geometry and the Case of the United Kingdom

A key challenge to the constitutionalisation of EU criminal law constitutes the avenue provided by the Lisbon Treaty for Member States not to participate in EU criminal law adopted under Title V TFEU. Conditions for non-participation (or 'opt-outs') are spelt out in a series of Protocols accompanying the Lisbon Treaty which determine the specific position of a number of EU Member States, in particular Denmark, Ireland and the United Kingdom. Protocol No 22 on the position of Denmark states that Denmark will not take part in the adoption of all Title V measures[239] and that no Title V measure will be binding upon or applicable to it.[240] Denmark may decide to opt into Schengen building measures adopted post-Lisbon, and in such cases the measures will create an obligation under international law between Denmark and the other Member States bound by the measure.[241] At any time Denmark may decide not to avail itself of all or part of the Protocol, in which case Denmark will apply in full all relevant measures then in force taken within the framework of the EU.[242] Moreover, at any time Denmark may notify the other Member States of the replacement of Part I of the Protocol with provisions attached in its annex, introducing, inter alia, an 'opt-in' mechanism similar to the arrangements for the UK and Ireland.[243] Denmark has also declared that it will not block measures which contain both provisions applicable to it and provisions not applicable to it.[244] In terms of the position of the United Kingdom and Ireland, Protocol No 19 on the Schengen *acquis* continues these Member States' pre-Lisbon position after Lisbon, stating in particular that they may at any time request to take part in some or all of the provisions of the Schengen *acquis* but that the Council must decide on this request by unanimity of the full Schengen members.[245] Moreover, Protocol No 21 extends the UK and

---

[239] Protocol No 22, Article 1(1).

[240] Article 2.

[241] Article 4(1).

[242] Article 7. At the time of writing, a date for a referendum enabling an 'opt-in' mechanism for Denmark on Title V measures has been announced for 3 December 2015: www.euractiv.com/sections/elections/danish-premier-announces-date-eu-referendum-316988.

[243] Protocol No 22, Article 8.

[244] Declaration 48 annexed to the Final Act of the Lisbon Treaty.

[245] Protocol No 19, Article 4.

Irish 'opt-out' (or rather the option for these Member States not to participate in Union law) also to EU criminal law, by covering all measures under Title V TFEU. The United Kingdom and Ireland may decide to take part in post-Lisbon Title V measures on a case-by-case basis.[246] For the United Kingdom, this extension has been deemed necessary to address concerns over undue transfer of sovereignty to the European Union after the abolition of the third pillar and the 'communautarisation' and constitutionalisation of EU criminal law. UK concerns regarding the impact of the entry into force of the Lisbon Treaty on the transfer of sovereign powers to the European Union in the field of criminal justice have resulted in a further political compromise, which has arguably served to avoid a referendum on the Lisbon Treaty in the UK. Protocol No 36 on Transitional Provisions retained the limited powers of EU institutions under the largely intergovernmental framework of the third pillar with regard to third pillar law for a period of five years after the entry into force of the Lisbon Treaty.[247] At least six months before the end of that period the United Kingdom could notify the Council of its non-acceptance of the full powers of the EU institutions in third pillar law.[248] In case of a decision not to accept these powers, third pillar law would cease to apply to the UK,[249] but the latter may notify the Council subsequently of its wish to participate in such legislation which has ceased to apply to it.[250] In addition to these country-specific provisions, the Lisbon Treaty has also introduced a more generalised legal possibility for the development of EU criminal justice à-la-carte, in the Treaty legal basis enabling the establishment of a European Public Prosecutor's Office. Reflecting Member States' concerns over the impact of such an agency on national sovereignty and legal diversity, Article 86 TFEU introduces an exception to the ordinary decision-making procedure by requiring unanimity in the Council for the establishment of the Office. However, if such unanimity is not forthcoming, the Treaty enables the establishment of enhanced cooperation with the participation of at least nine Member States.[251]

Focusing on the position of the United Kingdom is key in analysing the impact of these complex, multi-level enhanced cooperation arrangements for the content and direction of EU criminal justice policy after Lisbon. In terms of its position pursuant to Protocol No 21, and its position regarding participation in post-Lisbon EU criminal law, the United Kingdom has a mixed record.[252] It has participated

---

[246] See Articles 3 and 4 of Protocol No 21.

[247] Article 10(1) and 10(3) of Protocol No 36. For a background to the transitional provisions see A Hinarejos, JR Spencer and S Peers, *Opting out of EU Criminal Law: What Is Actually Involved?*, CELS Working Paper, New Series, vol 1, University of Cambridge Faculty of Law, September 2012.

[248] Protocol No 36, Article 10(4).

[249] Article 10(4).

[250] Article 10(5).

[251] Article 86(1) TFEU.

[252] For details see the regular annual reports by Ministry of Justice and Home Office, most recently: Ministry of Justice and Home Office, *Fifth Annual Report to Parliament on the Application of Protocols 19 and 21 to the Treaty on the European Union (TEU) and the Treaty on the Functioning of the European*

in a major judicial cooperation instrument, the Directive on the European Investigation Order,[253] which introduces a system of mutual recognition in the field of evidence and repeals for its signatories pre-existing EU law including the Framework Decision on the European Evidence Warrant, the Framework Decision on the freezing of evidence and the Council of Europe and European Union Mutual Legal Assistance Conventions.[254] The UK participation in the Directive on the European Investigation Order may be seen to have happened against the odds in view of the increasingly Euro-sceptic political climate at Westminster, but may be explained by the necessity to ensure that the United Kingdom remains in the first category of countries in an increasingly integrated system of judicial cooperation in the field of evidence. Less encouraging are the signs with regard to the UK's participation in post-Lisbon EU criminal law measures granting rights to individuals. While the UK has opted into the first measures adopted post-Lisbon on the rights of suspects and defendants in criminal procedure, it has not participated in a key instrument in the field, namely the Directive on the right of access to a lawyer.[255] The non-participation of the United Kingdom in this measure may come as a surprise given the fact that the Directive introduces minimum standards which would arguably lead to minimal—if any—legislative changes to domestic criminal procedure. However, non-participation may be explained by the Government's reluctance to participate in a constitutionalised post-Lisbon framework where institutions such as the Commission and the Court of Justice would have a say in evaluating the domestic implementation and proceeding to the interpretation of the terms of the Directive.[256] There may be a prospect—albeit politically unlikely in the current climate—of the UK deciding to participate in the Directive post-adoption pursuant to Article 4 of Protocol 21. This is the strategy that the United Kingdom has followed in relation to other measures, in particular the Directive on trafficking in human beings[257] to which the UK has opted in post-adoption. This 'wait and see' strategy is increasingly coupled with a strategy attempting to broaden the field of the measures where the UK 'opt-out' applies. In the field of

Union (TFEU) ('the Treaties') in Relation to EU Justice and Home Affairs (JHA) matters (1 December 2013–30 November 2014): Cm 9006, February 2015.

[253] Directive 2014/41/EU of the European Parliament and of the Council of 3 April 2014 regarding the European Investigation Order in criminal matters, [2014] OJ L130/1, 1 May 2014.

[254] Directive on the European Investigation Order, Article 34(1).

[255] Directive 2013/48/EU of the European Parliament and of the Council of 22 October 2013 on the right of access to a lawyer in criminal proceedings and in European arrest warrant proceedings, and on the right to have a third party informed upon deprivation of liberty and to communicate with third persons and with consular authorities while deprived of liberty, [2013] OJ L294/1, 6 November 2013.

[256] The Government's review of the Balance of Competences in the field of criminal justice included an extensive section on the potential impact of the Court of Justice in the field post-Lisbon—HM Government, *Review of the Balance of Competences between the United Kingdom and the European Union. Police and Criminal Justice*, December 2014, paragraphs 3.11–3.21.

[257] Directive 2011/36/EU of the European Parliament and of the Council of 5 April 2011 on preventing and combating trafficking in human beings and protecting its victims, and replacing Council Framework Decision 2002/629/JHA, [2011] OJ L101/1, 15 April 2011.

international agreements, the United Kingdom has argued that Articles 1 and 2 of Protocol No 21 'are not restricted to provisions in agreements concluded under a Title V legal base, but to those adopted or concluded "pursuant to" Title V'.[258] Moreover, the United Kingdom has questioned the legal basis of measures adopted outside Title V TFEU but which are deemed to include a criminal law component (such as the recently adopted fourth anti-money laundering Directive)[259] and has resisted efforts to reclassify Title V measures as measures which could be adopted under different legal bases under the Treaty (see the road traffic offences litigation above). As we will further see in the following chapter on the harmonisation of substantive criminal law after Lisbon, the choice of legal basis is crucial in determining not only the type of instrument (Regulation or Directive), but also whether enhanced cooperation can actually take place. The United Kingdom has challenged legal basis choices and has intervened in legal basis litigation before the Court of Justice with limited success.[260]

Of further interest is the position of the United Kingdom following the expiry of the five-year deadline set out in the Transitional Provisions Protocol.[261] The UK notified the Presidency of the EU that, pursuant to Article 10(4) of Protocol No 36, it did not accept the powers of the EU institutions; accordingly, third pillar law would cease to apply in the UK from 1 December 2014.[262] However, the UK eventually indicated that it would seek to opt back into 35 third pillar measures including the European Arrest Warrant Framework Decision. The five-year transitional period expired at the end of November 2014 and the continuation of the applicability of these 35 measures to the United Kingdom has been confirmed. Third pillar law will continue to apply to the United Kingdom vis-à-vis the vast majority of measures applying the principle of mutual recognition in criminal matters (including the Framework Decision on the European Arrest Warrant) and a number of other key measures, including legislation establishing Europol and Eurojust and legislation on joint investigation teams and criminal records.[263] Third

---

[258] House of Lords European Union Committee, The UK's Opt-In Protocol: Implications of the Government's Approach, 9th Report, Session 2014–15, HL Paper 136, paragraph 38.

[259] Directive (EU) 2015/849 of the European Parliament and of the Council of 20 May 2015 on the prevention of the use of the financial system for the purposes of money laundering or terrorist financing, amending Regulation (EU) No 648/2012 of the European Parliament and of the Council, and repealing Directive 2005/60/EC of the European Parliament and of the Council and Commission Directive 2006/70/EC, [2015] OJ L141/73, 5 June 2015.

[260] See Cases C-431/11 *UK v Council*, judgment delivered on 26 September 2013 (the EEA case); C-137/12, *Commission and Parliament v Council*, judgment of 22 October 2013; C-377/12, *Commission v Council*, judgment delivered on 11 June 2014 (*The Philippines case*); and C-81/13, *UK v Council*, judgment delivered on 18 December 2014 (*the Turkey case*), critically analysed in House of Lords European Union Committee, 'The UK's Opt-In Protocol: Implications of the Government's Approach', 9th Report, Session 2014–15, HL Paper 136.

[261] For an analysis see V Mitsilegas, S Carrera and K Eisele, *The End of the Transitional Period for Police and Criminal Justice Measures Adopted before the Lisbon Treaty. Who Monitors Trust in the European Justice Area?*, CEPS Paper in Liberty and Security in Europe, no 74, Centre for European Policy Studies, Brussels, December 2014.

[262] Council document 12750/13.

[263] See Annex to Decision 2014/836/EU, [2014] OJ L343/11.

pillar law which has ceased to apply to the United Kingdom following the expiry of
the transitional period includes, inter alia, a number of measures on substantive
criminal law, the Council Framework Decision on prevention and settlement of
conflicts of jurisdiction, and the Framework Decision on the mutual recognition
of probation decisions.[264] While the United Kingdom's 'opt back into' key measures of third pillar law has provided reassurance both domestically and at EU level,
the reluctance of the UK to opt in from the start to key instruments 'Lisbonising'
third pillar law, including new Regulations on Europol and Eurojust, perpetuates
legal uncertainty. Complex legal issues regarding the place of the United Kingdom
in Europe's area of criminal justice also arise from the non-participation of the UK
in the Regulation establishing the European Public Prosecutor's Office.[265]

The end of the transitional period on 1 December 2014 was a significant step
forward towards the constitutionalisation of EU criminal law by granting EU
institutions their full powers of scrutiny with regard to third pillar law still in
force after Lisbon. In addition to the enhanced powers of the Commission and
the Court to monitor the implementation of third pillar law by Member States, a
key constitutional change in this context is the normalisation of the Court's jurisdiction to give preliminary rulings. This impact is particularly visible in the case
of the United Kingdom, which did not grant its judiciary the power to interact
with the Court of Justice under the preliminary ruling procedure under the third
pillar. The limits of the involvement of the UK judiciary can be seen in case-law
concerning the interpretation of key concepts in the field of judicial cooperation
in criminal matters, and in particular mutual recognition, including the concept
of 'judicial authority'. The Supreme Court of the United Kingdom, which has not
been granted the right to send preliminary references to Luxembourg by the UK
Government under the third pillar arrangements, has had to grapple with the
question of the definition of judicial authority for the purposes of the Framework Decision on the European Arrest Warrant in two recent cases: the case of
Assange[266] and the case of *Bucnys*.[267] In the absence of the cooperative avenue of
preliminary references with regard to third pillar law for UK courts, the Supreme
Court could not avail itself of the assistance of the Court of Justice and thus had
to develop an autonomous concept of judicial authority on its own. In *Bucnys*, the
Court did so largely by reference to what it assumed Luxembourg would decide on
this matter. Subsequently, the Court of Justice put forward a definition of the concept of judicial authority for the purposes of the Framework Decision on mutual

---

[264] Notice 430/03, [2014] OJ C430/17.

[265] The European Union Act 2011 imposes a 'referendum lock' on the UK's participation on the
EPPO—European Union Act 2011, s 6 and in particular s 6(5)(c). See JR Spencer, 'The UK and EU
Criminal Law: Should we be Leading, Following or Abstaining?' in V Mitsilegas, P Alldridge and
L Cheliotis (eds), *Globalisation, Criminal Law and Criminal Justice. Theoretical, Comparative and
Transnational Perspectives* (Oxford, Hart Publishing, 2015) 135–52.

[266] *Assange v Swedish Prosecution Authority* [2012] UKSC 22.

[267] *Bucnys v Ministry of Justice, Lithuania* [2013] UKSC 71.

recognition of financial penalties in the case of *Baláž*.[268] The normalisation of the preliminary references jurisdiction of the Court of Justice after the end of the transitional period will be a considerable improvement in enabling national courts in all Member States, including UK courts, to send questions on the interpretation of third pillar law to Luxembourg and thus contribute decisively to legal certainty and the cooperative evolution of the EU *acquis* in the field.

These improvements notwithstanding, it is submitted that the position of the United Kingdom based on a 'pick-and-choose' model of differentiated integration becomes increasingly untenable in an interdependent and increasingly integrated Union area of criminal justice after Lisbon. The varied landscape with regard to the participation of the United Kingdom in EU criminal law measures post-Lisbon poses significant challenges for legal certainty, coherence and the protection of fundamental rights in Europe's area of criminal justice. These challenges became more complex following the end of the transitional period in Protocol No 36. To take the example of judicial cooperation under the principle of mutual recognition of judicial decisions in criminal matters: the day after 30 November 2014 has seen the United Kingdom participating fully in the Framework Decision on the European Arrest Warrant, without participating at the same time in a key measure on the rights of suspects and accused persons in criminal proceedings, the Directive on access to a lawyer. The selective participation of the United Kingdom in this context is problematic not only from the perspective of the protection of fundamental rights, but also from the perspective of the coherence of EU law. As will be analysed in detail in Chapter six, the legal basis for the Directive on access to a lawyer is Article 82(2) TFEU. This provision grants for the first time express competence to the European Union to legislate on aspects of criminal procedure (including explicitly the rights of the defence) where necessary to facilitate the operation of the principle of mutual recognition in criminal matters. The legality of post-Lisbon legislation on defence rights, including the Directive on access to a lawyer, is thus inextricably linked with the effective operation of mutual recognition in criminal matters, including of the Framework Decision on the European Arrest Warrant. It is questionable whether, from the point of view of legal certainty and coherence in the Area of Freedom, Security and Justice, the United Kingdom can pick and choose in this manner.[269] These challenges are likely to become more acute in the future if the United Kingdom chooses to opt out of future criminal procedure measures proposed under Article 82(2) TFEU, implementing the defence rights Roadmap (such as Directives on legal aid, presumption of innocence and detention), but also developing other areas of the *acquis*, such as minimum standards on the admissibility of evidence which will accompany the Directive on the European Investigation Order (to which, as seen above, the UK has opted in).

---

[268] Case C-60/12, *Baláž*, judgment of 14 November 2013.
[269] For further analysis, see Chapter 6 of this volume on defence rights.

Similar questions of coherence arise in the field of the protection of the Union's financial interests. At the time of writing, the United Kingdom is not bound by EU substantive criminal law on fraud (the Fraud Convention is not within the list of 35 third pillar measures in which the UK participates since 1 December 2014, and the UK has not opted into the post-Lisbon fraud Directive currently under negotiation in Brussels). The UK will further not participate in the Regulation establishing a European Public Prosecutor's Office. Yet the United Kingdom is currently participating in the work of OLAF, whose future is uncertain and which is likely to be subsumed by the European Public Prosecutor's Office in the future. The legal position of the United Kingdom in relation to the Prosecutor (and how it is going to interact with an EU agency in which it does not participate especially in cross-border or multi-offence cases) and to OLAF (if the latter ceases to exist) will become increasingly complex.[270] Moreover, the non-participation of the United Kingdom in EU substantive and procedural law on fraud sits very uneasily with the fact that the United Kingdom is bound by Article 325 TFEU on the protection of the Union's financial interests. In its recent ruling in *Taricco*,[271] the Court of Justice confirmed that EU Member States are obliged to counter fraud on the basis of the principle of assimilation and that this obligation stems directly from the Treaty, namely Article 325 TFEU.[272] The United Kingdom is bound by Article 325 TFEU, and *Taricco* confirms the interdependence between the need to ensure the effectiveness of EU law and the content and structure of domestic criminal justice systems. It may become increasingly difficult for the United Kingdom to meet its EU law obligations to protect effectively the budget of the European Union and to counter effectively fraud if the UK is not bound by substantive EU criminal law on fraud and if it does not participate in the key EU bodies and agencies entrusted with the fight against fraud, including Eurojust, OLAF and the European Public Prosecutor's Office.

VII. Conclusion

The entry into force of the Treaty of Lisbon has given significant momentum towards the constitutionalisation of EU criminal law. The immediate impact can be seen at the institutional level, where EU action in criminal matters—especially after the end of the transitional period imposed by Protocol No 36—is, with few exceptions, subject to the full powers of EU institutions. The move towards supranationalism in the field has not stopped legal basis litigation and has, if anything,

---

[270] For further analysis see Chapter 4 of this volume on prosecution.
[271] Case C-105/14, *Taricco*, n 19 above, judgment of 8 September 2015.
[272] ibid paragraphs 37 and 50.

alerted Member States further to the potential impact that European integration in the field can have on their national criminal justice systems. Legal basis litigation has emerged involving the reconfiguration of inter-institutional balance after Lisbon touching upon both internal and external dimensions of EU criminal law, as well as involving attempts by Member States (in particular the United Kingdom) to assert its legal position regarding the possibilities of an 'opt-out' from EU criminal law. The Court's case-law thus far has confirmed the Court's readiness to see criminal justice competence subsumed within other fields of EU action. Hence the Court has found that a transport legal basis takes precedence over a police cooperation legal basis on a measure relating to exchange of information on road traffic offences—a ruling which has a significant impact in obliging the Title V 'outsiders' (Denmark, Ireland and the United Kingdom) to now take part in this measure and in confirming the Court's functionalist approach towards criminal justice. In the same vein, the Court has found that EU legislation on terrorist sanctions is best adopted under an external action legal basis rather than under a Title V legal basis. This choice and the reasoning of the Court are also significant and cause concern in that they effectively cause counter-terrorism action by the EU to be subsumed under the framework of foreign and security policy, thus excluding any institutional and constitutional safeguards that the treatment of this legislation as an internal security matter would entail. The provisions of the Treaty related to the recognition of national legal diversity (in particular the emergency brake provisions) and subsidiarity have not been tested in detail at the time of writing, although the establishment of a European Public Prosecutor's Office may give rise to a specific subsidiarity-related legal challenge before the Court of Justice. The growing interdependence of the various strands of EU criminal justice policy renders the evolution of EU criminal justice à-la-carte increasingly untenable.

If the entry into force of the Lisbon Treaty has already had a significant effect on the intra-EU interinstitutional balance and the balance of power between the Union and Member States, its constitutionalising impact will be felt most strongly in relation to the relationship between the individual and the state in an increasingly integrated system of European Union criminal justice. Constitutionalisation means in this context that the constitutional principles of EU law, including the protection of fundamental rights, apply fully on EU criminal law. These principles (and, as will be seen later in this volume, secondary EU law on the rights of the individual) have the effect of placing the individual at the heart of Europe's area of criminal justice. Constitutionalisation means that not only is the protection of fundamental rights a sine qua non condition for the development of EU criminal law, but also that Member States, when implementing EU criminal law, are obliged to comply fully with the Union's constitutional principles. The application of these principles ensures both the decentralised and the centralised enforcement of EU law. In terms of decentralised enforcement, individuals can claim rights before national courts by evoking the principle of direct effect—this is very likely to be the case concerning key provisions of criminal procedural law. In terms of centralised enforcement, EU institutions have increased powers to scrutinise Member States' implementation of EU criminal law. Their scrutiny remit is extensive, entailing a holistic examination of domestic criminal justice systems to the extent that aspects of these systems are connected with the implementation of key EU criminal law instruments, including the Framework Decision on the European Arrest Warrant and the Directives on procedural rights in criminal proceedings. Monitoring implementation means monitoring conditions from the police station to the court to prison, in order to ensure that the requirement of effective protection of fundamental rights on the ground is complied with fully.[273]

---

[273] On this requirement, see further the analysis in Chapter 5 of this volume on mutual recognition and Chapter 6 on defence rights.

3

Defining EU Competence in Substantive Criminal Law: From Securitised to Functional Criminalisation

I. Introduction

The extent of the competence of the European Union (EU) to criminalise—namely to define criminal offences and adopt criminal sanctions—has traditionally been contested and remains contested notwithstanding the abolition of the third pillar and the normalisation of EU criminal law after the entry into force of the Lisbon Treaty. Concerns with regard to the impact of Union action to criminalise on national sovereignty and the diversity and integrity of national legal systems have led to the evolution of EU criminalisation competence in a series of fraught, incremental steps, reflecting a number of EU inter-institutional battles and necessitating the intervention of the Court of Justice. Informed by an overview of the evolution of EU competence in the field, this chapter will analyse the extent of the Union's power to define criminal offences and introduce criminal sanctions after Lisbon and the impact of such competence on the enforcement powers of the state. It will demonstrate that EU competence to criminalise can be justified in a twofold manner: by the need for the Union to address security threats (securitised criminalisation); and by the need for the Union to use criminal law in order to ensure the effectiveness of Union law (functional criminalisation). While the focus will be on an analysis of the Union's power to criminalise under Article 83 TFEU, the chapter will also test the wording of this article in relation to other Treaty legal bases and the practice of the institutions with regard to proposals on EU substantive criminal law after the entry into force of the Lisbon Treaty. These legal developments will also be evaluated in the light of the inter-institutional debate on EU criminalisation, as reflected in a series of policy documents published by the Commission, the Parliament, the Council and the European Council. The analysis will be complemented by an overview of the impact of European Union law on criminalisation at national level, and an examination of the impact of the Lisbon Treaty on national criminalisation in this context.

II. The Constitutional Politics of Criminalisation Before Lisbon: The Interplay Between Securitised and Functional Criminalisation

Although the Treaty of Rome did not envisage express powers for the European Community in the field of criminal justice, European integration has demonstrated that it has been increasingly difficult to disassociate Community action in the main areas of Community competence (including free movement and the completion of the internal market) from criminal justice policy. Calls for Community action in criminal matters have emerged in order to protect perceived EU-wide interests (such as fraud against the Community budget) and ensure the effectiveness of Community law; and calls have also arisen for Community law to respond to serious forms of criminality perceived as global security threats including drug trafficking, organised crime, money laundering and terrorism.[1] These two justifications for Union action in substantive criminal law—the need to safeguard interests, policies and objectives of the Union and to achieve effectiveness on the one hand (functional criminalisation), and the need to respond to security threats posed by serious criminality on the other (securitised criminalisation)— have recurred over time and, as will be seen below, are still highly relevant after the entry into force of the Lisbon Treaty.

As regards functional criminalisation, the Court further recognised in 1989 the principle of assimilation, placing national authorities under a duty to treat EU interests in an equivalent manner to domestic interests.[2] The absence of an express Community competence to define criminal offences and adopt criminal sanctions did not act as an obstacle to finding a legal basis in the Treaty of Rome to adopt Community anti-money laundering law.[3] In terms of constitutional politics, it is noteworthy that the Commission's initial proposal envisaged the express introduction of criminal offences and sanctions by a Community law instrument, arguing that such criminalisation was justified by the need to protect wider Community policies such as the stability of the financial system and thus the internal market. The Directive that was eventually adopted did not contain an express requirement for Member States to adopt criminal sanctions (the Directive called upon Member States to prohibit money laundering and to impose sanctions for non-compliance with the preventive duties set out therein). However, the Directive represented a considerable alignment of Community law with global

---

[1] For an overview see V Mitsilegas, *EU Criminal Law* (Oxford, Hart Publishing, 2009) ch 2.

[2] See, in particular, Case C-68/88 *Commission v Greece (Greek Maize)* [1989] ECR 2965.

[3] For an analysis, see V Mitsilegas, *Money Laundering Counter-Measures in the European Union: A New Paradigm of Security Governance versus Fundamental Legal Principles* (The Hague, Kluwer Law International, 2003).

criminal law standards in the field,[4] and resulted in the de facto criminalisation of money laundering in Member States when implementing the Directive.[5] From the perspective of constitutional politics, the debate over the adoption of the first Anti-Money Laundering Directive reflects a recurring strategy on behalf of the European Commission to frame the adoption of substantive criminal law by the EU within the broader objective of ensuring the effectiveness of EU law, in particular as regards the implementation of specific EU policies not necessarily related to criminal justice.

The third pillar under the Treaty of Maastricht introduced express legal bases enabling the adoption by the EU of concrete measures defining criminal offences and introducing criminal sanctions. An analysis of harmonisation of substantive criminal law today demonstrates that the Union *acquis* is a combination of instruments adopted post-Maastricht (eg the Fraud[6] and Corruption in the Public Sector Conventions),[7] post-Amsterdam (a series of framework decisions addressing security threats such as terrorism,[8] organised crime[9] and drug trafficking)[10] and post-Lisbon (see the recently adopted Directives on human trafficking[11] and sexual exploitation).[12] On a number of occasions, such as in the case of human trafficking and sexual exploitation, continuity in EU law has meant that harmonisation measures have been evolving substantively and institutionally over time. Overall, the EU legislator has adopted an expansive approach to EU competence in substantive criminal law under the third pillar. Harmonisation has not been limited to the fields of crime expressly mentioned in the Treaty but has also been extended to harmonisation in the fields of, inter alia, irregular migration,[13] corruption[14] and cyber-crime.[15] The existence of express harmonisation legal bases in the third pillar and the expansive approach to harmonisation adopted by Member States has not stopped the Commission from arguing that the Community (and not only the Union under the third pillar) also had competence to legislate in the field. The funding by the European Commission of an academic project resulting in proposals for harmonised, if not unified, criminal law under the *Corpus Juris* was

---

[4] V Mitsilegas, 'The EU and the Rest of the World: Criminal Law and Policy Interconnections' in M Evans and P Koutrakos (eds), *Beyond the Established Orders. Policy Interconnections between the EU and the Rest of the World* (Oxford, Hart Publishing, 2011) 149–78.

[5] Mitsilegas, *Money Laundering Counter-Measures* (n 3 above).

[6] [1995] OJ C316/49, 27 November 1995.

[7] [1997] OJ C195/2, 25 June 1997.

[8] See the 2002 Framework Decision on combating terrorism, [2002] OJ L164/3, 22 June 2002 as amended in 2008 ([2008] OJ L330/21).

[9] Framework Decision on organised crime, [2008] OJ L300/42.

[10] Framework Decision on drug trafficking, [2004] OJ L335/8, 11 November 2004.

[11] [2011] OJ L101/1, 15 April 2011.

[12] [2011] OJ L335/1, 17 December 2011.

[13] See the Framework Decision on the facilitation of unauthorised entry, transit and residence, [2002] OJ L328/1, 5 December 2002, and more recently the Directive on employers' sanctions, [2009] OJ L168/24, 30 June 2009.

[14] Framework Decision on corruption in the private sector, [1998] OJ L358/2, 31 December 1998.

[15] Framework Decision on attacks against information systems, [2005] OJ L69/67, 16 March 2005.

followed by a number of unsuccessful attempts by the Commission to introduce first pillar criminal law.[16] These attempts were based on the view that first pillar criminal law was necessary in order to achieve the effectiveness of Community law in relation to Community policies and objectives such as the protection of the Community's financial interests or the protection of the environment. With these attempts being eventually unsuccessful in the Council, the Commission initiated legal basis litigation in Luxembourg. In two important rulings, the Court of Justice found in favour of the existence of the Community competence to define criminal offences and impose criminal sanctions.[17] Community competence was deemed necessary to ensure the effective protection of the environment, which was viewed as an essential Community objective—with criminal law thus viewed not as a separate Union policy but rather as a means to an end of achieving effectiveness of Community policies.[18] However, it was not clear from the Court's case-law whether Community competence would extend beyond cases involving the protection of the environment, with the Commission adopting a maximalist approach and Member States disagreeing.[19] Moreover, following sustained opposition by Member States in the subsequent *Ship Source Pollution* litigation, the Court confirmed its *Environmental Crimes* ruling that the Community has competence to criminalise in the first pillar in order to achieve the effectiveness of Community law but at the same time limited Community competence in only defining criminal offences and imposing criminal sanctions *in abstracto*, with the concrete levels of sanctions to be established under the third pillar.[20] This case-law has led to the adoption of pre-Lisbon first pillar criminal law, but with all three measures adopted introducing only very limited harmonisation as to penalty levels.[21]

The debate over the extent of EU competence to criminalise was also reflected in the work of the Convention on the Future of Europe, entrusted with providing recommendations for the drafting of the Constitutional Treaty. The Final Report of Working Group X on 'Freedom, Security and Justice' produced a number of recommendations on the basis of the constitutional state of play of criminalisation under the third pillar and its members' perceived needs for Union legislative intervention in the field.[22] The Report called for clearer identification of the scope of Union legislation in the field, recognising that Articles 30 and 31

---

[16] In the areas of fraud and environmental crime. See Mitsilegas, *EU Criminal Law* (n 1 above) ch 2.

[17] Case C-176/03 *Commission v Council (Environmental Crime)* [2005] ECR I-7879, followed by Case C-440/05 *Commission v Council (Ship Source Pollution)* [2007] ECR I-9097.

[18] See V Mitsilegas, 'The Transformation of Criminal Law in the Area of Freedom, Security and Justice' 26 *Yearbook of European Law* 2007 1.

[19] COM(2005) 583 final, Brussels, 24 November 2005; Council doc 6077/06 (Presse 38).

[20] Case C-440/05 *Commission v Council (Ship Source Pollution)* [2007] ECR I-9097, paras 70–71.

[21] See Directive 2008/99 on the Protection of the Environment through Criminal Law (OJ 2008 L328/28); Directive 2005/35 on Ship Source Pollution and the Introduction of Penalties for Infringements ([2005] OJ L255/11); Directive 2009/52 providing for Minimum Standards on Sanctions and Measures against Employers of Illegally Staying Third-country Nationals ([2009] OJ L168/24). These three Directives contain general references to the introduction of 'effective, proportionate and dissuasive sanctions'.

[22] CONV 426/02, Brussels, 2 December 2002, WG X 14.

TEU, which constituted the applicable legal bases for criminal law, were 'too vague in many respects, and too narrow in some other aspects'.[23] The Working Group made specific recommendations, a great number of which found their way into the text of the Lisbon Treaty. It recommended the inclusion of a legal basis in the new Treaty permitting the adoption of minimum rules on constituent elements of criminal acts and of penalties in certain fields of crime where the crime in question is both of a particularly serious nature and has a cross-border dimension and where the crime is directed against a shared European interest which is already itself the subject of a common policy of the Union (for example counterfeiting of the Euro, the protection of the Union financial interest).[24] The Working Group thus advocated the constitutional recognition of both securitised and functional criminalisation.[25] The majority of the Working Group supported enumeration of those types of crime considered to have a transnational dimension and advocated—if this enumeration were to be exhaustive—that the Council, acting by unanimity, and after the assent of the EP (or for a few members, consultation) may amend this list in case of need in order for the Union to respond adequately to changing patterns of crime. According to a widespread view in the Working Party, the Treaty could provide that approximation of substantive criminal laws although this should be carried out in the form of directives only. As will be seen below, both these recommendations have been incorporated in the Lisbon Treaty.

III. EU Competence to Criminalise After Lisbon: Securitised and Functional Criminalisation Revisited

The dual securitised/functional criminalisation approach has been espoused by the drafters of the Lisbon Treaty, and in particular of Article 83 TFEU. The first paragraph of Article 83 confers upon the Union competence to establish, by means of directives,

> *minimum rules* concerning *the definition of criminal offences and sanctions* in the areas of *particularly serious crime with a cross-border dimension* resulting from the nature or impact of such offences or from a special need to combat them on a common basis (emphasis added).

---

[23] ibid, 8.

[24] ibid, 10. According to the Working Group, approximation of substantive criminal law should be part of the toolbox of measures for the pursuit of that policy whenever non-criminal rules do not suffice.

[25] The Working Group also called for further consideration to be given to the possible inclusion of a third criterion, which was proposed, namely 'when approximation is required to generate sufficient mutual confidence to enable the full application of mutual recognition of judicial decisions or to guarantee the effectiveness of common tools for police and judicial cooperation created by the Union'—however this criterion has not been explicitly included in the criminalisation legal basis of the Lisbon Treaty—ibid.

These areas of crime are enumerated exhaustively in Article 83(1). The list includes 'terrorism, trafficking in human beings and sexual exploitation of women and children, illicit drug trafficking, illicit arms trafficking, money laundering, corruption, counterfeiting of means of payment, computer crime and organised crime'. As per the recommendation of the Convention on Justice and Home Affairs Working Party, the list may be expanded 'on the basis of developments in crime' by the Council acting unanimously after obtaining the consent of the European Parliament. Article 83(1) thus affirms the acceptance of the added value of criminalisation at EU level in order to address perceived serious security threats. The second paragraph of Article 83 constitutes an attempt to translate the Court's functionalist interpretation of the extent of Community (and now Union) criminal law competence in *Environmental Crimes* and *Ship Source Pollution*. Article 83(2) TFEU thus grants the Union competence to approximate national criminal laws and regulations if such approximation 'proves *essential* to ensure the effective implementation of a Union policy in an area which has been subject to harmonisation measures'. For that purpose, 'directives may establish minimum rules with regard to the definition of criminal offences and sanctions in the area concerned'.

A. Securitised Criminalisation—Article 83(1) TFEU

Article 83(1) TFEU reflects the securitised criminalisation approach in determining EU competence in substantive criminal law. EU competence to criminalise is justified as necessary to combat specified areas of criminality the majority of which have been elevated after the Cold War by the international community and the Union as global security threats.[26] The objective of Article 83(1) TFEU to address security threats is also confirmed by the requirement for harmonisation to apply only to areas of particularly serious crime. The securitised view of Article 83(1) TFEU has been recently confirmed by the Court of Justice, according to which the very enumeration of an area of criminality under Article 83(1) suffices for criminality to be considered serious enough to justify the limitation of citizenship rights and the expulsion of EU citizens on public security grounds, although arguably the offences themselves did not necessarily represent a threat to the wider public as such.[27] In this manner, Article 83(1) TFEU—whose purpose is to define the extent of EU competence in substantive criminal law—has been used for a

---

[26] V Mitsilegas, 'Countering the Chameleon Threat of Dirty Money: "Hard" and "Soft" Law in the Emergence of a Global Regime against Money Laundering and Terrorist Finance' in A Edwards and P Gill (eds), *Transnational Organised Crime: Perspectives on Global Security* (London, Routledge, 2003).

[27] Case C-348/09 *P.I. v Oberbürgermeisterin der Stadt Remscheid* [2012] 3 CMLR 662. According to the Court, Art 28(3)(a) of the Citizens' Directive must be interpreted as meaning that it is open to the Member States to regard criminal offences such as those referred to in the second subparagraph of Article 83(1) TFEU as constituting a particularly serious threat to one of the fundamental interests of society, which might pose a direct threat to the calm and physical security of the population and thus be covered by the concept of 'imperative grounds of public security', capable of justifying an expulsion

very different purpose, namely to interpret exceptions to freedom of movement. By confirming the seriousness of the areas of crime enumerated in Article 83(1) *in abstracto*, the Court has transformed securitised criminal law into symbolic criminal law.

In an attempt to circumscribe EU competence in the field further, Article 83(1) TFEU contains an express enumeration of these areas of serious crime and specifies that these areas must have a cross-border dimension resulting from the nature or impact of such offences or from a special need to combat them on a common basis. This requirement has led commentators to argue that the justification for EU criminal law under Article 83(1) resides in its value-added function, drawing on a common capability to address the scale and nature of threats posed by transnational criminality.[28] While the wording of Article 83(1) can indeed be seen as an attempt to establish the added value of criminalisation at EU level, this added value is not limited to transnational criminality. The applicability of Article 83(1) to areas of serious crime with a cross-border dimension resulting from the nature or impact of such offences or from a special need to combat them on a common basis must be read as conferring on the Union competence to define criminal offences and adopt criminal sanctions in areas of crime which have a cross-border dimension but which do not involve cross-border or transnational criminality as such. Examples of areas of crime with a cross-border dimension resulting from their nature or impact or need to combat on a common basis— but which may involve criminality conducted purely at national level—include terrorism and corruption. In this way, the scope of Article 83(1) TFEU is broader than it appears at first sight.

This broad scope is confirmed by the fact that EU competence is defined on the basis of areas of crime, rather than on the basis of specific criminal offences. These areas of crime may actually correspond to a wide range of criminal offences or sanctions. A clear example of the potential to overstretch EU criminal law competence under Article 83(1) involves the use of the concept of organised crime. Not only is the definition of the concept vague and amorphous at EU level,[29] but it can also be used as a legal basis for harmonisation of a wide range of specific criminal offences and sanctions linked to the activities of a criminal organisation. Such a broad approach may serve to address some gaps in the Lisbon legal bases for criminal law, whose wording may be narrower than the third pillar legal bases and can thus be seen to exclude prima facie EU action in areas where the EU has legislated extensively under the third pillar. A prime example in this context is

---

measure under Art 28(3), as long as the manner in which such offences were committed discloses particularly serious characteristics, which is a matter for the referring court to determine on the basis of an individual examination of the specific case before it.

[28] C Harding and JB Banach-Gutierrez, 'The Emergent EU Criminal Policy: Identifying the Species' (2012) 37 *EL Rev* 758.

[29] V Mitsilegas, 'Defining Organised Crime in the European Union: The Limits of European Criminal Law in an Area of Freedom, Security and Justice' (2001) 26 *EL Rev* 565; Mitsilegas, *EU Criminal Law* (n 1 above) ch 2.

constituted by the recent Commission proposal for a directive on confiscation,[30] where the Commission has used Article 83(1) TFEU as a broad legal basis to justify EU action on confiscation and enable confiscation of the proceeds of crime to include all offences committed within the framework of organised crime. Limits to EU confiscation law appear to have been the side effects of EU efforts to clarify EU competence in criminal matters after Lisbon. If confiscation measures are to be considered measures of criminal procedure to facilitate mutual recognition, then their adoption is not possible under Article 82(2) TFEU as confiscation is not an area of criminal procedure expressly enumerated therein. If confiscation is to be considered a sanction, it can no longer apply on a catch-all basis to all offences in the light of the limits placed on EU competence by Article 83(1) TFEU. The broad interpretation of Article 83(1) TFEU by the Commission seeks to address this lacuna, and constitutes the first example of a measure adopted under Article 83(1) TFEU focusing specifically and horizontally on sanctions and not on the definition of criminal offences. The use of Article 83(1) TFEU in this manner may constitute a precedent for the adoption of EU instruments introducing a general framework of sanctions for the areas of crime enumerated therein. The solution eventually reached by the institutions in the adoption of the confiscation Directive has been to use the dual legal basis of Articles 82(2) and 83(1) TFEU.[31] This choice of legal basis may have served to evade the answer to the question of whether confiscation is a sanction or a judicial co-operation mechanism, but it has also led to the narrowing of the scope of confiscation measures at EU level. The use of Article 83(1) TFEU has meant that the harmonised confiscation regime applies only to criminal offences falling within the specifically enumerated fields in Article 83(1) TFEU and not across the board.[32]

B. Functional Criminalisation—Article 83(2) TFEU

The introduction of Article 83(2) TFEU in the Treaty of Lisbon confirms a functionalist view of criminal law. Rather than assuming the status of a self-standing Union policy, criminal law is thus perceived as a means to an end, the end being the effective implementation of other Union policies.[33] Criminal law is thus used as a tool to achieve the effectiveness of Union law.[34] Article 83(2) TFEU flows

---

[30] COM(2012) 85 final, 12 March 2012.

[31] Directive 2014/42/EU of the European Parliament and of the Council of 3 April 2014 on the freezing and confiscation of instrumentalities and proceeds of crime in the European Union, [2014] OJ L127, 29.4.2014, p 39.

[32] See Article 3 of the Directive.

[33] V Mitsilegas, 'The Transformation of Criminal Law in the Area of Freedom, Security and Justice' 26 *Yearbook of European Law 2007* 1.

[34] For a critical view, see M Kaiafa, 'The Importance of Core Principles of Substantive Criminal Law for a European Criminal Policy Respecting Fundamental Rights and the Rule of Law' (2011) 1 *European Criminal Law Review* 7, 19, arguing that the unique identity of criminal law cannot allow it to be reduced to a mere tool for the implementation of any policy.

naturally from the Court's interpretation of the Union's (then the Community's) criminalisation competence under the first pillar in the *Environmental Crimes* and *Ship Source Pollution* rulings. As the Court of Justice confirmed in its environmental crime ruling, while

> [a]s a general rule, neither criminal law nor the rules of criminal procedure fall within [EC] competence ... [this] does not prevent the [EC] legislature, *when the application of effective, proportionate and dissuasive criminal penalties* by the competent national authorities is an *essential measure* for combating serious environmental offences, from taking measures which relate to the criminal law of the Member States which it considers *necessary* in order to ensure that the rules which it lays down on environmental protection *are fully effective* (emphasis added).[35]

The Lisbon Treaty constitutionalises the Court's case-law on competence in the field of substantive criminal law, providing an express legal basis for functional criminalisation. This legal basis is not confined to the adoption of substantive criminal law in the field of environmental crime (which was viewed by the Court as an essential objective of the European Community),[36] but extends to any Union policy in an area which has been subject to harmonisation measures. This expansive constitutionalisation of the Court's functional criminalisation approach in Article 83(2) TFEU has raised concerns with regard to the extent of criminalisation powers conferred upon the European Union by the Lisbon Treaty.

The Treaty attempts to address concerns with regard to the extensive use of Article 83(2) by introducing two central requirements for the use of EU competence in the field: the requirement that measures are essential to achieve effectiveness; and the requirement that measures are 'essential to ensure the effective implementation of a Union policy *in an area which has been subject to harmonisation measures*' (emphasis added). By using the term 'essential', the Treaty has adopted a high threshold for EU intervention in the area of functional criminalisation, but it is unclear what kind of action meets this threshold.[37] Demonstrating the 'essential' character of EU intervention under Article 83(2) is prone to litigation in Luxembourg.[38] The interpretation of the second requirement of Article 83(2) TFEU—that measures are essential to ensure the effective implementation of a Union policy in an area that has been subject to harmonisation measures—may also prove to be contested. On the one hand, it is noteworthy

---

[35] Environmental crime ruling, n 17 above, paragraphs 47–48.

[36] Ibid, paragraphs 41 and 45–47.

[37] It has, eg been put forward that the requirement of action under Art 83(2) is essential includes a strict proportionality requirement—J Öberg, 'Union Regulatory Criminal Law Competence after the Lisbon Treaty' (2011) 19 *European Journal of Crime, Criminal Law and Criminal Justice* 289, 290.

[38] Already the German Constitutional Court has adopted a narrow view of the Union's criminalisation competence under Art 83(2) TFEU. In its Lisbon ruling, the Court found that such competence exists 'only if it is demonstrably established that a serious deficit concerning enforcement actually exists and that it can only be remedied by the threat of a sanction, this exceptional constituent element exists and the annex competence for legislation in criminal law may be deemed conferred': para 362. See BVerfG, 2 BvE 2/08, *Gauweiler, Die Linke v Act of Approval of the Lisbon Treaty ('Lisbon')*, 30 June 2009.

that effectiveness is related broadly to the implementation of Union policies and not of Union objectives.[39] On the other hand, the requirement that effectiveness must be in an area that has been subject to harmonisation measures may serve to limit the scope of EU competence under Article 83(2) TFEU. A lively academic discussion on the detail of this requirement (in particular on the temporal aspect of Article 83(2) and whether criminalisation can occur in cases where no previous harmonisation has taken place, as well as on the level of detail of harmonisation to be required) has ensued.[40] In this context, Peers argues that while it could not be said that there is a Union policy that needs implementing effectively in the absence of harmonisation in specific areas of law, there is nothing in the current legal framework of the Treaty of Lisbon that requires full harmonisation as a pre-condition.[41] Indeed, in interpreting the scope of Article 83(2), the key focus must be whether EU action is essential to ensure effectiveness of Union law in a policy area that has been subject to a degree of harmonisation.

C. The Extent of EU Competence to Criminalise: Minimum Rules

The articulation of EU competence to define criminal offences and impose criminal sanctions in the Lisbon Treaty may result in actually limiting the criminalisation powers of Member States. The limited conferral on the EU of competence in substantive criminal law only via the adoption of minimum rules can be potentially decisive in limiting Member States' criminalisation competence. Hans Nilsson has set out the limits that the minimum rules requirement may pose for national sovereignty in substantive criminal law:

> One may argue that the term 'minimum rules' should be seen from the point of view of the Member State, so that the Member States may adopt the constituent elements of the offence as set out in the Framework Decision or Directive, but they are free to have less constituent elements, and thus criminalise more acts than the minimum ones. This is however hardly defendable, both for reasons of logic, legal certainty and respect for the principle of the unity of the common market (in this case the criminal law part of it), as well as for the uniform application of Community/Union law, as laid down in the AETR case law.

> It would therefore appear to me that the 'minimum rules' in all substantive criminal law Framework Decisions would not only be minimum, but also maximum rules and that

---

[39] P Craig, *The Lisbon Treaty. Law, Politics, and Treaty Reform* (Oxford, Oxford University Press, 2010) 365.

[40] For a narrow interpretation, see Öberg (n 37 above) 314–16. For broader interpretations, see P Asp, *The Substantive Criminal Law Competence of the EU* (Skrifter Utgivna av Juridiska Fakulteten vid Stockholms Universitet Nr 79, 2013) 134; and S Peers, *EU Justice and Home Affairs Law*, 3rd edn (Oxford, Oxford University Press, 2011) 775–76.

[41] Peers, ibid, 775.

they would in principle be not only 'harmonising' but also 'unifying' instruments in the real sense of the word.[42]

Notwithstanding the uncertainty as to what constitutes a 'minimum rule' under Article 83,[43] Nilsson is right in arguing that the requirement of the EU to legislate via minimum rules under Article 83 TFEU places barriers to Member States over-criminalising and adopting more extensive substantive criminal law provisions than those which have been selected by the European legislator. This view is reinforced by the protective character of minimum harmonisation, which has been used traditionally in the context of the internal market as a means of addressing social concerns.[44] Similar concerns are addressed by the treatment of minimum harmonisation in the context of EU measures in the field of criminal procedure under Article 82(2) TFEU. The last indent of this Article states expressly that 'adoption of the minimum rules referred to in this paragraph' (which involve the adoption of largely protective standards including measures on the rights of the defendant in criminal proceedings) 'will not prevent Member States from maintaining or introducing a higher level of protection for individuals'. As Nilsson notes, Member States can go beyond minimum rules as expressly stated in Article 82(2) TFEU to protect individuals, but not so in Article 83 TFEU, as this is not expressly granted in the Treaty and would have the opposite effect.

IV. The Relationship Between Criminal and Adminstrative Law

A key question following the entry into force of the Lisbon Treaty concerns the interplay between criminal and administrative law after Lisbon in cases where EU measures are being put forward which envisage the adoption of both criminal and non-criminal (administrative) sanctions. This dual approach to sanctions has been adopted by the European Commission in its recent proposals

---

[42] H Nilsson, 'How to Combine Minimum Rules with Maximum Legal Certainty?' (2011) *Europaraettslig Tidskrift* 665. Nilsson refers to the analysis in the first edition of Klip's *European Criminal Law* (Oxford/Portland, Intersentia, 2009), where the author argued that it is necessary to look at the spirit of the instrument when one examines the impact of minimum rules (p 154). In its second edition, Klip mentions Nilsson's argument but continues to argue that the starting point is the objective of the legal instrument in question (p 167). A Klip, *European Criminal Law*, 2nd edn (Cambridge/Mortsel, Intersentia, 2012).

[43] There is also a debate on whether the minimum rules requirement allows the EU to adopt minimum maximum penalties as per the pre-Lisbon practice, or also minimum penalties as such: see Asp (n 40 above) 126. Asp argues that rules requiring a specific minimum penalty are not minimum rules as to require a certain minimum level would amount to full harmonisation as regards the minimum penalties. The post-Lisbon trend is for substantive criminal law measures to retain the 'minimum maximum' formula.

[44] M Dougan, 'Minimum Harmonization and the Internal Market' (2000) 37 *CML Rev* 53.

for revised post-Lisbon legislation introducing sanctions for insider dealing and market manipulation.[45] Unlike the case of its recent proposal on criminal law on fraud, the European Commission here has used Article 83(2) TFEU for the adoption of criminal law provisions, with an internal market legal basis being used for the regulation. This dual approach was ultimately confirmed by the Council and the Parliament in the adoption of two parallel instruments.[46] Two issues arise in this context in terms of criminalisation powers: the first, as mentioned above, is whether Member States are constrained by the adoption of criminal offences and sanctions under Article 83(2) TFEU in terms of their criminalisation choices at national level; the second, and related point, is whether Member States are similarly constrained by their choices of what to treat as an administrative infraction under the Regulation adopted under a separate legal basis. The requirement to ensure the effectiveness of Union law militates in favour of limiting national powers to criminalise in both cases. In the case of the interplay between EU administrative law and national criminal law, the choice by the EU legislator to address harmful behaviour (in this case market abuse) via merely administrative—and not criminal—sanctions would mean that the effectiveness of the EU policy and measure in question would be jeopardised if Member States adopted a harsher, criminal law approach. National criminalisation would also be contrary to the principle of proportionality, as enshrined in Article 49(3) of the Charter. In this manner, the adoption of Union law may actually limit criminalisation and lead to decriminalisation at the national level. The adoption of the marker abuse Regulation and Directive throw up a number of challenges in this regard. On the one hand, the Directive adopts a restrictive criminalisation approach, limiting criminalisation as a minimum measure to serious cases—although the Directive's reference to including 'at least' serious cases raises issues of legal certainty.[47] On the other hand, administrative sanctions imposed by the Regulation are 'without prejudice to any criminal sanctions'.[48] It is submitted that this approach undermines the effectiveness of the market abuse legal framework put forward by the combination of the Regulation and the Directive, as the relationship between the two instruments and their objectives becomes blurred and the added value of distinguishing between criminal and administrative law becomes unclear. The wording of the Regulation may result in cases where market abuse is punishable with administrative sanctions in one Member State

---

[45] Commission, 'Draft directive on criminal sanctions for insider dealing and market manipulation' COM(2011), 654 final, 20 October 2011 accompanying a 'Proposal for a regulation under Art 114 TFEU' COM(2011) 651 final, 20 October 2011.

[46] Regulation (EU) No 596/2014 of the European Parliament and of the Council of 16 April 2014 on market abuse (market abuse regulation) and repealing Directive 2003/6/EC of the European Parliament and of the Council and Commission Directives 2003/124/EC, 2003/125/EC and 2004/72/EC, [2014] OJ L173, 12.6.2014, p 1; and Directive 2014/57/EU of the European Parliament and of the Council of 16 April 2014 on criminal sanctions for market abuse (market abuse directive), [2014] OJ L173, 12.6.2014, p 179.

[47] See Articles 3(1), 4(1) and 5(1) of the market abuse Directive.

[48] Article 30(1) of the market abuse Regulation.

and by criminal sanctions in another. This raises serious issues of legal certainty vis-à-vis affected individuals and legal persons in Europe's area of criminal justice, rendering the prospect of double punishment (administrative and criminal) in cross-border cases a reality. It remains to be seen how the Court of Justice will apply its *ne bis in idem* case-law in such cases. It is submitted that the Court needs to take a protective approach towards affected parties, limiting the possibility of double punishment for the same acts, even if these are labelled as criminal in one Member State and administrative in another. The current criminal/administrative case-law applicable in domestic cases needs to be revisited in this context.[49]

V. Extending EU Competence to Criminalise Elsewhere in the Treaty

The attempt by the drafters of the Lisbon Treaty to determine more clearly the extent of EU competence in substantive criminal law under Article 83 TFEU may be undermined not only by the inherent flexibility in the competence requirements of Article 83(1) and 83(2) TFEU, but also by the question of whether these provisions are the sole legal bases for EU action in the field. It is contested in particular whether Article 83(2) is the only legal basis for the adoption of functionalist EU criminal law or whether criminal law can be adopted by the EU by using a different, policy-specific legal basis elsewhere in the Treaty. Using a legal basis other than Article 83(1) and 83(2) TFEU has significant constitutional consequences: it may enable the adoption of EU substantive criminal law measures in the form of regulations; it deprives Member States of the option of using the emergency brake introduced under Article 83(3) TFEU; and it forces the participation of Denmark, Ireland and the UK in EU criminal law if the legal basis for EU criminalisation is located in a part of the Treaty from which these states have not negotiated an opt-out. EU substantive criminal law rules adopted under a legal basis different to Article 83 TFEU may not necessarily be minimum rules. The adoption of regulations in the field of substantive criminal law challenges Treaty requirements to respect national diversity as outlined in Title V of the TFEU on the area of freedom, security and justice.[50] It also—at least in theory—raises the prospect for EU measures defining criminal offences and imposing criminal sanctions to have direct effect, thus reversing the protective function of the principle in domestic legal orders. While the Court of Justice has excluded the direct effect of directives in this context,[51] direct effect is not excluded in the case of regulations that do not require further implementing measures by Member

---

[49] See Case C-498/10, *Prokurator Generalny v Bonda*, judgment of 5 June 2012.
[50] See Art 67 TFEU.
[51] Cases C-387/02, C-391/02 and C-403/02 *Berlusconi and Others* [2005] ECR I-3565.

States.[52] However, it is difficult to see how in practice a regulation defining criminal offences and imposing criminal sanctions would be clear and unconditional enough not to require a degree of implementation in order to secure an adjustment to the specificities of national criminal justice systems.

The first potential legal basis for substantive criminal law outside Article 83 TFEU is Article 325 TFEU on the fight against fraud affecting the Union's financial interests. Article 325(4) confers to the Union competence to adopt

> the necessary measures in the fields of the prevention of and fight against fraud affecting the financial interests of the Union with a view to affording effective and equivalent protection in the Member States and in all the Union's institutions, bodies, offices and agencies.

A comparative analysis of Article 325(4) TFEU with its pre-Lisbon version[53] reveals that the last sentence of Article 280(4) has been deleted in the Lisbon text. This sentence stated that measures to combat fraud (an area which is not expressly listed in Article 83(1) TFEU but may be included in 83(2)) will not concern the application of national criminal law and the national administration of justice.[54] The fact that the adoption of criminal law measures is not excluded by Article 325(4) TFEU, in addition to the general wording of the provision, can be seen to militate in favour of the conferral on the EU of competence to define criminal offences and impose criminal sanctions in the field not under Article 83(2) TFEU but solely under Article 325 TFEU. It has been noted that such competence is justified by the fact that Article 325(4) TFEU contains a stronger obligation to legislate in comparison with Article 83 (by the use of the verb 'shall' instead of 'may') as well as by the fact that Article 325(4) calls for the adoption of 'necessary measures', instead of the more minimalistic requirement of Article 83 TFEU for the EU to adopt 'minimum rules'.[55] It should also be added in this context that Article 325 TFEU is a legal basis for the adoption of measures in a specific criminal justice field (fraud). In terms of policy areas, Article 325(4) can thus be considered as *lex specialis* in relation to Article 83(2). It is noteworthy in this context that the Commission has opted in favour of using exclusively Article 325 TFEU as a legal basis for its recent proposal for a directive on fraud.[56] However, in negotiations in the Council, Member States have opted for the use of Article 83(2) TFEU as the sole legal basis for the Directive.[57]

---

[52] For details, see V Mitsilegas, 'Article 49 (the Principles of Legality and Proportionality of Criminal Offences and Penalties)' in S Peers et al (eds), *The EU Charter of Fundamental Rights. A Commentary* (Oxford, Hart Publishing/Beck, 2014).

[53] Art 280(4) EC.

[54] A similar clause was deleted from Art 135 EC concerning customs cooperation (this is Art 33 in the TFEU).

[55] R Sicurella, 'Some Reflections on the Need for a General Theory of the Competence of the European Union in Criminal Law' in A Klip (ed), *Substantive Criminal Law of the European Union* (Antwerp, Maklu, 2011) 236–37.

[56] COM(2012) 363 final, Brussels, 11 July 2012. Article 325(4) TFEU.

[57] See Council document 8604/15, Brussels, 7 May 2015, from www.statewatch.org/news/2015/may/eu-council-fraud-dir-trilogue-8604-15.pdf (downloaded on 31 August 2015).

Attention should also been drawn to two further alternative legal bases for the adoption of EU substantive criminal law, one located within and the other outside the Treaty Title on the area of freedom, security and justice (Title V). Within Title V, the relevant provision is Article 86 TFEU, which enables the establishment of a European Public Prosecutor's Office. According to Article 86(2) TFEU, the European Public Prosecutor's Office will be 'responsible for investigating, prosecuting and bringing to judgment the perpetrators of, and accomplices in, offences against the Union's financial interests', as determined by the regulation establishing the Office provided for in Article 86(1). According to Article 86(4) TFEU, the powers of the European Public Prosecutor's Office may be subsequently extended by a decision of the European Council 'to include serious crime having a cross-border dimension and amending accordingly [Article 86(2)] as regards the perpetrators of, and accomplices in, serious crimes affecting more than one Member State'. The question thus arises whether legislation defining criminal offences and imposing criminal sanctions for the purposes of the operation of the European Public Prosecutor can be adopted not under Article 83, but under Article 86(2) and 86(4) TFEU—which would lead to the adoption of substantive criminal law under different legislative procedures, by different institutions (note the reference to the European Council in Article 86(4)) and by different instruments. The wording of Article 86(2), which calls for fraud offences to be 'determined' by a regulation under Article 86(1), is open enough not to exclude the adoption of substantive EU criminal law on fraud. However, the function of any criminalisation based on Article 86(2) TFEU would be limited to the operation of a European Public Prosecutor's Office and would not exclude the adoption of parallel EU measures under Article 83(2) or Article 325(4) TFEU—with the risk of proliferation and fragmentation of the criminal law on fraud being visible. Article 86(4) TFEU on the other hand—which refers to the inclusion of further areas of crime—should be read as mandating not a criminalisation process, but merely the listing of offences already defined elsewhere.[58]

Another alternative criminalisation legal basis discussed by commentators is the catch-all provision of Article 352(1) TFEU, which confers competence on the EU if action by the Union should prove necessary, within the framework of the policies defined in the treaties, to attain one of the objectives set out in the treaties, and the treaties have not provided the necessary powers.[59] It has been pointed out that Article 352(1) TFEU could lead to the adoption of EU substantive criminal law in cases where the requirement of Article 83(2) TFEU for harmonisation in the underlying policy area has not been met, and it has been argued that Article 352 should not apply in the light of this requirement[60]

---

[58] But see here the analysis of Sicurella, n 55 above, who argues that Art 86(2) TFEU also implies a listing function.

[59] See E Herlin-Karnell, *The Constitutional Dimension of European Criminal Law* (Oxford, Hart Publishing, 2012) ch 4.

[60] Asp (n 40) 138.

and in the light of the existence of the specific provisions in Title V TFEU.[61] However, this analysis cannot mask the paradox inherent in the constitutionalisation of functional criminalisation in the Lisbon Treaty. If substantive criminal law is, under Article 83(2) TFEU, merely a means to the end of achieving effectiveness of EU law based on the specific EU policies outlined in the treaties, it is difficult to see in principle why the Treaty legal bases related to these policies and located elsewhere in the treaties, in particular outside the Treaty Title on the area of freedom, security and justice, cannot be used as additional, or alternative, legal bases for the adoption of EU substantive criminal law. This is especially the case where the conditions of Article 83(2) TFEU are not met, in particular where an area has not been subject to harmonisation measures and there is an urgent need to address a social problem related to the implementation of an EU policy or objective.

VI. Policy Responses to the EU Competence to Criminalise After Lisbon

The redefinition of the Union's competence to criminalise by the Lisbon Treaty has led to an extensive inter-institutional policy debate over the extent and use of such competence. The European Council's intentions were revealed in the Stockholm Programme[62] which includes a special section on criminal law.[63] The Stockholm Programme confirms in this context that criminal behaviour in the areas of particularly serious crime with a cross-border dimension resulting from the nature or impact of such offences or from a special need to combat them on a common basis should become the object of common definitions of criminal offences and common minimum levels of maximum sanctions and that these are the serious criminal offences referred to in Article 83(1) TFEU. Priority should be given to terrorism, trafficking in human beings, illicit drug trafficking, sexual exploitation of women and children and child pornography and computer crime. The European Council invited the Commission in particular to examine whether the level of approximation is sufficient in relation to the adopted framework decisions and report on the need to establish common definitions and sanctions and to consider submitting new legislative proposals where further approximation is needed, adding that the relationship between approximation of criminal offences or their definition and the double criminality rule in the framework of mutual recognition should be further

---

[61] Herlin-Karnell (n 59) 87.
[62] The Stockholm Programme—An Open and Secure Europe Serving and Protecting Citizens, [2010] OJ C115/01.
[63] ibid, s 3.3.1.

explored. Particular emphasis has been placed upon the justification and limits or conditions for the adoption of EU substantive criminal law. According to the Stockholm Programme, criminal law provisions should be introduced when they are considered essential in order for the interests to be protected and, as a rule, should be used only as a last resort. Minimum rules with regard to the definition of criminal offences and sanctions may also be established when the approximation of criminal laws and regulations of the Member States proves essential to ensure the effective implementation of a Union policy which has been subject to harmonisation measures.

The Stockholm Programme was preceded by the adoption of Conclusions by the Council shortly before the entry into force of the Lisbon Treaty.[64] The Council's intervention can be seen as an attempt to set out a marker on what Member States consider the extent and limits of EU competence to criminalise after Lisbon. The Council predicted that the Lisbon Treaty was likely to have the effect that criminal law provisions would be discussed within the Council to an even greater extent than previously and that this might result in incoherent and inconsistent criminal provisions in EU legislation. In order to address this, the Council put forward a series of detailed guidelines for EU substantive criminal law. The Council emphasised in particular the requirement to assess the need for criminal provisions and stressed the application of principles including necessity and *ultima ratio* (namely that criminal law provisions should be introduced when they are considered essential in order for the interests to be protected and, as a rule, should be used only as a last resort), proportionality and subsidiarity. The Guidelines also emphasised the need to address clearly defined and delimited conduct, which cannot be addressed effectively by less severe measures, and added that when there seems to be a need to adopt new criminal provisions the following factors should be further considered: added value or effectiveness of criminal provisions compared to other measures; how serious and/or widespread and frequent the harmful conduct is both regionally and locally within the EU; and the possible impact of existing criminal provisions on EU law and on different legal systems. The Council Guidelines demonstrate a degree of ambiguity with regard to the impact of EU substantive criminal law on the domestic systems of penalties: it is stated that when it has been established that criminal penalties for natural persons should be included it may in some cases be sufficient to provide for 'effective, proportionate and dissuasive' criminal penalties and to leave it to each Member State to determine the actual level of the penalties but that in other cases there may be a need for going further in the approximation of the levels of the penalties.

---

[64] Draft Council conclusions on model provisions, guiding the Council's criminal law deliberations Council doc 16542/1/09 25 November 2009. See also Council doc 16798/09, 27 November 2009—endorsed by the JHA Council of 30 November—1 December 2009, doc 16883/1/09 REV 1 (Presse 355) 31.

The European Commission reacted to the entry into force of the Lisbon Treaty by the publication of a Communication on European Criminal Policy.[65] The Commission focused on what it considered to be the 'added value' of the harmonisation of substantive criminal law. This 'added value' was perceived to be fourfold: harmonisation of criminal law fosters the confidence of citizens in using their right to free movement and to buy goods or services from providers from other Member States through a more effective fight against crime; it prevents 'forum shopping' by criminals; it strengthens mutual trust among the judiciaries and law enforcement authorities of the Member States, facilitating mutual recognition and judicial cooperation in criminal matters; and it helps to prevent and sanction serious offences against EU law in important policy areas, such as the protection of the environment or illegal employment. This is a rather mixed bag of assertions whose credibility is difficult to ascertain—this was the case in particular when the Commission emphasised the subjective elements of EU criminal law as enhancing the confidence of citizens in exercising their Union law rights and as leading to greater mutual trust among national authorities.[66] Aware that such a vague approach might lead to fears that the Commission would be unduly activist in the field of substantive criminal law after Lisbon, the Commission proceeded to outline the principles that should guide EU criminal law.[67] These principles included subsidiarity and respect for fundamental rights. The Commission then called for a two-step approach in criminal law legislation: step one concerned the decision on whether to adopt criminal law measures at all, where it was stated that necessity and proportionality must be respected and that criminal law is a means of last resort (*ultima ratio*); step two concerned the principles guiding the decision on what kind of criminal law measures to adopt: these included the adoption of minimum rules; necessity and proportionality; the existence of clear factual evidence about the nature and effects of the crime in question and about a diverging legal situation in all Member States which could jeopardise the effective enforcement of an EU policy subject to harmonisation; and tailoring the sanctions to the crime. These principles should not, however, be read as a sign of the Commission's limited ambition as regards the adoption of further substantive criminal law at EU level. The last part of the Communication revealed the primary purpose of the document, which was to set out the Commission's vision as to the areas where further EU standards on criminal offences and sanctions would be developed on the basis of Article 83(2) TFEU.[68] The list of such policies provided

---

[65] Commission to the European Parliament, the Council, the European Economic and Social Committee and the Committee of the Regions, 'Towards an EU Criminal Policy: ensuring the effective implementation of EU policies through criminal law' (Communication) COM(2011) final, 20 September 2011.

[66] V Mitsilegas, 'The Limits of Mutual Trust in Europe's Area of Freedom, Security and Justice. From Automatic Inter-state Cooperation to the Slow Emergence of the Individual' 31 *Yearbook of European Law 2012* 319.

[67] Communication (n 65) 6–9.

[68] ibid, 9–11.

in the Communication is far-reaching. The Commission claimed that it had been established that criminal law measures were necessary in order to protect the financial sector, to fight against fraud and to protect the Euro against counterfeiting and that it would further reflect on the use of criminal law to tackle the illegal economy and financial crime, and on the use of criminal law in areas as diverse as road transport, data protection, customs rules, environmental protection, fisheries policy and internal market policies. Rather than following the principles set out earlier in the Communication, this list confirmed an expansive approach treating criminal law merely as a 'means to an end'.[69]

The European Parliament responded by the adoption of a resolution on an EU approach to criminal law.[70] The resolution focused on the principles that should govern EU action in the field of substantive criminal law. The European Parliament stressed the need for EU substantive criminal law to respect the principles of subsidiarity and proportionality and fundamental rights. It was also noted that, in the adoption of EU substantive criminal law, it is not sufficient to refer to abstract notions or to symbolic effect, but that the necessity of new substantive criminal law provisions must be demonstrated by the necessary factual evidence making it clear that damage has occurred; there are no less intrusive measures which can be adopted; that the crime in question is of a particularly serious nature or is having a direct negative impact on the effective implementation of a Union policy which has been subject to harmonisation measures; that there is a need to combat on a common basis; and that EU action is in conformity with Article 49(3) of the Charter and in particular that the severity of the proposed sanctions is not disproportionate to the criminal offence. The European Parliament also recognised the importance of the other general principles governing criminal law (such as the principle of non-retroactivity of criminal sanctions) and welcomed the recognition by the Commission that the first step in criminal law legislation should always be to decide whether to adopt substantive criminal law measures at all.

The differences in the policy approaches of EU institutions towards substantive criminal law are noteworthy. The European Council placed in the Stockholm Programme emphasis on the continuation of the adoption by the European Union of securitised criminal law. Member States in the Council aimed at pre-empting

---

[69] This expansionist tendency is also reflected in the willingness of the Commission to maintain legal basis litigation concerning criminal law. The latest example is a case before the ECJ in which the Commission obtained the annulment of a road traffic directive adopted under Art 87(2) TFEU (Directive 2011/82/EU facilitating the cross-border exchange of information on road safety related traffic offences, [2011] OJ L288/1, 5 November 2011), with the Commission successfully arguing in favour of the more supranational legal basis of Art 91(1) TFEU (Case C-43/12 *Commission Parliament and Council*, judgment of 6 May 2014, EU:C:2014:298). Although the case did not involve the adoption of substantive criminal law, it is a clear indication that the Commission will not hesitate to defend its choices or prerogatives in cases involving the use of Art 83(2) TFEU.
[70] Based on 'Report on an EU approach on criminal law' A7-0144/2012, 24 April 2012, rapporteur: Cornelis de Jong.

the supranationalisation brought forward by the entry into force of the Lisbon Treaty and emphasised conditions and limits to the exercise of Union competence under Article 83 post-Lisbon. The Commission attempted to demonstrate the added value of criminalisation at EU level and focused primarily on functional criminalisation. The European Parliament emphasised the need for EU substantive criminal law to comply with fundamental rights. A common theme in these institutional approaches has been the call to respect either fundamental principles of domestic criminal law (such as *ultima ratio*) or constitutional principles of Union law, including effectiveness, subsidiarity and proportionality. Institutional practice after the entry into force of the Lisbon Treaty in terms of the production of secondary substantive criminal law has not yet revealed a major change to the pre-Lisbon practice as regards new initiatives proposed by the Commission, with a number of proposals on both securitised and functional criminal law tabled and in the pipeline. Those who expected a fresh momentum towards EU harmonisation in the field of substantive criminal law by the post-Stockholm five-year plan will have been disappointed by the European Council conclusions of June 2014 which contained minimal—if any—references to criminal law harmonisation.[71] Whatever new initiatives appear in the future, it is the Union law constitutional principles—and in particular the principles of legality and proportionality as enshrined in Article 49 of the Charter—that will prove influential in the development of EU substantive criminal law.

VII. The Lisbon Treaty and the Impact on National Criminal Law

An analysis of the impact of the entry into force of the Lisbon Treaty on criminalisation cannot be complete without an analysis of the impact of European Union law on national criminal law. The interplay between EU law—and in particular the need to ensure its effective enforcement—and national criminal law is not new, having appeared in the Court's case-law much earlier than the entry into force of the Treaty of Lisbon.[72] This section will analyse this case-law, by pointing out that the interplay between EU law and national criminal law may lead to both over-criminalisation and de-criminalisation. The impact of the need to ensure the effective enforcement of European Union law on domestic criminal justice systems post-Lisbon will be highlighted in particular in the case of *Taricco*.

---

[71] European Council Conclusions of 26–27 June 2014, EUCO doc 79/14, Brussels, 27 June 2014.
[72] V Mitsilegas, 'From Overcriminalisation to Decriminalisation. The Many Faces of Effectiveness in European Criminal Law' (2014) 5 *New Journal of European Criminal Law* 415–24.

A. Effectiveness and National Criminal Law: Decriminalisation

The application of the principle of effectiveness can lead to decriminalisation in cases where EU law places limits on national criminal law in order to ensure the effectiveness of Union law. In a number of cases, the Court of Justice has confirmed that Community law places limits on the application of national criminal law, if the latter would have as its effect the limitation disproportionately of rights established by Community law, in particular rights related to free movement. As early as 1981, the Court stated in *Casati* that

> In principle, criminal legislation and the rules of criminal procedure are matters for which the Member States are still responsible. However, it is clear from a consistent line of cases decided by the Court, that Community law also sets *certain limits* in that area as regards the control measures which it permits the Member States to maintain in connection with the free movement of goods and persons. The administrative measures or penalties must not go beyond what is strictly necessary, the control procedures must not be concerned in such a way as to restrict the freedom required by the Treaty and they must not be accompanied by a penalty which is so disproportionate to the gravity of the infringement that it becomes an obstacle to the exercise of that freedom (emphasis added).[73]

The Court has reiterated this case-law on a number of occasions, placing limits on national criminalisation when this would constitute a disproportionate infringement of free movement rights.[74] In a significant post-Lisbon development, the Court has extended its case-law to include limiting national criminalisation on the grounds of ensuring the effectiveness of an instrument of immigration enforcement within the Area of Freedom, Security and Justice. In the case of *El-Dridi*,[75] which concerned the compatibility of national criminalisation of immigration offences with the EU returns Directive, the Court reiterated that although in principle criminal legislation and the rules of criminal procedure are matters for which the Member States are responsible, this branch of the law may nevertheless be affected by European Union law.[76] The Court added that Member States may not apply rules, even criminal law rules, which are liable to jeopardise the achievement of the objectives pursued by a Directive and, therefore, deprive it of its effectiveness.[77] It also confirmed the applicability of the principle of loyal cooperation as expressed in Article 4(3) TEU.[78] The Court's effectiveness reasoning in *El-Dridi* has been since reiterated by the Court in a number of cases concerning

---

[73] Case 203/80, *Casati* [1981] ECR 2595, paragraph 27.

[74] See inter alia Case C-193/94 *Skanavi and Chryssanthakopoulos* [1996] ECR I-929 and Joined Cases C-338/04, C-359/04 and C-360/04, *Placanica, Palazzese and Sorricchio*, [2007] ECR I-1891. For an overview see V Mitsilegas, *EU Criminal Law* (Oxford, Hart Publishing, 2009) chapter 2.

[75] Case C-61/11 PPU, *El-Dridi* [2011] ECR I-03015.

[76] Paragraph 53.

[77] Paragraph 55.

[78] Paragraph 56.

the compatibility of national criminalisation initiatives with the returns
Directive.[79] These cases are significant as they mark a departure from earlier
case-law: while traditionally, in rulings like *Casati*, the Court of Justice has placed
limits on national criminal law in order to achieve free movement objectives, in *El
Dridi* and its follow-up cases limits to national criminalisation are justified in order
to achieve the effectiveness of an *enforcement* measure, namely the EU returns
Directive.[80] In this context, the decriminalisation potential of the application of
the principle of effectiveness has increased considerably.[81]

B. Effectiveness as Assimilation: Over-criminalisation

Over-criminalisation may be the outcome of the application of the principle of
assimilation as a means of ensuring the effectiveness of EU law. Already in the' 70s,
the Court stated in *Amsterdam Bulb* that

> although Article 5 of the EEC Treaty places Member States under a duty to take all appro-
> priate measures, whether general or particular, to ensure fulfilment of the obligations
> resulting from action taken by the institutions of the Community, it allows the various
> Member States to choose the measures which they consider appropriate, including sanc-
> tions *which may even be criminal in nature* (emphasis added).[82]

Amsterdam Bulb is a clear reflection of the view that criminal law may be used to
achieve as a means to an end, with the end being the achievement of the effectiveness of Community law. In the late' 80s the Court went a step further in a landmark
ruling concerning the possibility of imposition of national criminal sanctions for
the protection of the financial interests of the Community. In the seminal ruling
of the Court in *Commission v Greece*,[83] the Court stated that:

> where Community legislation does not specifically provide any penalty for an infringe-
> ment or refers for that purpose to national laws, regulations and administrative provi-
> sions, Article 5 of the Treaty requires the Member States to take all measures necessary to
> guarantee the application and effectiveness of Community law.

> For that purpose, whilst the choice of penalties remains within their discretion, they
> must ensure in particular that infringements of Community law are penalised under
> conditions, both procedural and substantive, which are *analogous* to those applicable

---

[79] Case C-329/11 *Achughbabian v Préfet du Val-de-Marne* [2011] ECR I-12695; Case C-430/11
Sagor; Case C-297/12 *Filev and Osmani*.

[80] See V Mitsilegas, 'The Changing Landscape of the Criminalisation of Migration in Europe. The
Protective Function of European Union Law' in M Guia, M Van der Woude and J Van der Leun (eds),
Social Control and Justice. Crimmigration in an Age of Fear (The Hague, Eleven International Publish-
ing, 2012) 87–114; and V Mitsilegas, *The Criminalisation of Migration in Europe. Challenges for Human
Rights and the Rule of Law* (London, Springer, 2015) chapter 3.

[81] See Mitsilegas, 'From Overcriminalisation to Decriminalisation' (n 72 above).

[82] Case 50/76 *Amsterdam Bulb BV v Produktschap voor Siergewassen* [1977] ECR 137, paragraph 32.

[83] Case C-68/88 *Commission v Greece (Greek Maize)* [1989] ECR 2965.

to infringements of national law of a similar nature and importance and which, in any event, make the penalty effective, proportionate and dissuasive.

Moreover, the national authorities must proceed, with respect to infringements of Community law, *with the same diligence* as that which they bring to bear in implementing corresponding national laws (emphasis added).[84]

Based on the principles of effectiveness and equivalence,[85] the Court thus introduced the principle of assimilation: Community law must be 'assimilated' in national legal systems, and infringements of Community law must be treated in a manner analogous to the manner in which breaches of similar domestic law are treated. In this manner, criminalisation may occur at national level even in cases where such criminalisation is not expressly required by EU law. The Court stated subsequently that effective national measures in this context 'may include criminal penalties even where the Community legislation only provides for civil sanctions'.[86] This potential for over-criminalisation remains prominent after the entry into force of the Treaty of Lisbon as regards cases involving fraud against the EU budget. Article 325 TFEU consolidates the principle of assimilation based upon equivalence and effectiveness by requiring effective protection in the Member States and in the Union's institutions,[87] requiring Member States to take the same measures to counter fraud affecting the financial interests of the Union as they take to counter fraud affecting their own financial interests,[88] and calling for the adoption of EU law in the fields of the prevention of and fight against fraud with a view to affording effective and equivalent protection in the Member States and in all the Union's institutions, bodies, offices and agencies.[89] Effectiveness here applies not only at the national level (via the principle of assimilation) but also at the EU level, via action by EU institutions and adoption of EU law.

The question of the impact of European Union law on national criminal law in the context of the application of Article 325 TFEU has arisen recently in the case of *Taricco*.[90] The key question that the Court of Justice decided to answer was the extent to which national rules in relation to limitation periods for criminal offences in Italy were in compliance with EU law, and in particular with EU law on the protection of the Union's financial interests. The Court of Justice followed a three-step approach to answer this question: first, it identified specific EU law obligations in the field; secondly, it determined the effect of these obligations on

---

[84] ibid, paragraphs 23–25.

[85] On the relationship between effectiveness and equivalence, see Tridimas, *General Principles of EU Law*, 2nd edn (Oxford, OUP, 2007) 423.

[86] Case C-186/98 *Nunes and de Matos*, [1999] ECR I-4883, paragraph 14.

[87] Article 325(1) TFEU.

[88] Article 325(2) TFEU.

[89] Article 325(4).

[90] Case C-105/14 *Taricco and Others*, judgment of 8 September 2015, EU:C:2015:555.

national law; and thirdly, it assessed the compatibility of compliance by national authorities with these obligations with fundamental rights, and in particular with the principle of legality. In terms of the first step, namely the identification of specific EU law obligations, the Court established such obligations as emanating from both secondary and primary EU law. On the one hand, the Court found (by reference to its ruling in *Fransson*)[91] that Directive 2006/112, read in conjunction with Article 4(3) TEU on the principle of loyal co-operation, imposes on Member States 'not only ... a general obligation to take all legislative and administrative measures appropriate for ensuring collection of all the VAT due on their territory, but must also fight against tax evasion'.[92] Furthermore, also by reference to *Fransson*,[93] the Court reiterated that

> Article 325 TFEU itself obliges the Member States to counter illegal activities affecting the financial interests of the European Union through effective deterrent measures and, in particular, obliges them to take the same measures to counter fraud affecting the financial interests of the European Union as they take to counter fraud affecting their own interests

—hence stressing again the importance of the principle of assimilation.[94] The Court recalled its finding in *Fransson* that

> there is ... *a direct link between the collection of VAT revenue in compliance with the EU law applicable and the availability to the EU budget of the corresponding VAT resources*, since any lacuna in the collection of the first potentially causes a reduction in the second (emphasis added).[95]

The Court noted that

> [a]lthough the Member States have freedom to choose the applicable penalties ... in order to ensure that all VAT revenue is collected and, in so doing, that the financial interests of the European Union are protected in accordance with the provisions of [Directive 2006/112 and Article 325 TFEU ... *criminal penalties may nevertheless be essential to combat certain serious cases of VAT evasion* in an effective and dissuasive manner (emphasis added).[96]

The Court further recalled the duty of Member States

> under Article 2(1) of the PFI Convention ... to take the necessary measures to ensure that conduct constituting fraud affecting the European Union's financial interests is punishable by effective, proportionate and dissuasive criminal penalties, including, at least in cases of serious fraud, penalties involving deprivation of liberty.[97]

---

[91] *Åklagaren v Åkerberg Fransson*, C-617/10, EU:C:2013:105, paragraph 25.
[92] *Taricco and Others*, paragraph 36.
[93] *Fransson*, paragraph 26.
[94] *Taricco*, n 90 above, paragraph 37.
[95] Paragraph 38.
[96] Paragraph 39.
[97] Paragraph 40.

In a move which is also significant for the determination of the mandate of the European Public Prosecutor's Office,[98] the Court further found that the concept of 'fraud' as defined in Article 1 of the PFI Convention 'covers revenue derived from applying a uniform rate to the harmonised VAT assessment bases determined according to EU rules', a conclusion which 'cannot be called into question by the fact that VAT is not collected directly for the account of the European Union'.[99] The Court confirmed that the offences in the present case (inter alia, conspiracy to commit offences in relation to VAT and VAT evasion amounting to several million euros) 'constitute cases of serious fraud affecting the European Union's financial interests'[100] and confirmed that 'such cases of serious fraud are punishable by criminal penalties which are, in particular, effective and dissuasive' and that 'the measures adopted in that respect must be the same as those which the Member States adopt in order to combat equally serious cases of fraud affecting their own financial interests'.[101]

Having established obligations under EU law, the Court went on to spell out the effect of these obligations on national authorities. The Court noted that 'the national provisions at issue ... have the effect, given the complexity and duration of the criminal proceedings leading to the adoption of a final judgment, of neutralising the temporal effect of an event interrupting the limitation period'.[102] The Court added crucially that

> if the national court concludes that the application of the national provisions in relation to the interruption of the limitation period has the effect that, in a considerable number of case[s], the commission of serious fraud will escape criminal punishment, since the offences will usually be time-barred before the criminal penalty laid down by law can be imposed by a final judicial decision, it would be necessary to find that the measures laid down by national law to combat fraud and any other illegal activity affecting the financial interests of the European Union could not be regarded as being effective and dissuasive, which would be incompatible with Article 325(1) TFEU, Article 2(1) of the PFI Convention as well as Directive 2006/112, read in conjunction with Article 4(3) TEU.[103]

> ...

> In the event that the national court concludes that the national provisions at issue do not satisfy the requirement of EU law that measures to counter VAT evasion be effective and dissuasive, that court would have to ensure that EU law is given full effect, *if need be by disapplying* those provisions and thereby neutralising the consequence referred to in paragraph 46 above, without having to request or await the prior repeal of those articles by way of legislation or any other constitutional procedure (emphasis added).[104]

---

[98] For an analysis, see Chapter 4 of this volume on the Europeanisation of prosecution.
[99] Paragraph 41.
[100] Paragraph 42.
[101] Paragraph 43.
[102] Paragraph 46.
[103] Paragraph 47.
[104] Paragraph 49.

The Court stressed in this context that

> the Member States' obligation to counter illegal activities affecting the financial interests of the European Union through dissuasive and effective measures, and their obligation to take the same measures to counter fraud affecting those interests as they take to counter fraud affecting their own financial interests, are obligations imposed, inter alia, by EU primary law, namely Article 325(1) and (2) TFEU.[105]

> Those provisions of EU primary law impose on Member States a precise obligation as to the result to be achieved that is not subject to any condition regarding application of the rule, which they lay down.[106]

> The provisions of Article 325(1) and (2) TFEU therefore have the effect, in accordance with the principle of the precedence of EU law, in their relationship with the domestic law of the Member States, of rendering automatically inapplicable, merely by their entering into force, any conflicting provision of national law.[107]

The Court thus here confirms that Article 325 TFEU has direct effect, and primacy over national law which leads to the disapplication of conflicting national law.

As the third step in its response to the national court, the Court of Justice found that the disapplication of the national provisions in question would be compatible with the principle of legality as enshrined in Article 49 of the Charter of Fundamental Rights.

> [T]he sole effect of the disapplication of the national provisions at issue would be to not shorten the general limitation period in the context of pending criminal proceedings, to allow the effective prosecution of the alleged crimes, and to ensure, if necessary, that penalties intended to protect the financial interests of the European Union and those intended to protect the financial interests of the Italian Republic are treated in the same way.[108]

Such a disapplication of national law

> would in no way lead to a conviction of the accused for an act or omission which did not constitute a criminal offence under national law at the time when it was committed … nor to the application of a penalty which, at that time, was not laid down by national law. On the contrary, the acts which the accused are alleged to have committed constituted, at the time when they were committed, the same offence and were punishable by the same criminal penalties as those applicable at present.[109]

> The case-law of the European Court of Human Rights in relation to Article 7 [ECHR] … support[s] that conclusion. Thus according to that case-law, the extension of the limitation period and its immediate application do not entail an infringement of the rights guaranteed by Article 7 of that convention, since that provision cannot be interpreted as

---

[105] Paragraph 50.
[106] Paragraph 51.
[107] Paragraph 52.
[108] Paragraph 55.
[109] Paragraph 56.

prohibiting an extension of limitation periods where the relevant offences have never become subject to limitation.[110]

The judgment in *Taricco* has a major impact on the relationship between European Union law and national criminal law. The Court confirms in the strongest possible terms that national sovereignty in criminal matters is limited in order to ensure the effective enforcement of EU law. *Taricco* is significant in this context because it confirms that the obligation of national authorities to disapply national law may stem directly from a Treaty provision which is seen as having direct effect. Effectively, the Court here grants the principle of assimilation, as enshrined in Article 325 TFEU, direct effect. The Court has thus sent a very powerful message regarding the obligation of Member States to ensure the effective protection of the EU budget.[111] It confirmed that Article 325 TFEU has direct effect and primacy over national law, thus placing obligations upon national authorities to ensure the effectiveness of the fight against fraud in the strongest possible terms. *Taricco* is also of broader significance in confirming the inclusion of VAT fraud within the scope of the PFI Convention—it remains to be seen whether Member States will disregard the Court's finding in defining the concept of fraud for the purposes of the new fraud Directive, which will replace the PFI Convention and is currently under negotiation in Brussels. The outcome of this negotiation is important as it is likely that whatever is defined as 'fraud' in the Directive will also form the mandate of the European Public Prosecutor's Office. However, the significance of *Taricco* is broader than strictly the field of the protection of the Union's financial interests. The Court has opened the door for the disapplication of national law which is not in compliance with the achievement of objectives contained in primary law provisions when these provisions are deemed to impose precise obligations—thus extending the principle of functional criminalisation at the level of national enforcement. It remains to be seen whether the *Taricco* approach will be applicable with regard to Treaty provisions which, unlike Article 325 TFEU, do not necessarily include references to the principle of assimilation. Last, but not least, *Taricco* has a very significant impact on domestic criminal justice choices and the protection of fundamental rights. In a manner reminiscent of its case-law in *Pupino*[112] and *Advocaten voor*

---

[110] Paragraph 57, omitting references to *Coëme and Others v Belgium*, Application nos 32492/96, 32547/96, 32548/96, 33209/96 and 33210/96, § 149, ECHR 2000-VI; *Scoppola v Italy (no 2)* [GC], Application no 10249/03, § 110 and the case-law cited, 17 September 2009, and *OAO Neftyanaya Kompaniya Yukos v. Russia*, Application nos 14902/04, §§ 563, 564 and 570 and the case-law cited, 20 September 2011.

[111] See also the Opinion of Advocate General Kokott, who called for the referring court to refrain from applying a provision if that provision were to reflect a 'systemic shortcoming' which prevents the achievement of an outcome consistent with EU law—Opinion delivered on 30 April 2015, paragraph 11.

[112] Case C-105/03 *Pupino*, [2005] ECR I-5285. For an analysis, see V Mitsilegas, 'Constitutional Principles of the European Community and European Criminal Law' (2006) 8 *European Journal of Law Reform* 301–24.

de Wereld,[113] the Court interpreted narrowly the scope of substantive criminal law: it found that the principle of legality is not affected because the national provisions in question (here on limitation periods) do not involve substance, but procedure. There is a very thin line between substance and procedure, however, in this context, and *Taricco* has the effect of effectively overturning domestic criminal justice choices and in this manner lowering the level of fundamental rights protection at national level in the name of the effective fight against fraud.

VIII. Conclusion

The debate over the extent of EU competence to criminalise and introduce criminal sanctions under the Lisbon Treaty is inextricably linked with the broader discussion of the substance of the EU criminalisation policy. In the pre-Lisbon third pillar world, the focus by EU institutions has been largely to determine the constitutional parameters of Union competence in the field, without considering the potential over-criminalisation impact that this framing of the issue may have.[114] The entry into force of the Lisbon Treaty will not bring an end to the competence debate, but will serve to refocus the mind on the impact of the exercise of EU competence in substantive criminal law upon the Union's criminalisation policy. A key question in this context is whether, irrespective of the existence of EU competence to legislate, criminal law is the most effective way to address security threats or achieve the effective implementation of Union policies. This question is central especially in the light of the constitutional affirmation by the Lisbon Treaty of the Union's functional criminalisation competence. The use of the Lisbon legal bases on substantive criminal law will test this assumption. Post-Lisbon practice thus far has shown a rather measured use of the possibilities offered by the Lisbon Treaty and has highlighted a number of areas of remaining uncertainty and controversy with regard to the extent of the Union's powers to criminalise. What this chapter has attempted to demonstrate is that the development of EU substantive criminal law in conformity with constitutional principles of Union law, and in full respect of the Charter, should lead to a more measured use of criminal law. In this context, it should not be forgotten that supranational criminal law after Lisbon and the limits that this places on Member States' competence to criminalise may lead in practice not to over-criminalisation, but to a process of de-criminalisation.

---

[113] See in particular *Advocaten voor de Wereld VZW v Leden van de Ministerraad* and the Court's departure from Advocate General Sharpston's Opinion in *Radu*—for an analysis see Chapter 5 of this volume on mutual recognition.

[114] V Mitsilegas, 'The Third Wave of Third Pillar Law: Which Direction for EU Criminal Justice?' (2009) 34 *EL Rev* 523.

The constitutionalisation of functional criminalisation in the Lisbon Treaty and the debate over the potential use of other Treaty legal bases to introduce harmonisation of EU substantive criminal law have raised the prospect of over-criminalisation in EU criminal law.[115] However, a careful examination of both the content of the constitutional provisions as well as post-Lisbon institutional practice demonstrates that in fact the Treaty on the Functioning of the European Union contains a number of possibilities to limit criminalisation and in fact to lead to de-criminalisation.[116] One way of achieving limits to criminalisation is by placing limits on the *EU* competence to harmonise substantive criminal law, resulting largely from Member States' concerns regarding the impact of supra-national criminal law on their sovereignty and the integrity of national criminal justice systems. These limits appear in addition to the specific conditions for EU competence embedded expressly within Article 83(1) and 83(2) TFEU and which were subject to examination above. In this context, Article 67(3) TFEU calls for the approximation of criminal laws only if necessary—introducing thus in essence a proportionality test applicable to Article 83 TFEU as far as measures concerning the area of freedom, security and justice are concerned.[117] The respect for national legal diversity is further enshrined in Article 67(1) TFEU, according to which the Union shall constitute an area of freedom, security and justice with respect for fundamental rights and the different legal systems and traditions of the Member States. Respect for national diversity is also guaranteed by the emphasis of the Treaty on the respect of the principles of subsidiarity and proportionality, the use of directives to harmonise substantive criminal law under Article 83 TFEU, and the introduction of the emergency brake provision in Article 83(3) TFEU.[118] Criminalisation limits are also placed by the requirement for the Union to respect fully fundamental rights as enshrined in the ECHR (European Convention on Human Rights) and the Charter, in particular the principles of legality and proportionality in criminal offences and sanctions.[119] However, it is the limits that European Union law places on the powers of national law to criminalise which provide the main driver for de-criminalisation.

However, the potential for over-criminalisation post-Lisbon still remains, with such over-criminalisation being the outcome of the use of Article 83 TFEU for purposes other than originally envisaged, as well as the use of other Treaty provisions with the aim of enhancing the effective enforcement of EU law. In terms

---

[115] On the concept of over-criminalisation, see inter alia D Husak, *Overcriminalisation. The Limits of the Criminal Law* (Oxford, OUP, 2008).

[116] V Mitsilegas, 'From Overcriminalisation to Decriminalisation. The Many Faces of Effectiveness in European Criminal Law' (2014) 5 *New Journal of European Criminal Law* 415–24.

[117] But see the view of Satzger from a domestic criminal law perspective who argues that Art 67(3) TFEU correlates to the principles of subsidiarity and *ultima ratio*: H Satzger, *International and European Criminal Law* (Oxford, Beck/Hart/Nomos, 2012) 76.

[118] V Mitsilegas, 'European Criminal Law and Resistance to Communautarisation Post-Lisbon' (2010) 1 *New Journal of European Criminal Law* 458.

[119] Mitsilegas, ibid (Art 49 commentary).

of the use and misuse of Article 83, and in particular Article 83(1) TFEU, it will be demonstrated in detail further in this volume[120] that Article 83(1) has been used as symbolic criminal law in order to justify national decisions to limit citizenship rights and expel EU citizens from their territory. On the other hand, and not-withstanding the 'janus-faced' nature of the principle of effectiveness (which, as was seen above, may lead to both over-criminalisation and de-criminalisation at national level), the recent judgment of the Court of Justice in *Taricco* has demonstrated clearly the potential impact that EU law (including primary EU law) may have on national criminal justice choices. *Taricco* demonstrates that general principles of EU law, including primacy and direct effect, when applied to criminal law related provisions outside Title V, such as Article 325 TFEU, may have a significant influence on national criminal justice systems, compensating for any limits to the competence of the European Union to criminalise under Article 83 TFEU. This is in particular the case regarding the protection of the budget of the European Union, which is viewed by the Court clearly as a European interest worthy of extensive EU law protection.

---

[120] See Chapter 8 of this volume on citizenship.

4

The Rocky Road to European Prosecution: Caught Between Co-ordination and Centralisation

I. Introduction

A key challenge arising from the evolution of European integration in criminal matters has been how EU law can deal with the issue of prosecution in an area of freedom, security and justice without internal frontiers where the fundamental principle of freedom of movement is central. This challenge becomes more acute in cases of cross-border crime. At the heart of the matter lies the question of the extent to which EU law can impose upon national legal orders binding mechanisms of co-ordinating or mandating prosecution in cases with a European Union dimension. The latter include cases with a horizontal element including transnational *ne bis in idem* cases and cases of resolution of transnational conflicts of jurisdiction. They also include cases with a vertical dimension related to the role of EU criminal justice bodies and agencies (and in particular Eurojust and the European Public Prosecutor's Office) in the prosecution of cases falling within their mandate, including cases related to the protection of 'EU' interests such as the protection of the Union's budget. Should EU law grant these agencies powers to oblige Member States to initiate investigations and prosecutions? And, to take it a step further, can these agencies assume investigatory and prosecutorial powers per se in national legal orders? This chapter will examine how EU law has dealt with these questions thus far, in particular after the renewed *impetus* provided by the entry into force of the Lisbon Treaty towards further European integration in the field. The chapter will analyse the evolution of EU intervention in the field from prosecution to horizontal cooperation to vertical integration arrangements, and evaluate critically the impact of the current state of play on criminal justice. There are three main parameters underpinning this analysis: the impact of EU law on national legal diversity (especially in the light of the currently limited harmonisation of elements of national criminal justice systems, in particular in the field of criminal procedure); the impact of EU law on state sovereignty in criminal matters; and the impact of EU law on the protection of fundamental rights. The issue of the relationship between Europeanisation and mutual trust becomes central in the analysis of all three parameters, and will be highlighted throughout this chapter. The emerging picture will do justice to the claim that the effective protection of fundamental rights will provide a reference point in relation to which issues of trust, diversity and sovereignty in European prosecution can be resolved.

II. Horizontal Co-ordination via the Protection of Fundamental Rights: The Emergence of a Transnational *Ne Bis In Idem* Principle

A key challenge for EU criminal law has been to provide clear and legitimate answers to the question of how to achieve justice in cases of cross-border prosecutions. The determination of the substance and parameters of an EU law principle of *ne bis in idem* in criminal matters has been key in this context. At the national level, the determination of the parameters of the principle of *ne bis in idem* reflects the balance between state demands for delivering effective criminal justice on the one hand and the need to ensure legal certainty and the finality of judicial decisions on the other.[1] In this manner, *ne bis in idem* has both a rule of law and a human rights function. The rule of law function arises from the need to achieve legal certainty and finality with regard to state action in the field of criminal law. The human rights function—which is linked inextricably to the rule of law function—arises from the need to protect the rights of affected individuals and address the imbalance between individual rights and state power: the state should not be able to threaten individuals perennially with prosecution when criminal proceedings for the same conduct have been finalised once. The contrary would lead to a constant state of uncertainty and transform citizens into perennial suspects, eroding the relationship of trust between the individual and the state. On the other hand, limitations to the *ne bis in idem* principle have been advocated as necessary in order to enhance trust to the state as a security provider effectively delivering broader criminal justice objectives. Questions of the delimitation of the *ne bis in idem* principle have thus to address fundamental choices of justice and of the relationship between the individual and the state in a system based upon the rule of law. These questions are central in the determination of the parameters of the *ne bis in idem* principle in a domestic context, but are equally valid in the context of inter-state cooperation in criminal matters necessitating the development

---

[1] On various aspects of legal certainty in this context see C van den Wyngaert and G Stessens, 'The International *Non Bis In Idem* Principle: Resolving Some of the Unanswered Questions' (1999) 48 *ICLQ* 779–804. See also B Van Bockel, *The Ne Bis In Idem Principle in EU Law* (Alphen aan den Rijn, Kluwer Law International, 2010) chapter 2.

of a cross-border, or transnational *ne bis in idem* principle.[2] In Europe's Area of Freedom, Security and Justice transnational *ne bis in idem* has been introduced in Article 54 of the Schengen Implementing Convention.[3] Questions with regard to the relationship between trust, justice and the protection of human rights obtain further dimensions in the context of the Area of Freedom, Security and Justice, which is founded primarily upon the interaction of national criminal justice systems which have largely not been harmonised. Here, rather than addressing the question of whether the state can enforce criminal law over an individual more than once for the same conduct, the question is rather whether another state can enforce its criminal law over the same individual for the same conduct, or whether it is precluded from doing so in order to safeguard legal certainty and fundamental rights in an area without internal frontiers. Underpinning this question is the need to address the relationship between fundamental rights and fundamental EU law principles such as free movement on the one hand, and fundamental criminal policy choices of justice at the national level, arising from the expectation of national constituencies for justice to be delivered by their state authorities. The extent to which national authorities will forfeit their right to prosecute or enforce sentences on the basis of mutual trust and the respect of the prior undertaking of similar proceedings against the same individual in another state—precluding them thus from delivering criminal justice in their own jurisdiction—remains unsurprisingly contested.[4]

The Court of Justice has been called to deal with these contested issues in interpreting the scope of the *ne bis in idem* principle under Article 54 CISA. The Court has interpreted principle of *ne bis in idem* broadly focusing on the need to achieve a high degree of legal certainty in order to ensure free movement in a borderless Area of Freedom, Security and Justice. This broad interpretation is underpinned by the existence of mutual trust in an Area where national criminal procedural laws have not been harmonised. The need to achieve the effective enjoyment of free movement takes precedence over national priorities with regard to the delivery of criminal justice. This teleological approach is evident in the Court's interpretation of both elements of *bis* and *idem*. On the concept of *bis*, the Court has included

---

[2] J Vervaele, '*Ne Bis In Idem*: Towards a Transnational Constitutional Principle in the EU?' (2013) 9 *Utrecht Law Review* 211–29. R Roth, '*Non bis in idem* transnational: vers de nouveaux paradigmes?' in S Braum and A Weyembergh (eds), *Le Controle Juridictionnel dans l'Espace Pénal Européen* (Brussels, Editions de l'Université de Bruxelles, 2009) 121–41.

[3] A person whose trial has been finally disposed of in one Contracting Party may not be prosecuted in another Contracting Party for the same acts provided that, if a penalty has been imposed, it has been enforced, is actually in the process of being enforced or can no longer be enforced under the laws of the sentencing Contracting Party.

[4] See in this context the critical view of Caeiro, who notes that in the absence of a mechanism to allocate jurisdiction, the rule of *ne bis in idem* in Article 54 creates an awkward situation, where the first final decision pre-empts possible decisions from other jurisdictions. P Caeiro, 'Jurisdiction in Criminal Matters in the EU: Negative and Positive Conflicts, and Beyond' (2010) 93 *Kritische Vierteljahresschrift für Gesetzgebung und Rechtswissenschaft* 366, 376.

in the concept of 'finally disposed of' cases whose outcome was settled without involving a substantive examination of their merits. These include cases of a settlement ('transaction') between the defendant and the prosecution terminating the prosecution[5] as well as cases of time-barred prosecutions.[6] The Court's reasoning was put forward with great clarity in the landmark case of *Gözütok and Brügge* where the Court placed emphasis on the purpose of the integration of the Schengen *acquis* into the Union legal order. The Court noted that such integration 'is aimed at enhancing European integration and, in particular, at enabling the Union to become more rapidly the area of freedom, security and justice which is its objective to maintain and develop'.[7] Examining specifically Article 54 of the Schengen Convention, the Court emphasised its objective to ensure that no one is prosecuted on the same facts in several Member States on account of his having exercised his right to freedom of movement.[8] The Court stated that nowhere in the EU Treaty or the Schengen Convention 'is the application of Article 54 of the Convention made conditional upon harmonisation, or at least approximation, of the criminal laws of the Member States relating to procedures whereby further prosecution is barred'[9] and added that in those circumstances,

> there is a necessary implication that the Member States have *mutual trust* in their criminal justice systems and that each of them recognises the criminal law in force in the other Member States even when the outcome would be different if its own national law were applied (emphasis added).[10]

The Court's teleological approach thus presumes mutual trust in the absence of harmonisation of criminal justice systems.[11] Unlike its use in the European Arrest Warrant system, this presumption of trust serves here to enhance, and not to challenge, the protection of fundamental rights in Europe's Area of Freedom, Security and Justice. The Court's teleological interpretation emphasising the need to protect free movement has also based the Court's interpretation of *idem*. The Court has proceeded towards defining *idem* autonomously.[12] In the leading case of *Van Esbroeck*,[13] the Court rejected an approach defining *idem* on the basis of the legal classification of the act in national law noting that given that there is no

---

[5] Joined Cases C-187/01 and C-385/01, *Gözütok and Brügge* [2003] ECR I-1345.
[6] Case C-467/04, *Gasparini and Others*, [2006] ECR I-9199.
[7] Paragraph 37.
[8] See paragraphs 35–38. See also the Opinion of AG Ruiz-Jarabo Colomer, paragraphs 42–43.
[9] Paragraph 32.
[10] Paragraph 33. See also the Opinion of Advocate General Ruiz-Jarabo Colomer, delivered on 19 September 2002, paras 119–124, and para 55, where the AG states that 'the construction of a Europe without borders, with its corollary of the approximation of the various national legal systems, including the criminal systems, presupposes that the States involved will be guided by the same values'.
[11] See also the Court's similar reasoning in *Gasparini*, where the Court included time-barred prosecutions within the scope of Article 54 CISA notwithstanding the concerns by Advocate General Sharpston that this approach would disregard the fact that substantive justice has not been delivered in the present case.
[12] See the section on autonomous concepts below.
[13] Case C-436/04 *Van Esbroeck* [2006] ECR I-2333.

harmonisation of national laws, a criterion based on the legal classification or the legal interest protected at national level 'might create as many barriers to freedom of movement within Schengen as there are legal systems'.[14] On similar grounds, the Court has rejected the use of the concept of the legal interest (*Rechtsgut*) in national law as a determining factor for *idem*.[15] The Court has taken into account to a greater extent national considerations in cases on the determination of *bis* concerning the examination of the merits of the case in a trial.[16] The Court has required for the application of Article 54 that a decision was given after a determination had been made as to the merits of the case[17] and that a national decision definitely bars further prosecution at national level.[18] However, the decisive factor in the applicability of the *ne bis in idem* principle continues to be the law of the first Member State which has dealt with the case. In the case of *M*, the Court confirmed that the assessment of the 'final' nature of the criminal ruling at issue must be carried out on the basis of the law of the Member State in which that ruling was made.[19] This ruling re-affirms the priority of the requirement of legal certainty for the affected individual in Europe's area of criminal justice.

The relationship between mutual trust, the protection of fundamental rights and the respect of the national criminal enforcement choices of Member States in the development of a transnational *ne bis in idem* principle is being reconfigured further in the light of the gradual transformation of *ne bis in idem* from a principle to a fundamental right. Key in this context is the interaction of the transnational CISA *ne bis in idem* principle with international and supranational human rights norms which also apply to purely domestic cases. A first set of questions which has arisen in this context concerns the relationship between Article 54 CISA and *ne bis in idem* as enshrined in Article 4 of Protocol 7 of the ECHR. In a significant development, the Strasbourg Court has, in the case of *Zolothukin*, effectively aligned its interpretation of the scope of *ne bis in idem* in the Convention—and in particular of the element of *idem*—with that of the Court of Justice in relation to Article 54 CISA.[20] *Zolothukin* has reframed the Strasbourg Court's interpretation of *ne bis in idem* and has strikingly offered a coherent interpretation of ECHR domestic and EU transnational *ne bis in idem*. It has been influential and a key reference point for subsequent Strasbourg[21] and Luxembourg[22] case-law.

---

[14] ibid, paragraph 35.

[15] Case C-288/05, *Jürgen Kretzinger*, [2007] ECR I-6641, in particular paragraph 33.

[16] On the latter point see A Weyembergh and I Armada, 'The Principle of *ne bis in idem* in Europe's Area of Freedom, Security and Justice' in V Mitsilegas, M Bergström and T Konstantinides (eds), *Research Handbook on EU Criminal Law* (Cheltenham, Edward Elgar, forthcoming).

[17] Case C-469/03 *Miraglia*, EU:C:2005:156, paragraph 30.

[18] Case C-491/07, *Turanský* EU:C:2008:768, paragraph 36.

[19] Case C-398/12, *M*, judgment of 5 June 2014, paragraph 36.

[20] *Sergey Zolothukin v Russia*, Application no 14939/03 (ECtHR), paragraphs 78–84.

[21] See *Glantz v Finland*, Application no 37394/11 (ECtHR); *Nykänen v Finland*, Application no 11828/11 (ECtHR); *Rinas v Finland*, Application no 17039/13 (ECtHR); *Österlund v Finland*, Application no 53197/13 (ECtHR); *Kapetanios et al v Greece*, Application nos 3453/12, 42941/12 and 9028/13 (ECtHR).

[22] See case of *M*, n 19 above, paragraph 39.

The second set of questions which has arisen, especially post-Lisbon, concerns the relationship between Article 54 CISA and Article 50 of the Charter which enshrines *ne bis in idem* as a fundamental right in the EU constitutional order. Should the interpretation of *ne bis in idem* in Article 54 CISA and Article 50 of the Charter be aligned? And to what extent will the interpretation of Article 54 CISA in conformity with Article 50 of the Charter have an impact on the substance of *ne bis in idem* under both provisions? An exemplary test case to address these questions has arisen in the context of the interpretation of the third element of Article 54 (in addition to the elements of *bis* and *idem*), namely the determination of the content and limits of the enforcement condition required by Article 54. More than the other two elements of Article 54, the enforcement condition can test mutual trust between EU Member States. The relevant cases before the Court of Justice reveal lack of trust between national authorities and the questions referred to the Court by national courts imply that the latter doubt that legal systems in other Member States can deliver effective enforcement of criminal justice. The approach of the Court of Justice on this question has evolved over time to gradually narrow the protective scope of Article 54. From the highly protective approach adopted by the Court in *Bourquain*,[23] the Court moved on in *Kretzinger*[24] to insert a series of caveats to protection. The Court accepted that suspended custodial sentences constitute penalties within the meaning of Article 54 of the Schengen Convention, in so far as they penalise the unlawful conduct of a convicted person—with the penalty regarded as 'actually in the process of being enforced' as soon as the sentence has become enforceable and during the probation period.[25] However, the Court found that periods spent in police custody and/or remand pending trial must not be regarded automatically as the enforcement of a penalty for the purposes of Article 54.[26] Moreover, the Court rejected Mr Kretzinger's argument that the fact that it is legally possible under the Framework Decision on the European Arrest Warrant for the sentencing State to issue a Warrant in order to enforce a judgment which has become final and binding means that the enforcement condition must be regarded as satisfied.[27] The Court found that this factor cannot affect the interpretation of the notion of 'enforcement' under Article 54 of the Schengen Convention as the latter requires not only a conviction,

---

[23] Case C-297/07 *Bourquain*, where the Court found that *ne bis in idem* was applicable to criminal proceedings instituted in a Contracting State against an accused whose trial for the same acts as those for which he faces prosecution was finally disposed of in another Contracting State, even though, under the law of the State in which he was convicted, the sentence which was imposed on him could never, on account of specific features of procedure such as those referred to in the main proceedings, have been directly enforced (paragraph 54).

[24] *Kretzinger*, n 15 above.

[25] Paragraph 42.

[26] Paragraph 48 *et seq.*

[27] Paragraph 57.

but also the satisfaction of the enforcement condition.[28] The Court was thus not prepared to link *ne bis in idem* enforcement with the European Arrest Warrant, or rather with the *possibility* for a Member State to issue a European Arrest Warrant on a specific case. The Court seemed to recognise that this would pose an undue burden on domestic criminal justice systems, as well as an inroad to prosecutorial or judicial discretion: if Mr Kretzinger's argument were accepted, the decision not to issue a European Arrest Warrant would effectively shield defendants from prosecutions as it would in essence constitute an act equivalent to a decision triggering the *ne bis in idem* principle.[29]

The question of the extent of the limits that the enforcement condition can place on the protective scope of *ne bis in idem* under Article 54 CISA has arisen also after the entry into force of the Lisbon Treaty in another case brought forward to Luxembourg by a German Court, the case of *Spasic*.[30] This time, the Court of Justice also had to assess whether the limitation to the principle of *ne bis in idem* under Article 54 is compatible with Article 50 of the Charter, which does not make the application of *ne bis in idem* subject to the enforcement condition. The Court found that the additional condition laid down in Article 54 CISA constitutes a limitation of the *ne bis in idem* principle that is compatible with Article 50 of the Charter.[31] The Court accepted that argument put forward by the German and French governments that the condition laid down in Article 54 CISA does not call into question the *ne bis in idem* principle as such but is intended, inter alia, to avoid a situation in which a person definitively convicted and sentenced in one Contracting State can no longer be prosecuted for the same acts in another Contracting State and therefore ultimately remains unpunished if the first State did not execute the sentence imposed.[32] Moreover, the Court went on to find that the limitation of *ne bis in idem* was proportionate as it is intended to prevent, in the area of freedom, security and justice, the impunity of persons definitively convicted and sentenced in an EU Member State. According to the Court, by allowing, in cases of non-execution of the sentence imposed, the authorities of one Contracting State to prosecute a person definitively convicted and sentenced by another Contracting State on the basis of the same acts, the risk that the person concerned would enjoy impunity by virtue of his leaving the territory of the State in which he was sentenced is avoided.[33] The Court was not convinced by the Commission's argument that EU secondary law instruments providing for consultations between national authorities (including the Framework Decision on conflicts of jurisdiction)

---

[28] Paragraphs 59 and 63.
[29] V Mitsilegas, *EU Criminal Law* (Oxford, Hart Publishing, 2009), chapter 3.
[30] Case C-129/14 PPU *Spasic*, judgment of 27 May 2014.
[31] Paragraph 54.
[32] Paragraph 58 and reference to *Kretzinger*, n 15 above, paragraph 51.
[33] Paragraphs 63 and 64 respectively.

addressed this objective. The Court noted that these instruments do not lay down an execution condition similar to that of Article 54 CISA and, accordingly, are not capable of fully achieving the objective pursued.[34] According to the Court, the options made available to that Member State by those Framework decisions cannot ensure that, in the area of freedom, security and justice, persons definitively convicted and sentenced in the European Union will not enjoy impunity if the State which imposed the first sentence does not execute the penalties imposed.[35] The Court's approach in *Spasic* is striking. It is a marked departure from the View of Advocate General Jääskinen, who found that the generalised application of the execution condition in Article 54 CISA does not satisfy the proportionality criterion and cannot be regarded as a justified interference with the right not to be tried or punished twice in criminal proceedings within the meaning of Article 52 of the Charter.[36] The ruling is also at odds with the Court's case-law on *bis* and *idem*, but also with national trends towards extending the protective scope of Article 54 in the light of Article 50 of the Charter,[37] with the earlier emphasis on the presumption of mutual trust being transformed in *Spasic* to an institutionalisation of mutual distrust. The Court seems to have little time for the deliberative and consultative mechanisms introduced by EU law and aiming to facilitate inter-state cooperation in cases of conflicts of jurisdiction. The Court finds these mechanisms to be weak, but this weakness is explained by Member States' reluctance to harmonise standards further in the field. This lack of harmonisation is allowed here to ferment distrust and allow multiple interventions by national enforcement authorities for the same acts. This approach has profound consequences for the protective function of *ne bis in idem*. In *Spasic*, the Court effectively introduces a security rationale within a fundamental right. However, not only does this rationale (and the emphasis on the need to avoid impunity) not fall within the scope of *ne bis in idem*, but the Court's interpretation also opens the door towards divergent interpretations and levels of protection between domestic *ne bis in idem* cases involving the implementation of EU law (interpreted in conformity with Article 50 of the Charter) and transnational *ne bis in idem* cases under Article 54 CISA.[38] The Court's approach in *Spasic* also does very little for the achievement of legal certainty in Europe's area of criminal justice and raises the spectre of serious impediments to the enjoyment of free movement. It also poses a significant challenge to the essence of the *ne bis in idem* right as enshrined in Article 50 of the Charter.[39]

[34] Paragraph 68.
[35] Paragraph 69.
[36] View delivered on 2 May 2014, paragraphs 91–103.
[37] The Greek Supreme Court has found that Member States' reservations under Article 55 CISA have ceased to exist since Article 50 of the Charter does not provide for optional exceptions to the *ne bis in idem* principle similar to those enshrined in Article 55 CISA—Areios Pagos, Case 1/2011.
[38] See further M Wasmeier, 'Ne bis in idem and the Enforcement Condition: Balancing Freedom, Security and Justice?' (2014) 4 *New Journal of European Criminal Law*.
[39] See also the pending at the time of writing case of *Kossowski* (Case C-486/14), where the Court is called upon to rule on the compatibility of the derogations enshrined in Article 55(1)(a) of CISA with Article 50 of the Charter.

III. Horizontal Co-ordination via the Establishment of Common Standards—The Case of Decisions on Choice of Forum and Conflicts of Jurisdiction

The current fluidity with regard to the determination of which jurisdiction should be able to prosecute in the European Union and the issues of delivery of justice which have arisen from the Court's case-law on *ne bis in idem* have led some commentators to advocate the adoption of horizontal EU rules governing choice of forum and conflicts of jurisdiction matters.[40] There is currently no centralised binding mechanism of jurisdiction allocation in criminal matters in the European Union. The Decision establishing Eurojust[41] states that the organisation—acting through its national members or as a College—may ask the competent authorities of Member States to co-ordinate.[42] Eurojust may also ask these authorities 'to accept that one of them may be in a better position to undertake an investigation or to prosecute specific acts'.[43] Eurojust's non-binding powers in this context have been somewhat strengthened by its 2009 amending Decision[44] whereby a new provision has been inserted stating that where national members are not in agreement on how to resolve conflicts of jurisdiction cases with regard to the undertaking of investigations or prosecutions, the College will issue 'a written non-binding opinion on how the case should be solved'.[45] At present however there are no clear rules regulating decisions on choice of forum and conflicts of jurisdiction at EU level. Eurojust adopted in 2003, a series of (non-binding) 'Guidelines for deciding "which jurisdiction should prosecute?"'.[46] The Guidelines call for a 'preliminary presumption' that a prosecution should take place in the jurisdiction where the majority of criminality occurred or where the majority of the loss was sustained— in reaching the decision, prosecutors 'should balance carefully and fairly all the factors both for and against commencing a prosecution in each jurisdiction where it is possible to do so'.[47] The Guidelines contain a series of criteria to be taken into account including the location of the accused, capacity to extradite or surrender, centralising prosecutions of many suspects in one jurisdiction, and the attendance

---

[40] See M Luchtman, 'Choice of Forum and the Prosecution of Cross-Border Crime in the European Union—What Role for the Legality Principle?' in M Luchtman (ed), *Choice of Forum in Cooperation Against EU Financial Crime. Freedom, Security and Justice and the Protection of Specific EU Interests* (The Hague, Eleven International Publishing, 2013) 3–60.

[41] Council Decision of 28 February 2002 setting up Eurojust with a view to reinforcing the fight against crime, [2002] OJ L63, 6.3.2002, p 1.

[42] [2002] OJ L63, 6 March 2002, p 1. Articles 6(a)(iii) and 7(a)(iii) respectively.

[43] Article 7(a)(ii).

[44] Decision 2009/426/JHA on the strengthening of Eurojust and amending Decision 2002/187/JHA setting up Eurojust with a view to reinforcing the fight against serious crime [2009] OJ L138, 4.6.2009, p 14.

[45] New Article 7(2).

[46] Found in the Annex to Eurojust Annual Report 2003, pp 60 *et seq.*

[47] ibid, p 62.

and protection of witnesses and victims. According to the Guidelines, the relative sentencing powers of the courts must not be a 'primary' factor in deciding where to prosecute, but availability and use of evidence is a relevant factor. The absence of legally binding and detailed rules on choice of forum and conflicts of jurisdiction leave much to be desired from the perspective of upholding the rule of law, legal certainty and the rights of the individuals affected by such decisions—with the danger of prosecutorial 'forum shopping' being clear.[48] The situation has not been remedied by the adoption in 2009 of a Framework Decision on prevention and settlement of conflicts of jurisdiction,[49] which merely establishes channels of information exchange and consultation between national authorities.[50] The Framework Decision provides a role for Eurojust where it has not been possible to reach consensus,[51] but Member States do not appear to have made wide use of this provision.[52]

The entry into force of the Treaty of Lisbon has provided new *impetus* towards the adoption of EU rules on conflicts of jurisdiction. Article 82(1)(b) TFEU calls upon the Union legislators to adopt measures to prevent and settle conflicts of jurisdiction between Member States, while Article 85(1)(c) TFEU states that the tasks of Eurojust following the adoption of post-Lisbon secondary law may include the resolution of such conflicts. However, little progress has been made thus far on the ground. At the time of writing, no use of Article 82(1)(b) has been made, while the current proposals on a new legal framework on Eurojust do not contain any major changes in relation to the latter's role in the resolution of conflicts of jurisdiction.[53] These developments reflect the reluctance of Member States to introduce EU-level binding rules which would limit their capacity to prosecute and their real and perceived power to deliver justice in criminal matters for their citizens. Indeed, binding EU powers in the field would limit considerably the powers of Member States in the field: in cases of positive conflicts of jurisdiction, a binding EU decision excluding one Member State from prosecuting would raise serious questions on its capacity to deliver justice domestically (as seen above, similar questions have been raised in the context of *ne bis in idem* cases); in cases of negative conflicts of jurisdiction, a binding EU decision would have the effect of obliging a Member State to prosecute a case which it would not normally have

---

[48] V Mitsilegas, 'The Transformation of Criminal Law in the Area of Freedom, Security and Justice' 26 *Yearbook of European Law 2007* 1–32.

[49] Council Framework Decision 2009/948/JHA of 30 November 2009 on prevention and settlement of conflicts of exercise of jurisdiction in criminal proceedings, [2009] OJ L328, 15.12.2009, p 42.

[50] Articles 5–9 and 10–13 respectively.

[51] Article 12(2) of the Framework Decision.

[52] European Commission, Report from the Commission to the European Parliament and the Council on the implementation by the Member States of Framework Decision 2009/948/JHA of 30 November 2009 on prevention and settlement of conflicts of exercise of jurisdiction in criminal proceedings COM(2013) 313 final, 2.6.2014, pp 4–5.

[53] See section IV below.

prosecuted, something which would raise a number of legitimacy and efficiency concerns (similar concerns have been raised in the context of the debate on the application of proportionality in the operation of the European Arrest Warrant).[54] In all these cases, concerns related to the delivery of justice are exacerbated in the absence of detailed and clear remedies for affected individuals decisions affecting conflicts of jurisdiction. These concerns arise in particular in the context of the current negotiations on a Regulation establishing a European Public Prosecutor's Office, which includes provisions on choice of forum in relation to vertical investigations[55] and prosecutions.[56] While the draft Regulation puts forward a series of hierarchical criteria to determine the forum of prosecution (the place where the suspect or accused person has his/her habitual residence; the nationality of the suspect or the accused person; and the place where the main financial damage has occurred), it does not envisage (at least in the draft put forward by the European Commission) any form of judicial control in relation to the decision on where to investigate or to prosecute.[57]

To exclude the judicial review of decisions by the European Public Prosecutor on choice of forum, especially by EU courts, would amount to negating an effective remedy against acts which may have significant consequences for the protection of fundamental rights, including respect of the principles of legality

---

[54] See Chapter 5 of this volume.

[55] Article 21(3) of the latest draft states that a case must in principle be handled by a European Delegated prosecutor from the Member State where the focus of the criminal activity is or, if several connected offences within the competences of the Office have been committed, the Member State where the bulk of the offences has been committed. A Permanent Chamber may only instruct a European Delegated prosecutor of a different Member State to initiate an investigation where that Member State has jurisdiction for the case, taking into account the following criteria, in order of priority:

a. The place where the suspect or accused person has his/her habitual residence;
b. The nationality of the suspect or the accused person;
c. The place where the main financial damage has occurred.

[56] Article 27(3) of the latest draft states that the competent Permanent Chamber will determine, in close consultation with the European Delegated Prosecutor submitting the case, the Member State in which the prosecution must be brought. The Permanent Chamber must in principle bring the prosecution in the Member State of the European Delegated Prosecutor handling the case. The Chamber may determine another Member State, which has jurisdiction in the case, if there are sufficiently justified grounds related to the criteria for determining the EDP handling the case in Article 21(3).

[57] A number of commentators have criticised the absence of a remedy against EPPO choice of forum decisions: see M Wasmeier, 'The Choice of Forum by the European Public Prosecutor' in LH Erkelens, AWH Meij and M Pawlik (eds), *The European Public Prosecutor's Office. An Extended Arm or a Two-Headed Dragon?* (The Hague, Asser Press/Springer, 2015) 139–64; J Tricot, 'Observations Critiques sur la Proposition de Règlement portant Création du Parquet Européen' in G Giudicelli-Delage, S Manacorda and J Tricot (eds), *Le Contrôle Judiciaire du Parquet Européen. Nécessité, Modèles, Enjeux*, Collection de l'UMR de Droit Comparé de Paris (Université Paris 1) (Société de Législation Comparée, vol 37, 2015) 155–74; and S Manacorda, 'La Localisation de la Garantie Jurisdictionnelle du Parquet Européen' in G Giudicelli-Delage, S Manacorda and J Tricot (eds), *Le Contrôle Judiciaire du Parquet Européen. Nécessité, Modèles, Enjeux*, Collection de l'UMR de Droit Comparé de Paris (Université Paris 1) (Société de Législation Comparée, vol 37, 2015) 255–74.

(including foreseeability)[58] and equality before the law.[59] Lack of legal certainty with regard to choice of forum decisions at national level was found to be in violation of Article 7 ECHR by the European Court of Human Rights. In the case of *Camilleri v Malta*,[60] the Court found that national law providing for two different possible punishments depending on the procedure chosen by the Attorney General failed to satisfy the foreseeability requirement and provide effective safeguards against arbitrary punishment as provided in Article 7. The Court noted in this context that:

> It would therefore appear that the applicant would not have been able to know the punishment applicable to him even if he had obtained legal advice on the matter, as the decision was solely dependent on the prosecutor's discretion to determine the trial court.

> While it may be true that the Attorney General gave weight to a number of criteria before taking his decision, it is also true that any such criteria were not specified in any legislative text or made the subject of judicial clarification over the years. The law did not provide for any guidance on what would amount to a more serious offences or a less serious one…An insoluble problem was posed by fixing different minimum penalties … The decision was inevitably subjective and left room for arbitrariness, particularly given the lack of procedural safeguards.[61]

It is clear that this reasoning is likely to apply to transnational choice of forum decisions, including decisions by the European Public Prosecutor's Office, something which necessitates not only a clear procedure involving the defendant leading to the decision on the choice of forum but also effective remedies at European Union level against choice and transfer of forum decisions by the EPPO.[62]

IV. Towards Vertical Co-ordination: The Evolution and Powers of Eurojust

The establishment of Eurojust in 2002 is a clear example of the tension between voices demanding greater effectiveness of judicial cooperation and prosecution at

---

[58] On the principle of legality as foreseeability in this context see F Zimmermann, 'Choice of Forum and Choice of Law under the Future Regulation on the Establishment of a European Public Prosecutor's Office' in P Asp (ed), *The European Public Prosecutor's Office—Legal and Criminal Policy Perspectives* (Stifelsen Skrifter utgivna av Juridiska fakulteten vid Stockholms universitet, 2015) 156–77; and M Panzavolta, 'Choice of Forum and the Lawful Judge Concept' in M Luchtman (ed), *Choice of Forum in Cooperation Against EU Financial Crime. Freedom, Security and Justice and the Protection of Specific EU Interests* (The Hague, Eleven International Publishing, 2013) 143–66.

[59] See in this context also Fundamental Rights Agency, *Opinion of the European Union Agency for Fundamental Rights on a proposal to establish a European Public Prosecutor's Office*, FRA Opinion 1/2014, Vienna, 4 February 2014.

[60] *Camilleri v Malta* Application no 42931/10, judgment of 22.1.2013.

[61] ibid, paragraphs 42–43.

[62] V Mitsilegas, 'The European Public Prosecutor before the Court of Justice. The Challenge of Effective Judicial Protection' in G Giudicelli-Delage, S Manacorda and J Tricot (eds), *Le Contrôle*

EU level and concerns regarding the potentially adverse effect of Europeanisation in this context on state sovereignty in criminal matters and national legal diversity. The outcome of this tension has been the adoption of the Decision establishing Eurojust in 2002[63]—to a great extent in response to the integrationist proposals to establish a European Public Prosecutor in the late '90s—which reflected a political compromise: on the one hand, a specific EU body with powers in the field of judicial cooperation, investigation and prosecution in criminal matters would be established; on the other, this body would have a largely intergovernmental structure (in the form of a College) and limited powers in relation to what it could ask national authorities to do (Eurojust acting as a College could merely ask the competent authorities of Member States to undertake an investigation or prosecution of specific acts[64]—thus no binding powers were granted to Eurojust to oblige national authorities to initiate investigations or prosecutions).[65] The balance of powers between Eurojust and national authorities has not changed fundamentally after the amendment of the Eurojust Decision in 2009.[66] Eurojust has thus developed mainly as a co-ordination agency aiming to bring together national authorities in order to facilitate the resolution of cross-border cases, as well as liaising with other EU agencies in the field of criminal justice.[67] The entry into force of the Treaty of Lisbon has created the possibility of a reconfiguration of the role of Eurojust vis-à-vis national authorities. In addition to the legal basis on Eurojust's role in the resolution of conflicts of jurisdiction mentioned above, the Treaty calls for the adoption of secondary legislation determining Eurojust's structure, operation, field of action and tasks which may include *the initiation of criminal investigations*, as well as proposing the initiation of prosecutions conducted by competent national authorities.[68] Granting Eurojust binding powers to initiate criminal investigations—as well as granting express powers in resolving conflicts of jurisdiction—would amount to a significant increase of Eurojust's powers and a qualitative change in its role.[69] Much would depend in this context from

---

Judiciaire du Parquet Européen. Nécessité, Modèles, Enjeux, Collection de l'UMR de Droit Comparé de Paris (Université Paris 1) (Société de Législation Comparée, vol 37, 2015) 67–87.

[63] Council Decision of 28 February 2002 setting up Eurojust with a view to reinforcing the fight against crime, [2002] OJ L63, 6.3.2002, p 1.

[64] Article 7(a) of the 2002 Eurojust Decision.

[65] For further background and details on the establishment and powers of Eurojust, see V Mitsilegas, *EU Criminal Law* (Oxford, Hart Publishing, 2009) chapter 4.

[66] Decision 2009/426/JHA on the strengthening of Eurojust and amending Decision 2002/187/JHA setting up Eurojust with a view to reinforcing the fight against serious crime [2009] OJ L138, 4.6.2009, p 14.

[67] See M Labayle and HG Nilsson, 'The Role and Organisation of Eurojust: Added Value for Judicial Cooperation in Criminal Matters' in J Monar (ed), *The Institutional Dimension of the European Union's Area of Freedom, Security and Justice* (College of Europe Studies, Peter Lang, 2010) 195–216.

[68] Article 85(1)(a) TFEU.

[69] For an analysis of the potential of Article 85 for the future role of Eurojust, see the contribution of Eurojust President Michèle Coninsx, 'Eurojust' in V Mitsilegas, M Bergström and T Konstadinides (eds), *Research Handbook on EU Criminal Law* (Cheltenham, Edward Elgar, forthcoming).

negotiations on the establishment of the European Public Prosecutor's Office, which according to the Lisbon Treaty may be established 'from Eurojust'.[70]

A. The Commission's Proposal for a Eurojust Regulation

Developments thus far have shown that the Commission has prioritised and thrown its weight on the establishment of the European Public Prosecutor's Office, at the expense of a radical reform or increase of the powers of Eurojust. On 17 July 2013—and shortly after the celebration of Eurojust's tenth birthday—the Commission released a new proposal for a Regulation on Eurojust.[71] The proposal was presented as part of a package also including the EPPO proposal[72] and a Communication on reinforcing the role of OLAF.[73] Its overall objective is to modernise the legal framework of the Agency and streamline its functioning and structure in line with the Lisbon Treaty and the 2012 Common Approach on EU decentralised Agencies,[74] insofar as the nature of Eurojust allows it.[75] The draft Regulation is more oriented towards the restructuring of the Agency so as to alleviate the administrative burden from national members, who can then focus on their operational tasks. In this context, it proposes a new governance structure, according to which the College will meet in two distinct formations—one for operational issues and one for administrative issues[76]—and an Executive Board will be set up to assist the College and the Administrative Director.[77] Furthermore, the Commission will be represented in the College when discussing managerial matters[78] and in the Executive Board.[79] The next change involves the status and powers of national members, which have already been enhanced by the 2009 Eurojust Decision.[80] The draft Regulation explicitly sets out the operational powers that all national members must have, powers which have been further aligned in order to improve Eurojust's effectiveness.[81] Moreover, the proposal

---

[70] Article 86(1) TFEU.

[71] European Commission, Proposal for a Regulation of the European Parliament and of the Council on the European Agency for Criminal Justice Cooperation (Eurojust), COM(2013) 535 final, 17.7.2013 (proposal for Eurojust).

[72] European Commission, Proposal for a Regulation of the European Parliament and of the Council on the establishment of the European Public Prosecutor's Office, COM(2013) 534 final, 17.7.2013.

[73] European Commission, Communication from the Commission to the European Parliament, the Council, the European Economic and Social Committee and the Committee of the Regions 'Improving OLAF's governance and reinforcing procedural safeguards in investigations: A step-by-step approach to accompany the establishment of the European Public Prosecutor's Office', COM(2013) 533 final, 17.7.2013.

[74] For the Common Approach see Council of the European Union, Document 11450/12, 18.6.2012.

[75] Proposal for Eurojust, Explanatory Memorandum, 3.

[76] Articles 4, 5 and 14.

[77] Article 16.

[78] Articles 10(1)(b).

[79] Article 16(4).

[80] Se Articles 9a–9e of the 2009 Decision.

[81] Article 8.

provides for increased involvement of the European Parliament and the national parliaments in the evaluation of Eurojust's activities. In particular, its President will appear before the European Parliament and both the European and the national Parliaments will receive the Agency's annual reports and other relevant documentation.[82] However, the European Parliament will not be involved in the evaluation of operational aspects. Moreover, the rules on information exchange and data protection have been strengthened; while Regulation 45/2001[83] will become fully applicable, special rules on operational personal data have been inserted to reflect the specificity of Eurojust's activities.[84] In addition, the supervision of personal data processing will no longer be entrusted to the Joint Supervisory Authority, but to the European Data Protection Supervisor, as is the case with other EU Agencies. Finally, as regards the relations of Eurojust with other partners, the proposal includes rules concerning the links with Europol, the European Judicial Network and the future EPPO.[85] The Agency will no longer be able to negotiate international agreements with third countries or international organisations. Nevertheless, its representatives will still be involved in the negotiating procedures of future international agreements, all existing agreements will remain valid and the Agency will still be able to conclude working arrangements in order to implement adequacy decisions or international agreements concluded between the EU and third states.[86]

The extent to which the reforms on the tasks of Eurojust correspond to the potential of Article 85 TFEU is fairly limited. As it has been pointed out, while the proposal provides for some important changes, the text 'does not constitute a revolution'[87] and that it 'does not fully exploit the possibilities offered'.[88] In particular, the Commission chose to retain the status quo and not address the clauses of Article 85(1) that would allow for binding decisions from Eurojust

---

[82] Article 55.

[83] Regulation (EC) No 45/2001 of the European Parliament and of the Council of 18 December 2000 on the protection of individuals with regard to the processing of personal data by the Community institutions and bodies and on the free movement of such data, [2001] OJ L8/1, 12.1.2001.

[84] See Article 60, which excludes case-related documents from the EU regime.

[85] Articles 38–42. As regards the links between Eurojust and the European Judicial Network, no changes have been introduced despite the potential offered by Article 85(1)(c) TFEU. See also Council of the European Union, Document 11233/14, 27.6.14. The relationship with the future EPPO is regarded as 'special'; the EPPO will constitute a distinct entity next to Eurojust and the Agencies will share administrative, operational and management resources. However, the proposal does not contain much on their functional relationship, thus leaving numerous issues open. In addition, according to the Annex attached to the proposal, Eurojust will not have competence in respect of PIF crimes, as these will fall within the mandate of the EPPO. See Council of the European Union, Documents 17188/1/13, 4.12.2013, 34–42 and 5730/2015, 2.2.2015.

[86] Article 45.

[87] Council of the European Union, Document 17188/1/13, 4.12.13, p 6 (this quote is taken from the contribution of Lotte Knusden, then Director in DG Justice, European Commission, as reported in the Council Document).

[88] ibid, p 8 (this quote is taken from the contribution of Michelle Coninsx, President of Eurojust, as reported in the same Council Document).

vis-à-vis national authorities. In fact, neither the Explanatory Memorandum attached to the proposal, nor the Preamble include any reasons for this political choice.[89] In order to explain this reluctance to grant Eurojust binding powers, Weyembergh refers to the 'it is not the right moment' argument, according to which it is too early to entrust binding decision-making functions to Eurojust.[90] Despite the missed opportunity to enhance Eurojust's efficiency, its realm of action is extended; Article 2(1) stipulates that it

> shall support and strengthen coordination and cooperation between national investigating and prosecuting authorities in relation to serious crime affecting two or more Member States, or *requiring a prosecution on common bases*, on the basis of operations conducted and information supplied by the Member States' authorities and by Europol (emphasis added).[91]

The wording of the Article, which comes directly from Article 85(1) TFEU, suggests that, unlike the current Decision, Eurojust's action will not be limited to cases already opened (Article 3 of the current Eurojust Decision reads 'in the context of investigations and prosecutions').[92] However, the proposal does not adequately clarify what type of cases are included within the new mandate, in other words what constitutes a case of serious crime requiring a prosecution on common bases.[93] Recital 9 of the proposal provides an explanation, according to which '[s]uch cases should include investigations and prosecutions affecting only one Member State and a third State, as well as cases affecting only one Member State and the Union'. Nevertheless, this definition is not exhaustive and does not enhance Eurojust's competence, since it refers to situations that the Agency already covers.[94] Two further improvements can be traced in Article 2; by referring to any information 'collected by Eurojust itself', it seems that the strategic work of the Agency will be improved and there is an explicit reference to the possibility for Eurojust to act 'on its own initiative'. This reference implies that its proactive role is further enhanced, however, no further interpretation is provided.

---

[89] Anne Weyembergh, 'An Overall Analysis of the Proposal for a Regulation on Eurojust' (2013) 4 *The European Criminal Law Associations' Forum* 130. See also Council of the European Union, Document 17188/1/13, 4.12.2013, p 19.

[90] Weyembergh, ibid, 181.

[91] Article 2(1).

[92] Council of the European Union, Document 17188/1/13, 4.12.2013, p 22.

[93] A number of explanations have been put forward in this regard. In general, it could cover cases where common and coordinated action is required to address EU interests or to implement EU priorities. Such cases could include (a) cases which affect only one Member State but have an impact in other cases or deserve to be examined at EU level in order to involve and possibly coordinate other jurisdictions (eg a case of human smuggling where the prosecutor suspects that the existence of a criminal network in other Member States and the ask Eurojust's support); and (b) cases which are not cross-border but need a broader common action (eg on the basis of Europol's analysis) in order to achieve a result (eg investigations and prosecutions in several Member States on counterfeiting of medicines from China. Such cases have no obvious connection, but require common action in order to tackle the criminal group). See Council of the European Union, Document 17188/1/13, 4.12.2013, p 22.

[94] Weyembergh (n 89 above) 130.

In relation to the powers of Eurojust, Article 4(1) of the proposal includes an improvement by referring to a duty 'to inform the competent authorities' of investigations and prosecutions. The current wording of the Eurojust Decision requires Eurojust to 'ensure that the competent authorities inform each other'.[95] However, the rules on possible conflicts of jurisdiction have remained almost identical to Article 7 of the current Decision. The latter provides that in cases when two or more Member States cannot agree as to which will undertake an investigation or a prosecution, then Eurojust will be asked to issue a written non-binding opinion on the case unless the competent national authorities can reach mutual agreement. The Commission's draft has dropped the words 'non binding' and merely refers to a 'written opinion', whose binding status vis-à-vis receiving national authorities is unclear. More radical reforms are reserved for the powers of national members. Article 8 of the proposal further approximates the powers of national members and should thus be seen as a continuation of the developments launched by the 2009 Decision. In fact, in the light of the laconic wording of Article 2 compared to Article 8 of the proposal, Vervaele has pointed out that the powers of national members are much stronger than the tasks of Eurojust.[96] The clarification of the powers of national members may contribute towards enhancing the effectiveness of Eurojust, since the setting up of the Agency, it has been argued that the discrepancies between national members have considerably impeded its work.[97] More recently, the final report of the Sixth Round of Mutual Evaluations of Eurojust revealed that the discrepancies among Member States remain and some national members are not even provided with the ordinary powers set out in Article 9b.[98] In this context, there is no longer reference to the national members acting in their capacity as competent national authorities in accordance with national law; national members will always act as Eurojust.

Furthermore, Article 8 of the Commission proposal retains the division of powers (ordinary powers, powers exercised in agreement with the national competent authority and powers exercised in urgent cases), but new powers have been added or have moved category. In particular, in relation to the ordinary powers, national members shall have the power to 'facilitate and otherwise support the issuing and execution of any mutual legal assistance or mutual recognition request'. Currently, these powers can only be exercised in agreement with the competent national authority.[99] Admittedly, the reference to the 'facilitation and otherwise

---

[95] Article 7(b).

[96] Council of the European Union, Document 17188/1/13, 4.12.2013, p 19, 21.

[97] N Thwaites, 'Eurojust autre brique dans l'édifice de la coopération judiciaire en matière pénale ou solide mortier?' (2003) *Revue de science criminelle et de droit pénal comparé* 45, 51–52; A Suominen, 'The Past, Present and the Future of Eurojust' (2008) 15 *Maastricht Journal of European and Comparative Law* 217, 226.

[98] Council of the European Union, Document 14536/2/2014, 2.12.2014, p 28.

[99] Article 9c(1)(a) and (b) of the Eurojust Decision.

support' is quite vague. However, clarification is provided in Recital 11, which states that national members should be granted those powers that allow Eurojust to appropriately achieve its mission, including the 'issuing and executing mutual assistance and recognition requests'. This means that the proposal allows the issuance and execution of requests by national members without the involvement of a national competent authority.[100] Furthermore, national members will be able to contact directly and exchange information with both national or international authorities—in accordance with the commitments of their Member State—as well as participate in joint investigation teams (JIT's). Participation in joint investigation teams already takes place under the current regime, however Article 9f of the Eurojust Decision states that Member States may make the participation of the national member subject to the agreement of the competent national authority. National members will be able to issue, complete and execute requests for and decisions on judicial cooperation, order investigative measures and authorise and coordinate controlled deliveries in the Member State in accordance with national legislation.[101] The proposal retains the powers regarding investigative measures[102] and controlled deliveries and removes the references about the issuance and execution of requests, as these were included among the ordinary powers of national members. New powers have been added in urgent cases, namely the power to order investigative measures.[103] On the other hand, the proposal removes the possibility for Member States to grant their national members powers that go beyond those already prescribed, which currently is possible.[104] This issue has raised concerns because it could result in a reduction of powers of certain national members.[105] Finally, the national safeguard clause (Article 9e of the current Decision) is also removed.[106]

---

[100] It has been pointed out that in practice these powers would be difficult to use. First of all, the execution of a request would require an in-depth knowledge of the file. While in some Member States this power can be exercised by the national member, this cannot take place as a general rule, for example in relation to requests concerning EAWs that require formal acts of the judiciary. This would also not be in line with Article 85(2) TFEU. See Council of the European Union, Document 17188/1/13, 4.12.13, p 25.

[101] Article 8(2).

[102] In comparison with the wording of Article 9c(1)(c) of the Eurojust Decision, the meaning of the 'investigative measures' is unclear and may create conformity issues with national legal traditions and constitutions. See Council of the European Union, Document 17188/1/13, 4.12.2013, p 26.

[103] Article 8(2) and (3).

[104] Article 9A(2) of the Eurojust Decision states that each Member State each Member State shall grant its national member at least the powers described in Article 9b and, subject to Article 9e, the powers described in Articles 9c and 9d, which would be available to him as a judge, prosecutor or police officer, whichever is applicable, at national level.

[105] See for example Council of the European Union, Document 18172/13, 23.12. 2013, p 5.

[106] The national safeguard clause allows the powers exercised in agreement with a competent national authority or the powers exercised in urgent cases not to be granted, in cases in which granting any such powers to the national member is contrary to constitutional rules or fundamental aspects of the criminal justice system. The abolition of the national safeguard clause may pose difficulties in some Member States regarding the balance of powers between judges, prosecutors and the police. See Council of the European Union, Document 17188/1/13, 4.12.2013, p 9.

B. The Council General Approach

Negotiations have since taken place and resulted thus far in the adoption by the Council, in March 2015, of a General Approach.[107] The provisions regarding the relationship with the future EPPO have been excluded. Overall, the Council endorsed an alternative model of governance for Eurojust, which is designed to allow the College to focus primarily on its operational tasks by designating the preparations of all managerial matters to the new Executive Board,[108] rectified several points of concern[109] and made interventions in numerous respects. In relation to the tasks of Eurojust (Article 2 of the proposal), the General Approach does not provide for additions to the proposal. During the negotiations within the Council, the potential offered by Article 85(1) TFEU was discussed. It was pointed out that the Article could be further explored (and exploited), for example, with regard to an enhanced role of Eurojust in respect of the initiation of criminal investigations or the resolution of conflicts of jurisdictions.[110] The College of Eurojust also drew the attention to Article 85(1) TFEU—although focusing on the coordination of investigations and prosecutions- and suggested the replacement of the phrase 'support coordination' (Article 2 of the proposal) with the less restrictive 'shall coordinate the competent national authorities'.[111] Eventually, the calls for binding decisions from Eurojust did not materialise, thus Article 2 of the proposal setting out its tasks has remained basically unchanged.[112] The only changes concerning the tasks of Eurojust are two terminological clarifications. First, the General Approach provides an explanation of what type of cases fall within the category 'serious crimes requiring prosecution on common bases'. The revised Recital 9a states that

> [p]rosecution on a common bases refers to cases of prosecutions and investigations which may affect only one Member State and a third country where an agreement has been concluded or where there may be a specific need for Eurojust's involvement. It may also refer to cases which affect one Member State and the Union.[113]

---

[107] Council of the European Union, Document 6643/15, 27.2.2015.

[108] Early in the negotiations, the proposed model was met with serious reservations as to whether it would actually reduce the administrative workload of national members. This is because national members will continue to be entrusted with both management and operational tasks and for those national members that will participate in the Executive Board their role will be triple. The necessity of setting up an Executive Board was equally doubted, as well as the new role of the Commission. For the discussions on the revised model see Council of the European Union, Documents 8839/14, 16.4.2014; 9486/14, 19.5.2014.

[109] It restored the provision allowing for an extension of the Agency's competence to cases not included in the Annex. See Council of the European Union, Document 6643/15, 27.2.2015, p 22.

[110] Council of the European Union, Document 8617/14, 8.4.2014, p 5.

[111] Council of the European Union, Document 8488/14, 4.4.2014, pp 10–11.

[112] Council of the European Union, Document 6643/14, 27.2.2015, p 22.

[113] ibid, p 7. In this regard, relevant is the new Recital 10A according to which Eurojust may assist in investigations involving only that Member State but which have repercussions at Union level at the request of a Member State's competent authority or the Commission, This also covers cases which involve a significant number of Member States and could potentially require a coordinated European response. ibid, p 8.

Secondly, it is clarified what type of actions the Agency may perform 'on its own initiative'. According to the revised Recital 10, the Agency 'may take a more pro-active role in co-ordinating cases such as supporting the national authorities in their investigations and prosecutions'. In the Council's view, such functions include involving Member States who may not have initially been included in a particular case or discovering links on the basis of information retrieved from Europol, OLAF, EPPO or national authorities. In addition, Eurojust may produce guidelines, policy documents and casework-related analyses as part of its strategic work.[114]

Few changes have also been included regarding the powers of Eurojust. In essence, the content of Articles 7(2) and 8 of the current Decision is restored; the opinion issued by Eurojust in cases of conflicts of jurisdiction is explicitly characterised as non-binding.[115] Furthermore, the Council requires national authorities to respond without undue delay to Eurojust's requests and opinions and to inform the Agency in cases when Member States decide not to comply with a request or not follow a written opinion, including the reasons for such a decision. Member States are given the flexibility not to provide reasons in order to jeopardise essential national security interests or the safety of individuals.[116] As for the powers exercised by national members, the Council has significantly watered down the reforms envisaged in Article 8 of the proposal. The General Approach removes the participation of national members in joint investigation teams from their ordinary powers and adds it to those powers that can be exercised in agreement with the national competent authority or in urgent cases. This is not only a step backwards from the Commission proposal, but also a step backwards in comparison with the 2009 Decision, which left the requirement [or not] to ask for the agreement of the competent national authority at the discretion of Member States when implementing the Eurojust Decision. The issuance and execution of requests is also moved from the ordinary powers of national members. It thus seems that the uncertainty about whether such power could be effectively exercised in practice by national members seems to have played a significant role in reverting this power to sit among those that can only be exercised in agreement with the competent national authority.[117] Furthermore, the provision allowing Member States to grant additional powers to their national members[118] and the national safeguard clause[119] have been restored so as to allow for flexibility given the specificities of each national system. It is thus clear that the Council has not made use of the potential offered by Article 85 of the TFEU to enhance the role of Eurojust in the field of European investigation and prosecution. The powers of Eurojust remain

---

[114] ibid, 8.
[115] ibid, 24.
[116] ibid, 25.
[117] See n 47 above.
[118] Council of the European Union, Document 6643/15, 27.2.2015, p 30.
[119] ibid, 31.

limited and the current draft Decision does not change fundamentally the balance between EU law and national criminal law in the field. It seems that currently the main battlefield between EU institutions with regard to the relationship between EU law and national criminal law lies in the negotiations on the establishment of the European Public Prosecutor's Office.

V. Towards the Establishment of the European Public Prosecutor's Office—Ambitions and Limits to Centralisation

The entry into force of the Treaty of Lisbon has brought about a significant constitutional innovation in providing, for the first time in EU constitutional law, with a concrete and express legal basis for the establishment of a European Public Prosecutor's Office (Article 86 TFEU). Unsurprisingly for a constitutional provision, Article 86 is drafted in rather general terms. It calls for the establishment of a European Public Prosecutor's Office (EPPO) 'from Eurojust'[120] and states that the EPPO will be responsible for investigating, prosecuting and bringing to judgment the perpetrators of, and accomplices in, offences against the Union's financial interests. The EPPO will exercise the functions of prosecutor in the competent courts of the Member States in relation to such offences.[121] Secondary EU law will determine the general rules applicable to the European Public Prosecutor's Office, the conditions governing the performance of its functions, the rules of procedure applicable to its activities, as well as those governing the admissibility of evidence, and the rules applicable to the judicial review of procedural measures taken by it in the performance of its functions.[122] The wording of the Treaty has left a number of open questions with regard to the precise powers and structure of the EPPO and the relationship of the EPPO with national prosecutors and the operation of the EU agency within the criminal justice systems of Member States. Following the entry into force of the Lisbon Treaty and in the run up to the preparation of the Commission's proposal for a Regulation establishing the EPPO, a number of models on the structure and powers of the EPPO and its relationship with national legal systems have been put forward. These models viewed the EPPO from the perspective of the establishment of a vertical/hierarchical structure in relation to Member States (juxtaposing this model to strengthening horizontal cooperation under Eurojust), while other commentators have focused more on the degree of centralisation of prosecutorial

---

[120] Article 86(1) TFEU.
[121] Article 86(2) TFEU.
[122] Article 86(4) TFEU.

power within the EPPO and the relationship between a centralised and a decentralised prosecutorial model in this context.[123] In the course of negotiations on
the establishment of a European Public Prosecutor's Office, various incarnations
of these models have emerged. These range from a centralised, vertical model put
forward by the European Commission in its draft Regulation to a more intergovernmental, Collegiate model which has emerged following negotiations of the
Commission's draft in the Council of Ministers. Negotiations on the EPPO are a
moving target. The chapter will analyse the evolution of a number of key aspects
of the EPPO by tracking developments from the original Commission proposal
to the latest Presidency draft on parts of which Member States have reached a
'conceptual agreement'.

A. Structure and Powers of the European Public Prosecutor's Office

The Commission's proposal for a Regulation on the establishment of the
European Public Prosecutor's Office was tabled in the summer of 2013.[124]
The Commission has put forward a model of vertical cooperation based on a
combination of centralised and decentralised elements of prosecution. The EPPO
is established as a body of the Union with a decentralised structure[125] and legal
personality.[126] The structure of the EPPO comprises of a European Public Prosecutor, his/her Deputies and staff as well as European Delegated Prosecutors located
in the Member States.[127] The EPPO will have exclusive competence to investigate
and prosecute offences against the Union's financial interests.[128] The EPPO will
be headed by the European Public Prosecutor who will direct its activities and
organise its work. The EPPO will be assisted by four deputies.[129] The investigations and prosecutions of the EPPO will be carried out by the European Delegated
Prosecutors—who are appointed and may be dismissed by the European Public
Prosecutor[130]—under the direction and supervision of the European Public
Prosecutor. Where it is deemed necessary in the interest of the investigation or

---

[123] On key academic and policy discussions of various EPPO models, see V Mitsilegas (ed), 'The
Future of Prosecution After Lisbon', double special issue of the *New Journal of European Criminal
Law*. See in particular: K Ligeti and M Simonato, 'The European Public Prosecutor's Office: Towards a
Truly European Prosecution Service?' (2013) 4 *New Journal of European Criminal Law* 7–21; S White,
'Towards a *Decentralised* European Public Prosecutor's Office?' (2013) 4 *New Journal of European
Criminal Law* 22–39; and L Harman and E Szabova, 'European Public Prosecutor's Office—*Cui Bono?*'
(2013) 4 *New Journal of European Criminal Law* 40–58.
[124] COM(2013) 534 final, Brussels, 17.7.2013.
[125] Article 3(1).
[126] Article 3(2).
[127] Article 6(1).
[128] Article 11(4).
[129] Article 6(2) and (3).
[130] Article 10(1).

prosecution, the European Public prosecutor may also exercise his/her authority directly by reallocating the case to another Delegated Prosecutor or leading the case him/herself.[131] There will be at least one European Delegated Prosecutor in each Member State who will act under the exclusive authority of the European Public Prosecutor and follow only his/her instructions, guidelines and decisions when they carry out investigations and prosecutions assigned to them.[132] The Commission has thus put forward a centralised, hierarchical and vertical model of European prosecution. As it has been noted, the proposed regulation clearly goes beyond mutual recognition as it forms a passage from horizontal cooperation to vertical integration.[133] In the Commission's vision, centralisation is synonymous with independence and betrays a lack of trust towards the capacity or willingness of national authorities to combat effectively fraud against the budget of the Union:[134] after all, the EPPO has been legitimised primarily on the grounds of the current lack of effectiveness in combating fraud across the EU.[135] This link between effectiveness, independence and lack of trust towards Member States is epitomised in the following statement by a Commission official:

> The Commission considers that creating EPPO with an intergovernmental collegial structure would seriously hamper the independence of EPPO to take decisions on prosecutions … A collegial structure as foreseen for Eurojust allows pursuing national interests in the field of judicial cooperation and in this form contravenes the notion to create an independent prosecutorial office.[136]

The Commission's vision for a centralised EPPO has caused concerns in a number of EU Member States, both at the level of governments and at the level of parliaments. Some months before the Commission even tabled its proposal, the French and German Ministers of Justice sent a joint letter to the Justice and Anti—Fraud Commissioners expressing the view that the EPPO should be instituted at a collegial basis.[137] Since the tabling of the Commission's draft

---

[131] Articles 6(4) and 18(5).

[132] Article 6(5).

[133] K Ligeti and A Weyembergh, 'The European Public Prosecutor's Office: Certain Constitutional Issues' in LH Erkelens, AWH Meij and M Pawlik (eds), *The European Public Prosecutor's Office. An Extended Arm or a Two-Headed Dragon?* (The Hague, Asser Press/Springer, 2015) 53–78, at 59.

[134] According to Schutte, 'Member States which would support this draft regulation would implicitly recognise that at least with regard to EU fraud offences their public prosecution services are incompetent'. JJE Schutte, 'Establishing Enhanced Cooperation Under Article 86 TFEU' in LH Erkelens, AWH Meij and M Pawlik (eds), *The European Public Prosecutor's Office. An Extended Arm or a Two-Headed Dragon?* (The Hague, Asser Press/Springer, 2015) 195–208 at 197.

[135] The Commission's Explanatory Memorandum to the draft EPPO Regulation asserts that Member States' criminal investigation and prosecution authorities are currently unable to achieve an equivalent level of protection and enforcement—COM(2013) 534 final, p 2.

[136] V Alexandrova, 'Presentation of the Commission's Proposal on the Establishment of the European Public Prosecutor's Office' in LH Erkelens, AWH Meij and M Pawlik (eds), *The European Public Prosecutor's Office. An Extended Arm or a Two-Headed Dragon?* (The Hague, Asser Press/Springer, 2015) 11–20, at 15.

[137] Common Position of the Ministers of Justice of France and Germany on the European Public Prosecutor's Office (current as of 4 March 2013).

Regulation, national parliamentarians have raised subsidiarity concerns[138] and expressed their preference for the collegiate structure and for shared and not exclusive competence of the EPPO.[139] Negotiations in the Council of the European Union have revealed a strong preference of Member States for the Collegiate model. Successive Presidencies of the Council (Greece, Italy, Latvia) have produced substantially revised drafts of the opening part of the Regulation dealing with the structure of the EPPO, with the latest developments at the time of writing being that the Council has expressed 'broad conceptual support'[140] for the text of the first 16 articles of the draft finalised by the Latvian Presidency.[141] An analysis of this draft demonstrates clearly that Member States have adopted a much more intergovernmental model of an EPPO compared to the Commission's draft. The structure of the EPPO is now largely a Collegiate structure, with Member States having a greater say in the operation of the EPPO both at EU level and at national level. This move towards a Collegiate model—which is reminiscent of the structure of Eurojust, an EU body which was established partly as a response to the Commission's *Corpus Juris* initiative which was deemed too supranational by certain Member States[142]—has been accompanied by increased complexity in the structure of the EPPO, with additional layers of prosecutors being introduced in between the central EPPO Collegiate structure (which will be led not by a 'European Public Prosecutor' but by a 'Chief Prosecutor') and the work of European Delegated Prosecutors at national level. There is also a greater degree of participation of prosecutors from the Member State in whose territory EPPO investigations and prosecutions take place, which reveals a higher degree of trust towards the legal systems of affected Member States compared to the Commission's approach.

The EPPO is now 'an indivisible Union body operating as one single Office with a decentralised structure'.[143] The central level consists of a Central Office at the seat consisting of the College, Permanent Chambers, the European Chief Prosecutor, his/her deputies and the European Prosecutors.[144] The College will

---

[138] See Chapter 2 of this volume.

[139] Interparliamentary meeting on the EPPO, Assemblée Nationale, 17 September 2014. Common declaration on the proposal for a Council regulation on the establishment of the European Public Prosecutor's Office (COM(2013) 534), signed in their own name by members of national parliaments of the European Union, representing Members of parliament from 16 national parliaments' chambers of the European Union.

[140] Conclusions of the Justice and Home Affairs Council of 15 and 16 June 2015, Council doc 9951/15, p 5.

[141] Council doc 9372/15, Brussels, 12 June 2015. The same document includes a text of Articles 17–33, not agreed yet but which will inform the analysis further in this chapter.

[142] On the establishment, evolution and powers of Eurojust, see V Mitsilegas, *EU Criminal Law* (Oxford, Hart Publishing, 2009) chapter 4; and V Mitsilegas, 'The Third Wave of Third Pillar Law: Which Direction for EU Criminal Justice?' (2009) 34 *European Law Review* 523–60.

[143] Article 7(1).

[144] Article 7(3).

include a European Chief Prosecutor and one European Prosecutor per Member State.[145] The decentralised structure consists of European Delegated Prosecutors located in the Member States.[146] The *College* is responsible for the general oversight of the activities of the Office and for taking decisions in strategic matters and on general issues arising from individual cases but is not involved in taking operational decisions in individual cases.[147] On a proposal by the European Chief Prosecutor, the College will set up Permanent Chambers to direct and monitor the casework of the EPPO.[148] Unless otherwise stated, the College will take decisions by simple majority—with the Chief Prosecutor having the casting vote.[149] The *Permanent Chambers* will be chaired by the European Chief Prosecutor or one of the deputies and have two additional members.[150] In addition to the permanent members, the European Prosecutor who is supervising an investigation or a prosecution will participate in the deliberations of the Permanent Chamber.[151] Permanent Chambers will direct and monitor the investigations and prosecutions conducted by the European Delegated Prosecutors.[152] Directing and monitoring refers to certain clear powers to monitor and direct individual investigations and prosecutions when such directions appear necessary. This role is to be distinguished by supervision (which as will be seen below is entrusted to the European Prosecutors), which is understood as a closer and rather continuous oversight of investigations and prosecutions including, when necessary, intervening and giving instruction on investigations and prosecution matters.[153] However, Permanent Chambers may also give instructions in specific cases to the European Delegated Prosecutors.[154] Permanent Chambers will also ensure the coordination of investigations and prosecutions in cross-border cases and the implementation of decisions taken by the College on strategic or prosecution policy matters.[155] They will decide under simple majority, with the Chair having a casting vote.[156] The powers of the Permanent Chambers are key to the work of the EPPO as they have the final word on whether a case should be prosecuted[157] and they take decisions

---

[145] Article 8(1).
[146] Article 7(4).
[147] Article 8(2).
[148] Article 8(3).
[149] Article 8(5).
[150] Article 9(1).
[151] Article 9(6).
[152] Article 9(2).
[153] Footnote 9.
[154] Article 9(4).
[155] Article 9(2).
[156] Article 9(5).
[157] According to Article 27 in the Latvian Presidency draft, the European Delegated Prosecutor submits a summary/indictment to the European Prosecutor and Permanent Chamber for Review. Where it does not instruct to dismiss, the Permanent Chamber, acting through the competent European Prosecutor, must instruct the European Delegated Prosecutor to bring the case before the competent national court with an indictment, or refer it back for further investigations.

on conflicts of jurisdiction[158] the dismissal of a case[159] and the approval of transactions which may be proposed by European Delegated Prosecutors.[160] *The European Chief Prosecutor* will be the head of the EPPO. The Chief Prosecutor will organise the work of the Office, direct its activities and take decisions in accordance with the Regulation and rules of procedure[161] and will also assume representation functions.[162] *The European Prosecutors* will, on behalf of the Permanent Chamber and in compliance with its instructions, 'supervise the investigations and prosecutions for which the European Delegated Prosecutors handling the case *in their Member State of origin* are responsible' (emphasis added).[163] They will function as liaisons and channels of information between the Permanent Chambers and the European Delegated Prosecutors and will monitor the implementation of the tasks of the Office on their respective Member States in close consultation with the European Delegated Prosecutors.[164]

At the decentralised level, the *European Delegated Prosecutors* will be responsible for the investigations and prosecutions which they have initiated and will follow the direction and instructions of the Permanent Chamber in charge of the case as well as the instructions from the supervising European Prosecutor.[165] They will also be responsible for bringing a case to judgment.[166] The European Delegated Prosecutors will act on behalf of the EPPO in their respective Member States and will have the same powers as national prosecutors in respect of investigations,[167] prosecutions and bringing cases to judgment, in addition and subject to the specific powers and status conferred on them and under the conditions provided for in the EPPO Regulation.[168] They may also exercise functions as national prosecutors to the extent that this does not prevent them from fulfilling their obligations under the EPPO Regulation.[169] According to the second part of the Regulation, which has not been the subject of a general approach in the Council at the time of writing, where cross-border cases necessitate measures to be undertaken in a Member State other than the state of the European Delegated Prosecutor handling the case, the latter must assign the case to a European Delegated

---

[158] Article 27(2).

[159] Article 28.

[160] Article 29.

[161] Article 10(1) and (2).

[162] Article 10(3).

[163] Article 11(1).

[164] Article 11(3).

[165] Article 12(1), second indent.

[166] Article 12(1), third indent.

[167] According to Article 26, investigative measures will include, in cases of serious offences (punishable by a minimum maximum penalty of 4 years of imprisonment), search and seizure, freezing of instrumentalities or proceeds of crime and of future financial transactions and telecommunications interceptions. The European Delegated Prosecutors may also order or request arrest or pre-trial detention (Article 26b).

[168] Article 12(1), first indent. See also Article 25, which introduces the principle of assimilation by stating that The European Delegated Prosecutor handling the case must be entitled to order or request the same types of measures in his/her Member State which are available to the investigators/prosecutors according to national law in similar national cases.

[169] Article 12(3).

Prosecutor located in the Member State where that measure needs to be carried out.[170] Prosecutors in the second state are referred to as 'assisting' European Delegated Prosecutors,[171] adding thus an additional layer of prosecutorial intervention in the EPPO structure.

The latest draft produced by the Council has thus put forward a multi-level, complex and at first sight rather bureaucratic system of European prosecution with clear and strong intergovernmental elements as regards the structure, composition and decision-making underpinning the activities of the European Public Prosecutor's Office. Central to the function of the EPO are the Permanent Chambers, which operate in a Collegiate manner and include members from the states where investigations take place. This move is a clear signal to ensure ownership of the process by Member States. The introduction of intergovernmental elements is also clear in the provisions regarding the appointment of the EPPO. The European Chief Prosecutor and Deputies will be appointed by the Council and the European Parliament by common accord, with the Council acting by simple majority.[172] The Deputy Chief Prosecutors will be appointed by the EPPO College.[173] The European Prosecutors will be nominated by their respective Member States (who will nominate a pool of three candidates each) and will be appointed by the Council, acting by a simple majority and taking into account the opinion of a selection panel.[174] The European Delegated prosecutors, nominated by Member States, are appointed by the College on a proposal from the European Chief Prosecutor.[175]

B. Competence, Scope, Territoriality

From the outset, the Commission has introduced two strong federal elements in its vision of the EPPO: exclusive competence and European territoriality. By granting the EPPO exclusive competence, the Commission sent a strong signal to Member States that it is only the EPPO which is responsible and competent for the investigation and prosecution of the 'European Union' offences associated with fraud against the Union budget.[176] The powers of the EPPO in this context have been backed up by the application by the Commission of the principle of European territoriality. According to Article 25 of the Commission's draft, for the purpose of investigations and prosecutions conducted by the European Public Prosecutor's Office, the territory of the Union's Member States will be considered *a single legal area* in which the European Public Prosecutor's Office may exercise its competence

---

[170] Latvian Presidency draft, Article 26a(1). See also Article 23(2).
[171] See inter alia Articles 26a(4) and (5).
[172] Article 13(1).
[173] Article 13a(1).
[174] Article 14 (1) and (2).
[175] Article 15(1).
[176] Article 11(4) of the Commission's proposal.

(emphasis added).[177] The Commission's draft thus mirrors the approach taken by the drafters of the *Corpus Juris*.[178] The Guiding Principles of Corpus Juris introduced the principle of European territoriality by stating that for the purposes of investigation, prosecution, trial and execution of sentences concerning the Corpus Juris offences, the territory of the Member States of the European Union constitutes a single area, called the European judicial area and that the competence *ratione loci* of the European Public Prosecutor and of national prosecutors to issue warrants and judgments pursuant to the Corpus Juris extends to the entire European judicial area.[179] The principle is reflected in Article 18(1) of the *Corpus Juris*.[180] However, this single legal area does not signify the application of a single legislative framework to the operation of the EPPO but rather has to take into account the national legal systems of the Member States. The symbiotic relationship between the 'European' aspects of the EPPO and the applicability of national law is evident throughout the text of the Commission's draft, and in particular in the provisions regarding the applicability of national law in the context of EPPO investigations.[181] The references of the Commission's draft to the applicability of national law have led commentators to argue that the proposal leads to a situation where the investigative powers of the EPPO are defined by the national criminal procedural law of each Member State.[182]

Unsurprisingly, both the concepts of exclusivity and European territoriality have been rejected by the Council. The latest draft produced by the Latvian Presidency has replaced exclusive competence by priority competence of the EPPO, backed up by a right to evocation.[183] The Latvian Presidency draft also gives the final word to national authorities (and not to the EPPO) in cases of disagreement on whether the EPPO has ancillary competence[184] over offences linked to fraud

---

[177] Article 25(1) of the Commission's proposal.

[178] For a background to the *Corpus Juris*, see M Delmas-Marty, 'Guest Editorial: Combatting Fraud—Necessity, Legitimacy and Feasibility of the *Corpus Juris*' (2000) 37 *Common Market Law Review* 247–56.

[179] Guiding Principles of Corpus Juris 2000, at: ec.europa.eu/anti_fraud/documents/fwk-green-paper-corpus/corpus_juris_en.pdf.

[180] For the purposes of investigation, prosecution, trial and execution of sentences concerning the offences set out above (Articles 1 to 8 [of the *Corpus Juris*]), the territory of the Member States of the Union constitutes a single legal area. For an analysis of the concept of European territoriality in the evolution of proposals for a European Public Prosecutor, see J Vervaele, 'European Territoriality and Jurisdiction: The Protection of the EU's Financial Interests in Its Horizontal and Vertical (EPPO) Dimension' in M Luchtman (ed), *Choice of Forum in Cooperation Against EU Financial Crime* (The Hague, Eleven International Publishing, 2013) 167–84.

[181] See in particular Article 11(3) and Article 26(2) of the Commission's draft.

[182] K Ligeti, 'The European Public Prosecutor's Office' in V Mitsilegas, M Bergström and T Konstadinides (eds), *Research Handbook on EU Criminal Law* (Cheltenham, Edward Elgar, 2015).

[183] See Article 19(1) on priority competence and Article 21a on the right of evocation.

[184] According to Article 18(1), where an offence constituting a criminal offence referred to in Article 17 is based on a set of facts which are identical or inextricably linked to a set of facts constituting, in whole or in part under the law of the Member State concerned, a criminal offence other than those referred to in Article 17, the EPPO must also be competent for those other criminal offences, under the condition that the offence referred to in Article 17 is preponderant. Where the offence

crimes.[185] Decisions by national authorities will be preceded by consultations between them and the EPPO[186] in a system reminiscent of the model introduced by the Framework Decision on conflicts of jurisdiction.[187] The departure from exclusive EPPO competence is consistent with the general shift from a highly centralised to a more cooperative and interactive model. The Commission would confer exclusive competence in a field which under general EU constitutional law falls under shared EU/Member State competence.[188] Similarly, the Presidency's draft has abandoned the concept of European territoriality. While the original Commission proposal as seen above affirmed the principle by stating in Article 25(1) that for the purpose of investigations and prosecutions the territory of the Union's Member States will be considered a single legal area, the latest draft put forward by the Latvian Presidency merely states that when conducting investigations and prosecutions in the territory of the Union's Member States, the European Public Prosecutor's Office shall operate as *one single office*.[189] The Council draft thus rejects the view of the European Union as one single legal area and confirms the view of the Union consisting of a number of different national legal orders. The abandonment of European territoriality—and the in principle negation of action of European Delegated Prosecutors beyond the borders of their Member State this entails—has added an extra layer to the EPPO structure: in cross-border cases necessitating measures to be undertaken in a Member State other than the state of the European Delegated Prosecutor handling the case, the latter must assign the case to a European Delegated Prosecutor located in the Member State where that measure needs to be carried out.[190] Prosecutors in the second state are referred to as 'assisting' European Delegated Prosecutors.[191]

If developments in the Council with regard to bold Commission proposals on exclusive competence and European territoriality have not come as a surprise, further disagreements with regard to the powers and *ratione materiae* scope of the EPPO demonstrate deeper concerns in Member States regarding the potential impact of European prosecution on their national legal diversity and sovereignty. The first example of this kind is the resistance of some Member States to the attribution of mandatory investigation or prosecution powers to the

referred to in Article 17 is not preponderant, the Member State that is competent for the other offence must also be competent for the offence referred to in Article 17.

[185] Article 18(5).
[186] Article 18(4).
[187] Council Framework Decision 2009/948/JHA of 30 November 2009 on prevention and settlement of conflicts of exercise of jurisdiction in criminal proceedings, [2009] OJ L328, 15.12.2009, p 42.
[188] See also the comments of Asp, who argues that granting exclusive competence is not consistent with the principle of subsidiarity—P Asp, 'Jeopardy on European Level: What is the Question to which the Answer is the EPPO?' in P Asp (ed), *The European Public Prosecutor's Office—Legal and Criminal Policy Perspectives* (Stifelsen Skrifter utgivna av Juridiska fakulteten vid Stockholms universitet, 2015) 51–68, 64–65.
[189] Article 7(1).
[190] Latvian Presidency draft, Article 26a(1).
[191] See, inter alia, Articles 26a(4) and (5).

EPPO, arguing that this will have an impact on the discretionary nature of their domestic systems.[192] A number of Member States have also raised concerns with regard to the introduction of 'transactions' as a method of settlement of disputes in the Regulation, due to the absence of this method in their domestic systems.[193] If the term 'transaction' remains in the text, it is a prime candidate for autonomous interpretation by the Court of Justice.[194] Further disagreements arise with regard to the offences for which the EPPO will have competence to act. The draft Regulation defines such competence by reference to the offences which will be included in the currently negotiated fraud Directive. However, it has been noted that there is a degree of uncertainty as the said offences will be those resulting from the implementation of the Directive by Member States,[195] which may result in divergent criminalisation approaches.[196] A more fundamental question concerns what these offences will actually be. There is currently disagreement between Member States on the one hand and the European Parliament and the European Commission on the other with regard to the inclusion of VAT fraud in the scope of the Directive, with Member States taking the view that VAT fraud should not be included in the scope of the Directive as it is primarily a national issue.[197] Excluding VAT fraud from the scope of the Directive will most likely limit the scope of the EPPO considerably. This outcome will in turn cast doubt on the Commission's justification on the necessity of an EPPO, if one accepts that revenues from VAT fraud across the EU are indeed very substantial. It is perhaps in the light of these developments that the Court of Justice has sent a very strong signal in its ruling in *Taricco* by confirming that VAT fraud falls within the scope of the third-pillar fraud Convention which the new Directive will replace.[198] While the approach of

[192] See the reservations of France and the Netherlands in Article 21(1) of the latest Council draft, arguing that initiation of investigations should be discretionary. See also in the secondary literature the concerns of Smulders, who argues that the right to bring proceedings should not be mandatory but discretionary as one could not justify within a national system that financial damage to the EU always leads to criminal proceedings, but that similar harm to the national state will not—B Smulders, 'Is the Commission Proposal for a European Public Prosecutor's Office Based on a Harmonious Interpretation of Articles 85 and 86 TFEU?' in LH Erkelens, AWH Meij and M Pawlik (eds), *The European Public Prosecutor's Office. An Extended Arm or a Two-Headed Dragon?* (The Hague, Asser Press/Springer, 2015) 41–52, at 44.

[193] Article 29.

[194] On the role of autonomous concepts in the evolution of EU criminal law, see V Mitsilegas, 'Managing Legal Diversity in Europe's Area of Criminal Justice: The Role of Autonomous Concepts' in R Colson and S Field (eds), *EU Criminal Justice and the Challenges of Legal Diversity. Towards A Socio-Legal Approach to EU Criminal Policy* (Cambridge, Cambridge University Press, forthcoming).

[195] According to the latest draft, The EPPO will exercise this competence on the basis of the applicable national law implementing the fraud Directive (Article 17).

[196] D Flore, 'Garantie Judiciaire et Droit Applicable: Quelques Éléments de Réflexion' in G Giudicelli-Delage, S Manacorda and J Tricot (eds), *Le Contrôle Judiciaire du Parquet Européen. Nécessité, Modèles, Enjeux,* Collection de l'UMR de Droit Comparé de Paris (Université Paris 1) (Société de Législation Comparée, vol 37, 2015) 299–310, at 302.

[197] Informal JHA Council—Ministers of Justice discuss the protection of the EU's financial interests, the European Public Prosecutor's Office and the protection of the rights of the child, 10.7.2015, www.eu2015lu.eu/en/actualites/articles-actualite/2015/07/info-jai-justice/index.html, accessed 31.8.2015.

[198] Case C-105/14, *Taricco and Others,* judgment of 8 September 2015, paragraph 41. For an analysis, see Chapter 3 of this volume.

Member States can be seen as an attempt to guard their sovereignty in criminal matters in relation to the EPPO, disagreement at such deep level between the EU institutions is worrying in that it reveals ultimately a basic lack of understanding and agreement on what fraud against the EU budget is. If one cannot define the elements of fraud against the EU budget with a degree of certainty, then what is the hope of legal certainty backing the establishment of a European Public Prosecutor's Office?

C. Judicial Review of the European Public Prosecutor's Office at EU Level

The configuration of the powers and structure of the European Public Prosecutor's Office and its relationship with national legal orders are key in setting the parameters for judicial review of decisions and acts of the EPPO at European Union level. A common element in the drafts produced by the Commission and the Italian Presidency is the wide range of powers entrusted to the EPPO regarding investigation and prosecution of offences against the financial interests of the European Union. These powers are diffused downwards and exercised in different ways according to the different models of European prosecution put forward by the Commission and by Member States. Yet it is clear that, whatever the EPPO model eventually adopted, the establishment of a European Public Prosecutor's Office will lead to decisions and acts by an EU body which will have significant effects on the rights of affected individuals throughout the European Union. This part will highlight the legal and constitutional challenges that the current proposals for the EU judicial review of the EPPO entail, by evaluating these proposals in the light of EU constitutional and human rights law and drawing lessons from similar challenges which have arisen in investigations and prosecutions by EU bodies such as OLAF and Eurojust. These challenges will become more acute when certain current tasks of OLAF and Eurojust are streamlined within the operations of the EPPO.

i. Constitutional Challenges from Limiting EU Judicial Review for Acts of the EPPO

Notwithstanding the establishment of the EPPO as a European Union body operating within a single legal area, the Commission proposal excludes the judicial review of the EPPO at EU level. Article 36 of the Commission's draft states clearly that when adopting procedural measures in the performance of its functions, the European Public Prosecutor's Office will be considered as a *national* authority for the purpose of judicial review.[199] It is further added that where provisions of national law are rendered applicable by this Regulation, such provisions will

---

[199] Article 36(1).

not be considered as provisions of Union law for the purpose of Article 267 of the Treaty.[200] Shielding the EPPO from EU judicial scrutiny is also confirmed elsewhere in the Commission's draft where judicial review of certain EPPO decisions is excluded in general.[201] The Commission has justified the exclusion of EU judicial review on three main grounds: on the perceived specificity and difference of the EPPO from all other Union bodies and agencies which requires special rules on judicial review;[202] the strong link between the operations of the EPPO and the legal orders of the Member States;[203] and the need to respect the principle of subsidiarity.[204] The Commission's approach towards the limited judicial review of the EPPO at EU level is encapsulated in the Preamble to the draft Regulation as follows:

> Article 86(2) of the Treaty requires that the European Public Prosecutor's Office exercise its functions of prosecutor in the competent courts of the Member States. Acts undertaken by the European Public Prosecutor's Office in the course of its investigations are closely related to the prosecution which may result therefrom and have effects in the legal order of the Member States. In most cases they will be carried out by national law enforcement authorities acting under the instructions of European Public Prosecutor's Office, sometimes after having obtained the authorisation of a national court. It is therefore appropriate to consider the European Public Prosecutor's Office as a national authority for the purpose of the judicial review of its acts of investigation and prosecution. As a result, national courts should be entrusted with the judicial review of all acts of investigation and prosecution of the European Public Prosecutor's Office which may be challenged, and the Court of Justice of the European Union should not be directly competent with regard to those acts pursuant to Articles 263, 265 and 268 of the Treaty, since such acts should not be considered as acts of a body of the Union for the purpose of judicial review.

> In accordance with Article 267 of the Treaty, national courts are able or, in certain circumstances, bound to refer to the Court of Justice questions for preliminary rulings on the interpretation or the validity of provisions of Union law, including this Regulation, which are relevant for the judicial review of the acts of investigation and prosecution of the European Public Prosecutor's Office. National courts should not be able to refer questions on the validity of the acts of the European Public Prosecutor's Office to the Court of Justice, since those acts should not be considered acts of a body of the Union for the purpose of judicial review.

> It should also be clarified that issues concerning the interpretation of provisions of national law which are rendered applicable by this Regulation should be dealt with by national courts alone. In consequence, those courts may not refer questions to the Court of Justice relating to the interpretation of national law to which this Regulation refers.[205]

[200] Article 36(2).
[201] This applies to the decision to dismiss a case following a transaction—Article 29(4).
[202] Explanatory Report, paragraph 3.3.5.
[203] ibid.
[204] ibid, p 5.
[205] Preamble, recitals 37–39.

The Commission's treatment of the EPPO as a national body for the purposes of judicial review is strikingly at odds with its overall vision of the EPPO as a centralised body establishing a system of vertical cooperation in the field of investigation and prosecution in the European Union. The Commission emphasises the links of the EPPO with national legal orders, yet disregards the fact that EPPO acts and decisions are acts adopted by an EU agency—with the Commission's draft effectively creating a European agency lying outside European judicial control.[206] The Commission further justifies this exclusion on the basis of the special nature of the EPPO. However, if anything, the specificity of the EPPO in relation to other EU agencies—which consists of the fact that the EPPO is an operational body whose action has the potential to affect significantly fundamental rights across the EU—render EU judicial review even more imperative. Moreover, the possibilities allowed by the Treaty of Lisbon for specific rules concerning judicial review of EU agencies in general[207] and the EPPO in particular (Article 86(4) TFEU) do not mean that these rules can entail the total *exclusion* of EU judicial review for EU agencies, including the EPPO. The exclusion of such review would be a direct attack on the rule of law in the European Union and would challenge the obligation of the EU to uphold fundamental rights as enshrined in the ECHR and the Charter, and in particular Articles 47 and 49 of the Charter. Exclusion of EU judicial review of the EPPO would in particular be hard to reconcile with the right to effective judicial protection, which has assumed a central role in EU constitutional law in recent years.[208] Finally, the Commission's approach to the judicial review of the EPPO rests on a wrong understanding of the application of the principle of subsidiarity. The subsidiarity test to be met is whether the European Union level is the right level of legislative action with regard to the establishment of the EPPO in order to achieve the stated legislative objectives.[209] The question of judicial review is a meta-question concerning the functioning of the EPPO, which should arise after the decision on whether the establishment of an EPPO per se meets the requirements of the subsidiarity test.[210]

The issue of EU judicial review of the EPPO can be viewed from three separate but interrelated perspectives. First, one can distinguish between acts and decisions of the EPPO in its centralised functions on the one hand and under its decentralised formations on the other. Yet the centralise/decentralised distinction is increasingly harder to make, in particular after the additional layers in

---

[206] See in this context also established Luxembourg case-law according to which national courts have no jurisdiction themselves to declare the invalidity of measures taken by EU institutions—see Case 314/85, *Foto-Frost v Hauptzollamt Lübeck-Ost*, judgment of 22 October 1987.

[207] Article 263(5) TFEU.

[208] See for instance the Court's rulings in the *Kadi* litigation, and in particular the Court's findings in *Kadi II*—Joined Cases C-584/10 P, C-593/10 P and C-595/10 P, *European Commission v Kadi*.

[209] For a detailed and negative subsidiarity assessment of the Commission's draft EPPO Regulation, see House of Lords European Union Committee, *Subsidiarity Assessment: The European Public Prosecutor's Office*, 3rd Report, session 2013–14, HL Paper 65.

[210] On the EPPO and the principle of subsidiarity, see Chapter 2 of this volume.

the EPPO structure introduced in the Greek Presidency's draft. Moreover, it is clear that acts and decisions of the EPPO both in its centralised and its decentralised incarnations constitute acts taken by an *EU* body which should thus in principle be subject to *EU* judicial review within the constitutional parameters of the Treaties. The second perspective is to distinguish between judicial review of different *types of act* adopted by the EPPO—with *pre-prosecution* acts (eg investigation acts enumerated in Article 26 of the Commission's proposal) being left to national courts to deal with, while decisions *on prosecution* (including acts and decisions under Articles 27–29 of the Commission's draft) could be subject to EU judicial review.[211] However, this distinction would disregard the fact that both investigation and prosecution decisions are taken by the same *EU* body whose acts should in principle be subject to *EU* judicial review. More importantly, it would be contrary to the rule of law and a challenge to effective judicial protection if acts of an EU body which may have profound consequences for fundamental rights— such as investigation acts and decisions adopted by the EPPO—were shielded from EU judicial scrutiny. The third perspective would be to distinguish in terms of applicable law, with EPPO acts and decisions to which EU law applies being subject to EU judicial scrutiny, and acts and decisions to which national law applies being subject only to national judicial review. However, this perspective would also disregard the European Union nature of the EPPO and the acts and decisions adopted by this body, and could result in serious adverse consequences with regard to legal certainty as to which acts or decisions would qualify as 'national' for the purposes of judicial review. European Union judicial review should thus apply as extensively as possible to the acts and decisions of the EPPO. Effective use of the possibilities offered, in particular by Articles 263 and 267 TFEU, will contribute towards both effective judicial protection and the development of European Union law in this important field—which may lead to the reconfiguration of the relationship between the individual and the state in Europe via the introduction of a new, EU layer of investigation and prosecution—with the full involvement of the Court of Justice and the direction and clarification it may offer to national courts in this context.[212]

---

[211] The European Parliament has argued that decisions taken by the EPPO before or independently from the trial, such as those described in Articles 27, 28 and 29 concerning competence, dismissal of cases or transactions, should be subject to the remedies available before the Union Courts- European Parliament Resolution of 12 March 2014 on the proposal for a Council Regulation on the establishment of the EPPO, P7_TA (2014) 0234. For a discussion of judicial review options for EPPO dismissal decisions, see J Göhler, 'To Continue or Not: Who Shall Be in Control of the European Public Prosecutor's Dismissal Decisions?' (2015) 6 *New Journal of European Criminal Law* 102–25.

[212] Article 33 of the latest draft by the Latvian Presidency provides for two options for judicial review: one states that the EPPO must be considered as a national authority for the purpose of judicial review and the other seems to provide limited review of legality of measures determining ancillary competence and conflicts of jurisdiction (assuming that the enumeration of the relevant articles in the latest draft is understood to reflect the numbering in earlier drafts). However, this Article has not been subject to detailed discussion in the Council.

ii. Judicial Review of Investigation Decisions and Acts: Lessons from OLAF

In order to ensure effective judicial protection of individuals affected by EPPO operations it is necessary to provide for EU judicial review of the EPPO's investigative acts and decisions.[213] A key way to achieve this objective is the use of the action of annulment under Article 263 TFEU. According to Article 263(4) TFEU, any natural or legal person may institute proceedings against an act addressed to that person or which is of direct and individual concern to them, and against a regulatory act which is of direct concern to them and does not entail implementing measures. The Court of Justice has interpreted the standing criteria for natural and legal persons as applying if the binding legal effects of the contested act are capable of affecting the interests of the applicant by bringing about a distinct change in its legal position.[214] The standing criteria under Article 263(4) TFEU will apply to investigative acts and decisions by the EPPO. The need to ensure judicial review of these acts and decisions at EU level arises even more prominently in view of the very limited space given by the Court of Justice thus far to effective scrutiny of acts of OLAF, an approach which has resulted in the failure of actions for annulment of OLAF acts which are routinely declared inadmissible.[215] An emblematic case in this context is the case of *Tillack*,[216] where the Court of First Instance (CFI) found that the contested act (the transmission of information by OLAF to national authorities) 'does not bring about a distinct change in the applicant's legal position'[217] and that while national authorities are under a duty to examine the information forwarded by OLAF carefully, this does not mean that the forwarded information has binding effect, 'in the sense that the national authorities are obliged to take specific measures, since such an interpretation would alter the division of tasks and responsibilities as prescribed for the implementation of Regulation No 1073/99'.[218] The Court of First Instance thus shielded OLAF from judicial scrutiny, notwithstanding the fact that earlier in the procedure the European Ombudsman had found that the publication of allegations against Mr Tillack by OLAF without a factual basis was disproportionate

---

[213] For an analysis and categorisation of the different levels of EPPO action in this context, see Z Durdevic, 'Judicial Control in Pre-Trial Criminal Procedure Conducted by the European Public Prosecutor's Office' in K Ligeti, *Towards a Prosecutor for the European Union* (Oxford, Hart Publishing, 2013) 986–1010.

[214] Joined Cases C-463/10 P and C-475/P, *Deutsche Post and Germany v Commission* [2011] ECR I-9639. For an analysis of standing under Article 263(4) TFEU see K Lenaerts, I Maselis, K Gutman, *EU Procedural Law* (Oxford, Oxford University Press, 2014) para 7.21 (pp 268–69).

[215] JFH Inghelram, 'Fundamental Rights, the European Anti-Fraud Office (OLAF) and a European Public Prosecutor's Office (EPPO): Some Selected Issues' (2012) 95 *Kritische Vierteljahresschrift für Gesetzgebung und Rechtswissenschaft* 67–81; V Covolo, 'The Legal Framework of OLAF Investigations. What Lessons for the European Penal Area?' (2011) 2 *New Journal of European Criminal Law* 201–19.

[216] Case T-193/04, *Hans-Martin Tillack v Commission* [2006] ECR II-3995.

[217] ibid paragraph 68.

[218] Paragraph 72.

and constituted an act of maladministration, and that OLAF had made incorrect and misleading statements in its submissions to the Ombudsman in the context of this inquiry.[219] The CFI approach is also at odds with the subsequent ruling of the European Court of Human Rights which found that national measures taken against the applicant 'are disproportionate and thus have violated the applicant's right of freedom of expression under Article 10 ECHR'.[220] In reaching this conclusion, the Court took into account the fact that the applicant was a journalist (triggering thus freedom of the press issues).[221] It also looked at the measures taken by the Belgian authorities *in the light of the information provided to them by OLAF.* The Court agreeing with the European Ombudsman that the corruption suspicions against the applicant were founded upon 'simple rumours'—there was thus no preponderant imperative of public interest which could justify the measures taken by the national authorities.[222] Judicial protection for Mr Tillack—which was denied to him by the EU courts—was thus provided in the context of the examination of measures taken by *national* authorities.[223] The Court affirmed its reasoning on inadmissibility in the case of *Violetti,*[224] where the Court adopted a narrow view on the impact of the requirement of effective judicial protection on the interpretation of the standing criteria for actions of annulment.[225] It is however problematic to apply the Court's case-law on OLAF in the case of the EPPO. First, it is submitted that, from the perspective of the protection of fundamental rights, the Court's case-law sits at odds with the requirement of effective judicial protection as enshrined by the Charter, in particular after judicial developments in *Kadi II.*[226] Secondly, the legal position of investigate acts by the EPPO is qualitatively different to the acts of OLAF. Many of the investigative acts of the EPPO listed in the Commission proposal will clearly have the effect of bringing a distinct change in the legal position of affected individuals. Moreover, and unlike the system of cooperation established in the OLAF legal framework, investigative

---

[219] European Ombudsman, *Special Report to the European Parliament following the draft recommendation to the European Anti-Fraud Office in complaint 2485/2004/GG,* Strasbourg, 12 May 2005, at: ombudsman.europa.eu/special/pdf/en/042485.pdf.

[220] *Affaire Tillack c Belgique,* Requête no 20477/05, 27 November 2007 (final version 27.2.2008), paragraph 68.

[221] See paragraph 65.

[222] Paragraph 63.

[223] For further analysis, see Mitsilegas, *EU Criminal Law,* n 65 above, chapter 4.

[224] Case T-261/09 P *Commission v Violetti and Others,* EU:T:2010:215.

[225] ibid, paragraph 56. Covolo goes as far to say that according to the Court the lack of effective judicial protection is not, in itself, sufficient to justify the admissibility of an action for annulment—n 215 above, p 216.

[226] In *Kadi II,* the Court of Justice made express reference to the need for the European judiciary to ensure the in principle full review of the lawfulness of all Union acts in the light of fundamental rights and mentioned in particular the respect for the rights of the defence and the right to effective judicial protection as enshrined in the Charter—for an analysis, see 'The European Union and the Global Governance of Crime' in V Mitsilegas, P Alldridge and L Cheliotis (eds), *Globalisation, Criminal Law and Criminal Justice. Theoretical, Comparative and Transnational Perspectives* (Oxford, Hart Publishing, 2014) 153–98. For further analysis, see Chapter 9 of this volume.

acts by the EPPO may lead not to a national, but to a European prosecution by the EPPO itself—a fact which maintains the EU dimension of investigation and prosecution throughout the proceedings.

VI. The Quest for Coherence in Prosecution in a Fragmented Area of Criminal Justice

The development of EU law on vertical prosecution raises a number of questions regarding coherence in European prosecution. On the one hand, we are witnessing a proliferation of EU bodies and agencies with powers in the field of criminal investigation and prosecution. On the other, the establishment of the European Public Prosecutor's Office will signify the consolidation on a large scale of European integration in criminal matters à-la-carte. On the first point, when one examines the proliferation of EU actors in the field of criminal investigations and prosecutions, a number of questions arise regarding the relationship of the EPPO and other bodies in the field, in particular OLAF (currently responsible for administrative investigations on fraud against the Union's budget) and Eurojust (whose mandate *ratione materiae* is much broader than the EPPO, covering a whole range of serious criminality.[227] It remains to be seen whether OLAF will be subsumed within the EPPO and how the relationship between EPPO and Eurojust will develop with the respective Regulations being negotiated in parallel—after all, the Lisbon Treaty indicates that the EPPO will be established 'from Eurojust'. The relationship between the EPPO and OLAF and Eurojust is important and will depend upon and influence largely the relationship between the EPPO and non-participating EU Member States. The Lisbon Treaty envisages the possibility of the EPPO being established by enhanced cooperation, if unanimous agreement on the proposal is not reached, with a minimum of nine participating Member States.[228] Knowing that enhanced cooperation will be needed for the EPPO proposal to go ahead—and with the participation of the United Kingdom being excluded at the time of writing[229]—a number of questions arise on the relationship between the EPPO and non-participating Member States. The Commission's draft was largely silent on the matter. However, in practice there may be a number of occasions requiring cooperation between the EPPO and non-participating

---

[227] For background on the powers of OLAF and Eurojust see V Mitsilegas, *EU Criminal Law* (Oxford, Hart Publishing, 2009), chapter 4.

[228] Article 86(1) third indent TFEU.

[229] The European Union Act 2011 imposes a 'referendum lock' on the UK's participation on the EPPO- European Union Act 2011, cl 11, s 6 and in particular s 6(5)(c). See JR Spencer, 'The UK and EU Criminal Law: Should we be Leading, Following or Abstaining?' in V Mitsilegas, P Alldridge and L Cheliotis (eds), *Globalisation, Criminal Law and Criminal Justice. Theoretical, Comparative and Transnational Perspectives* (Oxford, Hart Publishing, 2015) 135–52.

Member States. These cases include in particular offences falling within the remit of the EPPO (such as fraud or money laundering) which however display a cross-border dimension (for instance a cross-border money laundering case between a participating and a non-participating Member State).[230] Another set of questions may arise if investigations focus on 'EPPO' offences together with ancillary offences deemed not to fall within the EPPO remit (this scenario may also involve Member States which actually take part in the EPPO). In both scenarios, the role of Eurojust is crucial, as Eurojust will normally be competent to coordinate and facilitate judicial cooperation for serious crime which does not fall within the remit of the EPPO[231] or which falls within the remit of the EPPO but also involves non-EPPO members. Indeed, the President of Eurojust views its future role as facilitating trust and addressing gaps arising from the complexities in the EPPO legal framework.[232]

With regard to the particular case of relations between the EPPO and the UK, Eurojust may not be able to assist in the future if the UK maintains its current opt-out from the new post-Lisbon Eurojust Regulation.[233] In this case, a model which could be followed (if the UK does not participate in the EPPO or in Eurojust) is the model involving UK relations with the European Border Agency (Frontex). Article 12(1) of the Frontex Regulation states that the Agency will facilitate operational cooperation of the Member States with [non-participating] Ireland and the UK in matters covered by its activities.[234] The United Kingdom has participated in several joint operations subject to the acceptance on a case-by-case basis of the Frontex Management Board, on which the UK has observer status.[235] A similar arrangement can be reached between the UK prosecution authorities and the

---

[230] For further detail see V Mitsilegas, Follow-up evidence to House of Lords European Union Committee for their inquiry on *The Impact of the European Public Prosecutor's Office on the United Kingdom* (4th Report, session 2014–15, HL Paper 53).

[231] On the potential role of Eurojust in relation to ancillary offences, but also in relation to cases of dismissal by the EPPO, see C Deboyser, 'European Public Prosecutor's Office and Eurojust: 'Love Match or Arranged Marriage'?' in LH Erkelens, AWH Meij and M Pawlik (eds), *The European Public Prosecutor's Office. An Extended Arm or a Two-Headed Dragon?* (The Hague, Asser Press/Springer, 2015) 79–100, 84.

[232] M Coninsx, 'The European Commission's Legislative Proposal: An overview of its Main Characteristics' in LH Erkelens, AWH Meij and M Pawlik (eds), *The European Public Prosecutor's Office. An Extended Arm or a Two-Headed Dragon?* (The Hague, Asser Press/Springer, 2015) 21–40.

[233] The UK has opted back into the pre-Lisbon Eurojust Decision by which it is currently bound but has opted out of the new post-Lisbon Regulation currently under negotiation in Brussels. See (then) Parliamentary Under Secretary of State for Security (James Brokenshire), written statement to Parliament—government will conduct a thorough review of the final agreed text to inform active consideration of opting into the Eurojust Regulation post adoption: www.gov.uk/government/speeches/european-commissions-proposals-on-eurojust-and-the-european-public-prosecutors-office, 2 December 2013, accessed on 1 September 2015.

[234] Council Regulation No 2007/2004 establishing a European Agency for the Management of Operational Cooperation at the External Borders of the Member States of the European union, [2004] OJ L349, 25.11.2004, p 1.

[235] House of Lords European Union Committee, *EU Police and Justice Measures: the UK's 2014 Opt-Out Decision*, 13th Report, session 2012–13, HL Paper 159, para 534.

Permanent Chambers in particular cases subject to the approval by the EPPO College. A number of questions however continue to remain open, including the fate of the participation of non-EPPO participating Member States in OLAF, should the latter be subsumed within the EPPO,[236] and whether non-participating states are under the duty to cooperate with EPPO requests, and if yes, under which legal framework.[237] Another way forward may be the treatment of the United Kingdom by the EPPO as a third country and co-operation via the conclusion of a mutual legal assistance agreement or a memorandum of understanding between the EPPO and the UK. Another important issue is the future of the UK's participation in OLAF if the latter is subsumed by the EPPO. These are complex issues which may have a profound impact on the national criminal justice systems of both participating and non-participating Member States as well as on Europe's area of criminal justice which may end up more fragmented following the adoption of the EPPO Regulation.

VII. Conclusion

The evolution of EU law regarding prosecution in Europe's area of criminal justice has been marked by controversy and a number of fundamental legal and constitutional challenges impacting on key aspects of the relationship between the European Union and Member States. The debate on the adoption of EU rules on prosecution triggers concerns related to the perceived adverse impact of Europeanisation on national legal diversity and state sovereignty on the one hand, while half-baked EU proposals oscillating between the need to achieve prosecutorial efficiency and the need to preserve state sovereignty raise a series of well-founded fundamental rights concerns on the other. The EU legislator (and in particular Member States) has been thus far reluctant to adopt wide-ranging EU rules governing horizontal cooperation including the settlement of *ne bis in idem*, choice of forum or conflicts of jurisdiction matters. Answers to transnational *ne bis in idem* questions are provided by the Court of Justice on the basis of the general wording of Article 54 CISA. Litigation thus far has demonstrated the limits of mutual trust, but also the Court's emphasis on the Area of Freedom, Security and Justice as an area of free movement. It appears that the Court is in the process of rebalancing its case-law by taking into account national mistrust to a greater extent, at the expense

---

[236] See the concerns expressed in this context by the House of Lords European Union Committee, *The Impact of the European Public Prosecutor's Office on the United Kingdom*, 4th Report, session 2014–15, HL Paper 53, paragraphs 66–67.

[237] It has been suggested that Member States are bound by the principle of loyal cooperation— see written evidence by Jorge Espina House of Lords European Union Committee, *The Impact of the European Public Prosecutor's Office on the United Kingdom*, 4th Report, session 2014–15, HL Paper 53, cited in paragraph 50 of the Report.

of the protection of fundamental rights and the achievement of legal certainty and free movement. The emancipation of the principle of *ne bis in idem* in the Lisbon Treaty and its elevation to a fundamental right in the Charter may serve to limit demands for restrictions to the protective scope of the transnational *ne bis in idem* principle. The constitutionalisation of the principle of *ne bis in idem* in this manner is also important in underpinning a mechanism of managing inter-state cooperation on prosecution with fundamental rights principles. In terms of the evolution of horizontal coordination mechanisms at EU level more broadly, the constitutionalisation of *ne bis in idem* serves to remind us of the necessity to underpin any EU law or practice on choice of forum and conflicts of jurisdiction with clear and effective safeguards for affected individuals. Further European integration in the field should not lead to prosecutorial forum shopping.

The evolution of EU mechanisms of vertical integration in the field of prosecution has been subject to controversy and poses fundamental questions about the *locus* and the substance of criminal justice in the European Union. Here the impact of the Lisbon Treaty has not been as pronounced in relation to the evolution of the powers of Eurojust, which do not seem likely to increase even after the insertion of Article 85 TFEU in the Treaty. A number of questions arise however from the current negotiations on a Regulation establishing the European Public Prosecutor's Office, which represents the clearest attempt to introduce a binding, vertical dimension in EU-wide prosecution. The Commission has produced a highly innovative and contested vision of centralised prosecution at EU level, replete with echoes of federalism via the use of concepts such as European territoriality and exclusive competence. National parliaments and governments were not convinced. A considerable number of national chambers have raised subsidiarity concerns on the establishment of a European Public Prosecutor's Office.[238] Member States on the other hand have replaced the Commission's federal vision with the usual intergovernmental, Collegiate vision present in a number of current EU judicial cooperation structures, and in particular Eurojust. Whether this toned down vision of European prosecution will resolve the issues arising from this highly complex legal endeavour remains to be seen. Member States' vision addresses issues of perceived lack of trust to state authorities by re-associating national prosecutors with cases involving their own Member State. On the other hand, the Collegiate model does not negate the fact that the EPPO will be a European Union body subject to EU law and all the duties stemming from the EU constitutional order. There is much to be discussed further in negotiations, including applicable law provisions and details on remedies, including judicial protection the provisions on which constitute the Achilles heel of the Commission proposal (which has chosen to treat its EU federal vision of the EPPO as a national body solely for the purposes of judicial control).

---

[238] See Chapter 2 of this volume.

The devil is in the detail, which will be negotiated further by the EU institutions in the coming months. However, the underlying question—and perhaps the elephant in the room—is the extent to which the fight against fraud affecting EU budget is a Union interest, separate and distinct from national interests, which merits a separate intervention from an EU body and whether such an approach can provide legal certainty in a constitutional landscape which allows the development of an EPPO à-la-carte. Once this question is answered in a clear manner, some of the details on the role and powers of the EPPO may fall into place. But in seeking to address these issues, one must not neglect to evaluate in detail the impact of the adoption of specific models of European prosecution on national legal systems and on affected individuals. In terms of national legal systems, it must be noted that the project for an EU prosecutor is not accompanied by a parallel project of separate EU rules for its functioning or EU offences for its mandate à-la-*Corpus Juris* and in a structure similar to a federal system. Rather, the EPPO will operate in national legal systems in co-existence and in accordance with national law, its mandate being defined by EU law as implemented by the Member States. The co-existence between EU and national law may have significant implications for the protection of fundamental rights, as it may create gaps in the legal protection for individuals. Issues related to the place and effective protection of fundamental rights in this new constitutional landscape tend to be lost in broader debates about subsidiarity, competence, powers and the structure and degree of centralisation of the EPPO. This has resulted thus far in drafts which give little consideration to the protection of fundamental rights which seems to come (if at all), as evidenced from the Commission's proposal on judicial review, as an afterthought. Yet it is ensuring effective protection of fundamental rights which will grant any EU project for further integration in the field of prosecution legitimacy and will address issues of lack of mutual trust between EU Member States and between Member States and the European Union and create further conditions of acceptance of the EPPO project by the European public.

5

Mutual Recognition and Mutual Trust in Europe's Area of Criminal Justice: The Centrality of Fundamental Rights

I. Introduction

Mutual recognition has been the motor of European integration in criminal matters for the past 15 years. Its application in the field of criminal law was premised upon the uncritical acceptance of presumed mutual trust between—and in—the legal systems of EU Member States. The Union legislator has established (mostly in the form of third pillar law) a comprehensive system whereby national judicial decisions in criminal matters are recognised and executed across the EU quasi-automatically, with a minimum of formality and with the aim of speedy execution. This model of mutual recognition—and its application in the sensitive sphere of criminal law—has raised fundamental questions on the relationship between national legal systems in the European Union, as well as questions on the feasibility of putting forward automaticity of mutual recognition in a system which may have significant negative consequences for the protection of the rights of affected individuals. These questions have become urgent after the entry into force of the Treaty of Lisbon and the constitutionalisation of the protection of fundamental rights, in particular by the Charter, that it entails. Conceptualising mutual trust and determining the relationship between mutual recognition and mutual trust is central to addressing these questions. This chapter will attempt to do so in four steps. First, it will examine the relationship between mutual trust and mutual recognition in European criminal law. The use of mutual trust to establish a pluralistic system of recognition will be juxtaposed with the perceived moral distance of mutual recognition based on uncritically accepted mutual trust in this context. The second step is to examine potential limits to trust, expressed as limits to automatic mutual recognition, via the introduction of express grounds of refusal to recognise and execute decisions on fundamental rights grounds. The third step will be to examine the extent to which concerns regarding mutual recognition based on the concept of presumed mutual trust can be addressed by introducing limits to recognition on the basis of the principle of proportionality. The fourth step is to examine mutual recognition and mutual trust from the perspective of the rule of law, by focusing on enhanced mechanisms of monitoring of national criminal justice systems and institutions that were introduced mainly as a follow-up to EU accession processes. The chapter will conclude by focusing on the need to move from perceived to earned trust in Europe's area of criminal justice, and highlight the centrality of ensuring the effective protection of fundamental rights as the key factor to achieve this aim.

II. Mutual Recognition as Legal Pluralism

In order to understand the relationship between mutual recognition and mutual trust in Europe's area of criminal justice it is necessary to cast light on the very design of the Area of Freedom, Security and Justice as such. While a key feature of the development of such an Area is the abolition of internal borders between Member States and the creation thus of a single European area where freedom of movement is secured, this single area of movement is not accompanied by a single area of law. The law remains territorial, with Member States retaining to a great extent their sovereignty, especially in the field of law enforcement. A key challenge for European integration in the field has thus been how to make *national* legal systems interact in the borderless Area of Freedom, Security and Justice. Member States have thus far declined unification of law in Europe's criminal justice area. The focus has largely been on the development of systems of cooperation between Member State authorities, with the aim of extending national enforcement capacity throughout the Area of Freedom, Security and Justice in order to compensate for the abolition of internal border controls. The simplification of movement that the abolition of internal border controls entails has led, under this compensatory logic, to calls for a similar simplification in inter-state cooperation via automaticity and speed. Following this logic, the construction of the Area of Freedom, Security and Justice as an area without internal frontiers intensifies and justifies automaticity in inter-state cooperation.[1] Automaticity in inter-state cooperation means that a *national* decision will be enforced beyond the territory of the issuing Member State by authorities in other EU Member States across the Area of Freedom, Security and Justice without many questions being asked and with the requested authority having at its disposal extremely limited—if any at all—grounds to refuse the request for cooperation. The method chosen to secure such automaticity has been the application of the principle of mutual recognition in the

---

[1] V Mitsilegas, 'The Limits of Mutual Trust in Europe's Area of Freedom, Security and Justice. From Automatic Inter-state Cooperation to the Slow Emergence of the Individual' 31 *Yearbook of European Law 2012* 319–72.

fields of judicial cooperation in criminal matters. Mutual recognition is attractive to Member States resisting further harmonisation or unification in European criminal law, as mutual recognition is thought to enhance inter-state cooperation in criminal matters without Member States having to change their national laws to comply with EU harmonisation requirements.[2] Mutual recognition creates extraterritoriality:[3] in a borderless Area of Freedom, Security and Justice, the will of an authority in one Member State can be enforced beyond its territorial legal borders and across this area. The acceptance of such extraterritoriality requires a high level of mutual trust between the authorities which take part in the system and is premised upon the acceptance that membership of the European Union means that all EU Member States are fully compliant with fundamental rights norms. It is the acceptance of the high level of integration among EU Member States which has justified automaticity in inter-state cooperation and has led to the adoption of a series of EU instruments which in this context go beyond preexisting, traditional forms of cooperation set out under public international law, which have previously afforded a greater degree of scrutiny of requests for cooperation. Membership of the European Union *presumes* the full respect of fundamental rights by all Member States, which creates mutual trust, which in turn forms the basis of automaticity in inter-state cooperation in Europe's area of criminal justice.

Framed in this manner, mutual recognition has emerged as the motor of European integration in criminal matters under the third pillar. The adoption in 2001 by the Council of a detailed programme of measures to implement the principle of mutual recognition of decisions in criminal matters[4] has been followed by the adoption of a wide range of Framework Decisions putting forward a comprehensive system of mutual recognition in the field of criminal justice. These Framework Decisions have been adopted essentially in three stages, one shortly post-9/11, an intermediary stage consisting of the adoption of the Framework Decision on the European Evidence Warrant (now superseded by the post-Lisbon Directive on the European Investigation Order) and another in the years leading to the adoption of the Lisbon Treaty.[5] Their ambit covers all stages of the criminal process extending from the pre-trial (recognition of Arrest Warrants,[6]

---

[2] V Mitsilegas, 'The Constitutional Implications of Mutual Recognition in Criminal Matters in the EU' (2006) 43 *Common Market Law Review* 1277–1311.

[3] K Nicolaidis and G Shaffer, 'Transnational Mutual Recognition Regimes: Governance without Global Government' (2005) 68 *Law and Contemporary Problems* 263–317; K Nicolaidis, 'Trusting the Poles? Constructing Europe through Mutual Recognition' (2007) 14 *Journal of European Public Policy* 682–98.

[4] [2001] OJ C12, 15 January 2001, p 10.

[5] V Mitsilegas, 'The Third Wave of Third Pillar Law: Which Direction for EU Criminal Justice?' (2009) 34 *European Law Review* 523–60.

[6] Framework Decision 2002/584/JHA of 13 June 2002 on the European Arrest Warrant [2002] OJ L190/1.

Evidence Warrants,[7] Freezing Orders,[8] Decisions on bail)[9] to the post-trial stage (recognition of confiscation orders,[10] of decisions on financial penalties,[11] of probation orders[12] and of decisions on the transfer of sentenced persons[13]). The system of mutual recognition was completed pre-Lisbon by a Framework Decision on judgments *in absentia*, which amended a number of the preceding Framework Decisions to specify cases when recognition of a judgment could or could not be refused in such cases.[14] The main features of the application of the principle of mutual recognition in criminal matters are automaticity, speed, and the execution of judicial decisions with a minimum of formality. Based on mutual trust, the system includes very limited grounds to refuse the recognition and execution of a judicial decision or to raise questions regarding the legal system of the Member State of the issuing authority.[15] Automaticity has presented a number of challenges, most notably with regard to the protection of the fundamental rights of affected individuals. These challenges have arisen in particular in the context of the Framework Decision on the European Arrest Warrant, which is emblematic of the application of the principle of mutual recognition in the field of criminal law. It is the first measure to be adopted in the field and the main mutual recognition measure which has been implemented fully and in detail at the time of writing. Automaticity in the operation of inter-state cooperation under the European Arrest Warrant Framework Decision has been introduced at three levels. First, cooperation must take place within a limited timeframe, under strict deadlines, and on the basis of a pro-forma document annexed to the Framework Decision—this means that in practice few questions can be asked by the executing authority beyond what has been included in the form.[16] Secondly, the executing authority is not allowed to verify the existence of dual criminality in respect of a list of 32 categories of

---

[7] Framework Decision 2008/978/JHA of 18 December 2008 on the European Evidence Warrant [2008] OJ L350/72. Post-Lisbon replaced by the Directive on the European Investigation Order—see below n 31.

[8] Framework Decision 2003/577/JHA of 22 July 2003 on the mutual recognition of orders freezing property or evidence [2003] OJ L196/45.

[9] Framework Decision 2009/829/JHA of 23 October 2009 on the application, between Member States of the European Union, of the principle of mutual recognition to decisions on supervision measures as an alternative to provisional detention [2009] OJ L294/20.

[10] Framework Decision 2006/783/JHA of 6 October 2006 on the mutual recognition of confiscation orders [2006] OJ L328/59.

[11] Framework Decision 2005/214/JHA of 24 February 2005 on the mutual recognition of judgments imposing financial penalties [2005] OJ L76/16.

[12] Framework Decision 2008/947/JHA of 27 November 2008 on the application of the principle of mutual recognition to judgments and probation decisions with a view to the supervision of probation measures and alternative sanctions [2008] OJ L337/102.

[13] Framework Decision 2008/909/JHA of 27 November 2008 on the transfer of custodial sentences (sentenced persons) [2008] OJ L327/27.

[14] Framework Decision 2009/299/JHA of 26 February 2009, [2009] OJ L81/24.

[15] V Mitsilegas, *EU Criminal Law* (Oxford, Hart Publishing, 2009) chapter 3.

[16] See Articles 15, 17 and 23 of the Framework Decision. The Court has confirmed the limited role of the executing authority in examining the content of the European Arrest Warrant in its ruling in Case C-261/09 *Gaetano Mantello* [2010] ECR I-11477.

offence listed in the Framework Decision[17]—this means that the executing state is asked to deploy its law enforcement mechanism, and to arrest and surrender an individual for conduct which is not an offence under its domestic law.[18] The third level of automaticity arises from the inclusion of limited grounds of refusal to recognise and execute a European Arrest Warrant under the Framework Decision. The Framework Decision includes only three, in their majority procedural, mandatory grounds for refusal[19] which are complemented by a series of optional grounds for refusal[20] and provisions on guarantees underpinning the surrender process.[21] Non-compliance with fundamental rights is not, however, included as a ground to refuse to execute a European Arrest Warrant.[22] This legislative choice reflects the view that cooperation can take place on the basis of a high level of mutual trust in the criminal justice systems of Member States, premised upon the presumption that fundamental rights are in principle respected fully across the European Union.

Designed in this manner, the application of the principle of mutual recognition in EU criminal law can be seen as a system of global legal pluralism. Mutual trust is used as a tool for pluralism in providing a procedural system enabling the free movement of judicial decisions across the EU via the recognition and execution of 'foreign' judgments with a minimum of formality and very limited grounds for refusal.[23] The executing authority is under a duty to enforce a 'foreign' judgment without essentially examining whether this judgment would have been issued under its own national rules. As Paul Schiff Berman has noted, enforcing a foreign judgment is viewed thus as being fundamentally different from issuing an original judgment, with judgment recognition implicating an entirely distinct set of concerns about the role of law in a multistate world.[24] In a borderless area of criminal justice, mutual trust serves to enhance co-operation and in doing so, to address justice concerns and priorities of the national legal order where the judgment to be recognised has been generated. However, this system of managed legal pluralism based on an extreme version of presumed mutual trust poses

---

[17] Article 2(2).
[18] See the Court's ruling in *Advocaten voor de Wereld* below n 35.
[19] Article 3.
[20] Article 4.
[21] Articles 5, 27 and 28.
[22] The general provision of Article 1(3) includes the general statement that 'this Framework Decision shall not have the effect of modifying the obligation to respect fundamental rights and fundamental legal principles as enshrined in Article 6 of the TEU'. References to fundamental rights are included also under a general wording in the Preamble to the Framework Decision (recital 12).
[23] Paul Schiff Berman, *Global Legal Pluralism. A Jurisprudence of Law Beyond Borders* (Cambridge, Cambridge University Press, 2012) 16. According to the author, while it does not offer substantive norms, a cosmopolitan pluralist approach may favour procedural mechanisms, institutions, and practices that provide opportunities for plural voices. Such procedures can potentially help to channel (or even tame) normative conflict to some degree by bringing multiple actors together into a shared social space.
[24] Berman, ibid, 296.

significant challenges for the perception of justice in EU Member States. Key in this context is what Roger Cotterrell has called the problem of 'moral distance', defined as the frequent remoteness or separation of law's normative expectations from many of those that are current and familiar in the fields of social interaction that it purports to regulate.[25] In a system of mutual recognition based on automaticity, the problem of moral distance may appear particularly acute in the executing Member State, where a judicial authority is required to recognise and execute a decision which is the outcome of the legal system of another Member State on the basis of almost blind trust. This 'one-size-fits-all and no questions asked' approach may appear too inflexible and lacking in democratic legitimacy, in that the substantive standards to be applied (rather than the procedure for inter-state cooperation) have not been the subject of deliberation in the executing state. It may also raise questions of compatibility of recognition with the societal and legal values of the executing state.[26] In the operation of the principle of mutual recognition in the field of EU criminal law, and in particular in the implementation of the Framework Decision on the European Arrest Warrant, a number of issues of moral distance have arisen along these lines. Key questions in this context are whether mutual trust can justify the recognition of judgments which may have a detrimental effect on the protection of the fundamental rights of the defendant, or the recognition of requests which appear disproportionate or contrary to the substantive criminal law of the executing Member State. An underlying question in this context has been whether mutual recognition on the basis of mutual trust can operate without a parallel degree of harmonisation of criminal procedural standards in Member States. All these are fundamental questions concerning not only the limits of mutual trust, but also the transformation of justice in a Union without internal frontiers.

III. Establishing Limits to Automatic Recognition: The Role of Fundamental Rights

The maximalist approach to mutual recognition adopted in the European Arrest Warrant Framework Decision led to reactions by commentators at the time who pointed out that EU Member States were not immune from convictions by the Strasbourg Court for breaches of the ECHR, and labelled the European Arrest Warrant 'a step too far too soon'.[27] Similar concerns led European and national

---

[25] R Cotterrell, *Law's Community. Legal Theory in Sociological Perspective* (Oxford, Clarendon Press, 1995) 304–5.

[26] The problems of lack of flexibility, lack of democratic legitimacy and values conflict have all been raised by Cotterrell as dimensions of moral distance—ibid, 305.

[27] S Alegre and M Leaf, 'Mutual Recognition in European Judicial Co-operation: A Step Too Far Too Soon? Case Study—The European Arrest Warrant' (2004) 10 *European Law Journal* 200–217.

legislatures to seek ways of accommodating fundamental rights considerations within the operation of the EU system of mutual recognition. There are three ways in which fundamental rights concerns have been addressed in legislation: via the use of parallel mutual recognition instruments to alleviate the adverse fundamental rights consequences of automaticity in the execution of mutual recognition requests; via the insertion of grounds of refusal on fundamental rights grounds in subsequent legislation; and via legislation addressing proportionality concerns.[28] In terms of the use of parallel mutual recognition measures, fundamental rights concerns can be addressed by the Framework Decision on the mutual recognition of bail decisions (the European Supervision Order), which would enable an individual surrendered under a European Arrest Warrant to spend the pre-trial period under bail conditions in the executing, and not the issuing, Member State.[29] In terms of the use of fundamental rights as a limit to mutual recognition, a number of Member States added non-compliance of surrender with fundamental rights as an express ground of refusal in their national law implementing the European Arrest Warrant Framework Decision.[30] Moreover, the post-Lisbon Directive on the European Investigation Order[31] expressly includes non-compliance with fundamental rights as a ground for refusal to recognise and execute a European Investigation Order.[32] Following case-law by the Strasbourg and Luxembourg Courts in the field of asylum law,[33] the Preamble to the Directive affirms that the presumption of compliance by Member States with fundamental rights is rebuttable.[34] However, as will be seen below, these legislative developments are not

---

[28] On proportionality, see more extensively section IV below.

[29] The use of the European Supervision Order as a means of addressing lengthy periods of pre-trial detention following the execution of a European Arrest Warrant was discussed and promoted in Sir Scott Baker, *A Review of the United Kingdom's Extradition Arrangements*, presented to the Home Secretary on 30 September 2011.

[30] On the implementation of the Framework Decision on the European Arrest Warrant, see Gisèle van Tiggelen, Anne Weyembergh and Laura Surano (eds), *The Future of Mutual Recognition in Criminal Matters* (Bruxelles, Éditions de l'Université de Bruxelles, 2009); and Valsamis Mitsilegas, 'The Area of Freedom, Security and Justice from Amsterdam to Lisbon: Challenges of Implementation, Constitutionality and Fundamental Rights' in Julia Laffranque (ed), *The Area of Freedom, Security and Justice, Including Information Society Issues, Reports of the XXV FIDE Congress, Tallinn 2012*, vol 3, 21–142 and national Reports included therein.

[31] Directive 2014/41/EU of the European Parliament and of the Council of 3 April 2014 regarding the European Investigation Order in criminal matters, [2014] OJ L130, 1.5.2014, p 1.

[32] Article 11—optional grounds for non-recognition or non-execution: 11(1)(f): where there are substantial grounds to believe that the execution of the investigative measure indicated in the EIO would be incompatible with the executing State's obligations in accordance with Article 6 TEU and the Charter.

[33] See section III.B below.

[34] The Preamble to the Directive, recital 19, reads as follows: 'The creation of an area of freedom, security and justice within the Union is based on mutual confidence and a presumption of compliance by other Member States with Union law and, in particular, with fundamental rights. However, that presumption is rebuttable. Consequently, if there are substantial grounds for believing that the execution of an investigative measure indicated in the European Investigation Order would result in a breach of a fundamental right of the person concerned and that the executing State would disregard its obligations concerning the protection of fundamental rights recognised in the Charter, the execution of the European Investigation Order should be refused'.

always consistent with the case-law of the Court of Justice on mutual recognition and mutual trust.

A. Fundamental Rights as Grounds for Refusal in the European Arrest Warrant Case-Law

A key step in conceptualising mutual trust in Europe's area of criminal justice is to address the extent to which the existence of such trust must be presumed automatically in the operation of the principle of mutual recognition in criminal matters. A central question in this context is whether, in a system of inter-state cooperation based on trust, executing authorities may refuse recognition on grounds of fundamental rights concerns. As seen above, the Framework Decision on the European Arrest Warrant has abolished the requirement of the verification of dual criminality for a wide range of categories of offences and has not included non-compliance with fundamental rights as an express ground of refusal to execute. The abolition of the requirement to verify dual criminality raises a key 'moral distance' question: should the executing state employ its law enforcement apparatus in cases involving conduct which is not a criminal offence under its own domestic legal system? The limits of recognition have since been tested by the Court of Justice. In its first ruling on the Framework Decision, *Advocaten voor de Wereld*—in what has in essence been a test case for the legality of the system—the Court upheld the legality of the structure of the mutual recognition system established by the Framework Decision.[35] The Court found that the abolition of the requirement to verify the existence of dual criminality is compatible with the principle of legality, as legality should be examined in accordance with the law of the *issuing* Member State which determines the definition of the offences and penalties included in Article 2(2) of the Framework Decision.[36] It is noteworthy in this context that Advocate General Jarabo-Colomer argued explicitly that 'the Framework Decision cannot be said to contravene the principle [of legality] because it does not provide for any punishments or even seek to harmonise the criminal laws of the Member States' but rather it is 'confined to creating a mechanism for assistance between the courts of different States during the course of proceedings to establish who is guilty of committing an offence or to execute a sentence'.[37] The Court added to this finding that, on the basis of Article 1(3) of the Framework Decision, the issuing state 'must respect fundamental rights and fundamental legal principles as enshrined in Article 6 EU and, consequently, the principle of the legality of criminal offences and penalties'.[38] The Court has stressed the co-operative

---

[35] Case C-303/05 *Advocaten voor de Wereld VZW v Leden van de Ministerraad* [2007] ECR I-3633.
[36] Paragraphs 52 and 53.
[37] Opinion of Advocate General Jarabo-Colomer delivered on 12 September 2006, paragraph 103.
[38] Judgment of the ECJ, 3 May 2007, paragraph 53.

structure of the mutual recognition system and the need to address the justice needs of the issuing Member State, and affirmed mutual trust by pointing out that it is for the issuing Member State to check on the compatibility of a request with fundamental rights. In this manner, the Court of Justice has moved from a narrow concept of the social contract covering the relationship between citizens and the state to a broader concept of social contract between citizens and the European Union as a whole. In an area of criminal justice without internal frontiers, co-operation must be ensured. Legality is measured in the issuing state in order to secure the delivery of justice therein.

Advocaten voor de Wereld was the first of a series of judgments where the Court of Justice has adopted a broad approach to mutual recognition, embracing a teleological interpretation and stressing the need to achieve the effectiveness of the Framework Decision by ensuring that in principle mutual recognition takes place in a speedy and simplified manner.[39] The entry into force of the Treaty of Lisbon has added a further dimension to the question of the extent to which fundamental rights concerns should be taken into account and form grounds of refusal in a system of mutual recognition based on mutual trust. The Lisbon Treaty has signified the constitutionalisation of the EU Charter of Fundamental Rights and it was only a matter of time before the Court of Justice would be asked to examine the compatibility of the system of mutual recognition with the Charter. The first major case in this context was the case of *Radu*,[40] in which the Court of Justice was asked for the first time in such a direct manner by a national court whether mutual recognition could be refused on fundamental rights grounds. In that case, the Court answered in the negative. The Court reaffirmed the adoption of a teleological interpretation, reiterating the purpose of establishing a simplified and more effective system of surrender based on mutual recognition.[41] Such a system will contribute to the Union's objective of becoming an area of freedom, security and justice by basing itself on the high degree of confidence which should exist between the Member States.[42] On the basis of this presumption of mutual trust, the Court found that the observance of Articles 47 and 48 of the Charter does not require that a judicial authority of a Member State should be able to refuse to execute a European Arrest Warrant issued for the purposes of conducting a criminal prosecution, on the ground that the requested person was not heard by the issuing judicial authorities before that warrant was issued.[43] Once again the Court placed effectiveness considerations at the forefront of its reasoning. It pointed out that such an obligation would inevitably lead to the failure of the very

---

[39] See inter alia: *Advocaten voor de Wereld*, n 35 above, paragraph 28; Case C-388/08 PPU, *Leymann and Pustovarov*, paragraph 42; Case C-192/12 PPU, *Melvin West*, paragraph 56; Case C-168/13 PPU, *Jeremy F*, paragraph 35; Case C-237/15 PPU, *Lanigan*, paragraphs 36 and 37.

[40] Case C-396/11, *Radu*, judgment of 29 January 2013.

[41] ibid, paragraphs 33 and 34.

[42] Paragraph 34.

[43] Paragraph 39.

system of surrender[44] and added that in any event, 'the right to be heard will be observed in the executing Member State *in such a way as not to compromise the effectiveness of the European arrest warrant system*' (emphasis added).[45] *Radu* thus follows the Court's earlier case-law in two respects: it confirms that it is satisfied with the provision of fundamental rights protection in one of the two states which take part in the cooperative mutual recognition system—here, it is the executing state which is under the duty to uphold the right to be heard; and it places the protection of fundamental rights within a clear framework of effectiveness of the enforcement cooperation system which is established by the Framework Decision on the European Arrest Warrant. Too extensive protection of fundamental rights (in both the issuing and the executing state) would undermine the effectiveness of law enforcement cooperation in this context.

The focus on the effective operation of mutual recognition was reiterated by the Court of Justice in the case of *Melloni*.[46] In *Melloni*, the Court effectively confirmed the primacy of third pillar law (the European Arrest Warrant Framework Decision as amended by the Framework Decision on judgments *in absentia*, interpreted in the light of the Charter) has primacy over national constitutional law providing a higher level of fundamental rights protection. In order to reach this far-reaching conclusion, the Court followed a three-step approach. The first step for the Court was to demarcate the scope of the Framework Decision on the European Arrest Warrant as amended by the Framework Decision on judgments *in absentia* (and in particular Article 4a(1) thereof) in order to establish the extent of the limits of mutual recognition in such cases. The Court reiterated its reasoning in *Radu* in adopting a teleological interpretation of the European Arrest Warrant Framework Decision and stressing that under the latter Member States are in principle obliged to act upon a European Arrest Warrant.[47] In the light of these findings, the Court adopted a literal interpretation of Article 4a(1), confirming that that provision restricts the opportunities for refusing to execute a European Arrest Warrant.[48] That interpretation is confirmed by the mutual recognition objectives of EU law.[49] The second step was to examine the compatibility of the above system with fundamental rights and in particular the right to an effective judicial remedy and the right to fair trial set out in Articles 47 and 48(2) of the Charter. By reference to the case-law of the European Court of Human Rights,[50] the Court of Justice found that the right of an accused person to appear in person at his trial is not absolute and can be waived.[51] The Court further stated that the objective of the

---

[44] Paragraph 40.
[45] Paragraph 41.
[46] Case C-399/11, *Melloni v Ministerio Fiscal*, judgment of 26.2.2013.
[47] Paragraphs 36–38.
[48] Paragraph 41.
[49] Paragraph 43.
[50] *Medenica v Switzerland*, Application no 20491/92 (ECtHR); *Sejdovic v Italy*, Application no 56581/00 (ECtHR); *Haralampiev v Bulgaria*, Application no 29648/03 (ECtHR).
[51] Paragraph 49.

Framework Decision on judgments *in absentia* was to enhance procedural rights whilst improving mutual recognition of judicial decisions between Member States[52] and found Article 4a(1) to be compatible with the Charter.

Having asserted the compatibility of the relevant provision with the Charter, the third step for the Court was to rule on the relationship between the secondary EU law in question with national constitutional law which provided a higher level of protection. The Court rejected an interpretation of Article 53 of the Charter as giving general authorisation to a Member State to apply the standard of protection of fundamental rights guaranteed by its own constitution when that standard is higher than that deriving from the Charter and, where necessary, to give it priority over the application of provisions of EU law.[53]

> That interpretation of Article 53 would undermine the principle of the primacy of EU law inasmuch as it would allow a Member State to disapply EU legal rules *which are fully in compliance with the Charter* where they infringe the fundamental rights guaranteed by that State's constitution (emphasis added).[54]

Article 53 of the Charter provides freedom to national authorities to apply national human rights standards 'provided that the level of protection provided for by the Charter, as interpreted by the Court, and the *primacy, unity and effectiveness* of EU law are not thereby compromised' (emphasis added).[55] In the present case, 'Article 4a(1) of Framework Decision 2002/584 does not allow Member States to refuse to execute a European arrest warrant when the person concerned is in one of the situations provided for therein'.[56] The Framework Decision on judgments *in absentia* 'is intended to remedy the difficulties associated with the mutual recognition of decisions rendered in the absence of the person concerned at his trial arising from the differences as among the Member States in the protection of fundamental rights' and 'reflects the consensus reached by all the Member States regarding the scope to be given under EU law to the procedural rights enjoyed by persons convicted *in absentia* who are the subject of a European arrest warrant'.[57]

> Consequently, allowing a Member State to avail itself of Article 53 of the Charter to make the surrender of a person convicted *in absentia* conditional upon the conviction being open to review in the issuing Member State … in order to avoid an adverse effect on the right to a fair trial and the rights of the defence guaranteed by the constitution of the executing Member State, by casting doubt on the uniformity of the standard of protection of fundamental rights as defined in that framework decision, *would undermine the principles of mutual trust and recognition which that decision purports to uphold and would, therefore, compromise the efficacy of that framework decision* (emphasis added).[58]

---

[52] Paragraph 51.
[53] Paragraphs 56–57.
[54] Paragraph 58.
[55] Paragraph 60.
[56] Paragraph 61.
[57] Paragraph 62.
[58] Paragraph 63.

In *Melloni*, once again the Court has given priority to the effectiveness of mutual recognition based on presumed mutual trust. Secondary pre-Lisbon third pillar law whose primary aim is to facilitate mutual recognition has primacy over national constitutional law which provides a high level of protection of fundamental rights. In reaching this conclusion, the Court has interpreted fundamental rights in a restrictive manner. It has emphasised the importance of the Framework Decision on judgments *in absentia* for the effective operation of mutual recognition, a Framework Decision which as the Court admitted restricts the opportunities for refusing to execute a European Arrest Warrant. This aim sits uneasily with the Court's assertion that the *in absentia* Framework Decision also aims to protect the procedural rights of the individual. By privileging the teleology of mutual recognition and upholding the text of the Framework Decision on judgments *in absentia* and the subsequently amended Framework Decision on the European Arrest Warrant—via the adoption also of a literal interpretation—over the protection of fundamental rights, the Court has shown a great—and arguably undue—degree of deference to the European legislator.[59] The Court's reasoning also seems to deprive national executing authorities of any discretion to examine the compatibility of the execution of a European Arrest Warrant with fundamental rights in a wide range of cases involving *in absentia* rulings.[60] This deferential approach may be explained by the fact that the Court was asked to examine the human rights implications of measures which have been subject to harmonisation at EU level, with the Court arguing that the Framework Decision reflects a consensus among EU Member States with regard to the protection of the individual in cases of *in absentia* rulings within the broader system of mutual recognition.[61] It has been argued that national constitutional standards will be more readily applicable in cases where EU law has not been harmonised.[62] The Court's ruling in the case of *Jeremy F*[63] has been cited as an example of this approach.[64] In *Jeremy F*, the

---

[59] LFM Besselink, 'The Parameters of Constitutional Conflict after Melloni' (2014) 39 *European Law Review* 531, 542; A Torres Pérez, '*Melloni* in Three Acts: From Dialogue to Monologue' (2014) 10 *European Constitutional Law Review* 308, 317–18.

[60] See also the Opinion of AG Bot, who linked national discretion to refuse surrender with the perceived danger of forum shopping by the defendant—paragraph 103.

[61] See also the Opinion of AG Bot, according to whom the Court cannot rely on the constitutional traditions common to the Member States in order to apply a higher level of protection (paragraph 84) and that the consensus between Member States leaves no room for the application of divergent national levels of protection (paragraph 126).

[62] See K Lenaerts and J Gutiérrez-Fons, 'The European Court of Justice and Fundamental Rights in the Field of Criminal Law' in V Mitsilegas, M Bergström and T Konstadinides (eds), *Research Handbook of European Criminal Law* (Cheltenham, Edward Elgar, forthcoming); B de Witte, 'Article 53' in S Peers, T Hervey, J Kenner and A Ward, *The EU Charter of Fundamental Rights. A Commentary* (Oxford, Hart Publishing, 2014); AG Bot, Opinion, paragraph 124. According to the Advocate General, it is necessary to differentiate between situations in which there is a definition at European Union level of the degree of protection which must be afforded to a fundamental right in the implementation of an action by the EU and those in which that level of protection has not been the subject of a common definition.

[63] Case C-168/13 PPU, *Jeremy F*, judgment of 30 May 2013.

[64] Lenaerts and Gutiérrez-Fons, n 62 above.

Court found that the Framework Decision on the European Arrest Warrant as amended by the Framework Decision on judgments *in absentia* did not preclude Member States from providing for appeals with suspensive effect, provided that such appeals comply with the time-limits set out in the European Arrest Warrant Framework Decision.[65] The Court noted that the absence of an express provision on the possibility of bringing an appeal with suspensive effect against a decision to execute a European Arrest Warrant does not mean that the Framework Decision prevents the Member States from providing for such an appeal or requires them to do so.[66] However, *Jeremy F* must be distinguished from *Melloni*: while *Melloni* concerned the possibility of refusing the execution of a mutual recognition request on fundamental rights grounds, *Jeremy F* did not question the essence of the mutual recognition system so fundamentally. Rather, the question in *Jeremy F* was a meta-question, concerning the specific procedural rules which apply in the process of the execution of a Warrant. Even in this case, the discretion left to Member States to protect fundamental rights is limited and circumscribed by the deadlines set out in the mutual recognition instruments aiming at achieving the desired speed linked to the perceived efficiency of the system.[67] The Court's deferential approach gives undue weight to what are essentially intergovernmental choices (the choices of Member States adopting a third pillar measure without the involvement of the European Parliament), which sit even more uneasily in the post-Lisbon, post-Charter era. The emphasis of the Court on the need to uphold the validity of harmonised EU secondary law over primary constitutional law on human rights (at both national and EU level) constitutes a grave challenge for human rights protection.[68] It further reveals, in the context of EU criminal law, a strong focus by the Court on the need to uphold the validity of a system of quasi-automatic mutual recognition in criminal matters which will enhance inter-state cooperation and law enforcement effectiveness across the EU.

B. Fundamental Rights as Limits to Automatic Recognition: Lessons from European Asylum Law

The restrictive approach of the Court of Justice with regard to the limited role fundamental rights considerations can play in limiting the automaticity of mutual

---

[65] *Jeremy F*, paragraph 74.

[66] Paragraph 38.

[67] See also the restrictive approach adopted by the Court in the more recent case of *Lanigan*, where the Court found that Article 12 of the Framework Decision read in conjunction with Article 17 thereof and in the light of Article 6 of the Charter must be interpreted as not precluding the holding of the requested person in custody even if the total duration for which that person has been held in custody exceeds the time-limits provided for in the European Arrest Warrant Framework Decision—Case C-237/15 PPU, *Lanigan*, paragraph 58.

[68] According to Besselink, attaching this importance to secondary legislation as 'harmonisation of EU fundamental rights' risks erasing the difference between the primary law nature of fundamental rights and secondary law as the subject of these rights. Besselink, n 59 above, p 542.

recognition in cases concerning the European Arrest Warrant may be tempered if the Court decides to import its own case-law and the case-law of the Strasbourg Court from the field of asylum to the field of criminal law.[69] The relevant legislation in EU asylum law is the 'Dublin system' of transfer of asylum seekers, which entails the automatic transfer of individuals between EU Member States if a series of criteria apply.[70] The very occurrence of any of these criteria sets in train a system of automatic inter-state cooperation which has been characterised as a system of negative mutual recognition.[71] Recognition can be viewed as negative in that the occurrence of one of the Dublin criteria creates a duty for one Member State to take charge of an asylum seeker and thus recognise the refusal of another Member State (which transfers the asylum seeker in question) to examine the asylum claim.[72] This system of automaticity based on the presumption of compliance by EU Member States with fundamental rights has been challenged in a series of rulings which have established a dialogue between the Strasbourg and the Luxembourg courts. The first key step in challenging automaticity and limiting mutual recognition on fundamental rights grounds was taken by the European Court of Human Rights in its *M.S.S.* ruling, where the Court found both the sending (Belgium) and the receiving (Greece) Member State implementing the Dublin Regulation to be in breach of the ECHR.[73] *M.S.S.* was followed by a landmark judgment by the Court of Justice in the joined cases of *N.S.* and *M.E.* (hereinafter *N.S.*).[74] In *N.S.*, the Court found that

> an application of [the Dublin Regulation] on the basis of the conclusive presumption that the asylum seeker's fundamental rights will be observed in the Member State primarily responsible for his application is incompatible with the duty of the Member States to interpret and apply [the Regulation] in a manner consistent with fundamental rights.[75]

Were the Regulation to require a conclusive presumption of compliance with fundamental rights, it could itself be regarded as undermining the safeguards which are intended to ensure compliance with fundamental rights by the European Union and its Member States.[76] Such presumption is rebuttable.[77] The Court's rejection of the conclusive presumption that Member States will respect the fundamental

---

[69] As seen above, such an import has occurred already by the legislator in relation to the post-Lisbon Directive on the European Investigation Order.

[70] On the Dublin system and mutual trust see V Mitsilegas, 'Solidarity and Trust in the Common European Asylum System' (2014) 2 *Comparative Migration Studies* 231–53.

[71] E Guild, 'Seeking Asylum: Storm Clouds between International Commitments and EU Legislative Measures' (2004) 29 *European Law Review* 198, at 206.

[72] Mitsilegas, n 1 above ('The Limits of Mutual Trust').

[73] European Court of Human Rights, *M.S.S. v Belgium and Greece*, judgment of 21 January 2011, Application no 30696/09. For a commentary see V Moreno-Lax, 'Dismantling the Dublin System: *M.S.S. v Belgium and Greece*' (2012) 14 *European Journal of Migration and Law* 1–31.

[74] Joined Cases C-411/10 and C-493/10, *N. S. v Secretary of State for the Home Department* and *M.E., A.S.M., M.T., K.P., E.H. v Refugee Applications Commissioner, Minister for Justice, Equality and Law Reform*, judgment of 21 December 2011 (Grand Chamber).

[75] *N.S.*, paragraph 99.

[76] Paragraph 100.

[77] Paragraph 104.

rights of asylum seekers has been accompanied, however, by the establishment of a high threshold of incompatibility with fundamental rights: a transfer under the Dublin Regulation would be incompatible with fundamental rights

> if there are *substantial grounds for believing that there are systemic flaws* in the asylum procedure and reception conditions for asylum applicants in the Member State responsible, resulting in inhuman or degrading treatment, within the meaning of Article 4 of the Charter [on the prohibition of torture and inhuman or degrading treatment or punishment], of asylum seekers transferred to the territory of that Member State (emphasis added).[78]

The Court found further that to ensure compliance by the European Union and its Member States with their obligations concerning the protection of the fundamental rights of asylum seekers,

> the Member States, including the national courts, may not transfer an asylum seeker to the 'Member State responsible' within the meaning of [the Dublin Regulation] where they *cannot be unaware* that systemic deficiencies in the asylum procedure and in the reception conditions of asylum seekers in that Member State amount to substantial grounds for believing that the asylum seeker would face *a real risk* of being subjected to inhuman or degrading treatment within the meaning of Article 4 of the Charter (emphasis added).[79]

The Court here relied heavily upon *M.S.S.* The Luxembourg Court referred to the Strasbourg Court's finding that Belgium

> had infringed Article 3 of the ECHR, first, by exposing the applicant to the risks arising from the deficiencies in the asylum procedure in Greece, since the Belgian authorities *knew or ought to have known* that he had no guarantee that his asylum application would be seriously examined by the Greek authorities and, second, by knowingly exposing him to conditions of detention and living conditions that amounted to degrading treatment (emphasis added).[80]

The Luxembourg Court extrapolated from *M.S.S.* that there existed in Greece, at the time of the transfer of the applicant, a systemic deficiency in the asylum procedure and in the reception conditions of asylum seekers.[81] The Court's ruling in *N.S.* has resulted in limiting automaticity in Dublin transfers by being incorporated in the latest instrument in the field (the so-called 'Dublin III' Regulation).[82] According to Article 3(2) of the Regulation, second and third indent,

> Where it is impossible to transfer an applicant to the Member State primarily designated as responsible because there are substantial grounds for believing that there are systemic flaws in the asylum procedure and in the reception conditions for applicants

---

[78] Paragraph 86.

[79] Paragraph 94.

[80] Paragraph 88—the Court referred to *M.S.S.*, n 73 above, paragraphs 358, 360 and 367.

[81] Paragraph 89.

[82] Regulation (EU) No 604/2013 of the European Parliament and of the Council of 26 June 2013 establishing the criteria and mechanisms for determining the Member State responsible for examining the application for international protection lodged in one of the Member States by a third-country national or a stateless person (recast), [2013] OJ L180/31, 29.6.2013.

in the Member State, resulting in a risk of inhuman or degrading treatment within the meaning of Article 4 of the Charter of Fundamental Rights of the European Union, the determining Member State shall continue to examine the criteria set out in Chapter III in order to establish whether another Member State can be designed as responsible.

Where the transfer cannot be made pursuant to this paragraph to any Member State designated on the basis of the criteria set out in Chapter III or to the first Member State with which the application was lodged, the determining Member State shall become the Member State responsible.

Notwithstanding the high threshold of systemic flaws it introduced, *N.S.* is of fundamental importance in limiting automaticity in mutual recognition by confirming that the presumption of EU Member States' compliance with fundamental rights is rebuttable and by introducing a ground of refusal to recognise and execute a judgment by another Member State on fundamental rights grounds. I have argued that the Court's approach in the field of asylum law is applicable in the field of criminal law as well, with both systems of enforced transfer of individuals operating in Europe's area of freedom, security and justice.[83] However, while the Dublin lessons have been learnt by the European legislator in the field of criminal law post-Lisbon (with the Directive on the European Investigation Order containing both a fundamental rights ground for refusal and an express confirmation of the rebuttability of the presumption of fundamental rights compliance by Member States), there has been considerable resistance by the Court of Justice to applying *N.S.* to the pre-Lisbon European Arrest Warrant Framework Decision. The chasm in the operation of mutual recognition in the fields of asylum and criminal law may deepen further following the Strasbourg Court's recent Dublin ruling in the case of *Tarakhel*,[84] where the Court stressed the obligation of states to carry out 'a *thorough and individualised examination* of the [fundamental rights] situation of the person concerned' (emphasis added).[85] In *Tarakhel*, the Court of Human Rights goes a step further than the approach of the Court of Justice in *N.S.* Rather than requiring a general finding of systemic deficiency in order to examine the compatibility of a state action with fundamental rights, the Strasbourg Court reminds us that the presumption of compliance with fundamental rights is rebuttable[86] and that effective protection of fundamental rights always requires an assessment of the impact of a decision on the rights of the specific individual

---

[83] Mitsilegas, n 1 above, ('The Limits of Mutual Trust').

[84] *Tarakhel v Switzerland*, Application no 29217/12, judgment of 4 November 2014 (ECtHR). For comments, see H Labayle, 'Droit d'Asile et Confiance Mutuelle: Regards Croisés de la Jurisprudence Européenne' (2014) 50 *Cahiers de Droit Européen* 501–34; and C Costello and M Mouzourakis, 'Reflections on Reading Tarakhel: Is "How Bad is Bad Enough" Good Enough?' in (2014) (10) *Asiel & Migrantenrecht* 404–11.

[85] *Tarakhel*, paragraph 104.

[86] Paragraph 103.

in the specific case before the Court.[87] In *Tarakhel*, this reasoning resulted in a finding of a breach of the Convention with regard to specific individuals even in a case where generalised systemic deficiencies in the receiving state had not been ascertained.[88] It is submitted that this finding is applicable not only to EU asylum, but also to EU criminal law, including the Framework Decision on the European Arrest Warrant. However, as will be seen below, the approach of the Court of Justice on the relationship between EU law and ECHR law casts serious doubts on the adoption of this view.

C. Mutual Trust and Fundamental Rights: The Impact of Opinion 2/13

The emphasis of the Court of Justice on the centrality of mutual trust as a factor privileging the achievement of law enforcement objectives via mutual recognition over the protection of fundamental rights has been reiterated beyond EU criminal law in the broader context of the accession of the European Union to the European Convention of Human Rights. The Court's Opinion 2/13[89] included a specific part dealing with mutual trust in EU law. The Court distilled its current thinking on mutual trust in the following two key paragraphs:

> it should be noted that *the principle of mutual trust between the Member States is of fundamental importance in EU law*, given that it allows an area without internal borders to be created and maintained. That principle requires, particularly with regard to the area of freedom, security and justice, each of those States, save in exceptional circumstances, *to consider all the other Member States to be complying with EU law and particularly with the fundamental rights recognised by EU law*

> Thus, when implementing EU law, the Member States may, under EU law, be required to presume that fundamental rights have been observed by the other Member States, so that not only may they not demand a higher level of national protection of fundamental rights from another Member State than that provided by EU law, but, save in exceptional cases, they may not check whether that other Member State has actually, in a specific case, observed the fundamental rights guaranteed by the EU (emphasis added).[90]

From the perspective of the relationship between EU criminal law and fundamental rights, this passage is striking. The passage follows a series of comments on the role of Article 53 of the Charter in preserving the autonomy of EU

---

[87] According to Halberstam, *Tarakhel* is a strong warning signal to Luxembourg that the CJEU's standard had better comport either in words or in practice with what Strasbourg demands or else the Dublin system violates the Convention. D Halberstam, '"It's the Autonomy, Stupid!" A Modest Defense of Opinion 2/13 on EU Accession to the ECHR, and the Way Forward', Michigan Law School, Public Law and Legal Theory Research paper Series, Paper No 432, February 2015, p 27:

[88] *Tarakhel*, paragraph 115.

[89] Opinion 2/13, delivered on 18 December 2014.

[90] Opinion 2/13, paragraphs 191–192.

law, with the Court citing the *Melloni* requirement for upholding the primacy, unity and effectiveness of EU law.[91] The Court then puts forward a rather extreme view of presumed mutual trust leading to automatic mutual recognition. It thus represents a significant challenge to our understanding of the EU constitutional order as a legal order underpinned by the protection of fundamental rights. The Court deifies mutual trust and endorses a system whereby the protection of fundamental rights must be subsumed by the abstract requirements of upholding mutual trust, instead of endorsing a model of a Union whereby cooperation on the basis of mutual trust must be underpinned by the effective protection of fundamental rights. The Court asserts boldly that mutual trust is not only a principle, but also a principle of fundamental importance in EU law. However, this assertion seems to disregard the inherently subjective nature of trust and the difficulties in providing an objective definition which meets the requirements of legal certainty. It is further clear that, although mutual trust is viewed by the Court as inextricably linked with the establishment of an area without internal borders (at the heart of which is the free movement principle and the rights of EU citizens), the Court perceives mutual trust as limited to trust 'between the Member States'—the citizen or individual affected by the exercise of state enforcement power under mutual recognition is markedly absent from the Court's reasoning. This approach leads to the uncritical acceptance of presumed trust across the European Union: not only are Member States not allowed to demand a higher national level of protection of fundamental rights than the one provided by EU law (thus echoing *Melloni*), but also, and remarkably, Member States are not allowed to check (save in exceptional circumstances) whether fundamental rights have been observed in other Member States in *specific* cases. This finding is striking as it disregards a number of developments in secondary EU criminal law aiming to grant executing authorities the opportunity to check whether execution of a judicial decision by authorities of another Member State would comply with fundamental rights. It also represents a fundamental philosophical and substantive difference in the protection of fundamental rights between the Luxembourg and Strasbourg Courts.

The Luxembourg Court's approach in Opinion 2/13 is strikingly at odds with the approach of the Strasbourg Court regarding the examination of state compliance with fundamental rights in systems of inter-state cooperation in *Tarakhel*. The willingness of the Court of Justice to sacrifice an individualised case-by-case assessment of the human rights implications of the execution of a mutual recognition order in the name of uncritical presumed mutual trust is a clear challenge for the effective protection of fundamental rights in the European Union and runs the risk of resulting in a lower level of protection of fundamental rights in systems of inter-state cooperation within the EU compared to that provided by the Strasbourg Court in ECHR cases. This difference in approaches raises the real prospect of a conflict between ECHR and EU law, especially in cases of inter-state cooperation

---

[91] Paragraph 188.

between EU Member States under the principle of mutual recognition. Eeckhout has commented that Opinion 2/13 confirms a radical pluralist conception of the relationship between EU law and the ECHR.[92] In the case of mutual recognition, this 'outward-looking', external pluralist approach, which can be seen as an attempt to preserve the autonomy of Union law, is combined with the parallel strengthening of an internal, intra-EU pluralist approach which stresses the importance of mutual trust, which is elevated by the Court to a fundamental principle of EU law. Both internal and external pluralist approaches undermine the position of the individual in Europe's area of criminal justice by limiting the judicial avenues of examination of the fundamental rights implications of quasi-automatic mutual recognition on a case-by-case basis.

IV. Proportionality as a Limit to Mutual Recognition

An issue which seems to have taken on a life of its own independently of the question of whether automaticity in mutual recognition should be limited by the requirement to examine compliance of mutual recognition with fundamental rights on a case-by-case basis, has been the issue of proportionality in the operation of mutual recognition. Proportionality concerns have been raised by governments and defendants alike and stem from the fear that mutual recognition instruments, and European Arrest Warrants in particular, will be issued for offences which are deemed to be minor or trivial in the executing state. These concerns are not alleviated by the extensive scope of the European Arrest Warrant Framework Decision[93] or by the abolition of the requirement to verify dual criminality. Calls for the introduction of a proportionality check in the operation of the principle of mutual recognition in criminal matters have been put forward in order to ensure that pressure on the criminal justice systems of executing Member States, and disproportionate results for the requested individuals, are avoided.[94] These calls are another reflection to some extent of the moral distance inherent in the system of mutual recognition: it is challenging for the authorities, the legal practitioners and the citizens of one EU Member State to accept the execution of a European Arrest Warrant for conduct which may be seen as constituting only a trivial offence or even not constituting a criminal offence at all in their domestic jurisdiction. On the other hand, demands to limit mutual recognition on proportionality grounds

---

[92] P Eeckhout, *Opinion 2/13 on EU Accession to the ECHR and Judicial Dialogue—Autonomy or Autarchy?*, Jean Monnet Working paper 01/15, p 36.

[93] See Article 2 of the EAW Framework Decision.

[94] For a discussion, see Joint Committee on Human Rights, *The Human Rights Implications of UK Extradition Policy*, Fifteenth Report, session 2010–12, pp 40–43; Sir Scott Baker, *A Review of the United Kingdom's Extradition Arrangements*, presented to the Home Secretary on 30 September 2011, paras 5.120–5.155.

may be seen as challenging demands to deliver justice, and even to uphold legality, in the issuing Member State. This debate has arisen prominently in the case of the issue of European Arrest Warrants by the Polish authorities, which has been viewed as disproportionate by a number of executing states, including in particular the United Kingdom.[95] Viewed from the perspective of the affected individual, demands for proportionality checks appear to be reasonable in ensuring checks and balances to automatic mutual recognition. However, the legal reality is much more complex. It is necessary first of all to pin down and specify which concept of proportionality is applicable to the discussion on mutual recognition in criminal matters. It is then essential to focus on determining in which way proportionality can enter the system of mutual recognition in criminal matters: by secondary law, or case-law? In the issuing state, in the executing state, or in both?

It is essential to highlight first of all that the principle of proportionality has many faces and many expressions in EU law. Post-Lisbon, it appears prominently in the Charter of Fundamental Rights in Article 49(3), as the principle of proportionality in criminal offences and penalties. According to the Charter Explanations, Article 49(3) 'states the general principle of proportionality between penalties and criminal offences which is enshrined in the common constitutional traditions of the Member States and in the case-law of the Court of Justice of the Communities'. Article 49(3) must thus be seen within the broader EU constitutional context. The Court of Justice confirmed recently its long-standing finding that the principle of proportionality is one of the general principles of European Union law and requires that measures implemented through provisions of European Union law be appropriate for attaining the legitimate objectives pursued by the legislation at issue and must not go beyond what is necessary to achieve them.[96] This is an iteration of two broad proportionality tests of suitability (focusing on the appropriateness of the chosen measures) and of necessity (focusing on their necessity).[97] The role of proportionality in limiting EU action is further confirmed in Article 5 TEU, according to which the use of Union competences is governed by the principle of proportionality.[98] Under the principle of proportionality, the content and form of Union action shall not exceed what is necessary to achieve the objectives of the Treaties.[99] This concept of proportionality is focused

---

[95] For an overview of the debate, see T Ostropolski, 'The Principle of Proportionality under the European Arrest Warrant—with an Excursus on Poland' (2014) 5 *New Journal of European Criminal Law* 167–91.

[96] Joined Cases C-539/10 P and C-550/10 P, *Al-Aqsa*. On the principle of proportionality see P Craig, *EU Administrative Law*, 2nd edn (Oxford, OUP, 2012) chapters 19 and 20, and T Tridimas, *The General Principles of EU Law*, 2nd edn (Oxford, OUP, 2006) chapters 3–5. The academic discussion has focused on whether the necessity test incorporates a third test, on *strict sensu* proportionality—even if there are no less restrictive means, it must be established that the measure does not have an excessive effect on the applicant's interests (see inter alia Tridimas, p 139).

[97] T Tridimas, *The General Principles of EU Law*, 2nd edn (Oxford, OUP, 2006) 139.

[98] Article 5(1) TEU.

[99] Article 5(4) TEU.

specifically on the control of the exercise of EU competence and serves to address concerns over the potential over-extension of the powers of the European Union. To these functions of proportionality can be added a concept of proportionality which is familiar to the evolution of the law of the ECHR, and which is focused on the protection of fundamental rights. This human rights concept of proportionality aims at minimising the limits introduced on the protection of fundamental rights, and is also reflected in the Charter. According to Article 52(1), subject to the principle of proportionality, limitations may be made only if they are necessary and genuinely meet objectives of general interest recognised by the Union or the need to protect the rights and freedoms of others. In this manner, European Union law has internalised—from a competence, good governance and human rights perspective—a principle which is common not only to the constitutional but also to the criminal justice traditions of Member States and which ultimately serves to limit state (and EU) power.[100]

The relevance of proportionality in relation to the operation of the European Arrest Warrant was raised by the European judiciary in the case of *Radu*. In her Opinion,[101] Advocate General Sharpston—while finding that the issue was not of direct relevance to the present case—highlighted the tension between Warrants issued for perceived trivial offences on the one hand and the principle of proportionality on the other:

> I would add one thing. At the hearing, counsel for Germany used the example of a stolen goose. If that Member State were asked to execute a European arrest warrant in respect of that crime where the sentence passed in the issuing Member State was one of six years, she thought that execution of the warrant would be refused. She considered that such a refusal would be justifiable on the basis of the doctrine of proportionality and referred the Court to Article 49(3) of the Charter, according to which 'the severity of penalties must not be disproportionate to the criminal offence'. This Court has yet to rule on the interpretation of that article. In the context of the Convention, the Court of Human Rights has held that while, in principle, matters of appropriate sentencing largely fall outside the scope of the Convention, a sentence which is 'grossly disproportionate' could amount to ill-treatment contrary to Article 3 but that it is only on 'rare and unique occasions' that the test will be met. It would be interesting to speculate as to the interpretation to be given to Article 49(3) of the Charter having regard to the interpretation given by the Court of Human Rights of the provisions of Article 3 of the Convention.[102]

The Court of Justice did not engage with this argument in its final ruling, which, as seen above, focused on the narrower issue of whether the execution of a European

---

[100] V Mitsilegas, 'Article 49—Principles of Legality and Proportionality of Criminal Offences and Penalties' in S Peers, T Hervey, J Kenner and A Ward (eds), *The EU Charter of Fundamental Rights. A Commentary* (Oxford, Hart Publishing/Beck, 2014) 1351–73.

[101] Opinion of Advocate General Sharpston delivered on 18 October 2012, Case C-396/11 *Radu*, n 40 above.

[102] Paragraph 103.

Arrest Warrant can be refused on the ground that the requested person had not been heard in the issuing Member State.[103]

Proportionality check requirements have, however, been introduced in policy documents and in secondary law. The need to address these proportionality concerns was acknowledged by the European Commission in its latest Report on the implementation of the Framework Decision.[104] The prevailing view has thus far been for proportionality to be dealt with in the issuing and not in the executing Member State. This is the interpretative guidance given in the revised version of the European Handbook on how to issue a European Arrest Warrant[105] and is an approach which has been endorsed by the European Parliament in its recommendations on the review of the European Arrest Warrant.[106] This approach has also been adopted by certain Member States in the implementation of European Arrest Warrant obligations.[107] The requirement to introduce a proportionality check in the issuing state has also been introduced at EU level in the Directive on the European Investigation Order, which states that the issuing authority may only issue a European Investigation Order where the issuing of the latter is necessary and proportionate and where the investigative measures indicated in the European Investigation Order could have been ordered under the same conditions in a similar domestic case.[108] The Directive thus links proportionality with the requirement to avoid abuse of law via the undertaking of 'fishing expeditions' by the authorities of the issuing state.

A step further with regard to the treatment of proportionality as a limit to mutual recognition has been taken in the United Kingdom, which in its latest version of the European Arrest Warrant implementing legislation (the Extradition Act 2003) has treated non-compliance with proportionality as a ground of

[103] See Case C-396/11, *Radu*, judgment of 29 January 2013.
[104] *Report from the Commission to the European Parliament and the Council on the implementation since 2007 of the Council Framework Decision of 13 June 2002 on the European Arrest Warrant and the surrender procedures between Member States* COM(2011) 175 final, Brussels, 11.4.2011, p 8.
[105] Council doc 17195/1/10 REV 1, Brussels, 17.12.2010. According to the Handbook, 'It is clear that the Framework Decision on the EAW does not include any obligation for an issuing Member State to conduct a proportionality check and that the legislation of the Member States plays a key role in that respect. Notwithstanding that, considering the severe consequences of the execution of an EAW with regard to restrictions on physical freedom and the free movement of the requested person, the competent authorities should, before deciding to issue a warrant consider proportionality by assessing a number of important factors. In particular these will include an assessment of the seriousness of the offence, the possibility of the suspect being detained, and the likely penalty imposed if the person sought is found guilty of the alleged offence. Other factors also include the effective protection of the public and taking into account the interests of the victims of the offence'.—p 14.
[106] European Parliament Resolution of 27 February 2014 with recommendations to the Commission on the review of the European Arrest Warrant, P7_TA-PROV (2014)0174.
[107] A number of changes to the Polish Code of Criminal Procedure come into force on 1 July 2015. These include an amendment to Article 607b, which now states that an arrest warrant will not be issued if it is not required by the interest of the administration of justice. The reference to the interest of the administration of justice can be seen as amounting to an implicit proportionality test. I am grateful to Celina Nowak for providing me the relevant information on Polish law.
[108] Article 6(1)(a) and (b) respectively.

refusal to execute a Warrant (and not merely as a requirement to be checked in the issuing state).[109] The amended provisions provide for an exhaustive list of matters to be taken into account by the judge when ruling on proportionality[110] and thus far English judges have interpreted these matters restrictively.[111] This restrictive approach notwithstanding, the amendment of the Extradition Act 2003 to expressly include breach of proportionality as a ground of refusal to execute a European Arrest Warrant poses a significant challenge to the system of mutual recognition based on mutual trust, as it effectively adds a new—and potentially far-reaching—ground of refusal to the European Arrest Warrant system. The approach in the Extradition Act diverges from current EU policy and legislative practice, as well as from the view of the UK Supreme Court,[112] of leaving proportionality to be checked by the issuing Member State and thus places further limits on mutual trust across EU Member States.

It appears thus that two *loci* of proportionality check have emerged, in the issuing and in the executing Member State. Proportionality checks seem to arise at two levels: proportionality in relation to the severity of the measures used; and proportionality in relation to the severity of the conduct for which a judgment has been issued. It remains to be seen how the European judiciary will deal with these approaches, and in particular with the approach taken in the Extradition Act should the proportionality approach endorsed therein be litigated. It is one thing for the executing authority to take into account proportionality considerations within its broader assessment of compliance of the execution with fundamental rights (which seems unavoidable if fundamental rights scrutiny is effective) and another to use proportionality to question surrender on the basis of the perceived triviality of conduct constituting an offence, which would seem to question the lawful (under EU law) power of the issuing authority to issue a judgment for conduct falling within the scope of the EU mutual recognition instruments. The added value of the proportionality test based on the severity of the alleged conduct remains also to be seen if the scope of the mutual recognition instruments—and the European Arrest Warrant Framework Decision in particular—is not limited to include fewer, only serious offences.

---

[109] Section 157 of the Anti-Social Behaviour, Crime and Policing Act 2014 has amended Section 21A of the Extradition Act 2003 to treat lack of proportionality as a ground for refusal (section 21A(1)(b)). See also the ruling of the Higher Regional Court of Stuttgart of 25 February 2010, reported by Joachim Vogel in (2010) 1 *New Journal of European Criminal Law* 145–52; see also the report and commentary to the ruling by Joachim Vogel and John Spencer in [2010] *Criminal Law Review* 474–82.

[110] Section 21A(2). These matters are: the seriousness of the conduct alleged to constitute the extradition offence; the likely penalty that would be imposed if the individual was found guilty of the extradition offence; and the possibility of the relevant foreign authorities taking measures that would be less coercive than the extradition sought—section 21(A)(3).

[111] See *Miraszewski v Poland* [2014] EWCH 4261 (Admin); *Celinski v Poland* [2015] EWHC 1274 (Admin).

[112] See the *Assange* ruling of the UK Supreme Court, [2012] UKSC 22, Lord Phillips in paragraph 90.

V. Mutual Recognition, Mutual Trust and the Rule of Law

The question of the limits of mutual trust in the context of the operation of the principle of mutual recognition in criminal matters has arisen prominently in the context of the eastward enlargement of the European Union. Accession negotiations were marked by concerns in EU Member States that the institutional and judicial capacity in candidate countries was not of a sufficient quality to inspire a high level of trust with regard to the operation of mutual recognition upon accession.[113] In this manner, questions related to the limits of mutual trust arising from concerns regarding the protection of fundamental rights across the EU have morphed essentially into rule of law questions: it is not enough to examine whether all EU Member States respect fundamental rights in individual cases; rather, it is also essential to ascertain that fundamental rule of law safeguards are applicable in practice, including the existence of an effective anti-corruption framework and of institutional independence, including the independence of the judiciary. It is the judiciary, after all, which is called to apply the principle of mutual recognition in the field of criminal law.

Fundamental rights and rule of law concerns led to the introduction, in the Act of Accession accompanying the 2004 'big bang' enlargement, of a 'safeguard clause' intended to address potential shortcomings in the implementation by new Member States of EU instruments relating to mutual recognition in criminal matters. According to the safeguard clause, in case of serious shortcomings or imminent risks thereof in the field, the Commission had the power to adopt, after consulting the Member States, safeguard measures including the temporary suspension of the provisions on judicial co-operation in criminal matters.[114] The safeguard clause could be invoked for three years after accession but was not ultimately used. A similar safeguard clause has been included in the Treaty accompanying the recent accession of Croatia to the European Union according to which 'the Commission may, until the end of a period of up to three years after accession, upon the reasoned request of a Member State or on its own initiative and after consulting the Member States, adopt appropriate measures' which may take the form of a temporary suspension of the application of relevant provisions and decisions in the relations between Croatia and any other Member State or Member

---

[113] See inter alia: V Mitsilegas, J Monar and W Rees, *The European Union and Internal Security: Guardian of the People?* (Basingstoke, Palgrave/Macmillan, 2003); and N Walker, 'The Problem of Trust in an Enlarged Area of Freedom, Security and Justice: A Conceptual Analysis' in M Anderson and J Apap (eds), *Police and Justice Co-operation and the New European Borders* (The Hague, Kluwer Law International, 2002) 19–34.

[114] Article 39 of the Accession Act. See C Hillion, 'The European Union is Dead. Long Live the European Union … A Commentary on the Treaty of Accession 2003' (2004) 29 *EL Rev* 583–612.

States.[115] While the Commission has threatened to use Article 39, changes in domestic Croatian law in relation to the European Arrest Warrant have resulted in the option of invoking the safeguard clause being withdrawn.[116]

A more intensive form of post-accession monitoring was introduced by the Treaty accompanying the accession of Bulgaria and Romania to the European Union in 2007. The introduction of this mechanism was linked with concerns regarding the capacity of the two countries to comply with the EU *acquis* pre-accession, with gaps in Bulgaria and Romania's institutional capacity raising broader questions regarding the feasibility of the 2007 accession date for both countries.[117] Approaching the accession date, the Commission published a critical monitoring Report, where it pointed out remaining gaps regarding progress in the two countries' justice systems and the fight against corruption, with Bulgaria also being singled out for gaps in the field of measures against organised crime and money laundering.[118] The Commission recommended—along with the introduction of a safeguard clause allowing the unilateral suspension of Member States' obligations with regard to judicial co-operation in civil and criminal matters vis-à-vis Bulgaria and Romania—the introduction, additionally, of a mechanism verifying progress by the newcomers after accession. The Commission's recommendations were taken up by Member States, with the Act of Accession including a safeguard clause in criminal matters similar to the one used in 2004,[119] and the Commission adopting two 'Decisions establishing a mechanism for co-operation and verification of progress' to address specific benchmarks in the areas of judicial reform and the fight against corruption and (specifically for Bulgaria) organised crime.[120] The benchmarks included are not limited to the mere implementation of the EU *acquis* in the field of criminal law but extend to broader and fundamental rule of law questions. Romania is asked to ensure a 'more transparent and efficient judicial process', and to combat corruption by establishing an integrity agency, conducting 'professional, non-partisan investigations' into allegations of high-level corruption, and taking 'further measures' to prevent and fight corruption in particular within the local government. The instrument on Bulgaria includes two further benchmarks aiming to ensure the independence of the judiciary and the implementation of a strategy to fight organised crime, focusing on serious crime, money laundering and confiscation.

---

[115] Article 39. See A Lazowski, 'EU Criminal Law and Enlargement' in V Mitsilegas, M Bergström and T Konstadinides (eds), *Research Handbook on European Criminal Law* (Cheltenham, Edward Elgar, forthcoming).

[116] Commission takes action to ensure Croatia correctly implements the European Arrest Warrant, European Commission Memo, Brussels, 18 September 2013.

[117] For a background, see A Lazowski, 'And Then They Were Twenty-Seven … A Legal Appraisal of the Sixth Accession Treaty' (2007) 44 *Common Market Law Review* 401–30.

[118] European Commission, *Monitoring Report on the state of preparedness for EU membership of Bulgaria and Romania*, COM(2006) 549 final, Brussels 26 September 2006, pp 4–5.

[119] Articles 37 and 38.

[120] [2006] OJ L354, 14 December 2006, p 56 and p 58 respectively.

The monitoring mechanism established is extensive and ongoing. Bulgaria and Romania are required to report once a year to the Commission on progress made in addressing each of these benchmarks.[121] The Commission may gather and exchange information on the benchmarks and organise expert missions for that purpose.[122] The benchmarks may be adjusted in the future by amending the two Decisions.[123] If Bulgaria and Romania fail to address the benchmarks adequately the Commission may apply safeguard measures based on Articles 37 and 38 of the Accession Act, including the suspension of Member States' obligations to recognise and execute, under the conditions laid down in Community law, judicial decisions from the two countries 'such as European arrest warrants'.[124] However, the progress verification Decisions do not preclude the adoption of safeguard measures at any time, if the conditions for such measures are fulfilled.[125] What is particularly noteworthy is that, in contrast to the 2004 Accession Treaty and the Treaty on the Accession of Croatia, there is no deadline set out for the expiry of the post-accession monitoring mechanism for Bulgaria and Romania.[126] The monitoring mechanism is still in place at the time of writing, eight years after accession. The continuation of the monitoring mechanism can be explained on the grounds of the persistence of mistrust from EU institutions and Member States towards the authorities in Bulgaria and Romania, in particular regarding matters of institutional capacity.[127] The need for enhancing institutional capacity and to focus on implementation was also highlighted by the Council of the European Union five years after the introduction of the Cooperation and Verification Mechanism[128] when the continuation of the Cooperation and Verification Mechanism was agreed.[129] The Commission has continued to monitor and report on progress, and

---

[121] Article 1 first indent of both Decisions.

[122] Article 1 second indent of both Decisions.

[123] Preamble, recital 9 in both Decisions.

[124] Preamble, recital 7 in both Decisions.

[125] Preamble, recital 8 in both Decisions.

[126] On this point see also Lazowski, 'EU Criminal Law and Enlargement', n 115 above.

[127] Such mistrust is evident in the words of the former enlargement Commissioner, Mr Füle, according to whom 'the last enlargement of Romania and Bulgaria brought a lot of questions about the credibility of the whole process. Because it was the first time that the EU decided to establish a special cooperation and verification mechanism on existing member states. The biggest challenge was to return the lost credibility to the enlargement process. It forces us to expand and tighten benchmarks. Candidate states should prove that the adopted legislation is working'.—'Füle: Bulgaria and Romania's accession questioned the credibility of EU enlargement', *EurActiv*, 26 June 2014.

[128] 'The existence of an impartial, independent and effective administrative and judicial system, with sufficient resources, is indispensable for EU policies to function properly and for citizens to benefit fully from all the opportunities offered by membership of the Union'—Council Conclusions on Cooperation and Verification Mechanism for Bulgaria and Romania, 3187th General Affairs Council meeting, Brussels, 24 September 2012.

[129] According to the Commission, the Co-operation and Verification Mechanism should continue, in order to lend its support to these efforts and to keep up the momentum of change towards a sustainable and irreversible reform process—a process sufficiently strong that the external intervention of the CVM is no longer needed: European Commission, *Report from the Commission to the European Parliament and the Council. On Progress in Bulgaria under the Co-operation and Verification Mechanism*, COM(2012) 411 final, Brussels, 18.7.2012, p 20.

still in recent Reports has found such progress insufficient, in particular in relation to Bulgaria.[130] The assessment of Romania has been more positive, but even there the Commission has called for the need to consolidate and systematise progress.[131]

While these less than enthusiastic assessments may cause concern with regard to the operation of mutual recognition across the European Union, they also render the need for the impact of a decision to execute a judicial decision on the fundamental rights of the affected individuals to be assessed on a case-by-case basis even more pressing. The ex post, ongoing monitoring of only selected Member States raises indeed issues of inter-state equality in the European Union,[132] may disregard positive developments arising in monitored states,[133] and may serve to deflect attention from fundamental rights and rule of law shortcomings in other EU Member States. However, the Cooperation and Verification Mechanism also serves to highlight the importance of compliance with the rule of law in order to ensure the effective operation of the principle of mutual recognition in criminal matters. What is assessed essentially here is compliance with the Copenhagen criteria. There can be no mutual recognition and no mutual trust without an independent judiciary. The emphasis of ex post monitoring on institutional capacity bodes well, together with the Commission's renewed emphasis on upholding the rule of law across the European Union.[134] As said above, it is not enough to assess narrowly the implementation by Member States of specific provisions of secondary EU law: an assessment of the effective implementation of the European Arrest Warrant Framework Decision is inextricably linked with an evaluation of detention conditions and the duration of judicial proceedings in Member States. In areas such as EU criminal law, where implementation involves serious fundamental rights challenges, a broader examination of Member States' criminal justice systems is thus essential. The evaluation of Member States' implementation under these mechanisms must further address broader institutional and rule of law questions. The requirement for an independent judicial authority will not be met if rule of law scrutiny is deficient; respect for defence rights will be challenged when the

[130] European Commission, *Report from the Commission to the European Parliament and the Council. On Progress in Bulgaria under the Co-operation and Verification Mechanism*, COM(2014) 36 final, Brussels, 22.1.2014, p 9; European Commission, *Report on Progress in Bulgaria under the Co-operation and Verification Mechanism*, COM(2015) 36 final, Brussels, 28.1.2015, pp 9–12.

[131] European Commission, *Report on Progress in Romania under the Co-operation and Verification Mechanism*, COM(2015) 35 final, Brussels, 28.1.2015, p 12.

[132] A von Bogdandy and M Ioannidis, 'Systemic Deficiency in the Rule of Law: What it is, what has been done, what can be done' (2014) 51 *Common Market Law Review* 59–96, 87.

[133] See for example the important preliminary reference for the interpretation of the European Arrest Warrant in the case of *Radu*, n 40 above. *Radu* follows the tradition of the judiciary in post-2004 EU Member States which has engaged constructively with the Court of Justice in the development of the interpretation of the European Arrest Warrant and the relationship between national (including constitutional) and EU law—for details see V Mitsilegas, *EU Criminal Law* (Oxford, Hart Publishing, 2009) chapter 3.

[134] European Commission, *Communication from the Commission to the European Parliament and the Council. A New EU Framework to strengthen the Rule of Law*, COM(2014) 158 final, Brussels, 11.3.2014.

institutional independence and stability of the judiciary is at stake; and it is naïve to expect the respect of the proportionality principle by national judiciaries which do not meet appropriate independence standards. Upholding the rule of law is in effect a key tool towards safeguarding fundamental rights across Europe's area of criminal justice. Both the normalised post-Lisbon powers of the Commission as a 'guardian of the Treaties' in EU criminal law and the new evaluation mechanism provided for in Article 70 TFEU provide avenues of enhanced scrutiny of Member States' compliance with the rule of law in this context.

VI. Conclusion: From Presumed to Earned Trust in Europe's Area of Criminal Justice

The application of mutual recognition in the field of European criminal law was originally based on a maximalist concept of mutual trust between national criminal justice systems. The existence of trust was presumed, unquestioned, taken for granted. EU mutual recognition measures have been designed to achieve quasi-automaticity in law enforcement cooperation across the European Union, with little space left for the examination of the consequences of recognition and execution for the affected individuals. Mutual trust meant that the system of interstate cooperation—not accompanied by any degree of harmonisation of criminal procedural law—was not questioned. However, the transnational character of cooperation has generated a number of questions related to the moral distance of mutual recognition from the affected individuals and communities—questions which have become more acute due to the significantly adverse fundamental rights consequences of a system of recognition privileging enforcement. One way to address these concerns is to set limits to the automaticity of recognition by allowing executing authorities to proceed to a substantive examination, on a case-by-case basis, of the fundamental rights impact of recognition and execution on the affected individuals. This is a line of reasoning promoted by the European Court of Human Rights in its case-law on the parallel system of mutual recognition in the field of asylum law, but it is a line currently vehemently resisted by the Court of Justice, which has elevated the inherently subjective concept of mutual trust into a fundamental principle of EU law in Opinion 2/13. This deification of mutual trust (without attempting to define it any further) poses, however, significant challenges on the effective protection of fundamental rights, which seems to be subordinated to the requirement to respect presumed and uncritically accepted trust. The approach of the Court of Justice seems increasingly at odds not only with the approach of the Strasbourg Court, but also with the way in which both the EU legislator and national legislators have attempted to place fundamental rights limits on the automaticity of mutual recognition in criminal matters. The approach taken in the post-Lisbon adoption of the Directive on the European

Investigation Order (which has introduced a fundamental rights ground for refusal, a proportionality check in the issuing Member State, and an express reference to the fact that the presumption of compliance by other Member States with fundamental rights is rebuttable) is an important step in addressing the need to ensure effective protection of fundamental rights in the system of mutual recognition, and must be applicable across the board to the pre-Lisbon, third pillar mutual recognition instruments, including the Framework Decision on the European Arrest Warrant. The requirement to examine the impact of mutual recognition on the affected individual on a case-by-case basis and refuse recognition when fundamental rights will be breached must be accompanied by positive duties on Member States to ensure effective respect for fundamental rights. The emphasis of the post-accession monitoring mechanisms on ongoing monitoring not only of the implementation of mutual recognition instruments, but of national institutional capacity and criminal justice systems from a broader rule of law perspective is a key way forward in this regard. Another key step in this direction, which will be examined in the following chapter, is accompanying mutual recognition by the harmonisation of national criminal procedural law, in particular by the adoption of EU measures related to the rights of the individual in criminal procedure. As will be seen in the following chapter, legislating for human rights in this manner can have a transformative effect for the protection of fundamental rights and can contribute decisively to the shift from presumed to earned trust in Europe's area of criminal justice.

6

Legislating for Human Rights:
The EU Legal Framework
on the Rights of Individuals
in Criminal Proceedings

I. Introduction

The entry into force of the Lisbon Treaty has enabled an unprecedented development in European Union criminal law: the adoption by the EU legislator of secondary legislation on human rights applicable in Europe's area of criminal justice. The legislation in question consists of a series of Directives introducing minimum standards on the rights of the individual in criminal proceedings. Legislating for human rights at EU level in this context has been made a reality following the inclusion in the Lisbon Treaty of an express legal basis—Article 82(2) TFEU—conferring on the Union express competence to adopt minimum standards on criminal procedure. This chapter will provide an analysis of the evolution and content of the EU legal framework on the rights of the defendant by beginning with an overview of the constitutional background underpinning substantive legislative developments in the field: an analysis of the pre-Lisbon difficulties in legislating on the rights of the defendant will be accompanied by an overview of the post-Lisbon possibilities to legislate in the light of the express legal basis provided in the TFEU. This analysis of the constitutional framework will be followed by an overview of the content of the substantive European Union law on the rights of the individual in criminal proceedings, by focusing on the Directives which have already been adopted at EU level at the time of writing (namely the Directives on the right to translation and interpretation, on the right to information, and on the right to access to a lawyer in criminal proceedings). The chapter will then assess the impact of EU law on procedural rights on the protection of fundamental rights in Europe's area of criminal justice (by focusing in particular on the strengthened enforcement avenues that the adoption of post-Lisbon secondary law in the field provides), but will also assess more broadly the impact of EU law on national legal systems, and in particular national legal diversity. The implications of the application of variable geometry for the protection of fundamental rights and the operation of EU criminal law (and in particular the principle of mutual recognition in criminal matters) will also be assessed, in the light of the United Kingdom's opting not to participate in the Directive on the right to access to a lawyer, which constitutes arguably the cornerstone of EU secondary law in the field of defence rights. The chapter will conclude with an analysis of the potential of EU defence rights law to transform justice in the development of European Union criminal law.

II. The Rocky Road Towards EU Law on the Rights of the Defendant Before Lisbon

Calls for the adoption of legislation on the rights of the defendant in criminal proceedings at European Union level emerged following the policy and legislative choice by EU institutions—and EU Member States in particular—to push forward with the application of the principle of mutual recognition in the field of criminal law, as the main motor of European integration in criminal matters post-Amsterdam and Tampere. Calls for EU action in the field of the rights of the defendant arose most prominently following the adoption in 2002 of the EU emblematic mutual recognition measure in the field of European criminal law, the Framework Decision on the European Arrest Warrant.[1] The operation of the European Arrest Warrant system—based on automaticity, speed and a minimum of formality—has caused grave concerns with regard to the impact of judicial co-operation under this system on the rights of affected individuals, in particular in view of the fact that non-compliance with fundamental rights has not been included as one of the grounds for refusal to recognise and execute a European Arrest Warrant under the Framework Decision.[2] In view of these challenges, the Commission started work on proposals for EU third pillar law on the rights of the defendant already in 2002, with its consultation continuing to mid-2003.[3] The Commission eventually tabled at the end of April 2004 a draft Framework Decision 'on certain procedural rights in criminal proceedings throughout the European Union'.[4] The proposal aimed at minimum standards and contains provisions on the right to legal advice, the right to translation and interpretation, the right to communication and specific attention and the duty to inform a suspect of his rights in writing through a common EU 'Letter of Rights'.

Although modest in its scope and aiming at establishing minimum EU standards, the Commission's proposal has proven to be controversial with Member States. A number of Member States fear that the proposal has potentially

---

[1] Framework Decision of 13 June 2002 on the European arrest warrant and the surrender procedures between Member States, 2002/584/JHA, [2002] OJ L190, 18.7.2002.

[2] V Mitsilegas, *EU Criminal Law* (Oxford, Hart Publishing, 2009) chapter 3.

[3] See C Morgan, 'Proposal for a Framework Decision on procedural safeguards for suspects and defendants in criminal proceedings throughout the European Union' (2003) 4 *ERA-Forum* 91.

[4] COM(2004) 328 final.

far-reaching implications for the integrity of their domestic criminal justice systems. This was also linked with a reluctance by certain Member States to accept that the European Union has competence in this matter and to bring issues of procedural rights within the framework of Union law. In negotiations, Member States voiced concerns regarding both the existence and extent of EU competence in the field, and the content of each individual article.[5] Member States' concerns, combined with decision-making by unanimity under the third pillar, resulted in considerable delay in negotiations. Although the adoption of the proposal was a priority under the Hague Programme, negotiations nearly stalled during the UK Presidency of the European Union in the second half of 2005. Inactivity led the Austrian Presidency of the European Union to relaunch a consultation with Member States, addressing fundamental issues such as the scope of the proposal, its relationship with the ECHR and the contested issue of the legal basis.[6] Efforts resulted in the inclusion of a statement on the necessity of measures on defence rights in the Hague Programme but not in an agreement on a legal text. A new legislative proposal was then tabled by the German Presidency of the Council of the European Union in 2007.[7] The proposal followed attempts by the Austrian Council Presidency to reach agreement, which were, however, undermined by the tabling of a parallel text for a non-binding Resolution by the United Kingdom, the Czech Republic, Ireland, Malta, Cyprus and Slovakia.[8] The German Presidency devoted a number of Council Working Group meetings to the proposal, and attempted to make it as consistent as possible with the European Convention on Human Rights, asking in this process the opinion of the Council of Europe.[9] With the German Presidency aiming to reach agreement on the proposal, its text has been watered down (in particular the 'Letter of Rights' provisions were dropped) and concessions appeared to have been made to Member States wishing to exclude from the scope of the measure proceedings against suspected terrorists.[10] However, agreement on the proposal has not proven to be possible.

The failure to reach agreement on EU legislation on the rights of the defendant under the third pillar is due to three interrelated concerns put forward by a

---

[5] See Council doc 12353/05.

[6] Council document 7527/06, Brussels, 27 March 2006.

[7] For an analysis of this draft and a comparison with the earlier Commission proposals see M Jimeno-Bulnes, 'The Proposal for a Council Framework Decision on Certain Procedural Rights in Criminal Proceedings throughout the European Union' in E Guild and F Geyer (eds), *Security versus Justice? Police and Judicial Cooperation in the European Union* (Aldershot, Ashgate, 2008) 171–202.

[8] See House of Lords European Union Committee, *Breaking the Deadlock: What Future for EU Procedural Rights?*, 2nd Report, session 2006–07, HL Paper 20. See also Council document 7349/07, Brussels, 13 March 2007.

[9] For background, see Council doc. 10287/07, Brussels, 5 June 2007. For the Council of Europe comments see Council document 5431/07, Brussels, 18 January 2007.

[10] See Preamble, indent 5, of doc 10287/07, stating: 'Without prejudice to Article 7 [a non-regression clause] the provisions of the Framework Decision are not intended to affect special measures based on national legal provisions to combat crime which is aimed at destroying the foundations of the rule of law. Prosecution of these serious and complex forms of crime, in particular terrorism, may justify restrictions on procedural standards, provided that such restrictions are strictly necessary and proportionate and that the procedural rights are not drained of their substance'.

number of Member States during negotiations: concerns over the existence and extent of EU competence to legislate in the field; concerns over the impact of EU legislation on the rights of the defendant on the diversity and the special characteristics of domestic criminal justice systems; and (not always voiced expressly but underlying legal diversity concerns), concerns over the impact of EU legislation on Member States' choices towards national law privileging security over the protection of human rights. With regard to competence, the proposed legal basis of the Commission's proposal was Article 31(c) TEU, which enabled common action to be taken on judicial cooperation in criminal matters 'ensuring compatibility in rules applicable in the Member States, as may be necessary to improve such cooperation'. The Commission defended this choice by stating that the proposal constitutes the 'necessary complement' to the mutual recognition measures that are designed to increase efficiency of prosecution.[11] However, it has been argued by Member States that the EU Treaty did not contain an express legal basis conferring upon the European Union powers to legislate in the field.[12] Negotiations have also been fraught with difficulties to reach a unanimous understanding of key criminal justice concepts which would underpin EU law on the rights of the defendant, including the concept of 'criminal proceedings'[13] and concepts such as individuals 'arrested' and 'charged' with a criminal offence.[14] Agreement at EU level of such concepts which would not be entirely consistent with domestic criminal law definitions was deemed by Member States to be an undue challenge to the diversity of their national criminal justice systems and (implicitly) also, for some, to their internal policy and the legal balance between the pursuit of security and the protection of fundamental rights.[15] As will be seen below, these concerns were also prevalent in the negotiation of EU defence rights law after Lisbon.

III. The Lisbon Breakthrough—The Attribution of an Express (Albeit Functional) Competence to the European Union to Legislate on the Rights of the Individual in Criminal Procedure

The entry into force of the Lisbon Treaty has tackled head on doubts about the existence of EU competence to adopt legislation on the rights of individuals in

---

[11] Commission n 4 above (COM(2004) 328 final), para 51.

[12] For details, see V Mitsilegas, 'Trust-building Measures in the European Judicial Area in Criminal Matters: Issues of Competence, Legitimacy and Inter-institutional Balance' in S Carrera and T Balzacq, *Security versus Freedom? A Challenge for Europe's Future* (Aldershot/Burlington VT, Ashgate, 2006) 279–89.

[13] The general definition used in Article 1 of doc 10287/07 was 'any proceedings which could lead to a criminal penalty ordered by a criminal court' (Article 1(1)).

[14] Article 1(2) states that these terms will be interpreted in accordance with the Strasbourg case-law.

[15] See the exceptions to the scope of the proposed Framework Decision in Article 1(5) of doc 10287/07.

criminal procedure. Article 82(2)(b) TFEU confers upon the European Union competence to adopt minimum rules on the rights of individuals in criminal procedure. EU competence in the field is not self-standing, but functional: competence to adopt rules on procedural rights has been conferred on the EU only to the extent necessary to facilitate mutual recognition (which, under Article 82(1) TFEU, is the basis of judicial cooperation in criminal matters) and police and judicial cooperation in criminal matters having a cross-border dimension. EU competence to legislate on the rights of the defence is thus conditional upon the need to demonstrate that defence rights are necessary for mutual recognition. In a strategy similar to the one followed in the pre-Lisbon Framework Decision, the ensuing Directives on procedural rights adopted post-Lisbon have been justified by linking the adoption of EU measures in the field with the enhancement of mutual trust. The Preamble to the Directive on the right to interpretation and translation states that

> mutual recognition of decisions in criminal matters can operate effectively in a spirit of trust in which not only judicial authorities but all actors in the criminal process consider decisions of the judicial authorities of other Member States as *equivalent* to their own, implying not only trust in the *adequacy* of other Member States' rules, but also trust that those rules are correctly *applied* (emphasis added).[16]

The same wording is used in the Preamble to the Directive on the right to information,[17] and the right to access to a lawyer.[18] In this manner, it can be argued that the European legislator attempts to address the consequences of the perceived moral distance inherent in mutual recognition via the harmonisation of criminal procedural law.[19] The emphasis on the need to ensure effective application of human rights rules in Member States is welcome. However, the use of mutual trust as an element justifying the adoption of EU measures in the field is problematic in two respects: it fails to provide a direct and clear link between the defence rights proposed and their necessity for the operation of mutual recognition; and it is based on a concept (of mutual trust) which is too subjective for it to meet the criteria set out by the Court of Justice when ascertaining the legality of EU instruments, namely that the choice of legal basis must be based on objective factors which are amenable to judicial review, including the aim and the content of the measure.[20]

[16] Recital 4 (n 35 below).
[17] Recital 4 (n 36 below).
[18] Preamble, recital 6 (n 37 below). while earlier drafts of the Directive on access to a lawyer expanded the link between defence rights and trust by stating that common minimum rules 'should increase confidence in the criminal justice systems of all Member States, which in turn should lead to more efficient judicial cooperation in a climate of mutual trust *and to the promotion of a fundamental rights culture in the Union*' COM Recital 3, (emphasis added). COM(2011) 326 final, Brussels, 8.6.2011. Council document 10467/12, Brussels, 31 May 2012.
[19] On the concept of moral distance and its applicability in the field of mutual recognition see chapter 5.
[20] See recently Case C-540/13 *European Parliament v Council*, judgment of 16 April 2015, EU: C: 2015:224, para 30; and Joined Cases C-317/13 and C-679/13 *European Parliament v Council*, judgment of 16 April 2015, EU:C:2015:223, para 40.

The concept of trust is subjective and not objective. An alternative way forward could be to justify EU defence rights measures as necessary to address the *effects* of the operation of automatic inter-state cooperation, as expressed by mutual recognition, on the individual. The aim and content of the measures in question are the strengthening of the protection of procedural rights. The necessity requirement of Article 82(2) TFEU would thus be viewed from the perspective of the individual and not of the state or of the authorities which are called upon to apply inter-state cooperation.[21] In any case, the functional framing of EU competence in the field of procedural rights effectively embeds procedural rights within Europe's area of criminal justice, by making the effective operation of mutual recognition conditional to a degree of harmonisation of procedural rights at European Union level. In this manner, procedural rights assume a central role in an increasingly integrated area of criminal justice. As will be seen below, this legal basis has been used to establish, via EU secondary law, human rights standards applicable across the board, embracing not only cross-border cases involving mutual recognition, but also purely domestic cases. In this manner, the functional legal basis of Article 82(2) TFEU has led to the adoption of self-standing EU human rights standards in the field of criminal procedure.

IV. The Renewed Momentum Towards EU Procedural Rights in the Light of Lisbon

At the time when the Treaty of Lisbon entered into force (on 1 December 2009), there was already renewed political momentum in the Council towards the adoption of EU legislation on procedural rights. Helped by the strengthening of defence rights by the European Court of Human Rights in the case of *Salduz*,[22] the fresh momentum for EU legislation in the field was created by the Swedish Presidency of the Council of the European Union in the second half of 2009. From the very outset of its Presidency, the Swedish Government tabled a 'Roadmap with a view to fostering protection of suspected and accused persons in criminal proceedings'.[23] On the basis of this plan, the Presidency secured the adoption by the Council of a Resolution on a Roadmap for strengthening procedural rights of suspected or accused persons in criminal proceedings, adopted one day before the

---

[21] V Mitsilegas, 'The Limits of Mutual Trust in Europe's Area of Freedom, Security and Justice. From Automatic Inter-state Cooperation to the Slow Emergence of the Individual' 31 *Yearbook of European Law* 2012 319–72.

[22] On the impact of *Salduz* in this context see J Jackson, 'Cultural Barriers on the Road to providing Suspects with Access to Lawyer' in R Colson and S Field (eds), *EU Criminal Justice and the Challenges of Legal Diversity. Towards A Socio-Legal Approach to EU Criminal Policy* (Cambridge, Cambridge University Press, forthcoming).

[23] Council doc 11457/09, Brussels, 1 July 2009.

entry into force of the Lisbon Treaty.[24] The Roadmap injected fresh momentum towards the adoption of EU legislation on procedural rights. Its Preamble recognised that there is further room for EU action in relation to and beyond the ECHR to ensure full implementation of and respect for the Convention standards and, where appropriate, to ensure consistent application of the applicable standards and to raise existing standards.[25] The Roadmap referred expressly to the need to rebalance the relationship between security and human rights in the European Union, and linked the protection of human rights with broader EU free movement objectives: according to the Preamble, efforts should be deployed to strengthen procedural guarantees and the respect of the rule of law in criminal proceedings, no matter where citizens decide to travel, study, work or live in the European Union.[26] In order to avoid the stagnation encountered in negotiations of procedural rights by previous EU Presidencies, Sweden adopted an incrementalist and gradual approach. Rather than resuscitating calls for the adoption of a single EU legal instrument on procedural rights, a 'roadmap' was proposed, anticipating the entry into force of the Lisbon Treaty and consisting of the step-by-step adoption of a series of specific measures on procedural rights, including measures on interpretation and translation (measure A), information on rights and information about the charges (measure B), legal advice and legal aid (measure C), communication with relatives, employers and consular authorities (measure D), special safeguards for suspected or accused persons who are vulnerable (measure E), and a Green paper on pre-trial detention (measure F). This gradual approach was justified in order to enable problems to be identified and addressed in a way that will give added value to each measure.[27] As will be seen further below, this step-by-step approach has led to the adoption of more detailed standards, while enabling EU institutions—and in particular Member States within the Council—to place focus on the challenges that EU harmonisation in the field of procedural rights may pose to the coherence domestic criminal justice systems.

Notwithstanding the renewed political impetus provided by the Roadmap, which has also been reflected in the Stockholm Programme adopted by the European Council during the Swedish Presidency,[28] the transition from the third pillar to the Lisbon Treaty has not been entirely straightforward from an institutional perspective. Following the Roadmap approach before the entry into force of the Lisbon

---

[24] Resolution of the Council of 30 November 2009 on a Roadmap for strengthening procedural rights of suspected or accused persons in criminal proceedings, [2009] OJ C29, 4.12.2009, p 1.

[25] Preamble, recital 2.

[26] Recital 10.

[27] Preamble, recital 11.

[28] European Council, *The Stockholm Programme—An Open and Secure Europe Serving and Protecting the Citizens*, [2010] OJ C115, 4.5.2010. The European Council invited the Commission to put forward the foreseen proposals in the Roadmap for swift implementation and to examine further elements of minimum procedural rights and to assess whether other issues, for instance the presumption of innocence, need to be addressed to promote better cooperation in this area—point 2.4.

Treaty, the Commission tabled in July 2009 a proposal for a Framework Decision on the right to interpretation and translation in criminal proceedings.[29] Although the Council did manage to reach a general approach in October 2009, it was not possible to adopt the Framework Decision before the entry into force of the Lisbon Treaty. This led to Member States calling for the exercise of their revised right of initiative post-Lisbon to table a new proposal on the right to interpretation and translation,[30] and to the eventual tabling by a number of Member States of a draft Directive in the field shortly after the entry into force of the Treaty (as early as 11 December 2009).[31] The tabling of this proposal demonstrated Member States' sensitivity and willingness to assert their powers of initiative at an early stage after the entry into force of the Lisbon treaty. The Commission's response was to propose its own initiative for a Directive on the right to interpretation and translation in criminal proceedings, tabled in March 2010.[32] The Commission's proposal can be seen as an attempt to defend its own right of initiative in the field of criminal law after Lisbon. The tabling of a new proposal in the field caused concerns in Member States who wrote to express concerns with regard to perceived confusion to the outside world including national parliaments and the potential of delay.[33] The Directive on the right to interpretation and translation was eventually deemed to be agreed as a Member State initiative[34] but the subsequently adopted measures on procedural rights have been adopted as Commission initiatives, with the decision-making process being now fully 'Lisbonised'.

V. The Content of EU Procedural Rights

The adoption of measures on procedural rights thus far has followed the Roadmap structure but not entirely the order envisaged by the Roadmap. In chronological order of adoption, procedural rights measures adopted post-Lisbon were: a Directive on the right to interpretation and translation;[35] a Directive on the right to information;[36] and a Directive on the right to access to a lawyer.[37] The Commission

---

[29] COM(2009) 338 final, Brussels, 8.7.2009.

[30] Council doc 16741/09, Brussels, 23 November 2009.

[31] Initiative for a Directive on the rights to interpretation and translation in criminal proceedings tabled by Belgium, Germany, Estonia, Spain, France, Italy, Luxembourg, Hungary, Austria, Portugal, Romania, Finland and Sweden, Council doc 16801/09, Brussels, 11 December 2009.

[32] COM(2010) 82 final, Brussels, 9.3.2010.

[33] Council doc 7598/10, Brussels, 17 March 2010.

[34] Preamble recital 2.

[35] Directive 2010/64/EU on the right to interpretation and translation in criminal proceedings, [2010] OJ L280, 26.10.2010, p 1.

[36] Directive 2012/13/EU on the right to information in criminal proceedings, [2012] OJ L142, 1.6.2012, p 1.

[37] Directive 2013/48/EU on the right of access to a lawyer in criminal proceedings and in European arrest warrant proceedings, and on the right to have a third party informed upon deprivation of liberty and to communicate with third persons and with consular authorities while deprived of liberty, [2013] OJ L294, 6.11.2013, p 1.

also published a Green Paper on the application of EU criminal justice legislation in the field of detention[38] and tabled, in November 2013, a number of draft Directives on legal aid,[39] procedural safeguards for children[40] and the presumption of innocence.[41] These proposals were accompanied by Commission Recommendations on the right to legal aid[42] and on procedural safeguards for vulnerable persons.[43] The current situation reflects legal and political complexities across the EU, as evidenced in particular by the move to exclude provisions on legal aid from negotiations on the access to a lawyer Directive and the decision to treat legal aid as a separate proposal in its own right. This move served to facilitate the adoption of the Directive on access to a lawyer, which contains a list of core rights in the field. The chapter will examine in detail the content of the measures which have already been adopted by the Council and the European Parliament.

A. The Directive on the Right to Interpretation and Translation

The Directive on the right to interpretation and translation strengthens the visibility of these rights by translating into secondary EU law rights that have been developed by the case-law of the European Court of Human Rights and at times extending the Strasbourg protection further.[44] With regard to the right to interpretation, the Directive places upon Member States a duty to

> ensure that suspected or accused persons who do not speak or understand the language of the criminal proceedings concerned are provided, without delay, with interpretation during criminal proceedings before investigative and judicial authorities, including during police questioning, all court hearings and any necessary interim hearings.[45]

Member States must

> ensure that, where necessary for the purpose of safeguarding the fairness of the proceedings, interpretation is available for communication between suspected or accused persons and their legal counsel in direct connection with any questioning or hearing during the proceedings or with the lodging of an appeal or other procedural applications.[46]

Member States must 'ensure that a procedure or mechanism is in place to ascertain whether suspected or accused persons speak and understand the language of the

---

[38] COM(2011) 327 final, Brussels, 14.6.2011.
[39] COM(2013) 824 final, Brussels, 27.11.2013.
[40] COM(2013) 822 final, Brussels, 27.11.2013.
[41] COM(2013) 821 final, Brussels, 27.11.2013.
[42] [2013] OJ C378/11, 24.12.2013.
[43] [2013] OJ C378/8, 24.12.2013.
[44] For an analysis see S Monjean-Decaudin, 'L'Union Européenne Consacre le Droit à l'Assistance Linguistique dans les Procédures Pénales. Commentaire de la Directive Relative aux Droits à l'interprétation et à la traduction dans les procedures pénales' (2011) 47 *Revue Trimestrielle du Droit Européen* 763–81.
[45] Article 2(1).
[46] Article 2(2).

criminal proceedings and whether they need the assistance of an interpreter'[47] and that,

> in accordance with procedures in national law, suspected or accused persons have the right to challenge a decision finding that there is no need for interpretation and, when interpretation has been provided, the possibility to complain that the quality of the interpretation is not sufficient to safeguard the fairness of the proceedings.[48]

Advocate General Bot has interpreted Articles 1(2) and 2(1) of the Directive as allowing an individual who is the subject of a judicial decision in criminal matters and who does not know the language of the proceedings to launch an appeal in her own language, while the onus for ensuring the enjoyment of this right falls upon the competent national court.[49] With regard to the right to translation, the Directive places Member States under a duty to

> ensure that suspected or accused persons who do not understand the language of the criminal proceedings concerned are, within a reasonable period of time, provided with a written translation of all documents which are essential to ensure that they are able to exercise their right of defence and to safeguard the fairness of the proceedings.[50]

Essential documents must include 'any decision depriving a person of his liberty, any charge or indictment, and any judgment'.[51] The competent authorities must, 'in any given case, decide whether any other document is essential. Suspected or accused persons or their legal counsel may submit a reasoned request to that effect'.[52] Exceptionally, 'an oral translation or oral summary of essential documents may be provided instead of a written translation on condition that such oral translation or oral summary does not prejudice the fairness of the proceedings'.[53] Member States must

> ensure that, in accordance with procedures in national law, suspected or accused persons have the right to challenge a decision finding that there is no need for the translation of documents or passages thereof and, when a translation has been provided, the possibility to complain that the quality of the translation is not sufficient to safeguard the fairness of the proceedings.[54]

B. The Directive on the Right to Information

The Directive on the right to information places Member States under an express duty[55] to

---

[47] Article 2(4).
[48] Article 2(5).
[49] AG Bot, Case C-216/14, *Criminal Proceedings against Gavril Covaci*, n 112 below, paragraph 81.
[50] Article 3(1).
[51] Article 3(2).
[52] Article 3(3).
[53] Article 3(7).
[54] Article 3(5).
[55] Preamble (18): 'The right to information about procedural rights, which is inferred from the case-law of the European Court of Human Rights, should be explicitly established by this Directive'.

ensure that suspects or accused persons are provided promptly with information concerning at least the following procedural rights, as they apply under national law, in order to allow for those rights to be exercised effectively:

(a)   the right of access to a lawyer;
(b)   any entitlement to free legal advice and the conditions for obtaining such advice;
(c)   the right to be informed of the accusation ...
(d)   the right to interpretation and translation;
(e)   the right to remain silent.[56]

Member States must 'ensure that the information ... is given orally or in writing, in simple and accessible language and taking into account any particular needs of vulnerable suspects or vulnerable accused persons'.[57] A key component of the right to information is the provision of a Letter of Rights. Member States must 'ensure that suspects or accused persons who are arrested or detained are provided promptly with a written Letter of Rights'. The Letter of Rights was one of the key innovations but forward by the Commission in its original proposal for a Framework Decision on procedural rights in 2004.[58] According to the Directive, suspects and accused persons must 'be given an opportunity to read the Letter of Rights and must be allowed to keep it in their possession throughout the time that they are deprived of liberty'.[59] In addition to the information set out in Article 3 of the Directive (which sets out the procedural rights for which the right to information applies as a minimum), the Letter of Rights must also

contain information about the following rights as they apply under national law:

(a)   the right of access to the materials of the case;
(b)   the right to have consular authorities and one person informed;
(c)   the right of access to urgent medical assistance; and
(d)   the maximum number of hours or days suspects or accused persons may be deprived of liberty before being brought before a judicial authority.[60]

The Letter of Rights must 'also contain basic information about any possibility, under national law, of challenging the lawfulness of the arrest; obtaining a review of the detention; or making a request for provisional release'.[61] The Letter of Rights must 'be drafted in simple and accessible language', with annex 1 to the Directive containing an indicative model Letter of Rights.[62] Member States must

ensure that suspects or accused persons receive the Letter of Rights written in a language that they understand. Where a Letter of Rights is not available in the appropriate language, suspects or accused persons [must] be informed of their rights orally in a language that

---

[56]   Article 3(1).
[57]   Article 3(2).
[58]   See section II above.
[59]   Article 4(1).
[60]   Article 4(2).
[61]   Article 4(3).
[62]   Article 4(4).

they understand. A Letter of Rights in a language that they understand [must] then be given to them without undue delay.[63]

The duty of Member States to ensure the provision of a Letter of Rights extends also to European Arrest Warrant proceedings.[64]

The right of information of the applicable procedural rights is complemented by provisions on the right to information about the accusation and the right of access to the materials of the case. The Directive thus reflects the case-law of the European Court of Human Rights which views the right to information in this context as inextricably linked with the defendant's right to an adversarial procedure.[65] As regards the right to information about the accusation, the Directive provides that Member States must

> ensure that suspects or accused persons are provided with information about the criminal act they are suspected or accused of having committed. That information must be provided promptly and in such detail as is necessary to safeguard the fairness of the proceedings and the effective exercise of the rights of the defence.[66]

Member States must 'ensure that suspects or accused persons who are arrested or detained are informed of the reasons for their arrest or detention, including the criminal act they are suspected or accused of having committed' and that,

> at the latest on submission of the merits of the accusation to a court, detailed information is provided on the accusation, including the nature and legal classification of the criminal offence, as well as the nature of participation by the accused person.[67]

Member States must further 'ensure that suspects or accused persons are informed promptly of any changes in the information given ... where this is necessary to safeguard the fairness of the proceedings'.[68] With regard to the right of access to the materials of the case, the Directive provides that this will be provided free of charge.[69]

> Where a person is arrested and detained at any stage of the criminal proceedings, Member States [must] ensure that documents related to the specific case in the possession of the competent authorities which are essential to challenging effectively, in accordance with national law, the lawfulness of the arrest or detention, are made available to arrested persons or to their lawyers.[70]

---

[63] Article 4(5).
[64] Article 5.
[65] Case of *Danayan v Turkey*, Application no 7377/03, 13 October 2009 (ECtHR), paragraphs 35 and 36.
[66] Article 6(1).
[67] Article 6(2) and (3).
[68] Article 6(4).
[69] Article 7(5).
[70] Article 7(1).

Member States must

> ensure that access is granted at least to all material evidence in the possession of the competent authorities, whether for or against suspects or accused persons, to those persons or their lawyers in order to safeguard the fairness of the proceedings and to prepare the defence.[71]

Access to these materials must be granted

> in due time to allow the effective exercise of the rights of the defence and at the latest upon submission of the merits of the accusation to the judgment of a court. Where further material evidence comes into the possession of the competent authorities, access [must] be granted to it in due time to allow for it to be considered.[72]

By way of derogation, but

> provided that this does not prejudice the right to a fair trial, access to certain materials may be refused if such access may lead to a serious threat to the life or the fundamental rights of another person or if such refusal is strictly necessary to safeguard an important public interest, such as in cases where access could prejudice an ongoing investigation or seriously harm the national security of the Member State in which the criminal proceedings are instituted. Member States [must] ensure that, in accordance with procedures in national law, a decision to refuse access to certain materials in accordance with this paragraph is taken by a judicial authority or is at least subject to judicial review.[73]

The Directive further includes express provisions on verification and remedies applicable to all rights contained therein. In particular, Member States must 'ensure that when information is provided to suspects or accused persons ... this is noted using the recording procedure specified in the law of the Member State concerned'.[74] Moreover, they must 'ensure that suspects or accused persons or their lawyers have the right to challenge, in accordance with procedures in national law, the possible failure or refusal of the competent authorities to provide information'.[75] The Directive thus re-affirms the backing up of the introduction of procedural rights with provisions on remedies.

C. The Directive on the Right of Access to a Lawyer

The right of access to a lawyer is the cornerstone of procedural rights in criminal proceedings. It has been characterised as a 'gateway' right, permitting the

---

[71] Article 7(2).
[72] Article 7(3).
[73] Article 7(4).
[74] Article 8(1).
[75] Article 8(2).

exercise of other rights and helping to make all these rights real and effective.[76] Notwithstanding its importance and the fact that the right of access to a lawyer is inextricably linked with the right to a fair trial, which all EU Member States are under the obligation to respect within the framework of the European Convention on Human Rights, negotiations on the Directive on access to a lawyer—which, as should be recalled, would have the modest aim of introducing merely minimum standards in the field under the legal basis of Article 82(2) TFEU—have proven to be complex. Negotiations focused on how best to achieve meaningful minimum standards without (as some Member States feared) jeopardising unduly national legal diversity in the field of criminal procedure.[77] The need to find compromises in order to reach agreement between the Council and the European Parliament in the post-Lisbon co-decision era has led to the adoption of a text accompanied by a lengthy Preamble consisting of no less than 59 recitals. As has been noted, the greater emphasis on the Preambular provisions reflects a strategy whereby areas where no agreement on the imposition of express obligations can be reached in negotiations are moved to the Preamble or where parties to negotiations (and in particular Member States) aim to achieve a high level of precision in the adopted standards.[78] A number of compromises had also to be reached within the main body of the Directive, which includes a number of provisions on exceptions and derogations. Having said that, and as with the other Directives discussed thus far, the Directive constitutes a decisive step towards strengthening procedural rights by translating into concrete secondary law the principles emanating from Strasbourg case-law and at times developing these principles further and providing for more extensive protection.[79] As will be seen below,[80] a further positive feature in expressly legislating for human rights in EU secondary law is the triggering of the application of fundamental rights and institutional and enforcement safeguards offered by the European Union legal order.

The scope and content of the right to access to a lawyer is spelt out in Article 3 of the Directive. The opening paragraph states as a general rule that

---

[76] See the submission of Fair Trials International in Case *A.T. v Luxembourg*, Application no 30460/13, 9 April 2015 (ECtHR), paragraph 58; and D Sayers, 'Protecting Fair Trial Rights in Criminal Cases in the European Union: Where does the Roadmap take Us?' (2014) 14 *Human Rights Law Review* 733–60, 748.

[77] On the main issues arising in negotiations see S Cras, 'The Directive on the Right of Access to a Lawyer in Criminal Proceedings and in European Arrest Warrant Proceedings, in (2014) 1 *EUCRIM* 32–44.

[78] H Nowell-Smith, 'Behind the Scenes in the Negotiation of EU Criminal Justice Legislation' (2012) 3 *New Journal of European Criminal Law* 381–93. On the application of this approach to the access to a lawyer Directive, see also Cras, n 77 above.

[79] For a positive assessment of the Directive on the right of access to a lawyer see J Hodgson, 'Criminal Procedure in Europe's Area of Freedom, Security and Justice: the Rights of the Suspect' in V Mitsilegas, M Bergström and T Konstadinides (eds), *Research Handbook on European Criminal Law*, (Cheltenham, Edward Elgar, forthcoming); and I Anagnostopoulos, 'The Right of Access to a Lawyer in Europe: A Long Road Ahead?' (2014) 4 *European Criminal Law Review* 3–18.

[80] Sections VI and VII of this chapter.

Member States must 'ensure that suspects and accused persons have the right of access to a lawyer in such time and in such a manner so as to allow the persons concerned to exercise their rights of defence practically and effectively'.[81] This provision reflects the approach of the Strasbourg Court, according to which the lawyer must be able to provide effective and concrete assistance, and not merely abstractassistance by virtue of the fact that he is present in the proceedings.[82]

> Suspects or accused persons [must] have access to a lawyer without undue delay. In any event, suspects or accused persons [must] have access to a lawyer from whichever of the following points in time is the earliest:
>
> (a) before they are questioned by the police or by another law enforcement or judicial authority;
> (b) upon the carrying out by investigating or other competent authorities of an investigative or other evidence-gathering act in accordance with point (c) of paragraph 3;
> (c) without undue delay after deprivation of liberty;
> (d) where they have been summoned to appear before a court having jurisdiction in criminal matters, in due time before they appear before that court.[83]

The right of access to a lawyer is further articulated as entailing the following elements:

> (a) Member States [must] ensure that suspects or accused persons have the right to meet in private and communicate with the lawyer representing them, including prior to questioning by the police or by another law enforcement or judicial authority;
> (b) Member States [must] ensure that suspects or accused persons have the right for their lawyer to be present and participate effectively when questioned. Such participation must be in accordance with procedures under national law, provided that such procedures do not prejudice the effective exercise and essence of the right concerned. Where a lawyer participates during questioning, the fact that such participation has taken place must be noted using the recording procedure in accordance with the law of the Member State concerned;
> (c) Member States [must] ensure that suspects or accused persons must have, as a minimum, the right for their lawyer to attend the following investigative or evidence-gathering acts where those acts are provided for under national law and if the suspect or accused person is required or permitted to attend the act concerned: identity parades; confrontations; reconstructions of the scene of a crime.[84]

> Member States [must] endeavour to make general information available to facilitate the obtaining of a lawyer by suspects or accused persons.

> Notwithstanding provisions of national law concerning the mandatory presence of a lawyer, Member States [must] make the necessary arrangements to ensure that suspects

---

[81] Article 3(1).
[82] *A.T. v Luxembourg*, n 76 above, paragraph 87.
[83] Article 3(2).
[84] Article 3(3).

or accused persons who are deprived of liberty are in a position to exercise effectively their right of access to a lawyer, unless they have waived that right in accordance with Article 9 [of the Directive].[85]

The Directive thus articulates in detail in EU secondary law the fundamental right of access to a lawyer as enshrined in Strasbourg case-law, and in particular in the case of *Salduz*.[86] The Directive clarifies and strengthens the impact of *Salduz* on national law, by narrowing the national margin of appreciation in implementing the access to a lawyer obligations and in particular by expressly extending the application of the right of access to a lawyer in cases where no deprivation of liberty is involved.[87]

The challenges which even minimum harmonisation of the right to access to a lawyer was perceived to pose for the integrity of national criminal justice systems and policies have led to the watering down of harmonisation in four main respects: in limiting the reach of the application of the Directive by attempting to exclude minor offences from its scope;[88] in introducing temporary derogations to rights;[89] in attempting to reach a compromise in the provision on confidentiality of communications between lawyers and defendants;[90] and in excluding from the scope of the present instrument provisions on legal aid, which (as seen above) are the subject of negotiations of a separate Directive under the Roadmap.[91] The same is the case with provisions on the rights of vulnerable persons, the detail of which is being negotiated under a separate Directive.[92] It is important to analyse here in detail the exceptions introduced by the Directive regarding minor offences and temporary derogations. With regard to minor offences, Article 2(4) states that without prejudice to the right to a fair trial, the Directive will only apply to the proceedings before a court having jurisdiction in criminal matters in respect of minor offences 'where the law of a Member State provides for the imposition of a

---

[85] Article 3(4). According to Article 9(1) of the Directive, 'without prejudice to national law requiring the mandatory presence or assistance of a lawyer, Member States must ensure that, in relation to any waiver of a right referred to in Article 3 ...: (a) the suspect or accused person has been provided, orally or in writing, with clear and sufficient information in simple and understandable language about the content of the right concerned and the possible consequences of waiving it; and (b) the waiver is given voluntarily and unequivocally'. Such waiver may be subsequently revoked (Article 9(3)).

[86] *Salduz v Turkey*, judgment of 27 November 2008 (ECtHR).

[87] See Article 2(1). See Cras, n 77 above; Hodgson, n 79 above.

[88] Article 2(4).

[89] Articles 3(5) and (6) and 5(3).

[90] See Article 4, according to which 'Member States [must] respect the confidentiality of communication between suspects or accused persons and their lawyer in the exercise of the right of access to a lawyer provided for under this Directive', with such communication including 'meetings, correspondence, telephone conversations and other forms of communication permitted under national law'. On the negotiations and the emergence of this compromise wording see Cras, n 77 above.

[91] According to Article 11, the Directive is 'without prejudice to national law in relation to legal aid, which [must] apply in accordance with the Charter and the ECHR'.

[92] The access to a lawyer Directive contains a general provision according to which Member States must 'ensure that the particular needs of vulnerable suspects and vulnerable accused persons are taken into account in [its] application' (Article 13).

sanction by an authority other than a court having jurisdiction in criminal matters, and the imposition of such a sanction may be appealed or referred to such a court', or 'where deprivation of liberty cannot be imposed as a sanction'. In any event, Article 2(4) continues by stating that the Directive will 'fully apply where the suspect or accused person is deprived of liberty, irrespective of the stage of the criminal proceedings'. Moreover, the Preamble to the Directive confirms that 'the scope of application ... in respect of minor offences should not affect the obligations of Member States under the ECHR'.[93] Even with these important caveats, this provision may act as a limit to the effective application of the right to access to a lawyer in a significant number of cases. This exception, which also applies in the Directives on the right to translation and interpretation and the right to information,[94] sits, however, at odds with the case-law of the European Court of Human Rights, and in particular the *Engel* jurisprudence according to which Article 6 ECHR is applicable in cases where there is a 'criminal charge' against the affected individual.[95] This inconsistency with the protection afforded by the Strasbourg Court is even more evident when one reads recital 13 to the Directive, according to which

> without prejudice to the obligations of Member States under the ECHR to ensure the right to a fair trial, proceedings in relation to minor offending which take place within a prison and proceedings in relation to offences committed in a military context which are dealt with by a commanding officer should not be considered to be criminal proceedings for the purposes of [the] Directive.

It is difficult to see how this blanket exclusion can apply without undermining the level of human rights protection provided by the ECHR.

In addition to limits to applicability with regard to minor offences, the Directive introduces a number of temporary derogations from the right to access to a lawyer.

> In exceptional circumstances and only at the pre-trial stage, Member States may temporarily derogate from [the right to access to a lawyer without undue delay after deprivation of liberty] where the geographical remoteness of a suspect or accused person makes it impossible to ensure the right of access to a lawyer without undue delay after deprivation of liberty.[96]

Similarly

> [i]n exceptional circumstances and only at the pre-trial stage, Member States may temporarily derogate from the application of the [access to a lawyer rights provided for in

---

[93] Recital 18.

[94] See also Art 1(3) right to interpretation Directive and Art 2(2) right to information Directive: 'Where the law of a Member State provides for the imposition of a sanction regarding minor offences by an authority other than a court having jurisdiction in criminal matters, and the imposition of such a sanction may be appealed to such a court, this Directive shall apply only to the proceedings before that court following such an appeal'.

[95] See also Sayers, n 79 above, p 740.

[96] Article 3(5).

Article 3(3) of the Directive] to the extent justified in the light of the particular circumstances of the case, on the basis of one of the following compelling reasons:

(a) where there is an urgent need to avert serious adverse consequences for the life, liberty or physical integrity of a person;

(b) where immediate action by the investigating authorities is imperative to prevent substantial jeopardy to criminal proceedings.[97]

A similar temporary derogation applies also to the right to have a third person informed of the deprivation of liberty, set out in Article 5 of the Directive.[98] Member States may also limit or defer the exercise of the right to communicate, while deprived of liberty, with third persons, provided in Article 6 of the Directive, 'in view of imperative requirements or proportionate operational requirements'.[99] The Directive sets out a number of general conditions of temporary derogations under Article 3(5) and (6) (access to a lawyer) or Article 5(3) (right to have a third person informed of the deprivation of liberty). According to Article 8 of the Directive, any temporary derogation under these provisions must '(a) be proportionate and not go beyond what is necessary; (b) be strictly limited in time; (c) not be based exclusively on the type or the seriousness of the alleged offence; and (d) not prejudice the overall fairness of the proceedings'.[100]

Temporary derogations under Article 3(5) or (6) may be authorised only by a duly reasoned decision taken on a case-by-case basis, either by a judicial authority, or by another competent authority on condition that the decision can be submitted to judicial review.[101]

'Temporary derogations under Article 5(3) may be authorised only on a case-by-case basis, either by a judicial authority, or by another competent authority on condition that the decision can be submitted to judicial review'.[102] The provisions on judicial review are consistent with the Directive's overall emphasis on the importance of remedies. According to Article 12 of the Directive,

---

[97] Article 3(6).

[98] Article 5(3). However, where Member States temporarily derogate from the application of this right in relation to a suspect or accused person under 18, 'they must ensure that an authority responsible for the protection or welfare of children is informed without undue delay of the deprivation of liberty of the child' (Article 5(4)).

[99] Article 6(2). However, no temporary derogation or limitation is envisaged regarding the right to communicate with consular authorities, set out in Article 7 of the Directive. According to the latter, 'Member States [must] ensure that suspects or accused persons who are non-nationals and who are deprived of liberty have the right to have the consular authorities of their State of nationality informed of the deprivation of liberty without undue delay and to communicate with those authorities, if they so wish' (Article 7(1)). 'Suspects or accused persons also have the right to be visited by their consular authorities, the right to converse and correspond with them and the right to have legal representation arranged for by their consular authorities, subject to the agreement of those authorities and the wishes of the suspects or accused persons concerned' (Article 7(2)). Article 7(3) states that the exercise of the rights laid down therein 'may be regulated by national law or procedures, provided that such law or procedures enable full effect to be given to the purposes for which these rights are intended'.

[100] Article 8(1).

[101] Article 8(2).

[102] Article 8(3).

Member States [must] ensure that suspects or accused persons in criminal proceedings, as well as requested persons in European arrest warrant proceedings, have an effective remedy under national law in the event of a breach of the rights under this Directive.[103]

The Directive further specifies that,

[w]ithout prejudice to national rules and systems on the admissibility of evidence, Member States [must] ensure that, in criminal proceedings, in the assessment of statements made by suspects or accused persons or of evidence obtained in breach of their right to a lawyer or in cases where a derogation to this right was authorised in accordance with Article 3(6), the rights of the defence and the fairness of the proceedings are respected.[104]

VI. Horizontal Issues: The Scope and Level of Protection of Procedural Rights After Lisbon

As has been demonstrated above, the entry into force of the Treaty of Lisbon has led to the adoption of a number of EU secondary law measures in the field of procedural rights in criminal proceedings, outlining in detail the protection of a number of these rights in EU law. Although the aim of these measures is modest—namely to establish merely 'minimum standards'—a careful reading of all Directives adopted thus far reveals that the scope and level of protection envisaged in EU law is considerable. With regard to the scope of application, it is important to note that, notwithstanding the link with mutual recognition that the legal basis to these instruments (Article 82(2) TFEU) entails, all adopted measures apply not only in cross-border cases involving the operation of the European Arrest Warrant system, but also in purely domestic cases.[105] This is an important development, as the implementation of the EU procedural rights measures in domestic law will have to cover all cases in the field of domestic criminal procedure which fall within the scope of the Directives. As Caeiro has noted, the Directives have thus created an autonomous, self-designed project for the protection of individual rights in criminal proceedings before the authorities of Member States.[106] In a further extension of the scope of protection under EU law, the Directive on access

---

[103] Article 12(1).

[104] Article 12(2).

[105] Directive on the right to interpretation and translation, n 35 above: Article 1(1); Directive on the right to information, n 36 above: Article 1; Directive on access to a lawyer, n 37 above: Article 1.

[106] P Caeiro, 'Introduction (or: Every Criminal Procedure Starts with a Bill of Rights)' in P Caeiro, *The European Union Agenda on Procedural Safeguards for Suspects or Accused Persons: the 'second wave' and its predictable impact on Portuguese law* (Instituto Jurídico, Faculdade de Direito, Universidade de Coimbra, 2015) 13–18, 17.

to a lawyer extends the applicability of this right not only to the executing,[107] but also to the issuing Member State.[108] However, in a provision reflecting the case-law of the Court of Justice on the requirement of speed regarding the operation of the European Arrest Warrant,[109] the Directive places the right to access to a lawyer in European Arrest Warrant proceedings under strict time-limits:

> The right of a requested person to appoint a lawyer in the issuing Member State is without prejudice to the time-limits set out in the [European Arrest Warrant Framework Decision] or the obligation on the executing judicial authority to decide, within those time-limits and the conditions defined under that Framework Decision, whether the person is to be surrendered.[110]

All three adopted Directives trigger the rights enshrined therein at an early stage and they apply the rights up to the point of finality of the criminal process: rights are applicable

> from the time that [suspects or accused persons] are made aware by the competent authorities of a Member State, by official notification or otherwise, that they are suspected or accused of having committed a criminal offence ... until the conclusion of the proceedings, which is understood to mean the final determination of the question whether they have committed the offence, including, where applicable, sentencing and the resolution of any appeal.[111]

EU law thus establishes a broad temporal scope of application of procedural rights.[112]

---

[107] Article 10: '1. Member States shall ensure that a requested person has the right of access to a lawyer in the executing Member State upon arrest pursuant to the European arrest warrant. 2. With regard to the content of the right of access to a lawyer in the executing Member State, requested persons shall have the following rights in that Member State: (a) the right of access to a lawyer in such time and in such a manner as to allow the requested persons to exercise their rights effectively and in any event without undue delay from deprivation of liberty; (b) the right to meet and communicate with the lawyer representing them; (c) the right for their lawyer to be present and, in accordance with procedures in national law, participate during a hearing of a requested person by the executing judicial authority. Where a lawyer participates during the hearing this shall be noted using the recording procedure in accordance with the law of the Member State concerned. 3. The rights provided for in Articles 4, 5, 6, 7, 9, and, where a temporary derogation under Article 5(3) is applied, in Article 8, shall apply, *mutatis mutandis*, to European arrest warrant proceedings in the executing Member State'.

[108] According to Article 10(4) 'the competent authority in the executing Member State shall, without undue delay after deprivation of liberty, inform requested persons that they have the right to appoint a lawyer in the issuing Member State. The role of that lawyer in the issuing Member State is to assist the lawyer in the executing Member State by providing that lawyer with information and advice with a view to the effective exercise of the rights of requested persons under Framework Decision 2002/584/ JHA'. Article 10(5) continues by stating that 'where requested persons wish to exercise the right to appoint a lawyer in the issuing Member State and do not already have such a lawyer, the competent authority in the executing Member State shall promptly inform the competent authority in the issuing Member State. The competent authority of that Member State shall, without undue delay, provide the requested persons with information to facilitate them in appointing a lawyer there'.

[109] Case C-168/13 PPU, *Jeremy F*, judgment of 30 May 2013, paragraph 65.

[110] Article 10(6).

[111] Directive on the right to interpretation and translation, n 35 above, Article 1(2). Directive on the right to information, n 36 above, Article 2(1). Directive on access to a lawyer, n 37 above, Article 2(1).

[112] See also in the context of the Directive on the right to interpretation and translation the remarks of AG Bot in his Opinion on Case C-216/14, *Criminal Proceedings against Gavril Covaci*, 7.5.2015, para 51; and in the context of the Directive on the right to information, the same Opinion, paragraph 100.

The EU Directives on procedural rights in criminal proceedings have translated, expanded and clarified rights enshrined in the ECHR—in particular in Articles 5 and 6—and in the EU Charter of Fundamental Rights, in particular in Articles 47 and 48.[113] The Directives themselves include provisions to address the key question of the relationship between general ECHR and Charter human rights norms and the specific provisions of EU secondary law on procedural rights. As regards the ECHR, it has been acknowledged from the outset that its provisions constitute the starting point and the benchmark by which the legality and legitimacy of EU secondary legislation on procedural rights should be judged. In the development of EU secondary legislation, every effort has been made from the outset[114] and throughout negotiations to ensure compliance with the ECHR by seeking the opinion of the Council of Europe on draft proposals.[115] Moreover, the Preambles to the adopted EU Directives include extensive references to their relationship with the ECHR. It is noted in particular that 'the right to interpretation and translation for those who do not speak or understand the language of the proceedings is enshrined in Article 6 of the ECHR, as interpreted in the case-law of the European Court of Human Rights' and that the Directive on the right to interpretation and translation 'facilitates the application of that right in practice'.[116] The Preamble to the Directive on the right to information states that 'Article 5 ECHR enshrine[s] the right to liberty and security of person', adding that 'any restrictions on that right must not exceed those permitted in accordance with Article 5 ECHR and inferred from the case-law of the European Court of Human Rights'.[117] The same provision makes reference to Article 6 of the Charter. The Directive on the right to access to a lawyer on the other hand, while continuing to refer to the ECHR, contains more detailed provisions and arguably demonstrates a greater emphasis on rights as enshrined in the Charter. It is stated that the conditions in which suspects or accused persons are deprived of liberty should fully respect the standards set out in the ECHR, in the Charter, and in the case-law of the Court of Justice of the European Union and of the European Court of Human Rights.[118] Moreover, the Preamble adopts a holistic approach to rights on the basis of the Charter, stating that the Directive

> upholds and should be implemented in accordance with the fundamental rights and principles recognised by the Charter, including the prohibition of torture and inhuman

---

[113] The EU Charter of Fundamental Rights includes a general provision on the right to a fair trial (Article 47) and a specific provision guaranteeing respect for the rights of the defence of anyone who has been charged (Article 48(2)).

[114] Roadmap Resolution: point 5: 'The Council will act in full cooperation with the European Parliament, in accordance with the applicable rules, and will duly collaborate with the Council of Europe'.

[115] Opinion of the Secretariat on the Commission's proposal for a Directive of the European Parliament and of the Council on 'the right to access to a lawyer in criminal proceedings and on the right to communicate upon arrest', Strasbourg, 9 November 2011. Opinion of the Secretariat on the Commission's proposal for a Directive of the European Parliament and of the Council on 'the right to information in criminal proceedings', Strasbourg, 8 December 2010.

[116] Preamble, recital 14.

[117] Preamble, recital 6.

[118] Preamble, recital 29.

or degrading treatment, the right to liberty and security, respect for private and family life, the right to the integrity of the person, the rights of the child, integration of persons with disabilities, the right to an effective remedy and the right to a fair trial, the presumption of innocence and the rights of the defence.[119]

Both the ECHR and the Charter constitute benchmarks for the provisions of the access to a lawyer Directive: 'the level of protection should never fall below the standards provided by the ECHR or the Charter as interpreted in the case-law of the Court of Justice and of the European Court of Human Rights'.[120]

The Preambular provisions to all Directives state that their provisions that correspond to rights guaranteed by the ECHR should be interpreted and implemented consistently with those rights, as interpreted in the relevant case-law of the European Court of Human Rights.[121] However, this wording leaves open the possibility of a higher level of protection for provisions which do not correspond to ECHR rights. Moreover, the possibility of offering a higher level of protection is further enshrined in the text of the Directives via the introduction of non-regression clauses, affirming that nothing in the Directives 'must be construed as limiting or derogating from any of the rights and procedural safeguards that are ensured under the Charter, the ECHR, or other relevant provisions of international law or the law of any Member State which provides a higher level of protection'.[122] This is the case particularly in situations not explicitly dealt with by EU law.[123] The non-regression clauses confirm that the Court's case-law in *Melloni* does not apply here:[124] national law which provides a high level of protection of procedural rights will apply, even if the level of protection is higher than that provided by the EU (in any case minimum) standards. The *Melloni* principles of unity, primacy and effectiveness of EU law take second place here, in particular as regards ensuring the operational effectiveness of the European Arrest Warrant system. As the Preamble to the access to a lawyer Directive states expressly, 'a higher level of protection by Member States should not constitute an obstacle to the mutual recognition of judicial decisions that those minimum rules are designed to facilitate'.[125] On the contrary, it is clear that a higher level of human rights protection would rather facilitate—and not hinder—mutual recognition.

[119] Preamble, recital 52.
[120] Preamble, recital 54.
[121] Directive on the right to interpretation and translation, n 35 above, recital 33 (referring also to the Charter and the interpretation by the CJEU); Directive on the right to information, n 36 above, recital 42; Directive on access to a lawyer, n 37 above, recital 53.
[122] Directive on the right to interpretation and translation, n 35 above, Article 8; Directive on the right to information, Article 10; Directive on access to a lawyer, n 37 above, Article 14.
[123] Directive on the right to interpretation and translation, n 35 above, recital 32; Directive on the right to information, n 36 above, recital 40.
[124] Case C-399/11, *Melloni*, judgment of 26 February 2013, EU:C:2013:107.
[125] Directive 2013/48/EU, n 37 above, Preamble, recital 54.

VII. The Impact of EU Procedural Rights on National Legal Systems: Enforcement and Implementation of Rights

The EU Directives on procedural safeguards will have a significantly positive impact on the protection of fundamental rights in domestic systems of criminal procedure. As seen above, the Directives translate, clarify and at times go beyond the standards enshrined by the ECHR and the European Court of Human Rights. The standards established therein apply not only to cross-border, but also to domestic cases. And although the aim of the Directives has been to establish minimum standards, in essence they have introduced a series of binding norms which are designed to ensure the respect of human rights and which must be interpreted broadly in order for their practical effectiveness to be ensured.[126] Largely mirroring the approach of the European Court of Human Rights, the Directives adopt a concept of active defence and aim to secure that the exercise of procedural rights is effective and concrete.[127] Effectiveness is thus key in the implementation of EU procedural rights Directives. There are four main ways in which the Directives on procedural rights in criminal procedure will enhance the protection of fundamental rights in EU Member States. First of all, a number of key provisions conferring rights in the Directives have direct effect. This means that, in a system of decentralised enforcement of EU law, individuals can evoke and claim rights directly before their national courts if the EU Directives have not been implemented or have been inadequately implemented. Direct effect means in practice that a suspect or accused person can derive a number of key rights—such as the right to an interpreter or the right to access to a lawyer—directly from EU law if national legislation has not made appropriate provision in conformity with EU law. Secondly, this avenue of decentralised enforcement is coupled with the high level of centralised enforcement of EU criminal law which has been 'normalised' after the entry into force of the Lisbon Treaty. The European Commission now has full powers to monitor the implementation of these Directives by Member States and has the power to introduce infringement proceedings before the Court of Justice when it considers that the Directives have not been implemented adequately. In view of the Court's approach regarding the applicability of the Charter, which will be examined below, and the broad objectives of the procedural rights Directives, the scope of the Commission's monitoring exercises is broader than to check merely the provision of national legislation adopted to implement

---

[126] Opinion of AG Bot, Case C-216/14, *Criminal Proceedings against Gavril Covaci*, 7.5.2015, paras 32–33, 74.

[127] See *A.T. v Luxembourg*, n 76 above, paragraph 88.

specifically the EU Directives in question. The Commission is also entitled to monitor national criminal procedure systems more broadly to ensure that effective implementation has taken place, as well as to ensure that rights are applied in practice and not only 'in the books'. Thirdly, and in line with the point above, national criminal procedural law must be applied and interpreted in compliance and conformity with the Directives. The procedural standards set out in the Directives will have an impact on a wide range of acts under national criminal procedure.[128] Fourthly, the implementation of the Directives must take place in compliance with the Charter of Fundamental Rights. The Charter will apply not only to national legislation which specifically implements the EU Directives on procedural rights, but also to all other elements of domestic criminal procedure which have a connection with EU law on procedural rights in criminal proceedings. In the case of *Fransson*,[129] the Court of Justice adopted a broad interpretation of the application of the Charter, including in cases where national legislation does not implement expressly or directly an EU criminal law instrument. Following *Fransson*, the Court of Justice ruled in *Siragusa*[130] that

> the concept of 'implementing Union law', as referred to in Article 51 of the Charter, requires a certain degree of connection above and beyond the matters covered being closely related or one of those matters having an indirect impact on the other.[131]

In the case of the Directives on procedural rights, there are a number of elements in domestic criminal procedures which, although not implementing specifically the Directives, meet this degree of connection required by the Court's case-law and thus trigger the applicability of the Charter. This view is reinforced by the Court's finding in *Siragusa* that

> it is important to consider the objective of protecting fundamental rights in EU law, which is to ensure that those rights are not infringed in areas of EU activity, whether through action at EU level or through the implementation of EU law by the Member States.[132]

VIII. The Impact of EU Procedural Rights on National Legal Diversity—The Role of Autonomous Concepts

One of the key challenges in reaching agreement on EU standards on procedural rights in criminal proceedings has been to accommodate Member States' concerns with regard to the potentially adverse impact of EU law in the field on the diversity

---

[128] See Opinion of AG Bot, n 126 above, in particular paragraphs 105–106.
[129] Case C-617/10, *Åklagaren v Hans Åkerberg Fransson*, judgment of 26 February 2013.
[130] Case C-206/13, *Cruciano Siragusa v Regione Sicilia*, judgment of 6.3.2014.
[131] ibid paragraph 24.
[132] Paragraph 31.

of national criminal justice systems. In order to address these concerns, the legal basis introduced in the Lisbon Treaty, Article 82(2) TFEU, provides a number of safeguards for national legal diversity, including the adoption of procedural rights measures in the form of Directives (which give Member States a certain leeway as to how the Directives will be implemented in national law as long as their objectives are met); the introduction of a low level of harmonisation (via the adoption of merely minimum rules); and the insertion in Article 82(2) TFEU of a sentence stating expressly that such rules must take into account the differences between the legal traditions of Member States. Faced with the diversity of national criminal justice systems,[133] negotiations on the specific EU Directives on procedural rights after Lisbon have proven to be complex, notwithstanding the limited ambition to introduce minimum standards based on the ECHR and leaving via the introduction of non-regression clauses, Member States free to maintain or introduce higher standards of protection. The price of reaching agreement has been the adoption of a number of provisions (especially as regards the access to a lawyer Directive) which have been the outcome of comparative law exercises and of criminal policy compromises, with the Directives containing a number of exceptions and lengthy Preambular provisions.[134] In spite of all these efforts, the existing EU Directives on procedural rights—even in their minimum standards form—will have a profound impact on national criminal justice systems. They will have an impact because, as Advocate General Bot has noted, the minimum standards character of EU law in the field does not mean that this is not equally binding as other standards of EU law—on the contrary, minimum standards must be interpreted broadly, to ensure the effectiveness of EU law in a field which is marked by considerable diversity between national legal systems.[135] Moreover, the Court will attempt to address the existence of national legal diversity in the field by developing autonomous concepts in the field of criminal procedure. The Court of Justice has developed autonomous concepts in order to ensure the uniform and independent interpretation of EU law, in cases where the latter does not refer expressly to national law as a tool for interpretation of the relevant EU law provisions. Autonomous concepts have been developed by the Court on the basis of a teleological and contextual interpretation, as well as on the basis of the need to ensure equality across the EU legal order.[136]

---

[133] For an overview of different national systems of criminal procedure in the investigative context, see inter alia E Cape, J Hodgson, T Prakken and T Spronken (eds), *Suspects in Europe. Procedural Rights at the Investigation Stage of the Criminal Process in the EU* (Antwerp, Intersentia, 2007).

[134] For an analysis, see Cras, n 77 above.

[135] AG Bot, *Covaci*, n 126 above, paragraphs 32–33.

[136] See inter alia Case C-195/06 *Kommunikationsbehörde Austria (KommAustria) v Österreichischer Rundfunk* [2007] ECR I-8817: 'It must be borne in mind that it follows from the *need for uniform application* of Community law *and from the principle of equality* that the terms of a provision of Community law *which makes no express reference to the law of the Member States* for the purpose of determining its meaning and scope *must normally be given an autonomous and uniform interpretation throughout the Community*, having regard to the *context* of the provision and the *objective* pursued by the legislation in question' (emphasis added)—para 24.

This approach is directly applicable to a number of provisions in EU criminal law, including the EU Directives on procedural rights in criminal proceedings.[137] The need to agree on common EU minimum standards in the field while respecting national legal diversity has led to the inclusion, in all three Directives adopted thus far, of general and broad terminology which remains undefined in the EU instruments and which is not to be defined in accordance with national law. This choice renders the potential of the future development of autonomous concepts by the Court of Justice as a key mechanism to flesh out the meaning of these terms considerable. Key concepts which have the potential to be defined as autonomous concern both the determination of the scope and the applicability of the defence rights Directives, as well as the interpretation of the content of the rights granted. With regard to the *scope* of the Directives, it is noteworthy that the terms 'suspect', 'accused' and 'criminal proceedings' are not defined in the text. Treating these concepts as autonomous EU law concepts is key to ensuring the effectiveness of the measures and achieving equality and the key objective of establishing a level playing-field of protection across Europe. Autonomous concepts will also have an influence on the interpretation of further specific provisions on the applicability of the Directives. The Directives limit access to a lawyer[138] and to an interpreter[139] to proceedings before courts having jurisdiction in criminal matters. However, this limitation must be interpreted consistently with the ruling of the Court of Justice in *Baláž*:[140] the Court has adopted a broad definition of the concept of a 'court having jurisdiction in criminal matters' as an autonomous concept of EU law. Notwithstanding detailed provisions in the Directives, aspects of the temporal scope of the Directive, including the precise time when rights become applicable or cease to become applicable, may be interpreted autonomously by the Court of Justice to create a level playing-field across the EU.[141]

Autonomous concepts will also be key in defining the *content* of the rights of suspects and accused persons. All three Directives oblige Member States to ensure

---

[137] V Mitsilegas, 'Managing Legal Diversity in Europe's Area of Criminal Justice: The Role of Autonomous Concepts' in R Colson and S Field (eds), *EU Criminal Justice and the Challenges of Legal Diversity. Towards A Socio-Legal Approach to EU Criminal Policy* (Cambridge, Cambridge University Press, forthcoming).

[138] Article 2(4) and Recitals 16 and 17.

[139] Article 1(3).

[140] Case C-60/12, *Baláž*, judgment of 14 November 2013.

[141] As seen above, the Directive on access to a lawyer applies 'to suspects or accused persons in criminal proceedings from the time when they are made aware that they are suspected or accused of having committed a criminal offence until the conclusion of the proceedings', which is understood to mean 'the final determination of the question whether the suspect or accused person has committed the offence, including, where applicable, sentencing and the resolution of any appeal' (Article 2(1)). For a similar wording, see Article 2(1) of the Directive on the right to information and Article 1(2) of the Directive on the right to interpretation and translation, n 35 above.

that rights are granted 'promptly'[142] 'without undue delay',[143] 'without delay',[144] 'in due time'[145] or 'within a reasonable period of time'.[146] The Court will be called to interpret these concepts autonomously, as they are not defined further in the Directives nor are they defined by reference to national law. Treating these concepts as autonomous will give flesh to the rights enshrined in the Directives. The same will potentially occur in the Court defining other key concepts inherent in the content of the rights provided by EU law, including what constitutes access to 'essential' documents for the purposes of the right to information[147] and right to translation,[148] what constitutes interpretation and translation 'of sufficient quality to safeguard the fairness of the proceedings' for the purposes of the said Directive,[149] and what is the meaning of the right of access to a lawyer 'in such time and in such a manner so as to allow the persons concerned to exercise their rights of defence practically and effectively'.[150] The treatment of these concepts as autonomous will influence significantly criminal law and practice in EU Member States, in particular in view of the fact that the Directives apply not only to cross-border, but also to purely domestic cases. By superimposing a Union meaning of key domestic law concepts, autonomous concepts become a mechanism of enforcement of EU law which has significant impact on domestic criminal justice systems and legal cultures, in changing both perceptions and practice in national criminal justice systems.[151] By carving out autonomous concepts of scope (who

---

[142] Key rights in the right to information Directive including the right to information about rights (Article 3(1)), the right to information about the accusation and relevant changes in such information (Article 6 paragraphs (1) and (4) respectively) and the provision of the Letter of Rights (Article 4(1)).

[143] See with regard to the Directive on access to a lawyer in particular: the right to access to a lawyer (Article 3(2)); the right to communicate with third persons and with consular authorities (Articles 6(1) and 7(1) respectively); the obligation to inform a person deprived of liberty in the execution of a European Arrest Warrant that they have the right to appoint a lawyer in the issuing Member State (Article 10(4)).

[144] The right to interpretation (Article 2(1) of the Directive on the right to interpretation and translation).

[145] See the Directive on the right to information on the right of access to the materials of the case, n 36 above (Article 7(3)).

[146] The right to translation (Article 3(1) of the Directive on the right to interpretation and translation, n 35 above).

[147] According to Article 7(1) of the right to information Directive, 'Member States [must] ensure access to documents related to the specific case in the possession of the competent authorities which are essential to challenging effectively, in accordance with national law, the lawfulness of the arrest or detention'.

[148] Article 3(1) of the Directive on the right to interpretation and translation grants a right to translation of essential documents: 'Member States [must] ensure that suspected or accused persons who do not understand the language of the criminal proceedings concerned are, within a reasonable period of time, provided with a written translation of all documents which are essential to ensure that they are able to exercise their right of defence and to safeguard the fairness of the proceedings'.

[149] Articles 2(8) and 3(9) respectively.

[150] Article 3(1).

[151] On the concept of legal culture as one encompassing these elements see D Nelken, 'Using Legal Culture: Purposes and Problems' in D Nelken (ed), *Using Legal Culture* (London, Wildy, Simmonds and Hill, 2012) 1–51. On a view of legal culture as embracing the participants' experience, see

is a suspect and an accused person?) and substance (what does it mean to grant rights promptly?), the Court of Justice will create a European legal culture of rights which Member States will be under a duty to accommodate.

IX. Variable Geometry and EU Procedural Rights—The Quest for Coherence

National concerns over the impact of EU harmonisation in the field of criminal procedure after Lisbon have led to a number of questions regarding the coherence of the EU legal framework on the protection of fundamental rights, in particular when viewed within the broader framework of its place in the EU system of mutual recognition of judicial decisions in criminal matters. These questions are exemplified by the position of the United Kingdom after the entry into force of the Treaty of Lisbon. The United Kingdom has negotiated an extension of its 'opt-out' Protocol after Lisbon to also apply to criminal justice measures adopted under Title V TFEU post-Lisbon.[152] On the basis of this protocol, the United Kingdom has chosen to opt into the Directives on the right to translation and interpretation and the right to information, but to opt out of the key Directive on the right to access to a lawyer in criminal proceedings, as the latter was deemed to be too disruptive for the UK criminal justice system.[153] At the same time, the end of the five-year transitional period from the entry into force of the Lisbon Treaty, set out in another Protocol on Transitional Provisions annexed to the Lisbon Treaty,[154] saw the United Kingdom opt out of all the EU pre-Lisbon third pillar *acquis*, but opt back into a list of 35 measures. These include the majority of the mutual recognition measures, and most significantly the Framework Decision on the European Arrest Warrant.[155] The selective participation of the United Kingdom in this context is problematic not only from the perspective of the protection of fundamental rights, but also from the perspective of the coherence of EU law.[156] The legal basis for the Directive on access to a lawyer (as with the other Directives implementing

---

R Cotterrell, 'Comparative Law and Legal Culture' in M Reimann and R Zimmermann (eds), *The Oxford Handbook of Comparative Law* (Oxford, OUP, 2008) 709–37.

[152] Protocol No 21 on the position of the United Kingdom and Ireland in respect of the area of freedom, security and justice.

[153] House of Lords European Union Committee, *The European Union's Policy on Criminal Procedure*, 30th Report, session 2010–12, HL paper 288, paragraph 99.

[154] Protocol 36 on 'Transitional provisions concerning acts adopted on the basis of Titles V and VI of the former version of the TEU prior the entry into force of the Treaty of Lisbon'.

[155] See Annex to Decision 2014/836/EU, [2014] OJ L343/11.

[156] V Mitsilegas, S Carrera and K Eisele, 'The End of the Transitional Period for Police and Criminal Justice Measures Adopted before the Lisbon Treaty. Who Monitors Trust in the European Justice Area?' 2014, *CEPS Paper in Liberty and Security in Europe*, no 74 (Brussels, Centre for European Policy Studies, 2014).

the Stockholm Roadmap) is Article 82(2) TFEU. This provision grants for the first time express competence to the European Union to legislate on aspects of criminal procedure (including explicitly the rights of the defence) where necessary to facilitate the operation of the principle of mutual recognition in criminal matters. The legality of post-Lisbon legislation on defence rights, including the Directive on access to a lawyer, is thus inextricably linked with the effective operation of mutual recognition in criminal matters, including of the Framework Decision on the European Arrest Warrant. This link is confirmed in the Preamble of the Directive on access to a lawyer itself,[157] which states that:

> Mutual recognition of decisions in criminal matters can operate effectively only in a spirit of trust in which not only judicial authorities, but all actors in the criminal process consider decisions of the judicial authorities of other Member States as equivalent to their own, implying not only trust in the adequacy of other Member States' rules, but also trust that those rules are correctly applied. Strengthening mutual trust requires detailed rules on the protection of the procedural rights and guarantees arising from the Charter, the ECHR and the ICCPR. It also requires, by means of this Directive and by means of other measures, further development within the Union of the minimum standards set out in the Charter and in the ECHR.[158]

The non-participation of the United Kingdom in measures on procedural rights, including the Directive on access to a lawyer, undermines the effective operation of the Framework Decision on the European Arrest Warrant as far as the UK is concerned. There is a direct causal link under EU constitutional law between the adoption of EU defence rights measures under Article 82(2) TFEU and the effective operation of mutual recognition in criminal matters. The non-participation of the UK in such measures poses fundamental challenges with regard to compliance by the UK with the fundamental rights obligations incumbent upon EU Member States participating in the system of mutual recognition in criminal matters. The UK's non-participation also challenges the coherence of EU criminal law in an integrated Area of Freedom, Security and Justice where EU criminal law measures are increasingly interconnected. It could be argued that from a black-letter perspective the current position of the United Kingdom is tenable: after all, under the Lisbon Treaty the UK can opt-in to (or opt out from) any post-Lisbon legislative proposal in the field of criminal justice on a case-by-case basis (and has decided not to participate in the access to a lawyer Directive). On the other hand, the day after the end of the transitional period of Protocol 36 will see the agreed participation of the UK in a list of enforcement measures including the Framework Decision on the European Arrest Warrant. However, this argument runs counter to a more teleological approach which respects fully the objectives

---

[157] [2013] OJ L294, 6.11.2013, p 1.

[158] Recital 6. The Preamble continues as follows: 'Common minimum rules should lead to increased confidence in the criminal justice systems of all Member States, which, in turn, should lead to a more efficient judicial cooperation in a climate of mutual trust and to the promotion of a fundamental rights culture in the Union' (recital 8).

and the integrated nature of the Area of Freedom, Security and Justice. There are important precedents by the Court of Justice in that respect in cases involving UK requests to participate in measures related to border controls. A key ruling in this context concerns the UK's request to participate in a third pillar Decision (Decision 2008/633) authorising access to the Visa Information System by law enforcement authorities.[159] The Decision is a third pillar measure (and at the time the Treaties did not include a Protocol extending the UK's opt-out arrangements to the third pillar). In applying for annulment of Decision 2008/633, the United Kingdom submitted that that decision does not constitute a development of provisions of the Schengen *acquis* in which the United Kingdom did not take part, but a police cooperation measure, as is also apparent from the Council's choice of legal basis, namely Articles 30(1)(b) EU and 34(c)(2) EU.[160] The Court however ruled against UK participation in the Decision. According to the Court,

> when classifying a measure as falling within an area of the Schengen *acquis*, or as a development of that *acquis*, the need for coherence of that *acquis*, and the need—where that *acquis* evolves—to maintain that coherence, must be taken into account.[161]

The Court added that

> the cooperation established by Decision 2008/633 could not, from both a functional and a practical point of view, exist independently of the VIS which falls, like Decision 2004/512 and the VIS Regulation on which the VIS is based, within the scope of the Schengen *acquis* concerning the common visa policy.[162]

The Court adopted a teleological and contextual approach focusing on the coherence of the Schengen *acquis*, following largely precedents in earlier rulings excluding the UK participation in the Frontex and biometrics Regulations.[163] The Court's rulings are also applicable with regard to the UK participation in EU criminal law measures. The legality of the adoption of procedural rights measures under Article 82(2) TFEU is inextricably linked with the effective operation of mutual recognition measures. As the Treaty is currently worded, defence rights measures under Article 82(2) TFEU cannot exist independently of measures on mutual recognition, including the Framework Decision on the European Arrest Warrant. Participating in the enforcement measures but not in the measures granting rights in order to facilitate judicial cooperation challenges the coherence of Europe's area of criminal justice and is contrary to EU law.

---

[159] Case C-482/08 *United Kingdom v Council*, judgment of 26 October 2010.
[160] ibid, paragraph 30.
[161] Paragraph 48.
[162] Paragraph 54.
[163] Case C-77/05, *United Kingdom v Council*, judgment of 18 December 2007 (*Frontex*), paragraph 55. Case C-137/05, *United Kingdom v Council*, judgment of 18 December 2007 (*Biometrics*).

X. Conclusion: Towards a Paradigm Change in Europe's Area of Criminal Justice

The entry into force of the Treaty of Lisbon has led to a paradigm shift in the development of Europe's area of criminal justice under the principle of mutual recognition. The inclusion in the Treaty of an express legal basis conferring upon the Union legislators authority to adopt measures harmonising criminal procedure has led to the European Union for the first time adopting secondary legislation on fundamental rights, in the form of a series of Directives on the rights of suspects and accused persons in criminal proceedings. In this manner, the construction of Europe's area of criminal justice has moved from a paradigm privileging the interests of the state and of law enforcement under a system of quasi-automatic mutual recognition to a paradigm where the rights of individuals affected by such system are brought to the fore, protected and enforced in EU law. The Lisbon legal basis enables the adoption of Directives containing only minimum standards. However, the significance of these Directives for the protection of human rights in Europe's area of criminal justice should not be underestimated. The Directives adopted thus far have a broad scope of application. Importantly, they go beyond the strict requirements of the Article 82(2) TFEU legal basis (which links harmonisation in the field of criminal procedure with the effective operation of mutual recognition) in applying not only to cross-border, but also to purely domestic cases. In this manner, national criminal procedural law—to the extent that it implements the Directives—must be applied in conformity with EU law. This means that national rules of criminal procedure must be applied in conformity with EU secondary human rights law (the Directives on procedural safeguards) as well as with EU constitutional human rights law (the Charter). The Court's case-law on the applicability of the Charter indicates that the latter is applicable not only in cases where national law implements specifically EU law, but also to cases where national law has a connection with EU law. These findings are applicable to a wide range of national provisions on criminal procedure, which—in integrated national systems—are closely linked with the achievement of the objectives and the effective implementation of the EU Directives on procedural rights, which will in turn result in the effective exercise of these rights on the ground.

In addition to these avenues of protection, the normalisation of large aspects of EU criminal law after Lisbon mean that secondary EU law on procedural rights enjoys the enhanced supranational enforcement mechanisms of EU law. At the level of decentralised enforcement, affected individuals can claim direct effect before national courts. At the level of centralised enforcement, the Commission now has full powers to monitor the effectiveness of the implementation of the procedural rights Directives in Member States and take action before the Court of Justice if such implementation is unsatisfactory. In view of the analysis above, the scope of the Commission's monitoring exercises is broader than to check merely the provision of national legislation adopted to implement specifically the EU Directives in question. The Commission is also entitled to monitor national criminal procedure systems more broadly to ensure that effective implementation has taken place, as well as to monitor compliance on the ground in addition to compliance on paper. Achieving effective implementation and enforcement of the Directives on procedural rights will be one of the key objectives in order to ensure that the individual emerges as the key focal point of Europe's area of criminal justice. The emphasis on fundamental rights is relevant not only in relation to mutual recognition, but throughout EU criminal law—with proposals on the establishment of a European Public Prosecutor's Office including specific cross-references to procedural rights in criminal proceedings. EU harmonisation and the enforcement of EU secondary fundamental rights law may be a challenge in view of the considerable diversity in national criminal procedure systems and standards. However, the very existence of EU law in the field triggers the intervention of EU institutions, and in particular the Court of Justice. It will be the task of the Court to develop an effective level playing-field of fundamental rights protection across the European Union. The Court's case-law on managing diversity (via the development of autonomous concepts in EU law), stressing the coherence of EU law (via setting limits to the choices of states with opt-out privileges with regard to participation in integrated measures in the Area of Freedom, Security and Justice), and ensuring the effective applicability of fundamental rights provides clear guiding principles in this context.

7

The Place of the Victim in Europe's Area of Criminal Justice

I. Introduction

The past 15 years have witnessed the transformation of the European Union into an Area of Freedom, Security and Justice, marked by the evolution of the EU constitutional framework in the field via the entry into force of the Treaties of Amsterdam and Lisbon, as well as by significant growth in secondary EU legislation in the field. The development of European integration in criminal matters has been a key part of this process, leading to the gradual configuration of a European area of criminal justice. The establishment of such an area faces a number of challenges, which are inextricably linked with the special place that criminal law occupies in the legal and political systems of EU Member States. Any attempt towards further European integration in the field of criminal justice has inevitably to address questions regarding the impact of EU action in the field on state sovereignty with regard to the exercise of state power in criminal matters. These sovereignty questions are accompanied by questions related to the impact of Europeanisation on national legal diversity, bearing in mind that domestic criminal justice systems reflect diverse and long-standing national legal traditions and concepts of justice. These questions have led to a number of complex solutions to accompany the supranationalisation of EU criminal law post-Lisbon, both as regards the extent of Union competence to legislate in the field and as regards the means and principles underlying EU legislative intervention. The impact of EU criminal law on state sovereignty, national legal diversity and national concepts of justice thus remains contested. This is the case in particular with regard to the place of the victim in the criminal justice system. When examined at a purely national level, calls to strengthen the position of the victim in criminal procedure have been accompanied by a series of questions and concerns with regard to the impact that victims' rights could have on the balance of interests in the criminal justice process, and in particular with regard to the potentially negative impact on the rights of the defendant in criminal proceedings. Different legal systems in Europe have provided different answers to these questions, leading to a considerable diversity in the protection of the victim and the content and extent of victims' rights in the domestic criminal justice system. It is in the context of this debate on the rights of victims in criminal procedure and their impact on criminal justice and the rights of the defendant in a landscape of considerable legal diversity among EU Member States that EU intervention with respect to victims' rights has taken place. Informed by these factors, the aim of this chapter is to provide a legal analysis of the place of the victim in EU criminal law and the EU area of criminal justice more generally. The chapter will begin by putting forward a typology of victims' rights in EU criminal law, by analysing the three different levels within which EU law addresses the position of the victim in the criminal justice process. This typology will be followed by a discussion of the three key challenges facing the evolution of EU criminal law on victims: first, the chapter will address the constitutional challenge, which is related to the extent to which the European Union has used its powers to legislate appropriately in the context of legislation on victims' rights; secondly, the chapter will deal with the challenge of national legal diversity, which involves an analysis of the extent to which EU victims' law has had or can have an impact on the domestic criminal justice systems of EU Member States, and of the extent to which EU harmonisation in the field can challenge national diversity; thirdly, the chapter will address the broader question of the challenge that EU criminal law on the victim poses to concepts of criminal justice in the EU Member States and in the European Union itself. The analysis will focus on the actual and potential impact of EU victims' law on the rights of the defence and on the balance of interests in the criminal justice process.

II. Victims' Rights in EU Criminal Law—A Typology

Victims' rights stem from multiple sources (including both legislation and case-law) and have been put forward in various stages of European integration, with preoccupation with victims' rights dating from before the attribution to the European Union of an express Treaty competence to legislate in criminal matters. EU law has established victims' rights related to the criminal justice process in three main ways. The first way has been to limit the power of Member States with regard to the national choices made in the field of criminal justice in order to ensure the protection of the rights of the victim who is an EU citizen—state sovereignty in criminal matters is limited by the need to ensure free movement and to respect fundamental principles of EU law. The second avenue for establishing victims' rights at EU level has been to ensure the extraterritorial reach of national decisions granting rights to victims and their enforcement by authorities in other EU Member States by applying the principle of mutual recognition in criminal matters[1]—the aim here being again to ensure the free movement of

---

[1] On the principle of mutual recognition see V Mitsilegas, 'The Constitutional Implications of Mutual Recognition in Criminal Matters in the EU' (2006) 43 *Common Market Law Review* 1277–1311.

the victim in a borderless Area of Freedom, Security and Justice. The third, and more direct, avenue of victim protection has been the adoption of specific EU legislation setting out a series of rights for the victim in criminal proceedings—such EU harmonisation measures have evolved over time, with the Treaty of Lisbon (Treaty on the Functioning of the European Union—TFEU) granting an express competence to the Union to adopt minimum standards on the rights of the victim. The rationale for EU intervention here goes beyond the justification of the other avenues for victim protection: the perceived need for the adoption of EU legislation establishing minimum standards on the rights of victims is not limited only to the achievement of the effective enjoyment of free movement in the European Union, but is linked more broadly to the need to ensure the effectiveness of the application of the principle of mutual recognition in criminal matters in the European Union (Article 82(2) TFEU). In addition to these three general avenues of ensuring the protection of the rights of victims in the criminal justice process by European Union law, a number of further EU law measures related to the victim have been adopted, ranging from specific measures on victims' rights in the context of terrorism,[2] trafficking in human beings[3] and sexual exploitation legislation[4] to legislation on victims' compensation[5] and the mutual recognition of civil protection orders.[6] These measures may be linked on occasion with the development of the EU criminal justice *acquis*, but will not be analysed in detail by this chapter which aims to focus on the general EU framework for the protection of victims in the criminal justice process.

A. Victims' Rights as Free Movement Rights

The first intervention with regard to ensuring the rights of the victim in the criminal process came by the Court of Justice in the 1980s. In an era when the (then) European Community did not possess express competence to legislate in criminal matters, the Court, in a series of rulings, found nevertheless that Community law did have an impact on criminal law by placing limits on national criminal law in cases where the latter was found to be contrary to fundamental principles of Community law such as free movement.[7] The application of this line of judgments in the case of victims of crime led the Court to find that national legislation restricting compensation to victims who were nationals of an EU

---

[2] Council Framework Decision 2002/475/JHA on combating terrorism [2002] OJ L164/3.

[3] Directive 2011/36/EU of the European Parliament and of the Council on preventing and combating trafficking in human beings and protecting its victims [2011] OJ L101/1.

[4] Directive 2011/93/EU of the European Parliament and of the Council on combating the sexual abuse and sexual exploitation of children and child pornography [2011] OJ L335/1.

[5] Council Directive 2004/80/EC relating to compensation to crime victims [2004] OJ L261/15.

[6] Regulation (EU) 606/2013 of the European Parliament and of the Council on mutual recognition of protection measures in civil matters [2013] OJ L181/4.

[7] See V Mitsilegas, *EU Criminal Law* (Oxford, Hart Publishing, 2009) ch 2.

Member State or holders of a residence permit was contrary to Community law. In the well-known *Cowan* ruling,[8] the Court found that the prohibition of discrimination

> must be interpreted as meaning that in respect of persons whose freedom to travel to a Member State, in particular as recipients of services, is guaranteed by Community law that State may not make the award of State compensation for harm caused in that State to the victim of an assault resulting in physical injury subject to the condition that he hold a residence permit or be a national of a country which has entered into a reciprocal agreement with that Member State.[9]

The Court reiterated its earlier case-law on the impact of Community law on national criminal law[10] to state that although in principle criminal legislation and the rules of criminal procedure, among which the national provision is to be found, are matters for which the Member States are responsible, the Court has consistently held that Community law sets certain limits to their power. In the present case such legislative provisions may not discriminate against persons to whom Community law gives the right to equal treatment or restrict the fundamental freedoms guaranteed by Community law.[11] By treating tourists as recipients of services and limiting national legislative choices as regards compensation of the victims of crime in order to ensure the effectiveness of Community law, the Court of Justice in *Cowan* provided the first major avenue for the protection of victims' rights when exercising free movement rights. Unlike in other cases, where the result of the Court's interference in national criminal justice choices has been to limit national criminalisation or punishment which was deemed to be disproportionate to the achievement of the effectiveness of Community law and thus enhance the rights of the defendant,[12] in *Cowan* the need to respect Community law has resulted in extending the scope of the rights of the victim in the criminal process.

B. Mutual Recognition

More than 20 years after the Court's ruling in *Cowan*, European integration in criminal matters has made spectacular steps forward: from the EC Treaty in the 1980s, which did not contain an express Community competence to legislate in criminal matters, to the entry into force of the Lisbon Treaty in 2009, which has largely 'supranationalised' EU criminal law, via the 'half-way house' Maastricht, Amsterdam and Nice Treaties. Yet the passage of time and the ensuing

---

[8] Case 186/87 *Cowan v Le Trésor Public* [1989] ECR 195.
[9] ibid, para 20.
[10] See in particular Case 203/80 *Casati* [1981] ECR 2595.
[11] Case 186/87 *Cowan*, n 8 above, para 19.
[12] See eg Case C-193/94 *Skanavi and Chryssanthakopoulos* [1996] ECR I-929.

constitutional developments at EU level do not seem to have altered the fundamental aim of granting rights to victims in order to ensure their freedom of movement, this time in a borderless Area of Freedom, Security and Justice. Rather than
relying exclusively on the case-law of the Court of Justice, the EU legislator has
opted for the adoption of a specific post-Lisbon legislative instrument to ensure
the protection of victims when they exercise free movement rights in the European Union. The measure in question is Directive 2011/99/EU on the European
Protection Order.[13] The Directive, which was adopted under a legal basis related to
judicial cooperation in criminal matters,[14] aims to apply the principle of mutual
recognition in criminal matters to orders issued to protect victims in one Member
State when these victims find themselves in other EU Member States—in other
words, it is intended that the recognition of a European Protection Order by the
authority in the executing Member State will mean that the protection will 'follow'
the victim to the Member State they have moved to. A European Protection Order
is defined as

> a decision, taken by a judicial or equivalent authority of a Member State in relation to a
> protection measure, on the basis of which a judicial or equivalent authority of another
> Member State takes any appropriate measure or measures under its own national law
> with a view to continuing the protection of the protected person.[15]

It may only be issued

> when a protection measure has been previously adopted in the issuing State, imposing
> on the person causing danger one or more of the following prohibitions or restrictions:
>
> (a) a prohibition from entering certain localities, places or defined areas where the
>   protected person resides or visits;
> (b) a prohibition or regulation of contact, in any form, with the protected person,
>   including by phone, electronic or ordinary mail, fax or any other means; or
> (c) a prohibition or regulation on approaching the protected person closer than a
>   prescribed distance.[16]

The objective of the European Protection Order Directive is to set out

> rules allowing a judicial or equivalent authority in a Member State, in which a protection
> measure has been adopted with a view to protecting a person against a criminal act by
> another person which may endanger his life, physical or psychological integrity, dignity,
> personal liberty or sexual integrity, to issue a European protection order enabling a com-
> petent authority in another Member State to continue the protection of the person in
> the territory of that other Member State, following criminal conduct, or alleged criminal
> conduct, in accordance with the national law of the issuing State.[17]

---

[13] Directive 2011/99/EU of the European Parliament and of the Council of 13 December 2011 on
the European Protection Order [2011] OJ L338/2.
[14] Art 82(1)(a) and (d) TFEU.
[15] Art 2(1).
[16] Art 5.
[17] Art 1.

Upon receipt of a European Protection Order

> the competent authority of the executing State [must], without undue delay, recognise
> that order and take a decision adopting any measure that would be available under its
> national law in a similar case in order to ensure the protection of the protected person.[18]

The executing authority is granted limited grounds for non-recognition.[19] The
Directive also puts forward the principle of assimilation, by stating that

> a European Protection Order [must] be recognised with the same priority which would
> be applicable *in a similar national case*, taking into consideration any specific circum-
> stances of the case, including the urgency of the matter, the date foreseen for the arrival
> of the protected person on the territory of the executing State and, where possible, the
> degree of risk for the protected person (emphasis added).[20]

The free movement rationale of the Directive is evident in the Preamble, where it
is stated that

> [i]n a common area of justice without internal borders, it is necessary to ensure that the
> protection provided to a natural person in one Member State is maintained and contin-
> ued in any other Member State to which the person moves or has moved

and that

> [i]t should also be ensured that the legitimate exercise by citizens of the Union of their
> right to move and reside freely within the territory of Member States, in accordance
> with Article 3(2) of the [TEU] and Article 21 TFEU does not result in a loss of their
> protection.[21]

C. Harmonisation

The process of harmonisation of national systems with regard to the rights of the
victims in criminal procedure began in the era of the third pillar, with the adoption, under Articles 31 and 34(2)(b) TEU, of the Framework Decision on the standing of victims in criminal proceedings.[22] The Framework Decision introduced a
number of provisions on the place of the victim in the criminal process.[23] It opens
with a rather general provision on 'respect and recognition', calling upon Member
States to 'ensure that victims have a real and appropriate role' in their criminal

---

[18] Art 9(1).

[19] Art 10.

[20] Art 15.

[21] Preamble, recital 6.

[22] Council Framework Decision 2001/220/JHA on the standing of victims in criminal proceedings
[2001] OJ L82/1.

[23] For an overview of the Framework Decision, see S de Biolley and A Weyembergh, 'L'Espace Pénal
Européen et les Droits des Victimes' (2005) 31 *Revue de la Faculté de Droit, Université Libre de Bruxelles*
93–122.

justice systems and to 'continue to make every effort to ensure that victims are treated with due respect for the dignity of the individual during proceedings' and to 'recognise the rights and legitimate interests of the victims with particular reference to criminal proceedings'.[24] Specific provisions in the Framework Decision call upon Member States to 'safeguard the possibility for victims to be heard during proceedings and to supply evidence',[25] and establish a right to receive information,[26] a series of communication safeguards[27] and details on specific assistance to the victim.[28] Member States must further 'afford victims who have the status of parties or witnesses the possibility of reimbursement of expenses incurred as a result of their legitimate participation in criminal proceedings'[29] with victims also being 'entitled to obtain a decision within reasonable time ... on compensation by the offender' in criminal proceedings.[30] Member States will 'seek to promote mediation in criminal cases'.[31] Most importantly, in the context of criminal procedure, the Framework Decision provides with a 'right to protection' which includes a duty for Member States to

> ensure that, where there is a need to protect victims—particularly those most vulnerable—from the effects of giving evidence in open court, victims may, by decision taken by the court, be entitled to testify in a manner which will enable this objective to be achieved, by any appropriate means compatible with [their] basic legal principles.[32]

The Framework Decision thus aims in general to enhance the position of the victim in criminal procedure across the European Union—as is noted in its Preamble, 'Member States should approximate their laws and regulations to the extent necessary to attain the objective of affording victims of crime a high level of protection, irrespective of the Member State in which they are present'.[33] However, its provisions are drafted in rather general terms and do not provide a high standard of legal certainty. This may be explained by the considerable diversity as regards the position of the victim in the national criminal justice systems of Member States, the decision-making limits placed by unanimity in third pillar law, and Member States' concerns with regard to the impact that the Framework Decision could have on their criminal justice systems—with the Preamble attempting to ensure minimum interference by stating that its provisions 'do not impose an obligation on Member States to ensure that victims will be treated in a manner equivalent to that of a party to proceedings'.[34] Although as seen below the Framework Decision

---

[24] Framework Decision 2001/220/JHA, Art 2(1).
[25] Art 3, first indent.
[26] Art 4.
[27] Art 5.
[28] Art 6.
[29] Art 7.
[30] Art 9(1).
[31] Art 10(1).
[32] Art 8(4).
[33] Preamble, recital 4.
[34] Preamble, recital 9.

on the rights of victims in criminal procedure has now been replaced by a post-Lisbon Directive, it remains significant in that its provisions have formed the basis for the development of the case-law of the Court of Justice in the field.[35] The Framework Decision also forms an important benchmark in relation to which post-Lisbon developments can be assessed.

The entry into force of the Lisbon Treaty led to the adoption of a new Directive on the rights of the victims of crime.[36] A deliverable under the so-called Budapest Roadmap on the rights of victims in criminal proceedings,[37] the Directive was adopted under Article 82(2) TFEU which confers upon the European Union competence to establish minimum rules on the rights of the victims of crime to the extent necessary to facilitate mutual recognition of judgments and judicial decisions and police and judicial cooperation in criminal matters having a cross-border dimension. According to Article 82(2), such minimum rules must take into account the differences between the legal traditions and systems of the Member States. The Directive thus constitutes an attempt to establish minimum rules on the rights of victims in the face of the considerable diversity in national criminal justice systems as regards the position and rights of the victim. The Preamble to the Directive reflects this diversity by recognising that

> the role of victims in the criminal justice system and whether they can participate actively in criminal proceedings vary across Member States, depending on their national system, and is determined by one or more of the following criteria: whether the national system provides for a legal status as a party to criminal proceedings; whether the victim is under a legal requirement or is requested to participate actively in criminal proceedings, for example as a witness; and/or whether the victim has a legal entitlement under national law to participate actively in criminal proceedings and is seeking to do so, where the national system does not provide that victims have the legal status of a party to the criminal proceedings.[38]

As will be seen below,[39] national legal diversity is further reflected in the text of the Directive by the inclusion of a number of references to national procedural rules as regards the enforcement of the rights set out in the Directive. According to the Preamble, 'Member States should determine which of [the criteria mentioned above] apply to determine the scope of rights set out in this Directive where there are references to the role of the victim in the relevant criminal justice system'.[40] A notable exception to the definition of rights by reference to national

---

[35] See section IV below.
[36] Directive 2012/29/EU of the European Parliament and of the Council establishing minimum standards on the rights, support and protection of victims of crime, and replacing Council Framework Decision 2001/220/JHA [2012] OJ L315/57.
[37] Council Resolution on a roadmap for strengthening the rights and protection of victims, in particular in criminal proceedings [2011] OJ C187/1.
[38] Directive 2012/29/EU, Preamble, recital 20.
[39] See section IV below.
[40] Preamble, recital 20.

systems constitutes the adoption of a 'European' definition of the victim which is, according to the Directive,

i.   a natural person who has suffered harm, including physical, mental or emotional harm or economic loss which was directly caused by a criminal offence; [and]
ii. family members of a person whose death was directly caused by a criminal offence and who have suffered harm as a result of that person's death.[41]

The Directive also contains a definition of family members[42] but further allows for the limitation and prioritisation of family members by Member States.[43]

As regards the content of the rights, the Directive introduces a multi-level system of protection of the victim. According to Article 1(1), its purpose is 'to ensure that victims of crime receive appropriate information, support and protection and are able to participate in criminal proceedings'. The rights of the victims are structured into three broad categories. The first category involves the provision of information and support to the victim.[44] This includes the right of the victim to understand and be understood;[45] the right to receive information from the first contact with a competent authority;[46] the rights of the victim when making a complaint;[47] the right of the victim to receive information about their case;[48] the right to interpretation and translation;[49] the right to access victim support services;[50] and the establishment of minimum rules on support from victim support services.[51] Another category of provisions involves the protection of victims and recognition of victims with specific protection needs.[52] These include the right to protection, under which Member States must ensure that measures are available to protect victims and their family members from secondary and repeat victimisation[53] and the right to avoid contact between victim and offender,[54] both of which could be seen as overlapping with the provisions of the Directive on the European Protection Order; the right to protection of victims during criminal investigations;[55] the right to protection of privacy;[56] provisions on the individual assessment of victims to identify specific protection needs;[57] and

---

[41] Art 2(1)(a).
[42] Art 2(1)(b).
[43] Art 2(2).
[44] Chapter 2 of the Directive.
[45] Art 3.
[46] Art 4.
[47] Art 5.
[48] Art 6.
[49] Art 7.
[50] Art 8.
[51] Art 9.
[52] Chapter 4 of the Directive.
[53] Art 18.
[54] Art 19.
[55] Art 20.
[56] Art 21.
[57] Art 22.

provisions on the right to protection of victims with specific protection needs during criminal proceedings[58] and the right to protection of child victims during criminal proceedings.[59] A number of the Directive's provisions on the right to protection of the victim may have a significant impact on the rights of the defendant in criminal proceedings, and the drafters of the Directive have been careful to state that a number of these rights are without prejudice to the rights of defence and in accordance with rules of judicial discretion.[60]

The most significant impact on the position of the defendant in criminal proceedings in relation to the victims may arise from the third category of rights set out in the Directive, namely rights related to participation in criminal proceedings. The Directive grants the victim the right to be heard during criminal proceedings,[61] rights in the event of a decision not to prosecute,[62] the right to safeguards in the context of restorative justice services,[63] a right to legal aid,[64] and rights to reimbursement of expenses,[65] to the return of property[66] and to a decision on compensation from the offender in the course of criminal proceedings.[67] The Directive also contains a provision on the rights of victims resident in another Member State.[68] However, these rights are largely dependent on national law, with the Directive attempting again to achieve a compromise between the introduction of EU minimum standards and the respect of national diversity in the field. Hence the Directive provides repeatedly that the procedural rules governing the exercise of a number of key rights including the right to be heard, the right to legal aid, the right of reimbursement of expenses, the right to return of property and the rights of the victims in the event of a decision not to prosecute will be determined by national law.[69] Moreover, the Directive grants considerable discretion to Member States as regards the content of certain rights: as regards the right to be heard, Member States must 'ensure that victims *may* be heard during criminal proceedings and may provide evidence' (emphasis added);[70] Member States must ensure the right of the victim to review a decision not to prosecute '*in accordance with the victim's role in the relevant criminal justice system*' (emphasis added).[71] In addition to these limitations and references to national legal systems, a number of rights are

---

[58] Art 23.
[59] Art 24.
[60] Arts 20 and 23. See also Art 18 on the right to protection which is without prejudice to the rights of defence.
[61] Art 10.
[62] Art 11.
[63] Art 12.
[64] Art 13.
[65] Art 14.
[66] Art 15.
[67] Art 16.
[68] Art 17.
[69] Arts 10(2), 13, 14, 15 and 11(1) and (2) respectively.
[70] Art 10(1).
[71] Art 11(1).

not set out in detail in the text of the Directive, but greater detail on their scope is provided in the Preamble. The Preamble of the Directive contains no fewer than 72 recitals and a number of them are detailed and serve to explain and (as demonstrated in the case of the right to reimbursement of expenses) limit the rights set out in the text of the Directive.[72] The use of extensive Preambular provisions has been explained as a means of addressing Member States' concerns with regard to the perceived lack of legal certainty in the Commission's original proposal, with the recitals acting as an aid to interpreting the operative Articles of the Directive when they are perceived as ambiguous, but also as a means of enabling the Council and the European Parliament to reach agreement on the Directive with recitals being used to mention issues where the legislators could not agree real obligations in the operative text.[73]

III. The Place of the Victim in Europe's Area of Criminal Justice: Constitutional Implications

The adoption of measures on victim' rights at EU level does not always sit easily with the limits of EU competence to legislate in criminal matters. Questions of the legality of both pre-Lisbon and post-Lisbon victims' rights instruments arise, in particular as regards the appropriateness of the legal basis used for their adoption. On the one hand, the extent to which measures on the rights of the victim in criminal procedure can be adopted on the basis of EU competence to legislate in criminal matters is not always clear. On the other hand, national legal diversity concerning means of protecting the victim (and the use of civil and not criminal law in this context) raises the question of whether a criminal law legal basis is appropriate and/or sufficient for the Union to legislate in this context. The latter question has arisen prominently with regard to the adoption of the Directive on the European Protection Order. The Preamble to the Directive clarifies that the latter 'applies to protection measures adopted in criminal matters and does not therefore cover protection measures adopted in civil matters'. It adds however that

[f]or a protection order to be executable in accordance with this Directive, it is not necessary for a criminal offence to have been established by a final decision. Nor is the

---

[72] According to recital 47, 'victims should not be expected to incur expenses in relation to their participation in criminal proceedings. Member States should be required to reimburse only necessary expenses of victims in relation to their participation in criminal proceedings and should not be required to reimburse victims' legal fees ... The right to reimbursement of expenses in criminal proceedings should not arise in a situation where a victim makes a statement on a criminal offence. Expenses should only be covered to the extent that the victim is obliged or requested by the competent authorities to be present and actively participate in the criminal proceedings'.

[73] See H Nowell-Smith, 'Behind the Scenes in the Negotiation of EU Criminal Justice Legislation' (2012) 3 *New Journal of European Criminal Law* 381–93, 384.

criminal, administrative or civil nature of the authority adopting a protection measure relevant. This Directive does not oblige Member States to amend their national law to enable them to adopt protection measures in the context of criminal proceedings.[74]

This flexibility as regards the nature of the authority issuing a European Protection Order and the nature of the protection measure undertaken in the executing state is maintained in the operative part of the Directive. While a protection measure is defined as a decision 'in criminal matters' adopted in the issuing Member State,[75] a European Protection Order is defined as

> a decision, taken by a judicial *or equivalent* authority of a Member State in relation to a protection measure, on the basis of which a judicial *or equivalent* authority of another Member State takes any appropriate measure or measures under its own national law with a view to continuing the protection of the protected person (emphasis added).[76]

However, the Directive does not require these authorities to be part of Member States' criminal justice systems, with the Directive not excluding the possibility that such authorities are administrative or civil bodies. According to the Preamble, the Directive takes into account 'the fact that effective protection can be provided by means of protection orders issued by an authority other than a criminal court'.[77] Flexibility is retained also with regard to the nature of the European Protection Order. In executing the European Protection Order, 'the executing State may apply, in accordance with its national law, *criminal, administrative, or civil measures*' (emphasis added).[78] The Directive thus allows the transformation of what is a decision in criminal matters in the issuing state to its execution as an administrative or a civil law measure in the executing state. While such flexibility may reflect the considerable diversity in national legal systems in the field,[79] as well as the need to reassure Member States that the adoption of the Directive will not alter their domestic criminal justice systems,[80] it is questionable whether Article 82(1) TFEU on judicial cooperation in criminal matters is sufficient as a sole legal basis for this instrument. A joint legal basis of Article 82 and Article 81 TFEU (on judicial cooperation in civil matters) would reflect more accurately the content and the cooperation mechanism set out in the Directive.[81] The adoption of the European Protection Order Directive under multiple legal bases could

---

[74] Directive 2011/99/EU of the European Parliament and of the Council of 13 December 2011 on the European protection order, Preamble, recital 10.

[75] Art 2(2) of the Directive.

[76] Art 2(1).

[77] Preamble, recital 8.

[78] Art 9(1).

[79] See also Preamble, recital 20.

[80] According to the Preamble to the Directive, the latter 'does not create obligations to modify national systems for adopting protection measures nor does it create obligations to introduce or amend a criminal law system for executing a European protection order' (recital 8).

[81] See S van der Aa and J Ouwerkerk, 'The European Protection Order: No Time to Waste or a Waste of Time?' (2011) 19 *European Journal of Crime, Criminal Law and Criminal Justice* 267–87, 280.

further serve to focus the mind of the EU legislators on the potential overlap of a number of the Directive's provisions with other EU law instruments which may affect the position of the victim in similar circumstances, including mutual recognition instruments in both the civil and criminal law spheres.[82]

Legality questions have also arisen with regard to the adoption of EU legislation aiming to harmonise national laws on the rights of the victims of crime. The third pillar Framework Decision on the standing of victims in criminal proceedings was adopted under the general legal basis of Article 31 TEU on common action on judicial cooperation in criminal matters, without specifying further which subparagraph of this provision applies. Article 31 TEU was thus used in a flexible manner in order to translate the political will of Member States to be seen to be taking action in favour of victims of crime into legal reality. Yet the link between the Framework Decision and the facilitation of judicial cooperation in criminal matters, which is the main objective of Article 31 TEU, has not been demonstrated and remains questionable. Indeed, approximation under the Framework Decision has been justified as 'necessary to attain the objective of affording victims of crime a high level of protection, irrespective of the Member State in which they are present'.[83] This approach reflects the need to achieve primarily a free movement objective, rather than an objective geared towards the facilitation of judicial cooperation in criminal matters. Notwithstanding the introduction of an express legal basis by the Lisbon Treaty conferring upon the European Union competence to adopt legislation on the rights of victims under Article 82(2) TFEU, the new Directive on the rights of the victims of crime is not devoid of similar legality shortcomings. Article 82(2) TFEU confers upon the European Union competence to establish minimum rules on the rights of the victims of crime 'to the extent necessary to facilitate mutual recognition of judgments and judicial decisions and police and judicial cooperation in criminal matters having a cross-border dimension'. However, it is questionable whether the Directive on the rights of the victims of crime meets the legality criteria set out by Article 82(2) TFEU. It has not been demonstrated in particular *how* the Directive will serve to facilitate mutual recognition or judicial cooperation in criminal matters having a cross-border dimension. In the Explanatory Memorandum to its original draft Directive, the Commission attempted to substantiate a link between the rights of victims of crime and the facilitation of mutual recognition as follows:

> Mutual recognition can only operate in a spirit of confidence, whereby not only judicial authorities but all those involved in the criminal justice process and others who have a legitimate interest in it can trust in the adequacy of the rules of each Member State and trust that those rules are correctly applied. Where victims of crime are not subject to the

---

[82] The Preamble to the Directive contains detailed references on the relationship between the various EU law measures which may be of relevance—see recitals 16 and 33 and 34 for criminal law and civil law measures respectively.

[83] Council Framework Decision 2001/220/JHA (n 22 above) Preamble, recital 4.

same minimum standards throughout the EU, such trust can be reduced due to concerns over the treatment of victims or due to differences in procedural rules.

> Common minimum rules should thus lead to increased confidence in the criminal justice system of all Member States, which in turn should lead to more efficient judicial cooperation in a climate of mutual trust as well as to the promotion of a fundamental rights culture in the European Union. They should also contribute to reducing obstacles to the free movement of citizens since such common minimum rules should apply to all victims of crime.[84]

However, as I have noted elsewhere in the context of the justification by the Commission of the adoption of EU minimum rules on the rights of the defendant in criminal proceedings,[85] the use of mutual trust as an element justifying the adoption of EU measures in the field of criminal procedure is problematic in two respects: it fails to provide a direct and clear link between the rights proposed and their necessity for the operation of mutual recognition; and it is based on a concept (of mutual trust) which is too subjective for it to meet the criteria set out by the Court of Justice when ascertaining the legality of EU instruments, namely that the choice of legal basis must be based on objective factors which are amenable to judicial review.[86] Compared with EU legislation in the field of the rights of the defendant, where minimum EU rules can be justified on specific human rights grounds and where EU standards can be linked directly with the operation of specific mutual recognition instruments such as the Framework Decision on the European Arrest Warrant,[87] the link between EU minimum rules on the victims of crime and the facilitation of mutual recognition and judicial cooperation in criminal matters is much less direct. It is perhaps no coincidence that the Commission's statement attempting to link the adoption of EU-wide minimum standards on victims of crime with the facilitation of mutual recognition has not been replicated in the finally adopted text of the Directive. However, in this way the EU legislators have not provided any detailed or specific explanation of the link between the Directive and the criteria set out by its legal basis, namely Article 82(2) TFEU. The political will to legislate on victims' rights post-Lisbon has resulted in a rather flexible use of the Treaty provisions enabling EU action on the harmonisation of national laws of criminal procedure.

---

[84] Proposal for a Directive of the European Parliament and of the Council establishing minimum standards on the rights, support and protection of victims of crime, COM(2011) 275 final, Brussels, 2–3.

[85] V Mitsilegas, 'Trust-building Measures in the European Judicial Area in Criminal Matters: Issues of Competence, Legitimacy and Inter-institutional Balance' in S Carrera and T Balzacq (eds), *Security versus Freedom? A Challenge for Europe's Future* (Aldershot, Ashgate, 2006) 279–89. The argument has been developed further in V Mitsilegas, 'The Limits of Mutual Trust in Europe's Area of Freedom, Security and Justice. From Automatic Inter-state Cooperation to the Slow Emergence of the Individual' 31 *Yearbook of European Law 2012* 319–72.

[86] See inter alia Case C-300/89 *Commission v Council* [1991] ECR I-2867 (*Titanium Dioxide*).

[87] Mitsilegas, 'The Limits of Mutual Trust', n 85 above.

IV. The Impact of EU Law on Victims' Rights on National Criminal Justice Systems

As seen above, one of the key challenges in developing EU criminal law on victims has been how to adopt EU-wide standards in the face of considerable diversity in terms of the legal position of the victim in domestic criminal justice systems. Throughout the development of EU criminal law on victims, the European Union institutions have been called upon to address the tension between the perceived need to create an EU level playing-field as regards the rights of victims and the need to maintain a degree of flexibility and breathing space for national systems in the light of the considerable differences in national criminal laws on victims. The challenge of adopting EU-wide standards on the rights of victims while taking into account national legal diversity has emerged in different ways, but forcefully, at all levels of EU legislative action in the field: from establishing victims' rights via the use of the principle of mutual recognition in criminal matters to legislative efforts to harmonise Member States' national law on victims' rights. The evolution of EU harmonisation measures from the largely intergovernmental third pillar to the post-Lisbon, more supranational, reality has not put an end to these challenges.

A. Mutual Recognition

One of the ways in which EU law has addressed the need to respect national legal diversity has been via the use of mutual recognition as a method of advancing victims' rights, with the prima facie advantage of mutual recognition in this context being that, unlike harmonisation instruments, Member States may not be required to introduce immediate and specific changes to their domestic criminal law and procedure as a result of implementing EU law in the field.[88] In the field of victims' rights, the Directive on the European Protection Order aims to achieve the protection of the victim by putting forward a system of interaction of national legal orders resulting in the recognition and execution of a national protection decision by the authorities of another Member State. Yet, even in this context of mutual recognition, the European Protection Order contains a number of further provisions aimed at managing the high degree of flexibility in national legal orders. The Preamble sets out a general flexibility clause stating that the Directive 'takes account of the different legal traditions of the Member States as well as the fact that effective protection can be provided by means of protection orders issued by an authority other than a criminal court'. It adds at the same time however that the Directive 'does not create obligations to modify national systems for adopting

---

[88] See Chapters 4 and 5 in this volume.

protection measures nor does it create obligations to introduce or amend a criminal law system for executing a European protection order'.[89] The tension between ensuring the effectiveness of the Directive in ensuring maximum flexibility while respecting national legal diversity and not challenging national sovereignty in criminal matters is evident in the wording of this provision.

In addition to this general flexibility provision, the Directive contains a number of provisions aiming to ensure flexibility in how the mutual recognition system established therein will work. In the first place, the Directive aims at ensuring flexibility with regard to the *authorities* which will be competent to operate the mutual recognition system regarding European Protection Orders. This need for flexibility is confirmed in the Preamble, according to which

> since, in the Member States, different kinds of authorities (civil, criminal or administrative) are competent to adopt and enforce protection measures, it is appropriate to provide a high degree of flexibility in the cooperation mechanism between the Member States under this Directive.[90]

The text of the Directive attempts to capture national legal diversity by allowing the issuing of a European Protection Order by '*judicial or equivalent* authorit[ies] … in accordance with the national law of the issuing State' (emphasis added).[91] The designation of the judicial or equivalent authorities responsible for issuing and recognising European Protection Orders is left to Member States.[92] There are two questions in relation to the determination of the authorities competent to act within the framework of the Directive. The first question is whether the use of non-criminal judicial authorities is compatible with the legal basis of the Directive, which focuses on judicial cooperation *in criminal matters*.[93] The second question is whether the use of 'equivalent' authorities is allowed by a legal basis which focuses on *judicial* cooperation. Not only do the answers to these questions have considerable legality implications, but they also have a considerable impact on the protection of fundamental rights. In the context of the implementation of another mutual recognition measure, the Framework Decision on the European Arrest Warrant, serious doubts have been raised by national courts on the extent to which non-judicial authorities are sufficiently independent to provide appropriate human rights safeguards.[94] While the European Protection Order Directive follows the example of other mutual recognition instruments and aims to ensure flexibility by leaving the designation of competent authorities to Member States, national courts have expressed doubts as to whether such

---

[89] Directive 2011/99/EU, Preamble recital 8.
[90] Preamble, recital 20.
[91] Art 1.
[92] Art 3.
[93] *Bucnys v Ministry of Justice, Lithuania* [2013] UKSC 71. See Lord Mance, para 23.
[94] See *Assange v The Swedish Prosecution Authority* [2012] UKSC 22.

designation plays a definitive role regarding the assessment of whether an authority is sufficiently independent to be considered a judicial authority for the purposes of these instruments.[95] The discretion given to Member States by the European Protection Order to designate authorities, combined with the potentially extensive scope and diverse nature of these authorities, is likely to prove counter-productive to speedy mutual recognition, as executing authorities are likely to undertake to assess themselves the independence of the issuing authority, especially in cases where the legal systems of the issuing and the executing Member States are markedly different. More concrete answers are likely to be provided by the Court of Justice, with the definition of 'judicial or equivalent authority' for the purposes of the European Protection Order constituting an autonomous concept of EU law. The Court of Justice has already found that the meaning of 'court having jurisdiction in particular in criminal matters' for the purposes of the Framework Decision on the mutual recognition of financial penalties cannot be left to the discretion of each Member State but constitutes an autonomous concept in EU law.[96]

The need to accommodate national diversity with regard to the protection of victims is also reflected in efforts to achieve flexibility with regard to *the measures of protection* which will follow the recognition of a European Protection Order. Thus,

> the competent authority in the executing State is not required in all cases to take the same protection measure as those which were adopted in the issuing State, and has a degree of discretion to adopt any measure which it deems adequate and appropriate under its national law in a similar case in order to provide continued protection to the protected person in the light of the protection measure adopted in the issuing State as described in the European protection order.[97]

'The executing State may apply, in accordance with its national law, criminal, administrative, or civil measures'.[98] These and subsequent measures must, 'to the highest degree possible, correspond to the protection measure adopted in the issuing [Member] State'.[99] However, as mentioned above Member States are not obliged to change their law to introduce new protection measures.[100] As is recognised in the Preamble,

> in view of the different legal traditions of the Member States, where no protection measure would be available in the executing State in a case similar to the factual situation described in the European protection order, the competent authority of the executing

---

[95] In the context of the European Arrest Warrant, see the ruling of Lord Mance in *Bucnys*, n 93 above, para 22.
[96] Case C-60/12 *Baláž* (CJEU, 14 November 2013) paras 25–26.
[97] Directive 2011/99/EU, Preamble, recital 20.
[98] Art 9(1).
[99] Art 9(2).
[100] See Preamble, recital 8.

State should report any breach of the protection measure described in [the Order] of which it is aware to the competent authority of the issuing State.[101]

The Directive also includes a number of provisions clarifying applicable law and the respective areas of responsibility between the issuing and the executing states in the aftermath of the recognition of the European Protection Order. The law of the executing state will govern the adoption and enforcement of the Order and the consequences of its breach[102] while the issuing state will remain competent for 'the renewal, review, modification, revocation and withdrawal of the protection measure' as well as for 'the imposition of a custodial measure as a consequence of revocation'.[103] The executing authority further has the power to discontinue a European Protection Order in a number of cases,[104] including 'where, according to its national law, the maximum term of duration of the measures adopted in execution of [the Order] has expired'.[105] The Directive thus attempts to establish a system of mutual recognition which will ensure continuous protection while respecting to the extent possible the legal system of the executing Member State.

B. Harmonisation

The challenge of ensuring EU-wide protection of victims while at the same time respecting national legal diversity has arisen with greater prominence in EU harmonisation efforts in the field. Both the Framework Decision and its successor Directive on the rights of victims have attempted to strike a balance between Europeanisation and the respect of national diversity on the one hand by including a number of broadly drafted provisions on victims' rights while on the other hand leaving considerable discretion to Member States as regards implementation. In the case of the Framework Decision, the specificities in the legal effects of third pillar measures would mean that its reach in national legal orders could remain limited. The tension between Europeanisation and the respect of national legal diversity, and its impact on enforcement and legal certainty as regards the Framework Decision on the rights of victims have now been tested before the Court of Justice. The first—and now landmark—ruling of the Court in this context was its judgment in the case of *Pupino*.[106] In *Pupino*, the Court was asked to interpret the broad provisions of the Framework Decision, and in particular Article 8 on the right to protection in court proceedings, in the light of their applicability to a specific domestic situation. The case arose after a reference by an Italian court asking to what extent the Italian Code of Criminal Procedure could be interpreted, in the light of the Framework Decision, as allowing children allegedly having suffered

---

[101] Preamble, recital 27.
[102] Art 11.
[103] Art 13.
[104] Art 14.
[105] Art 14(1)(b).
[106] Case C-105/03 *Maria Pupino* [2005] ECR I-5285.

a number of forms of abuse by their teacher to testify under a special procedure, and not in normal court proceedings, against the defendant. The Italian Code of Criminal Procedure allowed for this possibility for children under 16 only in cases of sexual offences or offences with a sexual background. In a landmark ruling, the Court established that third pillar Framework Decisions, while lacking direct effect, had indirect effect: in other words the national judge was under the duty to interpret domestic law in conformity with Framework Decisions. Having established the principle of indirect effect and its limits, the Court went on to examine the specific case.[107] It confirmed that the achievement of the aims of the Framework Decision on the rights of victims in criminal proceedings 'require that a national court should be able, in respect of particularly vulnerable victims, to use a special procedure', such as the one provided for already in Italian law.[108] However, in the light of the concerns raised regarding the potential impact of such an interpretation on the rights of the defendant, the Court added two caveats: that, in the light of the Framework Decision, the adopted conditions for giving evidence 'must ... be compatible with the basic legal principles of the Member State';[109] and that the national court must ensure that 'the application of those measures is not likely to make the criminal proceedings against [the defendant] considered as a whole, unfair within the meaning of Article 6 of the [ECHR], as interpreted by the European Court of Human Rights'.[110]

The Court's priority in *Pupino* appears to have been the clarification of the constitutional position of third pillar measures in EU law by affirming the binding legal effect of Framework Decisions and ensuring their enforcement in national legal orders via the application of the principle of indirect effect.[111] However, the impact of the application of the interpretative obligation to the national judge is significant. In *Pupino*, the Luxembourg Court has in reality rewritten the Italian Code of Criminal Procedure. Following the Court's guidance the Italian judge had little choice but to allow minors in this case to take advantage of the Code's protective provisions, although minors were not originally covered by the legislation. This interpretation raises important questions regarding the impact of the application of the principle of indirect effect on the internal coherence of national criminal justice systems, whose balance may be disturbed by piecemeal attempts by national judges to accommodate Union law demands in specific cases. Judges themselves may be faced with difficult balancing exercises, especially in cases where Union law itself—like in the case of the Framework Decision in question—is drafted in broad terms, having to take into account all complex parameters and interests involved in a criminal trial.

[107] ibid, paras 50–61.
[108] Para 56.
[109] Para 57. The Court referred in particular to Art 8(4) of the Framework Decision.
[110] Para 60.
[111] V Mitsilegas, 'Constitutional Principles of the European Community and European Criminal Law' (2006) 8 *European Journal of Law Reform* 301–24.

While *Pupino* should be seen within this specific constitutional context, where the Court of Justice attempted to ensure the enforceability of third pillar law at a time when Treaty reform no longer appeared imminent, the Court has since developed a substantial body of case-law resulting from a number of references for preliminary rulings by national courts seeking clarification of various aspects of the Framework Decision and its application in national law.[112] In all these cases, the Court was faced with the challenge of interpreting the provisions of the Framework Decision—a number of which were drafted in a broad, if not aspirational manner—in a way which would achieve the key objectives of the Framework Decision while respecting national legal diversity. The Court has attempted to accommodate national diversity and to address concerns with regard to the potentially negative impact of EU victims' law on state sovereignty and established criminal policy choices made at national level in a number of ways. First of all, the Court emphasised that the Framework Decision does not have an impact on domestic legislative choices with regard to criminalisation and the choice, form and level of penalties imposed under national criminal law.[113] The Court found that this is the case even when upholding national law would result in an outcome which is contrary to the wishes of the victim, as

> it must be borne in mind that where a Member State in the exercise of its powers to enforce the law ensures that the criminal law offers protection against acts of domestic violence, the objective is not only to protect the interests of the victim as he or she perceives them but also other more general interests of society.[114]

The Court has further declined to extend the scope of the Framework Decision and thus influence domestic legislative choices by defining the concept of a victim broadly to include within its scope legal persons.[115] This does not mean that the

---

[112] For an overview of early case law from the perspective of the dialogue between national courts and the Court of Justice in this context, see R Parizot, 'Les Interactions en Procédure Pénale: La Victime, Vecteur Symbolique de la Circulation du Jurisprudence' in G Giudicelli-Delage and S Manacorda (eds), *Cour de Justice et Justice Pénale en Europe* (Paris, Société de Législation Comparée, 2010) 177–202.

[113] Joined Cases C-483/09 and C-1/10 *Gueye and Sanchez* [2011] ECR I-8263. According to the Court, 'the Framework Decision contains no indication that the EU legislature, within the limits of the powers conferred on it by the EU Treaty, intended to harmonise or, at the least, approximate the legislation of Member States in respect of the forms and levels of criminal penalties' (para 51). Moreover, 'Article 8 of the Framework Decision cannot be interpreted in such a way that it restricts the choice by Member States of the criminal penalties they establish in their domestic legal systems' (para 68).

[114] See *Gueye*, para 61. According to the Court, 'the procedural right to be heard under the first paragraph of Article 3 of the Framework Decision does not confer on victims any rights in respect of the choice of form of penalties to be imposed on the offenders in accordance with the rules of the national criminal law nor in respect of the level of those penalties' (para 60).

[115] Case C-467/05 *Dell'Orto* [2007] ECR I-5557. According to the Court, 'there is no indication in any other provision of the Framework Decision that the European Union legislature intended to extend the concept of the victim for the purposes of the application of the Framework Decision to legal persons. The converse is in fact the case, as several provisions in the Framework Decision confirm that the legislature's objective was to limit its scope exclusively to natural persons who are victims of harm resulting from a criminal act' (para 55).

Framework Decision precludes Member States from enacting legislation treating legal persons as victims:

> since the Framework Decision does not undertake a complete harmonisation of the field in question, a decision that its provisions are also to be applicable where the victim is a legal person is one that Member States are neither prevented by the Framework Decision from taking nor obliged to take.[116]

On the other hand, the Court has ruled that the Framework Decision 'contains no indication that the European Union legislature intended to oblige Member States to provide that legal persons are to be liable in criminal law'.[117] Last, but not least, the Court of Justice has emphasised on a number of occasions that the Framework Decision grants a considerable degree of discretion to Member States as regards its implementation.[118] The tension between Member States' discretion and the need to ensure the effectiveness of the Framework Decision has been clearly reflected in the case of *Katz*, where the Court of Justice was asked whether a victim who can act as private prosecutor under national law can also be a witness in criminal proceedings instituted in this context. In a fine balancing act, the Court attempted to find a middle ground by ruling as follows:

> It must therefore be concluded that the Framework Decision, while requiring Member States, first, to ensure that victims enjoy a high level of protection and have a real and appropriate role in their criminal justice system and, second, to recognise victims' rights and legitimate interests and ensure that they can be heard and supply evidence, leaves to the national authorities a large measure of discretion with regard to the specific means by which they implement those objectives.
>
> However, in order not to deprive the first paragraph of Article 3 of the Framework Decision of much of its practical effect or to infringe the obligations stated in Article 2(1) of the Framework Decision, those provisions imply, in any event, that the victim is to be able to give testimony in the course of the criminal proceedings which can be taken into account as evidence.[119]

In *Katz*, the Court was faced with the considerable challenge of interpreting the broadly drafted provisions of the Framework Decision in a manner which would ensure the latter's effectiveness while at the same time adjusting and recognising a very specific policy choice by a national criminal justice system. This challenge is compounded by the fact that any answer that the Court would give would have an impact on the balance of power between the parties in the domestic criminal proceedings and ultimately on the delivery of criminal justice.[120] The Framework

---

[116] Case C-205/09 *Eredics and Sápi* [2010] ECR I-10231, para 29.
[117] Case C-79/11 *Giovanardi* (CJEU, 12 July 2012), para 45.
[118] See *Gueye*, para 58; *Eredics*, para 38.
[119] Case C-404/07 *Katz v Sós* [2008] ECR I-07607, paras 46–47.
[120] By quoting *Pupino*, the Court in *Katz* paid lip-service to the need to protect fundamental rights, and in particular the right to fair trial, and delegated this task to the national court—ibid, paras 48–49.

Decision has now been replaced by a post-Lisbon Directive, which is a significant development both from a substantive and from a constitutional perspective.
In terms of substance, the Directive contains a more extensive list of provisions
on victims' rights. From a constitutional perspective, the Directive is in principle
a more supranational instrument than the Framework Decision and is subject
to the full scrutiny of EU institutions. However, a number of questions remain
concerning legal certainty and the development of EU standards on the rights of
victims while respecting national diversity. First of all, as per the Directive's legal
basis of Article 82(2) TFEU, EU law can currently only provide minimum standards on victims' rights. Secondly, as seen above, the Directive maintains throughout its text—and very prominently as regards the rights of the victims relating to
criminal procedure and the trial itself—a high degree of discretion for national
authorities.[121] It can be said that in this context the *existence* of these rights is
provided by EU law, while their *exercise* is largely regulated by national law. This
legislative choice means that it is highly unlikely that autonomous EU concepts
will be developed in relation to the exercise of victims' rights in criminal procedure and that the Court of Justice will face similar interpretative challenges to
those it has faced when called to interpret the Framework Decision on victims.
Thirdly, while the Directive is 'Lisbonised', key provisions with regard to victims'
rights in criminal procedure—and in particular the right to be heard[122]—do not
fulfil the requirements which would grant them direct effect. A key enforcement
avenue with regard to these rights at national level is thus lost. Having said that,
national judges are still under a duty of consistent interpretation, and domestic
criminal law must be interpreted to the extent possible in conformity with the
key objectives of the Directive. Reconciling the Directive's objectives with national
legal diversity will thus remain a challenge for national and European courts.

V. The Impact of Victims' Rights on Justice in Europe

Questions on the impact of EU criminal law on victims' rights on national legal
diversity and the internal coherence of the criminal justice systems of Member
States cannot be considered independently from the fundamental question of the
impact of the proliferation of victims' rights on the rights of the defendant and,
more broadly, of the impact of the strengthening of the position of the victim on

---

[121] For a criticism of the extensive discretion left to member states, see R Letschert and C Rijken,
'Rights of Victims of Crime: Tensions Between an Integrated Approach and a Limited Legal Basis for
Harmonisation' (2013) 4 *New Journal of European Criminal Law* 226–55. They argue that the procedural autonomy that Member States have with regard to several provisions needs to be monitored
(pp 247 and 255).

[122] See Art 10(1) of the Directive, according to which 'Member States shall ensure that victims
may be heard during criminal proceedings and may provide evidence' (emphasis added).

criminal justice at national and EU level. The strengthening of the position of the victim in the criminal justice process reflects what I have characterised elsewhere as 'the individualisation of security' whereby the security needs of the individual take centre stage in justifying the expansion of state power: in addition to protecting the state from a number of perceived security threats, the individual is to be protected too.[123] Conferring rights upon victims is a key part of this process. Garland has called this 'the return of the victim', explaining that

> the new political imperative is that victims must be protected, their voices must be heard, their memory honoured, their anger expressed, their fears addressed. The rhetoric of penal debate routinely invokes the figure of the victim—typically as a child or a woman or a grieving family member—as a righteous figure whose suffering must be expressed and whose security must henceforth be guaranteed.[124]

However, taking into account the interests of the victim in the criminal justice system changes fundamentally the balance of power and interests in the criminal justice process and ultimately the relationship between the individual and the state. The need to protect the individual as defendant in criminal proceedings from the power of the state is watered down by the perceived need to protect the interests of another category of individual, the victim. Commentators have noted in this context the juxtaposition of the interests of offenders and victims in a zero-sum game[125] and the government rhetoric, in particular in the UK, of 'rebalancing the criminal justice system in favour of the law-abiding majority *and the* victim' (emphasis added).[126] In this kind of discourse, the focus on the protection of collective security (of the security of the law-abiding majority) is coupled with the individualisation of security as expressed in the protection of the rights of the victim.

In this light, the increased prominence of victims' interests in the criminal justice system has profound implications for the relationship between the individual and the state on the one hand, and the relationship between various categories of individuals in the criminal justice process on the other. A number of questions need to be answered in this context: What is the criminal process for? What is justice in this context? Whose interests are to be protected? Individualising security via calls to protect victims in the criminal justice system, especially at the pre-trial and trial stage, presents profound challenges to fundamental rights, in

---

[123] V Mitsilegas, 'Security versus Justice: The Individualisation of Security and the Erosion of Citizenship and Fundamental Rights' in S Ugelvik and B Hudson (eds), *Justice and Security in the 21st Century. Risks, Rights and the Rule of Law* (Abingdon, Routledge, 2012) 199–216.

[124] D Garland, *The Culture of Control. Crime and Social Order in Contemporary Society* (Oxford, Oxford University Press, 2001) 11.

[125] M Matravers, 'The Victim, the State and Civil Society' in A Bottoms and JV Roberts (eds), *Hearing the Victim. Adversarial Justice, Crime Victims and the State* (Cullompton, Willan, 2010) 1–16, 3.

[126] M Tonry, '"Rebalancing the Criminal Justice System in favour of the Victim": the Costly Consequences of Populist Rhetoric' in A Bottoms and JV Roberts (eds), *Hearing the Victim. Adversarial Justice, Crime Victims and the State* (Cullompton, Willan, 2010) 72–103, 73.

particular the presumption of innocence. At the same time, the individualisation of security serves as a justification for the increase of state power vis-à-vis the defendant by introducing exceptions to rules of criminal procedure aimed at protecting the defendant and to ensure a balance of power between the prosecution and the defence. The individualisation of security thus has profound justice implications: by placing one category of individual (the victim) against another category of individual (the defendant and alleged offender), the prioritisation of victims' claims may serve to redistribute justice by weakening procedural safeguards in criminal proceedings.[127]

The potential reconfiguration of the relationship between the individual and the state by individualising security via privileging the interests of the victim is apparent in a number of EU policy documents. The protection of the interests of the victim is central in both the Stockholm Programme[128] and the EU Internal Security Strategy.[129] In its Communication accompanying a package of proposals on the rights of victims, the European Commission outlined its vision on criminal justice focusing on the rights of the victim in greater detail.[130] According to the Commission, with this package the EU 'will contribute to making crime *victims' needs a central part of the justice systems, alongside catching and punishing the offenders*' (emphasis added).[131] The Commission also notes that:

> One of the European Union's objectives is to offer its citizens an area of freedom, security and justice in which their freedom of movement is ensured. However, without effective EU-wide application of a minimum level of rights for victims, mutual trust is not possible. This means that judicial systems should have full faith in each other's standards of fairness and justice, and citizens should have confidence that the same level of minimum rules will be applied when they travel or live abroad … Member States need to raise standards on victims' rights and the EU must ensure that victims benefit from a level playing field. A certain minimum level of safeguards and standards that are applied in all Member States will facilitate judicial cooperation and increase the quality of justice *and also improve people's confidence in the very notion of 'justice'* (emphasis added).[132]

---

[127] Mitsilegas, 'The Individualisation of Security', n 123 above.

[128] Point 2.3.4 of the Stockholm Programme on victims of crime, including terrorism reads as follows: 'Those who are most vulnerable or who find themselves in particularly exposed situations, such as persons subjected to repeated violence in close relationships, victims of gender based violence, or persons who fall victim to other types of crimes in a Member State of which they are not nationals or residents, are in need of special support and legal protection. Victims of terrorism also need special attention, support and social recognition'.

[129] Council doc 5842/2/10 REV 2, Brussels, 23 February 2010. The Internal Security Strategy is aimed at 'protection of all citizens, especially the most vulnerable, with the focus on victims of crime such as trafficking in human beings or gender violence, including victims of terrorism who also need special attention, support and social recognition' (emphasis added).

[130] Commission Communication, Strengthening victims' rights in the EU, COM(2011) 274, Brussels.

[131] ibid p 2.

[132] ibid p 3.

The Commission thus puts forward a vision of European criminal justice whereby the interests of the victim are central. Minimum standards on victims' rights are viewed as essential to create mutual trust not only between judicial authorities, but also between citizens in the EU. As seen above, references to mutual trust have been used by the Commission in order to be able to justify EU competence to legislate in the field under Article 82(2) TFEU. However, the above passage goes beyond the Commission's statements in the Explanatory Memorandum to the victims' Directive, by focusing specifically on the link between the establishment of EU rules on the rights of victims and confidence in 'the very notion of justice'. As with the references to mutual trust, this passage is very vague; the link between victims' rights and the achievement of justice is not substantiated and appears tenuous, to say the least. What is noteworthy in the Commission's Communication on victims is that it does not attempt to place the development of victims' rights in the context of criminal justice in Europe within the general framework of the development of legislation on the rights of the defendant at EU level, legislation which has been long pursued by the Commission and achieved after the introduction of a specific legal basis in Article 82(2) TFEU.[133]

These broad references to the achievement of mutual trust and confidence in the very notion of justice have not survived the finally adopted Directives on victims' rights. The impact on the balance of powers in the criminal justice system of the current EU legislative framework on victims, and in particular of the Directive on the rights of victims, remains to be seen. The Directive does include a series of provisions related to victims' rights and puts forward a general objective that victims must receive appropriate information, support and protection and be able to participate in criminal proceedings,[134] an objective which must guide the implementation and interpretation of the Directive. However, as seen above, Member States have been granted considerable discretion as to how to achieve this objective, with the enforcement of key victims' rights prescribed by the Directive being left to national law. The Directive thus attempts to achieve a delicate balance between introducing minimum rules on victims' rights at EU level and not distorting the balance of powers and the expression of justice thus far settled in the various domestic criminal justice systems of individual Member States. When looking at the interpretation of victims' rights at EU level, it is essential not to view victims' rights in isolation but to interpret these in accordance with fundamental rights, in particular the rights of the suspect or the defendant. The Directive on the rights of the victim contains a number of references to the need to respect defence rights in this context,[135] and consistent Court of Justice

---

[133] Mitsilegas, *EU Criminal Law*, n 7 above, ch 3.

[134] Art 1(1).

[135] According to the Preamble, the rights set out in the Directive are 'without prejudice to the rights of the offender. The term "offender" refers to a person who has been convicted of a crime. However, for the purposes of this Directive, it also refers to a suspected or accused person before any acknowledgement of guilt or conviction, and it is without prejudice to the presumption of innocence'—recital 12. See also Arts 18, 20 and 23 of the Directive.

case-law[136] has confirmed this need. The requirement to interpret victims' rights in conformity with fundamental rights and in particular defence and fair trial rights arises even more prominently in the post-Lisbon, post-Charter era. The Court's case law on the applicability of the Charter of Fundamental Rights[137] calls for a systemic examination of national provisions on the position of the victim in criminal proceedings and their impact on fundamental rights, even if such provisions do not constitute a direct and specific implementation of the standards set out in the EU victims' rights Directives.

VI. Conclusion

The evolution of legislation on victims' rights at EU level reflects a clear political commitment by the EU institutions to be seen to be active in strengthening the position of the victim in the criminal justice process. The EU has legislated on victims notwithstanding the considerable limits of EU competence in the field and notwithstanding the considerable diversity in national legal systems with regard to the protection of victims and their place in the criminal justice process. The political imperative to legislate on victims' rights has thus taken precedence over considerations of legality and legal certainty. As has been noted with regard to the evolution of victims' rights in the US context, 'the symbolic strength of the term "victim's rights" overrides careful scrutiny: Who could be anti-victim?'[138] The translation of this political will into legal reality in EU law has led to a situation whereby the general objective of strengthening the position of the victim in criminal justice across the European Union is to be achieved either by a system of mutual recognition aimed at providing maximum flexibility to national criminal justice systems, or by the introduction of EU-wide minimum standards on victims' rights whose implementation depends largely on the specificities of the criminal justice systems of Member States. The 'Lisbonisation' of victims' rights has not fundamentally changed the picture—at least as far as the drafting of EU law in the field is concerned—as regards legal certainty, some of the effects of Union law on national legal orders (in particular direct effect) and the degree of discretion left to Member States. Key pieces of the puzzle of the interaction between EU and national criminal law on victims' rights will thus continue to be filled by the Court of Justice, which has already been faced with the significant challenge of ensuring the effectiveness of EU law on victims while recognising national specificities and interests in the field of criminal justice. The Court of Justice—and national courts in their duties of ensuring the enforcement of EU law

---

[136] *Pupino*, n 106 above, para 59; *Katz*, n 119 above, para 48.
[137] See in particular Case C-617/10 *Åklagaren v Hans Åkerberg Fransson* (CJEU, 26 February 2013).
[138] LN Henderson, 'The Wrongs of Victim's Rights' (1985) 37 *Stanford Law Review* 937–1021, 952.

on victims at the domestic level and interpreting national law in conformity with EU law—will continue to face fundamental questions on the extent to which EU law on victims will change the balance of powers and the concept of justice at the national level. In this context, in the post-Lisbon era in particular, the judiciary is required to interpret provisions on victims' rights in conformity with fundamental rights and in particular fair trial and defence rights as enshrined in the Charter. Political discourse on the rights of victims as well as the piecemeal and functional characteristics of EU criminal procedure competence under Article 82(2) TFEU have led to legislation on victims' rights being developed largely in isolation from legislation on the rights of the defendant. If legislation on the rights of the victim aims to reflect broader concepts of justice at the national and EU level and their intersection, the need for a more holistic approach, viewing victims' rights in the light of fundamental rights and taking full account of the position of the suspect and the defendant in criminal proceedings is essential.

8

The Uneasy Relationship Between EU Criminal Law and Citizenship of the Union

I. Introduction

EU criminal law and the law of EU citizenship have traditionally evolved in parallel, but separate ways. However, recent years have witnessed growing interconnections between these two fields of EU law. On the one hand, aspects of EU citizenship law have emerged in the adoption of EU criminal law instruments. This has been the case in particular regarding the adoption of instruments applying the principle of mutual recognition in criminal matters, including the Framework Decision on the European Arrest Warrant and the Framework Decision on the Transfer of Sentenced Persons. On the other hand, aspects of EU criminal law have become increasingly relevant in the evolution of EU citizenship law, most notably in playing a part in determining the scope of exceptions to citizenship rights in the case-law of the Court of Justice. This chapter will examine the interrelationship between EU criminal law and EU citizenship law from these two perspectives, mapping the evolution of EU law in the field and casting light on the impact of the entry into force of the Lisbon Treaty in this regard. It will be argued that the current relationship between EU criminal law and EU citizenship law is rather uneasy, with both fields of law used out of their ordinary context when they interact in EU law. This approach is at odds with the objective of establishing a European area of freedom and justice and leads to a dilution of rights both in EU criminal law and in EU citizenship law.

II. Citizenship in EU Criminal Law

The first level of interaction between EU criminal law and EU citizenship law arises when citizenship aspects emerge in the adoption of secondary EU criminal law measures. This has been the case in the adoption of two mutual recognition measures, the Framework Decision on the European Arrest Warrant[1] and the Framework Decision on the Transfer of Sentenced Persons.[2] In the European Arrest Warrant system, citizenship considerations have arisen from the fact that in principle the system of surrender established by EU law would depart from traditional extradition arrangements in allowing the surrender of own nationals— with the Framework Decision tempering the extent of this change by including a provision shielding from surrender own nationals and those resident and staying in the executing Member State.[3] The Framework Decision on the Transfer of Sentenced Persons on the other hand aims to simplify the transfer of sentenced persons across the EU, irrespective of any citizenship links they may have with the executing state.[4] The implications of these two measures for EU citizenship rights will be examined in turn below.

A. EU Citizenship in the European Arrest Warrant

The Court of Justice has had the opportunity to examine limits to automaticity in the recognition and execution of European Arrest Warrants in the context of preliminary references concerning the interpretation of Article 4(6) of the Framework Decision, which may serve to protect own nationals, residents and individuals who are staying in the executing Member State from surrender. The first such case has been the case of *Kozlowski*,[5] where the Court was asked to interpret the meaning of 'residence' and 'stay' under Article 4(6) but also whether the transposition of the Framework Decision making it impermissible to surrender own nationals whilst allowing the surrender of nationals of other Member States was compatible with EU law, in particular non-discrimination and citizenship. The Court began by reaffirming the cooperative objective of the Framework Decision on the basis of mutual recognition[6] and answered the first question by putting forward three important findings: that the terms 'resident' and 'staying' in Article 4(6) of the Framework Decision are concepts having an autonomous meaning under European Union law;[7] that Article 4(6) of the Framework Decision has in particular the

---

[1] Framework Decision 2002/584/JHA of 13 June 2002 on the European Arrest Warrant [2002] OJ L190/1.

[2] Framework Decision 2008/909/JHA of 27 November 2008 on the transfer of custodial sentences (sentenced persons) [2008] OJ L327/27.

[3] Article 4(6). For an analysis, see V Mitsilegas, 'The Constitutional Implications of Mutual Recognition in Criminal Matters in the EU' (2006) 43 *Common Market Law Review* 1277–311.

[4] See section II.B below.

[5] Case C-66/08, *Kozlowski* [2008] ECR I-06041.

[6] See paragraph 31 (and the reference to paragraph 28 of Case C-303/05 *Advocaten voor de Wereld VZW v Leden van de Ministerraad* [2007] ECR I-3633) and 32.

[7] Since the objective of the Framework Decision, as indicated in paragraph 31, is to put in place a system of surrender, as between judicial authorities, of convicted persons or suspects for the purpose of enforcing judgments or of criminal proceedings, based on the principle of mutual recognition— a surrender which the executing judicial authority can oppose only on one of the grounds for refusal provided for by the Framework Decision—the terms 'staying' and 'resident', which determine the scope of Article 4(6), must be defined uniformly, since they concern autonomous concepts of EU law— paragraph 43.

objective of the reintegration of the requested person;[8] and that, in assessing their meaning, national authorities must embark on an individual examination of the facts of each case on the basis of a series of objective factors. The Court found in particular that the terms 'resident' and 'staying' cover, respectively, the situations in which the person who is the subject of a European Arrest Warrant has either established his actual place of residence in the executing Member State or has acquired, following a stable period of presence in that state, certain connections with that state which are of a similar degree to those resulting from residence.[9] It added that

> in order to determine whether, in a specific situation, there are connections between the requested person and the executing Member State which lead to the conclusion that that person is covered by the term 'staying' within the meaning of Article 4(6) of the Framework Decision, it is necessary to *make an overall assessment of various objective factors* characterising the situation of that person, which include, in particular, the length, nature and conditions of his presence and the family and economic connections which he has with the executing Member State (emphasis added).[10]

Although the Advocate General opined in detail on the second question referred to by the Oberlandesgericht Stuttgart,[11] the Court declined to answer the question in *Kozlowski*. The Court had to deal with the essence of this question however in the subsequent case of *Wolzenburg*.[12] The case concerned the interpretation of the Dutch legislation implementing Article 4(6) of the European Arrest Warrant Framework Decision. Unlike the German implementing law examined by the Court in *Kozlowski*, the Dutch law imposed specific criteria for the implementation of the ground for refusal to execute a European Arrest Warrant set out in Article 4(6): surrender would not take place if the individual involved was a Dutch national or a foreign national in possession of a residence permit of indefinite duration. The case involved a European Arrest Warrant for the surrender to Germany of Mr Wolzenburg, who, although employed in the Netherlands for a number of years, did not meet the conditions for grant of a residence permit of indefinite duration for the Netherlands on the ground that he had not yet resided in the Netherlands for a continuous period of five years.[13] In the light of the above, the Rechtbank Amsterdam referred a number of questions to Luxembourg, including whether persons staying in or residents of the executing Member State for the purposes of Article 4(6) of the Framework Decision include nationals of other EU Member States lawfully residing in the executing Member State regardless of the duration of their lawful residence, and if not, how long that residence period should be and under what requirements. The Dutch Court also asked whether

---

[8] Article 4(6) of the Framework Decision 'has in particular the objective of enabling the executing judicial authority to give particular weight to the *possibility of increasing the requested person's chances of reintegrating into society when the sentence imposed on him expires*'—paragraph 45 (emphasis added).

[9] Paragraph 46.

[10] Paragraph 48.

[11] View of AG Bot delivered on 28 April 2008, Case C-66/08, *Kozlowski*, paragraphs 40–112.

[12] Case C-123/08 *Wolzenburg*, [2009] ECR I-09621.

[13] Paragraphs 26–38.

domestic legislation differentiating between Dutch nationals and nationals of other EU citizens resulted in discrimination under Article 12 EC.

The Court addressed these questions by adopting a three-step approach. The first step was to examine the purpose and objectives of the Framework Decision on the European Arrest Warrant as a reflection of the application of the principle of mutual recognition in criminal matters. The second step was to define the concept of residence by evaluating the margin of discretion that Member States have in implementing Article 4(6) of the Framework Decision. And the third step was to assess whether the domestic implementing legislation in question (which differentiated between nationals of the executing Member State and nationals of other EU Member States) is compatible with the principle of non-discrimination as enshrined in the Treaty. As a first step, the Court made a number of observations regarding the system of surrender introduced by the European Arrest Warrant Framework Decision and in particular Article 4(6) thereof.[14] By reference to the earlier judgment in *Kozlowski*[15] (which in turn referred to the Court's key ruling in *Advocaten voor de Wereld*),[16] the Court then made extensive reference to the purpose of the European Arrest Warrant Framework Decision, which is to replace the multilateral system of extradition between Member States with a system of surrender, as between judicial authorities, of convicted persons or suspects for the purpose of enforcing judgments or of criminal proceedings, that system of surrender being based on the principle of mutual recognition.[17] By reference to its ruling in *Leymann*,[18] the Court noted that the principle of mutual recognition means that Member States are in principle obliged to act upon a European Arrest Warrant.[19] A narrow definition of optional grounds for refusal to execute a European Arrest Warrant is compatible with this obligation: according to the Court,

> a national legislature which, by virtue of the options afforded it by Article 4 of the Framework Decision, chooses to limit the situations in which its executing judicial authority may refuse to surrender a requested person *merely reinforces* the system of surrender introduced by that Framework Decision *to the advantage of an area of freedom, security and justice.*[20]

> …[B]y limiting the situations in which the executing judicial authority may refuse to execute a European arrest warrant, such legislation *only facilitates the surrender of requested persons*, in accordance with the principle of mutual recognition set out in Article 1(2) of Framework Decision 2002/584, which constitutes *the essential rule introduced by that decision* (emphases added).[21]

---

[14] Paragraph 55.
[15] *Kozlowski*, n 5 above, paragraph 31.
[16] *Advocaten voor de Wereld*, above n 6, paragraph 28.
[17] Paragraph 56.
[18] Case C-388 PPU *Leymann and Pustovarov* [2008] ECR I-08993, paragraph 51.
[19] Paragraph 57.
[20] Paragraph 58.
[21] Paragraph 59.

While accepting in principle that the essence of the European Arrest Warrant Framework Decision is the facilitation of surrender, the Court was asked to examine the compatibility with this Framework Decision of national legislation introducing grounds of refusal to surrender which was marked by two special features: it differentiated between nationals of the executing Member State and nationals of other EU Member States; and it introduced in automatic surrender of those EU nationals whose residence in the Netherlands did not fall under the specific residence requirements set out in the Dutch implementing law. In assessing the compatibility of national law with the Framework Decision, the Court's starting point was to accept that, when implementing Article 4 of the Framework Decision and in particular paragraph 6 thereof, Member States have 'of necessity' a certain margin of discretion.[22] The reintegration objective of Article 4(6) set out in *Kozlowski* cannot prevent the Member States, when implementing the Framework Decision, from limiting, in a manner consistent with the essential rule stated in Article 1(2) thereof, the situations in which it is possible to refuse to surrender a person who falls within the scope of Article 4(6).[23] The Court justified this departure from *Kozlowski* and upheld the Dutch limitation of exclusion of a great number of EU nationals from the protective scope of Article 4(6) by accepting the logic of abuse put forward by the Dutch Government, which justified the adoption of the Dutch implementing law on the basis of the 'high degree of inventiveness in the arguments put forward in order to prove that they have a connection to Netherlands society'.[24] Developing further this approach, the Court placed the objective of reintegration within the framework of the broader discussion on integration, by accepting that the executing Member State is entitled to pursue reintegration objectives only in respect of persons who have demonstrated a certain degree of integration in the society of that Member State.[25] Based on this approach, the Court then embarked on an assessment of the *integration* of the various categories of individuals covered by (and differentiated by) Dutch law for the purposes of implementing Article 4(6) of the European Arrest Warrant Framework Decision. The Court upheld the Dutch approach and found it compatible with the principle of non-discrimination by accepting a series of presumptions which have been distilled in the paragraph below:

> In the present case, the single condition based on nationality for its own nationals, on the one hand, and the condition of residence of a continuous period of five years for nationals of other Member States, on the other, may be regarded as being such as to ensure that the requested person is sufficiently integrated in the Member State of execution. *By contrast, a Community national who does not hold the nationality of the Member State of execution and has not resided in that State for a continuous period of a given length generally*

---

[22] Paragraph 61.
[23] Paragraph 62.
[24] Paragraph 65.
[25] Paragraph 67.

has more connection with his Member State of origin that with the society of the Member State of execution (emphasis added).[26]

The Court's ruling in *Wolzenburg* sends mixed and at times contradictory messages with regard to the operation of the system of mutual recognition in criminal matters and the place of mutual trust therein. The Court bases its reasoning on the objective of the European Arrest Warrant Framework Decision, and adopts a prima facie expansive approach by highlighting the principle of the Framework Decision—which is the execution of requests to surrender—and consequently privileging a limited construction of the exceptions to this principle, namely grounds to refuse to execute a Warrant. Yet this expansive interpretation of recognition—which is linked with the establishment of an Area of Freedom, Security and Justice—is contradicted by the Court's acceptance that possessing the nationality of the executing Member State can automatically trigger the ground for refusal set out in Article 4(6) of the Framework Decision. The automatic exemption of own nationals from the scope of the Framework Decision challenges one of the main innovations of this instrument (which is to abolish the limits to the surrender of own nationals)[27] and sits at odds with the construction of the Union as a borderless Area of Freedom, Security and Justice, where the European Arrest Warrant serves to compensate for the ease with which those wanted to face justice may move from one Member State to another.[28] The automaticity embraced by the Court is also at odds with the Area of Freedom, Security and Justice in that it is based upon the presumption that a national of an EU Member State has more connection with his/her Member State of origin than with another Member State and thus cannot be better reintegrated in another Member State,[29] and disregards the approach of the Court in *Kozlowski*, where an individual assessment of whether the Article 4(6) exception applies on the basis of a number of criteria was put forward.[30] The Court's acceptance of Member States' margin of discretion in implementing Article 4(6) also contradicts the Court's ruling in *Kozlowski*, which emphasised that the terms 'staying' and 'resident' in Article 4(6) of the Framework Decision are autonomous EU law concepts.

---

[26] Paragraph 68. A scheme based on these assumptions was not excessive and not contrary to the anti-discrimination principle in EU law (paragraphs 69–74).

[27] See also the Opinion of AG Bot delivered on 24 March 2009, *Wolzenburg*, EU:C:2009:183, paragraph 132, according to whom 'Member States have surrendered their sovereign power to shield their own nationals from the investigations and penalties of other Member States' judicial authorities'. The AG bases this conclusion, citing the *ne bis in idem* case-law, on the high level of confidence in the Area of Freedom, Security and Justice (paragraphs 133–136). He takes the view that 'Member States cannot, without undermining the effectiveness of the Framework Decision, take decisions in their domestic law which, in one way or another, would have the effect of reintroducing an automatic exception in favour of their nationals' (paragraph 152).

[28] See V Mitsilegas, 'The Limits of Mutual Trust in Europe's Area of Freedom, Security and Justice. From Automatic Inter-state Cooperation to the Slow Emergence of the Individual' 31 *Yearbook of European Law 2012* 319–72.

[29] See in this context also the Opinion of AG Bot, paragraphs 103–106.

[30] See also the Opinion of AG Bot who argued in favour of a case-by-case assessment—paragraph 63.

In the light of the above observations, the Court's approach to mutual recognition in the context of the European Arrest Warrant system in *Wolzenburg* is far from coherent. The Court has in essence accepted that the Article 4(6) ground for refusal can be interpreted restrictively in cases concerning a great number of EU citizens exercising EU law rights in a Member State other than the one of their nationality, but that the same ground for refusal can be interpreted in a maximalist manner granting full protection against surrender to nationals of the executing Member State. In addition to accepting discrimination on grounds of nationality as justified, the Court upheld the system adopted by Dutch law, using the high residence threshold established by the citizenship Directive in isolation from the developed legal framework and objectives of EU citizenship law to differentiate between various categories of citizens of the Union.[31] It is noteworthy that in assessing the proportionality of the Dutch implementing law, the Court chose to base its ruling on the restrictive approach it had adopted in the citizenship case of *Forster*, which concerned the granting of rights to EU citizens.[32] However, it is submitted that *Forster* is not the appropriate ruling to be applicable in the case of *Wolzenburg*, as the latter is not a case concerning the granting of rights to EU citizens, but is a case concerning essentially security of residence in another EU Member State according to Article 4(6) of the European Arrest Warrant Framework Decision. Framing the case within a security of residence context would trigger the application of the security of residence and protection from expulsion provisions of the Citizens' Directive, which introduces a very high threshold of threat to the host society, to be assessed on an individual basis, before security of residence is watered down. The Court's reasoning in *Wolzenburg* has resulted in the Court—contrary to the Opinion of Advocate General Bot—accepting that an EU citizen who has been resident and employed in a Member State other than the one of his nationality for a number of years is not covered by the protective bar to the execution of a European Arrest Warrant against him.

This approach can be explained if *Wolzenburg* can be seen as an immigration case rather than as a criminal law case, involving the protection of national identity as a state interest. The Court accepted uncritically the sharp distinction put forward by the Dutch Government between an inclusionary approach towards own nationals and long-term resident EU citizens and an exclusionary approach towards other EU citizens. In doing so, the Court privileged the interests of the state in maintaining and projecting a national identity over the interests of the affected individuals in the Area of Freedom, Security and Justice: reintegration (the accepted objective of Article 4(6) of the Framework Decision) is subject to mutual recognition when nationals of other EU Member States are concerned,

---

[31] For a criticism of this approach see L Marin, '"A Spectre Is Haunting Europe": European Citizenship in the Area of Freedom, Security and Justice' (2011) 17 *European Public Law* 705–28. Directive 2004/38/EC of the European Parliament and of the Council of 29 April 2004 on the right of citizens of the Union and their family members to move and reside freely within the territory of the Member States [2004] OJ L158/77.

[32] Case C-158/07 *Forster* [2008] ECR I-08507.

and is made conditional upon the perceived 'integration' of EU citizens in the executing Member State. By using immigration law terms and logic in this manner, the concept of mutual trust between Member States or authorities executing European arrest warrants is transformed into blind trust in favour of own nationals and blind distrust vis-à-vis nationals of other EU Member States. While the Court's ruling may be explained as an attempt to address—following its reticence in *Kozlowski*—concerns expressed in a number of Member States as regards the surrender of own nationals to other EU Member States, the confusion of immigration law with the law related to citizens of the Union, the acceptance of discrimination between various categories of EU citizens, the undue emphasis on national discretion, and the acceptance of automaticity instead of a case-by-case assessment of the applicability of Article 4(6) are backward steps which do not address the development of the Union into an Area of Freedom, Security and Justice without internal borders.[33]

The Court subsequently attempted to rebalance its approach to the definition of stay and residence for the purposes of Article 4(6) of the Framework Decision on the European Arrest Warrant in the case of *Da Silva Jorge*.[34] The case concerned the compatibility with EU law of the French implementing law, according to which refusal to execute a European Arrest Warrant was optional and applicable only in relation to French nationals and on condition that the competent French authorities had undertaken to enforce the sentence themselves. The Court reiterated the obligation of Member States as a rule to act upon a European Arrest Warrant[35] but also referred to its ruling in *Wolzenburg* to affirm that Member States have a margin of discretion in implementing the ground for refusal in Article 4(6) of the Framework Decision and that they may limit the scope of Article 4(6) by making its application 'subject to the condition that the person requested has lawfully resided for a certain period in that Member State', where that person is a national of another Member State having a right of residence on the basis of Article 21(1) TFEU.[36] However, the Court then continued by referring back to its ruling in *Kozlowski*, confirming that 'the terms "resident" and "staying" must be defined uniformly in all the Member States since they concern autonomous concepts of European Union law'.[37] While Member States have a margin of discretion, 'they are not entitled to give those terms a broader meaning than that which derives from a uniform interpretation of that provision in the Member States as a whole'.[38]

The Court not only attempted to use autonomous concepts to set limits on national discretion here, but continued by introducing a new teleological element

---

[33] Mitsilegas, above n 28.
[34] Case C-42/11, *Da Silva Jorge*, judgment of 5 September 2012.
[35] Paragraphs 28–29.
[36] Paragraphs 33–34.
[37] Paragraph 36.
[38] Paragraph 37.

in the interpretation of Article 4(6) by stating that, in transposing the latter, 'Member States are required to comply with Article 18 TFEU'.[39]

> [I]t cannot be accepted that a requested person who, without being a national of the executing Member State, has been staying or been resident there for a certain period of time is not in any circumstances capable of having established connections with that State which could enable him to invoke that ground for optional non-execution.[40]

It is for the executing judicial authority

> to determine whether, in a specific situation, there are connections between the requested person and the executing Member State which lead to the conclusion that that person 'is staying' or 'resident' within the meaning of Article 4(6) of that framework decision.

In order to do this, the authority must

> make an overall assessment of various objective factors characterising the situation of that person, which include, in particular, the length, nature and conditions of his presence and the family and economic connections which he has with the executing Member State.[41]

However, these principles were not followed by the French legislator in the implementation of the Framework Decision. The Court found that

> if Member States transpose Article 4(6) of Framework Decision 2002/584 into their domestic law, they cannot … limit ground[s] for optional non-execution solely to their own nationals, by excluding automatically and absolutely the nationals of other Member States who are staying or resident in the territory of the Member State of execution irrespective of their connections with that Member State.

This would be to undermine the principle that there should be no discrimination on the grounds of nationality[42] In this manner, the Court has laid down minimum ground rules for the definition of residence and stay as autonomous concepts for the purposes of the execution of European Arrest Warrants, consisting at least of an individual assessment of the degree of connection of an EU national with the executing Member State. However, *da Silva Jorge* does not negate the influence that domestic integration agendas may have in the development of the EU as an area of criminal justice.

B. EU Citizenship in the EU System on Transfer of Prisoners

The Framework Decision on the transfer of sentenced persons aims to go beyond existing public international law instruments in the field by enhancing

---

[39] Paragraph 38.
[40] Paragraph 41, by reference to *Kozłowski*, paragraph 37.
[41] Paragraph 43, by reference to *Kozłowski*, paragraphs 48 and 49, and *Wolzenburg*, paragraph 76.
[42] Paragraph 50. See also the Opinion by Advocate General Mengozzi, delivered on 20 March 2012. According to the Advocate General, the line of argument put forward by certain governments to the effect that, in such circumstances, nationals are not in a situation comparable to that of nationals of other Member States is untenable (paragraph 50).

automaticity in inter-state cooperation.[43] This step forward is justified on the basis of the existence of 'special mutual confidence' among EU Member States' legal systems which enables mutual recognition.[44] This elevated mutual trust justifies automaticity to such an extent that

> notwithstanding the need to provide the sentenced person with adequate safeguards, his or *her involvement in the proceedings should no longer be dominant* by requiring in all cases his or her consent to the forwarding of a judgment to another Member State for the purpose of its recognition and enforcement of the sentence imposed (emphasis added).[45]

Hence, while in theory the objective of the Framework Decision includes the facilitation of the social rehabilitation of the sentenced person,[46] in practice the Framework Decision introduces a system of maximum automaticity with little consideration for the position of the affected individual. Automaticity in the Framework Decision is introduced at four levels. The first three levels correspond largely to the automaticity elements analysed in the context of the Framework Decision on the European Arrest Warrant. First, cooperation is based on speed and a minimum of formality based on a pro-forma document annexed to the Framework Decision.[47] Secondly, the verification of the existence of dual criminality has been abolished for a list of categories of offence.[48] While in the case of the European Arrest Warrant the abolition of the verification of dual criminality led to legality concerns due to the obligation of the executing Member State to deploy its law enforcement powers for conduct which is not a criminal offence under its legal system, the same abolition in the transfer of sentenced persons Framework Decision leads to an equally complex challenge for the executing Member State which is required to keep in prison an individual for conduct which does not constitute an offence under its law. This is why Member States are given the opportunity not to apply this provision.[49] Thirdly, the Framework Decision contains limited grounds for refusal (here, unlike the European Arrest Warrant Framework Decision, these grounds are only optional) and non-compliance with fundamental rights does not constitute such ground.[50] The Framework Decision introduces an additional element of automaticity: it removes the need for consent

---

[43] Council Framework Decision 2008/909/JHA of 27 November 2008 on the application of the principle of mutual recognition to judgments in criminal matters imposing custodial sentences or measures involving deprivation of liberty for the purpose of their enforcement in the European Union, Preamble, recital 4.

[44] Preamble, recital 5.

[45] ibid.

[46] See Article 3(1) of the Framework Decision according to which its purpose is 'to establish the rules under which a Member State, with a view to facilitating the social rehabilitation of the sentenced person, is to recognise a judgment and enforce the sentence'.

[47] Article 12 and 15.

[48] Article 7(1).

[49] Article 7(4). For a discussion, see V Mitsilegas, 'The Third Wave of Third Pillar Law: Which Direction for EU Criminal Justice?' (2009) 34 *European Law Review* 523–60.

[50] Article 9. See also Article 3(4) of the Framework Decision which is drafted in a similar manner to Article 1(3) of the European Arrest Warrant Framework Decision.

of the sentenced person in a number of cases, including where the judgment is forwarded 'to the Member State of nationality in which the sentenced person lives', and where the judgment is forwarded 'to the Member State to which the sentenced person will be deported once he or she is released from the enforcement of the sentence on the basis of an expulsion or deportation order included in the judgment or in a judicial or administrative decision or any other measure consequential to the judgment'.[51]

The Framework Decision on the transfer of sentenced persons is an instrument designed with the interests of the state firmly in mind and with very little consideration for the position of the affected individuals. The latter are part of a particularly vulnerable category of population. Unlike the Framework Decision on the European Arrest Warrant (which targets individuals wanted to face justice), this Framework Decision deals with the unwanted individuals whom Member States wish to remove from their territory. The removal of the requirement of consent in this context introduces maximum automaticity, which is reinforced in practice by the implementation of the Framework Decision in Member States.[52] Automaticity is based on a double presumption: that the Member State of nationality in which the sentenced person lives is the Member State where the reintegration of this person will be best achieved; and that fundamental rights breaches—in particular breaches of Article 3 ECHR or Article 4 of the Charter—will never arise in the Member State of nationality. The system introduced also disregards any consequences of an enforced transfer for the right to private and family life of the sentenced person. It also sits at odds with the provisions of the Citizens' Directive on security of residence and expulsion of EU citizens in that it essentially ensures that the imprisonment of an EU citizen has the same effects as his/her expulsion, although the imposition of a custodial sentence does not in itself constitute a ground for expulsion under EU law and the threat posed to the host society must be individually assessed.[53] The automatic transfer of a sentenced person to his or her state of nationality sits at odds with the requirement of individual assessment put forward by EU citizenship law. Automaticity based on the above presumptions also serves to shield the Framework Decision from an examination of whether the system it introduces is compatible with the objective of establishing an Area of Freedom, Security and Justice. While the Framework Decision is justified partly on the grounds of ensuring the interests of the affected individuals—namely their

---

[51] Article 6(2)(a) and 6(2)(b) respectively. The other case involves transfer 'to the Member State to which the sentenced person has fled or otherwise returned in view of the criminal proceedings pending against him or her in the issuing State or following the conviction in that issuing State'— Article 6(2)(c).

[52] European Commission, *Report from the Commission to the European Parliament and the Council* on the implementation by the Member States of the Framework Decisions 2008/909/JHA, 2008/947/JHA and 2009/829/JHA on the mutual recognition of judicial decisions on custodial sentences or measures involving deprivation of liberty, on probation decisions and alternative sanctions and on supervision measures as an alternative to provisional detention, COM(2014) 57 final, Brussels, 5 February 2014, paragraph 4.1, p 8.

[53] See Articles 28 and 33(1) of Directive 2004/38/EC ([2004] OJ L158/77, 30.4.2004).

reintegration—it is difficult to see how this objective is met by a system which removes the need for consent and does not give affected individuals any decisive say on the execution of the judgment ordering their transfer. If the objective of reintegration is not met, it is hard to see which objective is met by the Framework Decision beyond cutting costs with regard to prison maintenance and operation in Member States. This objective in itself is not, however, sufficient to justify the adoption of EU law under an Area of Freedom, Security and Justice legal basis. The enforced transfer of persons who are already serving a sentence in one Member State which does not contribute to their reintegration does not address freedom, security or justice in an area without internal frontiers.[54]

III. EU Criminal Law in EU Citizenship

EU criminal law considerations have emerged in recent attempts by the Court of Justice to determine the scope of derogations to the protection afforded by the citizenship Directive.[55] The Court has delivered two landmark rulings post-Lisbon in the field: *Tsakouridis*, which involved the impact on citizenship rights of conduct which would be punishable under secondary EU criminal law (the third pillar Framework Decision on drug trafficking); and *P.I.*, which involved the impact on citizenship rights of conduct which was enumerated in the Treaty legal basis for securitised criminalisation under Article 83(1) TFEU (sexual offences). The evolving interpretation by the Court of the impact of EU criminal law on citizenship rights will be examined in this section.

A. The Impact of Secondary EU Criminal Law on EU Citizenship—*Tsakouridis*

The CJEU first considered the impact of EU criminal law on the meaning of 'imperative grounds of public security' in the case of *Tsakouridis*.[56] Mr Tsakouridis was born a Greek national in Germany in 1978, where he acquired an unlimited residence permit in 2001. Between March and November 2004 he ran a pancake stall in Rhodes where he returned in October 2005. A few months later he was arrested in Greece on the basis of an international arrest warrant issued by a German Court. Mr Tsakouridis had already been convicted in Germany more than once for crimes of assault and possession of an illegal object. In August 2008, he acquired another conviction of six years and six months for dealing in narcotics as part of an organised

---

[54] Mitsilegas, above n 28 ('The Limits of Mutual Trust').
[55] I would like to thank Niovi Vavoula for her excellent research assistance in the preparation of this section. The usual disclaimer applies.
[56] Case C-145/09 *Land Baden-Württemberg v Tsakouridis*, judgment of 23 November 2010.

group. Under German law a term of imprisonment of at least five years for an intentional offence was the threshold for triggering an expulsion on the basis of 'imperative grounds of public security' as set out in Article 28(3) of the Citizens Directive.[57] Consequently, national authorities ordered the expulsion of Mr Tsakouridis. He successfully brought an action against that decision.[58] However on appeal the national court decided to request a preliminary ruling and ask whether the concept of public security covered only irrefutable threats to the external or internal security of the Member State specifically linked to the existence and function of the state, the survival of its population, its foreign relations and the peaceful coexistence of nations. In other words, what was at stake was whether the personal conduct of Mr Tsakouridis represented a sufficiently serious threat to one of the core interests of German society that could justify his expulsion on imperative public security grounds. It further inquired about the consequences of repeated absences from the host state to the enhanced protection offered to an EU citizen after 10 years of residence in the host state.

The questions of the referring Court were addressed in detail by Advocate General Bot.[59] The Advocate General devoted a large part of his Opinion to an analysis on what constitutes an imperative ground of public security. From the outset, he made two remarks: first, that the length of stay in the territory of the host Member State is a decisive factor for determining the conditions of an expulsion measure, as it is indicatory of the level of integration in that state's society.[60] Secondly, that the principle that a criminal sanction must function as a means of achieving the rehabilitation of the convicted person is a general principle of EU law, which is applicable also in the context of the Area of Freedom, Security and Justice.[61] The Advocate General examined the distinction between the concepts of public security and public policy by pointing out that no judgment of the CJEU contains a definition of public security and that it is merely stated that it includes both internal and external security.[62] By invoking a series of judgments by the CJEU as well as the wording of the EU Citizens Directive as such, he opined that a clear-cut distinction of the two concepts and a definition with exhaustive content is difficult and even artificial, since their common objective is the protection of the fundamental interests of society.[63] 'Member States are free to determine public policy

---

[57] Paragraph 6(5) of the Gesetz über die allgemeine Freizügigkeit von Unionsbürgern (FreizügG/ EU). See para 10 of the judgment. Directive 2004/58/EC of the European Parliament and of the Council of 29 April 2004 on the right of citizens of the Union and their family members to move and reside freely within the territory of the Member States (Citizens Directive).

[58] For an overview of the arguments presented by the Administrative Court see paras 18–20 of the judgment.

[59] Opinion of Advocate General Bot, delivered on 8 June 2010, EU:C:2010:322.

[60] Paras 42–45 of the Opinion.

[61] Paras 46–50 of the Opinion.

[62] See Case C-367/89 *Richardt and Les Accessoires Scientifiques SNC* [1991] ECR I-4621, paragraph 22, Case C-83/94 *Leifer and Others* [1995] ECR I-3231, paragraph 26 and Case C-285/98 *Kreil v Bundesrepublik Deutschland* [2000] ECR I-69, paragraph 17.

[63] Para 68 of the Opinion.

and public security requirements in accordance with their national needs' and therefore the EU legislator and jurisprudence have deliberately left Member States with a certain margin of discretion.[64] As regards drug trafficking in particular, he pointed out that it could pose a direct threat to the physical safety of the population in cases, which occur very often, where drug traffickers are organised into armed gangs provoking urban violence.[65] Therefore, in his view public security should not be confined as including only 'the security of the Member State and its institutions', but also 'all the measures designed to combat serious threats to the values essential to the protection of its citizens'.[66] Consequently, this would inevitably bring under the scope of public security certain grounds that are also covered by the scope of public policy.[67]

However, this would not, according to the Advocate General, reduce the safeguards prescribed to limit the adoption of expulsion decisions against EU citizens. National authorities would still need to prove that the public security grounds are of imperative character.[68] In the assessment of the proportionality of an expulsion order, the justification must be of superior level and have regard to the extreme seriousness of the conduct alleged.[69] National authorities should explain with precision 'in what way [an expulsion] decision does not prejudice the offender's rehabilitation'. Overall, a balance between the interests of the individual and the EU must be found. This is because even if a person is expelled from a Member State and prohibited from returning, he will still be able to exercise his freedom of movement in the other Member States. 'It is therefore in the general interests [of the EU] that the conditions of his release should be such as to dissuade him from committing crimes and, in any event not risk pushing him back into offending'.[70] In addition, according to the Advocate General, a number of criteria need to be taken into consideration, such as the classification of the offence and the penalty framework, the involvement in the criminal activity and the specific sanction in comparison with the maximum sentence for the crime; the personal circumstances of the personal concerned such as the family ties and the exercise of economic activity in the host state as well as 'the effects produced or the information provided, regarding the degree of reintegration or the risk of re-offending, by the aid, advice and surveillance measures which accompanied his conditional release'.[71]

While the Court of Justice in its ruling did not fully follow the line of argument of the Advocate General, it reached a similar conclusion and adopted a wide interpretation of the concept of 'imperative grounds of public security'. Rather than

---

[64] Paras 69–71 of the Opinion.
[65] Para 72 of the Opinion.
[66] Para 77 of the Opinion.
[67] Para 78 of the Opinion.
[68] Para 80 of the Opinion.
[69] Para 91 of the Opinion.
[70] Para 95 of the Opinion.
[71] Para 96 of the Opinion.

exploring the correlation between public policy and public security more generally, the Court focused on the extent to which drug trafficking could be covered by the concept of 'imperative grounds of public security'. Therefore, the concept of public security was interpreted in an autonomous way without any express association with the notion of public policy.[72] In this regard, although a literal interpretation of Article 28(3) could perhaps lead to confining the application of the provision only to particularly serious conduct which threatens state security and puts into jeopardy the survival of the population,[73] the Court adhered to a wide interpretation of the notion—just like the Advocate General—by stating that the fight against crime in connection with dealing in narcotics as part of an organised group is not necessarily excluded from the concept of public security. In order to support this claim, the Court took into account the existence of an EU criminal law instrument, namely Framework Decision 2004/757/JHA, which lays down minimum rules regarding the constituent elements of criminal acts and penalties in the area of illicit drug trafficking.[74] In particular, the Court pointed out that Recital 1 of the Framework Decision includes security among the public interests threatened by the crime.[75] The second factor that the Court highlighted was the special characteristics of this criminal activity, in particular the negative consequences of drug addiction for the individual, its extraordinary economic and operational resources and its transnational links. In the light of the above, it concluded that dealing 'in narcotics as part of an organised criminal group could reach a level of intensity that might directly threaten the calm and physical security of the population as a whole or a large part of it', thus making it a threat that could lead to an expulsion on imperative public security grounds.[76]

This expansive interpretation adopted by the Court essentially blurs the distinction between the second and third paragraphs of Article 28 and leaves leeway to Member States to apply the public security concept in criminal offences that are also covered by the public policy ground, thus potentially lowering the enhanced level of protection provided by Article 28(3).[77] It appears that the underlying

---

[72] G Anagnostaras, 'Case Comment—Enhanced protection of EU nationals against expulsion and the concept of internal public security: comment on the PI case' (2012) 37 *European Law Review* 632.

[73] Kostakopoulou and Ferreira term this interpretation as a restrictionist approach in contrast with the Court's view which is regarded as the counter-restrictionist. See D Kostakopoulou and N Ferreira, 'Testing Liberal Norms: The Public Policy and Public Security Derogations and the Cracks in European Union Citizenship' (Legal Studies Research Paper No 2013-18, University of Warwick, School of Law) 10–11.

[74] Council Framework Decision 2004/757/JHA of 25 October 2004 laying down minimum provisions on the constituent elements of the criminal acts and penalties in the field of illicit drug trafficking, [2004] OJ L335/8.

[75] In particular, recital 1 of the Framework Decision states that illicit drug trafficking poses a threat to health, safety and the quality of life of citizens of the Union, and to the legal economy, stability and security of the Member States.

[76] Case C-145/09 *Tsakouridis*, para 47 of the judgment.

[77] Anagnostaras, n 72 above, 633; Kostakopoulou and Ferreira, n 73 above, 10; In fact, the Court admitted that dealing in narcotics was indeed covered by both the concepts of public policy and public security. See paras 54–56 of the judgment.

rationale behind the Court's approach is that when assessing expulsion decisions national authorities should not give precedence to determining precisely the classification of the threat, whether it is a public policy or a public security one, as these concepts cannot easily be distinguished and their meaning at national level can significantly vary. Instead, the focus must be placed to the 'exceptional circumstances' surrounding the criminal conduct and the 'high level of seriousness' of the threat.[78] The importance attached to the exceptional nature of the threat could be interpreted as also meaning that an overlap between the concepts of public policy and public security cannot occur on a common basis and would depend on the impact of the personal conduct in question on the calm and physical security of at least a part of the general population.[79] Regrettably, apart from examining the case of Mr Tsakouridis, the Court did not clarify what type of conduct would pose such exceptional security threats that could justify an expulsion of permanent residents.[80] However, it noted that an individual assessment of each case is necessary on the basis of the possible penalties and the sentences imposed, the degree of involvement in the criminal activity, and, if appropriate, the risk of reoffending. Echoing the arguments of Advocate General Bot, the Court stated that the personal conduct of the EU citizen should be balanced against the risk of compromising the social rehabilitation of the EU citizen in the host state in which he has become genuinely integrated.[81]

B. The Impact of Primary EU Criminal Law on EU Citizenship: Article 83(1) TFEU and *P.I.*

Less than two years after the release of the *Tsakouridis* judgment, another German Court sought an interpretation of Article 28(3) by the CJEU, this time with regard to criminal offences concerning the sexual exploitation of a minor. The case involved Mr I, an Italian national who had resided in Germany since 1987. In 2006 he was convicted and sentenced to seven and half years' imprisonment for sexually abusing his 14-year old stepdaughter from 1990 till 2001. In 2008, the German authorities adopted an expulsion order, which was unsuccessfully challenged. On appeal, the national Court decided to stay the proceedings and refer a single question to the CJEU. Its wording was almost identical to the first question in *Tsakouridis*, as discussed above, and was rephrased as meaning whether the crimes committed by Mr I were covered by Article 28(3).

Advocate General Bot delivered his Opinion on 6 March 2012.[82] The Advocate General took the view that the crimes in question, though particularly serious and

---

[78] See paras 40–41 of the judgment.
[79] Anagnostaras, n 72 above, 633.
[80] ibid.
[81] *Tsakouridis*, paras 48–50 of the judgment.
[82] Case C-348/09 *P.I. v Oberbürgermeisterin der Stadt Remscheid*, Opinion of AG Bot, delivered on 6 March 2012.

repulsive in character, posed a threat to public policy but could not give rise to 'imperative grounds of public security'. In line with his views in *Tsakouridis*, the Advocate General elaborated further his views on the distinction between the concepts of public security and public policy. In this regard, he explained that criminal law rules are in essence public policy rules, whereby each Member State defines the conduct it prohibits and sanctions.[83] In this context, an infringement of these rules will signify the imposition of a penalty, the level of which corresponds to the disturbance caused to public policy.[84] By contrast, public security covers a narrower category of criminal law which is determined first by the criminal conduct as such which is of particularly serious nature and second by its effects, which go beyond the individual harm caused to the victim.[85] Therefore, the Advocate General distinguished the nature of the act from the severity of the punishment; it is the nature of the crime in question that is of primary importance in asserting whether the offender poses a threat to public security, rather than the penalty imposed or the risk of reoffending.[86] As regards the crimes of Mr I, he recalled the definition provided by the Court in *Tsakouridis* that a threat to public security should be a 'diffuse form of crime [that] could reach a level of intensity that might directly threaten the calm and physical security of the population as a whole or a large part of it'.[87] Given the particularities of the case where the criminal offences took place exclusively in a family context, he held that Mr I did not pose a threat to public security despite the moral contempt attached to his crimes. Any other interpretation would signify that the objective seriousness of the offence as determined by the penalty imposed may justify an expulsion decision on imperative grounds of public security.[88]

Notwithstanding this finding, the Advocate General took the view that Mr I could not benefit from the protection enshrined in Article 28(3) of the Directive. Drawing from the CJEU's ruling in the *Kol* case,[89] he stated that expulsion from the host Member State can have harmful effects only to those EU citizens who are genuinely integrated in the host Member State.[90] In this regard, the Directive provides only for a 'presumption of integration', which is rebuttable.[91] This is because in his view, the level of integration of an individual is conditional not only upon territorial and time factors, but also upon qualitative elements. In the case of Mr I he found that such integration had not taken place since he started committing his criminal acts three years after he obtained his residence permit and

---

[83] Para 36 of the Opinion.
[84] Para 37 of the Opinion.
[85] Para 38 of the Opinion.
[86] Para 39 of the Opinion.
[87] Para 42 of the Opinion.
[88] Paras 43–45 of the Opinion.
[89] Case C-285/95 *Kol v Land Berlin* [1997] ECR I-3069. *Kol* involved a Turkish worker who had got a residence permit under fraudulent papers and subsequently got employment on the basis of this permit. The Court stated that he could neither derive any rights nor have any legitimate expectations.
[90] Para 53 of the Opinion.
[91] Para 56 of the Opinion.

continued throughout the years and within the 10-year period required by the Directive.[92] The commission of such crimes within this time-frame proved his complete lack of willingness to truly integrate into the German society.[93]

While the first part of his Opinion provides valuable remarks on the relationship between the notions of public policy and public security, his innovative line of thinking as regards the rebuttable character of the presumption of integration is questionable and has attracted much criticism.[94] In essence, the Advocate General suggested that in order for an EU citizen to enjoy the protection offered by the Directive, certain actions proving true integration need to be undertaken by the individual concerned.[95] Inability or unwillingness to conform to these requirements is ranked higher than the length of residence and could result in the disqualification and exclusion of any enhanced protection as set out in both Articles 28(2) and 28(3), thus depriving these articles of their *effet utile*.[96] Thus, the AG seems to have introduced an exception from this status of enhanced protection, an exception which is related specifically to the commission of a crime.[97] However, these proclamations are at odds with the spirit and philosophy of the Directive, which seeks to establish a meaningful status of permanent residence for EU citizens. Although the Preamble to the Directive refers to integration into society as the main cause behind the recognition of a status of permanent residence,[98] there is no indication in the instrument that presumption of integration can be rebutted.[99]

In its judgment, the Grand Chamber did not follow the approach of the Advocate General either in his distinction between public policy and public security or in his views regarding the dependence of true integration upon whether an EU citizen is law-abiding or not.[100] After recalling its findings in *Tsakouridis*, it emphasised that EU law does not impose on Member States a uniform scale of values as regards the assessment of a conduct as contrary to public security.[101] However, while the Court recognised that Member States enjoy the discretion to

---

[92] In this regard, Kostakopoulou notes that 'the perception of the risk posed by the criminal conduct of an EU citizen is flowing backwards in order to unsettle an actual fact, namely, residence exceeding 10 years. PI's past presence did not merely create a risk but was transformed into a real harm which had escaped the authorities' attention'. See D Kostakopoulou, 'When EU Citizens become Foreigners' (2014) 20 *European Law Journal* 459.

[93] Paras 59–60 of the Opinion.

[94] Anagnostaras, n 72 above, 3–8; D Kochenov and B Pirker, 'Deporting the EU citizens within the European Union: A counter-intuitive trend in Case C-348/09, *P.I. v Oberbürgermeisterin der Stadt Remscheid*' (2013) 19 *Columbia Journal of European Law* 384–86; Kostakopoulou and Ferreira, n 73 above, 13.

[95] Kochenov and Pirker, n 94 above, 384.

[96] D Kochenov, AG Bot in *P.I.* (Case C-348/09): Committing a crime disqualifies EU Citizens from permanent residence: europeanlawblog.eu/?p=281 (13.3.2012). Kochenov and Pirker, n 94 above, 385.

[97] Anagnostaras, n 72 above, 367.

[98] Recital 24 of the Directive.

[99] Kochenov and Pirker, n 94 above, 385.

[100] Case C-348/09, *P.I. v Oberbürgermeisterin der Stadt Remscheid*, judgment of 22 May 2012.

[101] Para 21 of the judgment.

determine the meaning of public security and public policy in accordance with their needs and their own appreciation of values, it stressed that they must do so within the limits of EU law and 'under the control of the institutions of the European Union'.[102] In order to determine whether the criminal offences of Mr I could give rise to imperative public security considerations, the Grand Chamber again took into account the legislative developments at EU level. First, it referred to the EU competence in adopting legislation in criminal matters and in particular in Article 83(1) TFEU, which includes the sexual exploitation of children among the crimes of a particularly serious nature and cross-border dimension where the EU legislature may intervene.[103] Secondly, it made reference to Directive 2011/93 as the result of exercising this competence,[104] which states that sexual abuse and sexual exploitation of children constitute grave violations of fundamental rights and provides a set of minimum maximum penalties that correspond to the seriousness of the offences in question.[105] According to the Court these references implied that sexual exploitation of children as well as all the criminal offences stated in Article 83(1) TFEU may constitute a serious threat to the calm and physical security of the population and thus fall within the concept of 'imperative grounds of public security' so long as the way these acts were committed carries particularly serious characteristics. Whether or not this is the case for a specific individual, this is for the referring court ultimately to determine after an individual assessment.[106] The Court thus introduced another criterion for assessing the existence of a public security ground; it is not only the exceptional nature of the threat posed by a certain criminal conduct, but also the seriousness of the criminal offence as such.[107] The gravity of certain offences is specifically evidenced by the EU competence to adopt minimum rules and the existence of secondary legislation as a form of exercise of this competence. Such serious offences may constitute particularly grave threats to one of the fundamental interests of society, which in turn may directly threaten 'the calm and physical security of the population'.[108]

Having provided a rather expansive interpretation of the threat posed by serious criminal offences, at least those enlisted in Article 83(1), the Court cautiously noted that the finding that a criminal offence poses such a threat should not necessarily lead to an expulsion of the EU citizen in question. It made clear that the particular circumstances of a person's life must be balanced against the legitimate security considerations of the state. A number of factors to be assessed by national

---

[102] Para 23 of the judgment. See in this regard, Case 36/75 *Rutili v Ministre de l'intérieur*, [1975] ECR 1219, paras 26–27 and Case C-50/06 *Commission v Netherlands*, [2007] ECR I-4383.

[103] *P.I.*, para 25 of the judgment.

[104] Directive 2011/92/EU of the European Parliament and of the Council of 13 December 2011 on combating the sexual abuse and sexual exploitation of children and child pornography, and replacing Council Framework Decision 2004/68/JHA, [2011] OJ L35/1, 17.12.2011.

[105] *P.I.*, paras 26–27 of the judgment.

[106] Para 28 of the judgment.

[107] Anagnostaras (n 72 above) 634.

[108] *P.I.*, para 28 of the judgment.

authorities were highlighted in this regard; the personal conduct of the individual must represent a 'genuine, present threat affecting one of the fundamental interests of society', which implies that a propensity to act in the same way in the future must exist.[109] According to Article 33(2) of the Directive, such propensity needs to be verified as still existing when the expulsion order is enforced more than two years after it was issued.[110] Additionally, the factors listed in Article 28(1) of the Directive, namely the length of stay in the host Member State, the age, state of health, family ties, economic situation, social and cultural integration in the host state, and existence and extent of links with the state of origin must also be assessed.[111]

The judgment in *P.I.* not only confirmed the shift in the focus from the public policy/public security divide to the exceptional character of the threat posed by the criminal conduct, but also significantly widened the scope of the public security derogation.[112] While in *Tsakouridis* the Court seemed to imply that a potential overlap between the two concepts would be a rare occurrence since the calm and physical security of the whole population or at least part of it would need to be under threat, in *P.I.* it was suggested that even cases involving specific individuals without such far-reaching repercussions could be considered as threats giving rise to imperative public security considerations as long as the manner in which the offence was committed involves particularly serious characteristics, which would be determined by the national authorities.[113] It is noteworthy in this regard, that the reference to the 'calm and physical security of the population as a whole or at least large part of it' was substituted by a mere reference to the 'calm and physical security of the population'.[114] Consequently, the Grand Chamber seems to understand the family context as part of a broader social sphere that the state owes to protect,[115] thus adding an 'everyday dimension' to the public security derogation which further blurs the distinction between the notions of public security and public policy.[116]

On the one hand, this wide interpretation by the Court, which encompasses large parts of the public policy notion, would satisfy Member States as it gives them leeway to expand their scope of manoeuvre and introduce additional limits to the free movement of persons in compliance with the judgment. In this

---

[109] Paras 29–30 of the judgment. The concept of 'propensity to act in the same in the future' is drawn from *Bouchereau*, Case 30/77 *Bouchereau*, [1977] ECR 1999. For an analysis of the different meaning between *P.I.* and *Bouchereau* see, L Azoulai and S Coutts, 'Restricting Union citizens' residence rights on grounds of public security. Where Union citizenship and the AFSJ meet: *P.I.* Case C-348/09, *P.I. v Oberbürgermeisterin der Stadt Remscheid*, judgment of the Court of Justice (Grand Chamber) of 22 May 2012' (2013) 50 *Common Market Law Review* 557.

[110] *P.I.*, para 31 of the judgment. Citizenship Directive 2004/38/EC, n 31 above, Art 33(2).

[111] Para 32 of the judgment.

[112] Kostakopoulou and Ferreira, n 73 above, 12.

[113] Anagnostaras, n 72 above, 634.

[114] Azoulai and Coutts, n 109 above, 559–60.

[115] ibid, 560. Azoulai and Coutts refer to the Court's approach as the socialisation of the concept of public security.

[116] Kostakopoulou and Ferreira, n 73 above, 12.

framework, the judgment creates an interesting paradox, as at the same time the Grand Chamber carefully called for a strict interpretation of public policy and public security requirements at the national level.[117] On the other hand, the content of Article 28(3) is reformed in a way that seems to be in contrast with the wording and rationale of the Directive, which was specifically designed in order to make expulsions for EU citizens more difficult depending on their level of integration in the society of the host Member State based on the length of residence, and thus promote the EU citizenship status.[118] As Azoulai and Coutts have pointed out, the judgment could be seen as complementing the rights enshrined in the Directive with correlative obligations.[119]

However, the fact that Article 28(2) makes reference to both public policy and public security grounds while Article 28(3) merely refers to 'imperative grounds of public security' clearly calls for a distinct interpretation of the concept of public security. A distinction between the notions is corroborated by the Commission Report on the implementation of the Directive, where it is highlighted that the competent national authorities must not extend the concept of public security to instruments that should be covered by public policy.[120] Elsewhere, the Commission stressed the importance of clearly identifying the protected interests of society and of distinguishing between public policy and public security, by noting that the former concept is generally to be interpreted along the lines of preventing the disturbance of the social order, while the latter intends to preserve the integrity of the territory of a Member State and its institutions.[121] In this context, by putting aside the distinction between the two concepts, the Court allowed Member States to interpret the Directive in a manner that waters down the high level of protection offered to EU citizens against expulsions and more generally undermines the effectiveness of the Directive.[122] As Acosta and Martire have noted, the Court's approach seems to suggest that '[r]ather than treating long-term EU citizens as quasi-nationals, the approach is to consider them … "eternal guests" whose integration can always be questioned'.[123]

---

[117] Anagnostaras, n 72 above, 634.

[118] Kostakopoulou and Ferreira, n 73 above, 13.

[119] Azoulai and Coutts, n 109 above, 569.

[120] Commission, Report to the European Parliament and the Council on the application of Directive 2004/38 on the rights of citizens of the Union and their family members to move and reside freely within the territory of the Member States, COM(2008) 840 final, 10.12.2008.

[121] Commission, Communication from the Commission to the European Parliament and the Council on guidance for better transposition and application of Directive 2004/38/EC on the right of citizens of the Union and their family members to move and reside freely within the territory of the Member States, COM(2009) 313 final, 2.7.2009, 10.

[122] D Kostakopoulou, 'When EU Citizens become Foreigners' (2014) 20 *European Law Journal* 447, 458. Some commentators have regarded the Court's approach as an ultra-vires action and unacceptable judicial activism and the interpretation of the EU Citizens Directive as *contra legem*. See Kochenov and Pirker n 94 above, 372.

[123] D' Acosta Arcarazo and J Martire, 'Trapped in the lobby: Europe's revolving doors and the others as Xenos' (2014) 39 *European Law Review* 374.

The emphasis of the Grand Chamber on the role of Article 83(1) TFEU seems to suggest the existence of an EU list of particularly grave offences, which may raise public security concerns and potentially lead to the expulsion of EU citizens. As regards these crimes there is no requirement to 'affect the calm and physical security of the general population *as whole or at least of a large part of it'*. The inclusion of a crime in Article 83(1) TFEU seems to satisfy the Court that the crime is sufficiently serious, so an EU citizen may be expelled on the basis of imperative public security grounds 'if the manner in which it was committed discloses particularly serious characteristics'.[124] In this context, Article 83(1) is transferred from its traditional context of judicial co-operation in criminal matters to the EU citizenship framework and acquires additional functions that are unrelated to the purpose it serves and were certainly not intended when the Lisbon Treaty was drafted.[125] First, it provides guidance to national authorities by indicating criminal conduct of a serious nature that could thus be covered by the concept of 'imperative public security grounds'. Secondly, rather than being used for controlling national definitions of fundamental interests as mentioned by the Court, it seems to affirm enforcement choices made at national level, with some commentators arguing even that it serves to define a set of EU values.[126] The Court has made clear that all listed crimes on the basis of which the EU legislature may intervene in accordance with Article 83(1) TFEU could imperil public security in an imperative manner and therefore could result in an expulsion order after considering the set of factors provided by the Court.[127]

In this manner, the Court has used Article 83(1) TFEU out of context: Article 83(1) TFEU serves as a legal basis circumscribing the *competence* of the European Union to adopt legislation on criminal offences and sanctions, and not as a legal basis for interpreting exceptions to EU free movement and citizenship rights. In any case, EU intervention under Article 83(1) TFEU takes the form of Directive, leaving Member States a discretion as to how specifically the criminalisation objectives of EU law adopted under this legal basis are implemented. The use of Article 83(1) TFEU by the Court in *P.I.* has thus a dual transformational effect: in terms of EU citizenship, it serves to dilute the protection offered by EU law; in terms of EU criminal law, by elevating the enumeration of the conduct listed in Article 83(1) to a ground justifying exceptions to rights granted under EU

---

[124] Anagnostaras, n 72 above, 635. In his view, the line of argumentation of the Court seems rather circular in the sense that by default a particularly serious criminal activity consists of particularly serious characteristics. The Court could have provided further clarifications as to what kind of particularly serious characteristics a serious offence should carry in order raise imperative public security concerns, but it merely left the matter for determination by national authorities, thus further obscuring the matter.

[125] Mancano views this development as enhancing the legitimacy of EU criminal law. See L Mancano, 'Criminal conduct and lack of integration into the society under EU citizenship: this marriage is not to be performed' (2015) 6 *New Journal of European Criminal Law* 53–77.

[126] Azoulai and Coutts, n 109 above, 564.

[127] *P.I.*, para 28 of the judgment.

law, it affirms an uncritical securitised vision of EU criminal law and transforms Article 83(1) TFEU into symbolic criminal law.[128]

IV. Conclusion: Towards a Paradigm Change in Citizenship and EU Criminal Law

The development of EU law in recent years on the relationship between EU criminal law and EU citizenship, in particular via the case-law of the Court of Justice, has resulted in a paradigmatic change in terms of both the effect and significance of EU criminal law provisions and in terms of the perception and content of citizenship rights. EU citizenship law has been distorted and thus undermined the objectives and effectiveness of EU criminal law; and EU criminal law has been used to undermine long-standing protections under EU citizenship law. In terms of the place of citizenship rights in the development of EU criminal law, both the legislator and the Court of Justice have demonstrated remarkable—and, it has been argued, undue—deference on the choices of EU Member States as to who is deemed to be sufficiently integrated into their territory to be able to remain. The irony here is that this approach is counter-productive to the stated aims of the EU criminal law instruments in question: discriminating between own nationals and citizens of other EU Member States is contrary to a key aim of the European Arrest Warrant system, namely to ensure justice across Europe's Area of Freedom, Security and Justice regardless of the nationality of the individual affected by the surrender procedure; the removal of the need for consent in the transfer of sentenced persons on the other hand, even if these individuals are EU citizens with strong integration links to the Member State which wishes to transfer them, is at odds with the stated aims of the instrument to reintegrate and rehabilitate. In both cases, the approach taken by the EU legislature and judiciary undermines key protections under EU citizenship law. Similar deference to Member States' security perceptions can be discerned also at the level of the use of EU criminal law in the case-law on derogations from the EU citizenship Directive. This trend has also been discernible with regard to the role of the use of domestic criminal law and its enforcement in limiting citizenship rights.[129] In terms of the impact of *European Union* criminal law on citizenship rights, the Court of Justice seems to accept that criminalisation at EU level—either by secondary law or by the Treaty itself—is a sufficient ground to justify *domestic* choices to restrict citizenship rights. National enforcement choices and security perceptions are legitimised by

---

[128] On Article 83(1) TFEU as a reflection of 'securitised criminalisation' see Chapter 3 of this volume.
[129] See in this context in particular the Court's ruling in *Onuekwere v Secretary of State for the Home Department*, which involved the impact of imprisonment on citizenship rights: Case C-378/12, judgment of 16 January 2014, EU:C:2014:13; for a comment see S Coutts, 'Union Citizenship as Probationary Citizenship: *Onuekwere*' (2015) 52 *Common Market Law Review* 531–46.

reference to the *EU* Treaty, and in particular Article 83(1) TFEU. In this manner, as Nic Shuibhne has noted in relation to *P.I.*, 'the Court converted an exceptional protection *against* expulsion into a route *towards* it'.[130] This approach not only transforms EU citizenship by altering fundamental presumptions of integration, but also signifies a fundamental change as regards the place of EU criminal law in the EU constitutional order. Post-*P.I.*, Article 83(1) TFEU can be seen as not only a conferral provision—namely a provision which serves to determine the extent of EU competence to adopt minimum rules on the definition of criminal offences and the imposition of criminal sanctions—but also, much more broadly, as a provision which treats the conduct enumerated therein as a security issue and thus justifies Member State choices to curtail long-established fundamental rights and freedoms at EU level. The combination of the two strands of law and policy leads to a vicious circle: by limiting citizenship rights and facilitating expulsion following *P.I.*, transfer to another Member States without consent under the Framework Decision on the transfer of prisoners is allowed. This twin-track approach disregards the objectives and internal coherence of both EU criminal law and EU citizenship law and poses significant challenges to the position of the citizen in Europe's area of criminal justice.

---

[130] N Nic Shuibhne, 'Limits Rising, Duties Ascending: The Changing Legal Shape of Union Citizenship' (2015) 52 *Common Market Law Review* 889–938, at 925.

9

The European Union and Preventive Justice. The Case of Terrorist Sanctions

I. Introduction

The analysis of the impact of post-Lisbon EU criminal law on the transformation of justice in the European Union cannot be complete without a critical engagement with the evolution of a preventive justice agenda at EU level. Preventive justice is understood here as the exercise of state power in order to prevent future acts which are deemed to constitute security threats. Preventive justice is thus forward- rather than backward-looking; it aims to prevent potential threats rather than punishing past acts; and in this manner it introduces a system of justice based on the creation of suspect individuals on the basis of on-going risk assessment. This model of preventive justice, based on the identification of suspect individuals and organisations on the basis of risk assessment, has been central to the US responses post-9/11 and has been imposed globally via the United Nations Security Council.[1] From the perspective of domestic criminal law, prominent theoretical preventive justice accounts have emerged in the United Kingdom,[2] Germany (where the concept of 'enemy criminal law' has been put forward),[3] and, post-9/11, in the United States.[4] What this chapter will attempt to demonstrate is that the European Union itself has also developed a model of preventive justice. This model has been the product of post-9/11 counter-terrorism responses and is centered on the imposition of sanctions on individuals who are suspected of being associated with terrorism. These sanctions—and in particular the freezing

---

[1] On various aspects of the link between risk assessment and counter-terrorism see L Amoore and M de Goede (eds), *Risk and the War on Terror* (Abingdon/New York, Routledge, 2008).

[2] See in particular A Ashworth and L Zedner, *Preventive Justice* (Oxford, Oxford University Press, 2014).

[3] On the concept of the criminal law of the enemy (Feindstrafrecht) see G Jakobs, 'Bürgerstrafrecht und Feindstrafrecht' (2004) *Höchstrichterliche Rechtsprechung zum Strafrecht* 88–94. On prevention and criminal justice see inter alia P-A Albrecht, 'La Politique Criminelle dans L'État de Prévention' (1997) 21 *Déviance et Société* 123–36.

[4] See inter alia D Cole, 'The Difference Prevention Makes: Regulating Preventive Justice' (2015) 9 *Criminal Law and Philosophy* 501: papers.ssrn.com/sol3/papers.cfm?abstract_id=2459976.

of property and the imposition of travel bans—are considered to be preventive in that they do not require a criminal conviction and that they target specific individuals or entities who are suspected of being associated with terrorism. The emergence of the EU preventive justice regime in this context has two key features: it has developed in response to global counter-terrorism initiatives, and in particular in response to action by the United Nations Security Council; and, in this manner, it is a response which is primarily based on executive action. The chapter will attempt to map the evolution of the EU preventive justice model in relation to terrorist sanctions, by analysing the development of the scope and content of EU terrorist sanctions ranging from the post-9/11 sanctions regimes to recent initiatives on foreign fighters. The relationship between EU law and international executive action at the level of the United Nations Security Council will be critically evaluated. The chapter will then explore the consequences of these measures for the transformation of justice in the EU by examining two key questions: the impact of the EU preventive justice regime on affected individuals and the protection of their fundamental rights; and the impact of the preventive justice regime on the rule of law, and in particular the relationship between the executive and the judiciary. While the two questions are closely interrelated, it will be demonstrated that the responses provided by EU institutions, and in particular by the European judiciary, privilege a concept of procedural justice instead of—or perhaps more critically at the expense of—a concept of substantive justice based on the need to ensure compliance with substantive—and not only procedural—rights.

II. Preventive Justice via 'Global Administrative Law': The Role of the UN Security Council

Calls for global, emergency counter-terrorism action post-9/11 have not resulted in the adoption of measures in the form of the traditional multilateral 'hard law' Conventions at the level of the United Nations. Rather, global standards in the field of preventive justice have been adopted and promoted principally via what legal scholars have labelled 'global administrative law'.[5] It has been noted that

> underlying the emergence of global administrative law is the vast increase in the reach and forms of transgovernmental regulation and administration designed to address the consequences of globalized interdependence in such fields as security ... much in the detail and implementation of such regulation is determined by transnational administrative bodies—including international organizations and informal groups of officials that perform administrative functions but are not directly subject to control by national

---

[5] B Kingsbury, N Krisch and RB Stewart, 'The Emergence of Global Administrative Law' (2004–2005) 68 *Law and Contemporary Problems* 15.

governments or domestic legal systems or, in the case of treaty-based regimes, the states parties to the treaty.[6]

It is contested whether all or some of the norms included under the rubric of 'global administrative law' can really be classified as 'law'.[7] However, the term is a useful analytical tool in focusing on the *process* of the adoption of norms and in this context highlighting key differences between the development of global norms in this context and the traditional adoption of multilateral, legally binding treaties. The production of normative standards at the level of 'global administrative law' or 'government networks' differs from the adoption of multilateral, expressly legally binding standards at the multilateral level in four main respects: standards are put forward by a limited number of states without the need for a global consensus; standards are adopted with a minimum of transparency; standards are adopted speedily (a factor which may explain the appeal of this form of normative production in times of perceived emergency); and standards are not explicitly legally binding rules of general application, but in reality have far-reaching consequences for law reform around the world. All these features confirm the dominance of the executive in the development and adoption of 'global administrative law'.

The adoption of preventive counter-terrorism sanctions by the UN Security Council constitutes a prime example of global administrative law in this context. The production of normative standards in criminal matters by the UN Security Council has been linked to global counter-terrorism efforts as part of a two-fold strategy. The first element of this strategy has been the adoption, which began before 9/11, of a set of Resolutions specifically targeting the Taliban, Osama bin Laden, Al-Qaida and those associated with them. The first step in this direction was Resolution 1267 (1999), which imposed a series of restrictive measures against the Taliban, including an arms embargo, banning travel and the freezing of funds. In the latter context, paragraph 4(b) of the Resolution called on states to

> [f]reeze funds and other financial resources, including funds derived or generated from property owned or controlled directly or indirectly by the Taliban, or by any undertaking owned or controlled by the Taliban ... and ensure that neither they nor any other funds or financial resources so designated are made available, by their nationals or by any persons within their territory, to or for the benefit of the Taliban or any undertaking owned or controlled, directly or indirectly, by the Taliban, except as may be authorized ... on the grounds of humanitarian need.

The designation of those targeted by such measures and the consideration of exceptions will be made by a Sanctions Committee, established in paragraph 6 of the Resolution. Resolution 1333 (2000) extended the freezing regime expressly to individuals in the Al-Qaida organisation and requested the Sanctions Committee

---

[6] ibid, 16.

[7] See, in this context, B Kingsbury, 'The Concept of 'Law in Global Administrative Law' (2009) 20 *European Journal of International Law* 23; and A Somek, 'The Concept of 'Law' in Global Administrative Law: A Reply to Benedict Kingsbury' (2009) 20 *European Journal of International Law* 985.

to maintain an up-to-date list of the individuals and entities designated as being associated with bin Laden, including those in Al-Qaida.[8] The next substantive amendment to the sanctions regime came about after 9/11, with Resolution 1390(2002).[9] The latter adjusted the content of Resolution 1267 to take into account political developments since its adoption but continued and consolidated the freezing regime established in paragraph 4(b) thereof. The Resolution urged

> all States to take immediate steps to enforce and strengthen through legislative enactments or administrative measures, where appropriate, the measures imposed under domestic laws or regulations against their nationals and other individuals or entities operating in their territory, to prevent and punish violations of the measures referred to in paragraph 2 of this resolution,

including the freezing of funds.[10] The substantive and procedural elements of these Resolutions have been revised since, without changing fundamentally the emphasis on economic sanctions against specific individuals as a key Security Council counter-terrorism strategy.[11]

The emphasis on the adoption of legislative measures is even more prominent in the second element of the Security Council counter-terrorism strategy. Resolution 1373 (2001), adopted less than three weeks after the 9/11 attacks, called upon all states in particular to 'prevent and suppress the financing of terrorist acts'; criminalise terrorism financing; and extend the freezing regime to cover in general 'persons who commit or attempt to commit terrorist acts or participate in or facilitate the commission of [such] acts, ... entities owned or controlled directly or indirectly by such persons, and ... persons and entities acting on [their] behalf or ... direction'.[12] Resolution 1373 expressly called upon all states to

> [e]nsure that any person who participates in the financing, planning, preparation or perpetration of terrorist acts or in supporting terrorist acts is brought to justice, and to ensure that, in addition to any other measures against them, such terrorist acts are established as serious criminal offences in domestic laws and regulations and that the punishment duly reflects the seriousness of such terrorist acts.[13]

It also called upon all states, inter alia, to 'become parties as soon as possible to the relevant international conventions and protocols relating to terrorism, including the International Convention for the Suppression of the Financing of Terrorism of 9 December 1999'.[14]

---

[8] Resolution 1333 (2000), para 8(c).

[9] In the meantime, Resolution 1363 (2001) had established a mechanism to monitor the implementation of Resolutions 1267 and 1333.

[10] Resolution 1390 (2002), para 8.

[11] See, in this context, inter alia, Resolution 1452 (2002) amending the scope of sanctions of Resolutions 1267 and 1390; and Resolutions 1735 (2006) and 1822 (2008) introducing in particular changes in the procedures of the Sanctions Committee.

[12] Resolution 1373(2001), para 1(a)–(c).

[13] Para 2(e).

[14] Para 3(d).

In this manner, the international community witnessed the production of global normative standards in the field of counter-terrorism outside the framework of the multilateral treaty. This shift did not go unnoticed by international lawyers, who stressed the Security Council's 'legislative' role.[15] In this context, it has been pointed out that Resolution 1373 is of general and abstract character and does not name a single country, society or group of people;[16] that with Resolution 1373, together with the related efforts of its 1267 Sanctions Committee, the Council is no longer responding with discrete action directed at a particular state because of a concrete threat to peace arising from a specific incident;[17] and that Resolution 1373 imposed general obligations on all states for an indefinite period, while Resolution 1267 set up a sanctions committee with court-like powers to identify and freeze the assets of individuals, groups and corporations.[18] This production of normative standards by the Security Council has been criticised as undemocratic on the grounds of the limited transparency of Security Council negotiations,[19] of the adoption of the Resolutions (in particular 1373) speedily as emergency measures,[20] and last, but not least, on the ground of the selective membership of the Security Council. It has been forcefully pointed out that 'a patently unrepresentative and undemocratic body such as the Council is arguably unsuitable for international lawmaking' and that: 'Council practice may be criticised as contrary to the basic structure of international law as a consent-based legal order'.[21] It has also been argued that the Resolutions 'circumvent the "vehicle *par excellence* of community interest", namely the multilateral treaty', and that as such they serve to promote the interests of a limited number of state actors.[22] It must be noted in this context that the Resolutions do not only impose an extensive normative restrictive counter-terrorism framework, but also aim to ensure and accelerate the implementation of the enforcement standards adopted in a pre-existing multilateral treaty, the 1999 Convention on Terrorist Finance.[23] In a departure from the

---

[15] See, in particular, S Talmon, 'The Security Council as World Legislature' (2005) 99 *American Journal of International Law* 175; JE Alvarez, 'Hegemonic International Law Revisited' (2003) 97 *American Journal of International Law* 873.

[16] Talmon, 'The Security Council as World Legislature', above n 15, 176–77.

[17] Alvarez, 'Hegemonic International Law Revisited', above n 15, 874.

[18] I Johnstone, 'Legislation and Adjudication in the UN Security Council: Bringing Down the Deliberative Deficit' (2008) 102 *American Journal of International Law* 275, 283.

[19] See, in particular, Talmon, above n 15, 190.

[20] See ibid, 15, and the detailed analysis of Johnstone, 'Legislation and Adjudication in the UN Security Council', above n 18, 284.

[21] Talmon, above n 15, 179.

[22] Alvarez, above n 15, 874–75. Alvarez examines in detail US influence in the passage of the Security Council Resolutions. See also, Johnstone, above n 18, 300 who points out that multilateral treaty negotiations tend to balance global concerns, leading to trade-offs and bargains that account for a wider range of interests than typically come out of Security Council negotiations.

[23] See, in this context, the criticism of Alvarez, who notes that: 'In Resolution 1373 the Council selected certain provisions of the then recently concluded International Convention for the Suppression of the Financing of Terrorism, added to others, and omitted other portions of the Convention (such as the explicit deference to other requirements of international law, including the rights due to persons charged with terrorism-related offences, the rights of extradited persons, the requisites of international humanitarian law, and the provisions on judicial dispute settlement', above n 15, 875.

consensus required for the adoption of legally binding provisions in a multilateral international treaty, in the case of the UN Security Council far-reaching norms are produced by a body operating with a limited agenda, membership, transparency and scrutiny. What makes this departure even more striking is that, in the counter-terrorism Resolutions, the individual (targeted by a series of sanctions) directly enters the realm of a system primarily designed to address inter-state relations.[24] What renders the reach of these Resolutions even wider is that, in addition to the fact that they target individuals directly, the Resolutions (in particular Resolution 1267) leave states and international organisations such as the EU with very limited discretion as to how to implement them. As Krisch has eloquently noted,

> insofar as Member State implementation is necessary to give measures effect, States' action is reduced to a subordinate, non-discretionary role in the overall administrative machinery directed by the Council and its committees, resulting in a significant reduction of the distance between national and international law in this domain and leading to an increasing enmeshment between those layers.[25]

III. Implementation of the UN Security Council Resolutions by the European Union

From the outset, the European Union has demonstrated strong political will to implement the Security Council Resolutions in terrorist sanctions. This was notwithstanding the three pillar constitutional complexity of the EU legal order before the entry into force of the Treaty of Lisbon. The European Union legislator managed to overcome this complexity by using creatively the Treaty options with regard to the use of potential legal bases establishing the Community and the Union's competence to adopt measures implementing the Security Council's sanctions regimes in the EU legal order. The latter were implemented at EU level via a combination of cross-pillar legal instruments. Implementation of the first set of Resolutions, targeting the Taliban, bin Laden and Al-Qaida and their associates, followed shortly after the adoption of the measures by the Security Council and consisted of second pillar Common Positions combined with first pillar Regulations. Council Common Position of 15 November 1999 concerning restrictive measures against the Taliban (1999/727/CFSP),[26] adopted under Article 15 TEU, stated that action by the Community is needed in order to implement the

---

[24] See, especially, in this context, PC Szasz, 'The Security Council Starts Legislating' (2002) 96 *American Journal of International Law* 901; Johnstone, above n 18, 295.

[25] N Krisch, *Beyond Constitutionalism. The Pluralist Structure of Postnational Law* (Oxford, Oxford University Press, 2010) 156–57.

[26] Council Common Position of 15 November 1999 concerning restrictive measures against the Taliban (1999/727/CFSP) [1999] OJ L294/1.

measures cited therein[27] and called, inter alia, for flight bans[28] and for funds and other financial resources held abroad by the Taliban under the conditions set out in UNSCR 1267(1999) to be frozen.[29] The Common Position was accompanied by Council Regulation (EC) No 337/2000 of 14 February 2000 concerning a flight ban and a freeze of funds and other financial resources in respect of the Taliban of Afghanistan,[30] adopted under Articles 60 and 301 EC. Counter-terrorism action under the first pillar was justified by stating that the measures set out in paragraph 4 of Resolution 1267 (1999) fall under the scope of the Treaty and, therefore, notably with a view to avoiding distortion of competition, Community legislation is necessary to implement the relevant decisions of the Security Council as far as the territory of the Community is concerned.[31] The Regulation stated inter alia that all funds and other financial resources designated by the Taliban Sanctions Committee will be frozen and that 'no funds or other financial resources designated by the Taliban Sanctions Committee ... [will] be made available to or for the benefit of the Taliban or any undertaking owned or controlled, directly or indirectly, by the Taliban'.[32] Thus, the Regulation, in combination with the Common Position, established a system of sanctions at Community level by reference to the sanctions adopted at the UN Security Council.

The same approach was adopted in order to implement Resolution 1333 (2000). A Council Common Position was adopted under Article 15 TEU,[33] accompanied by a first pillar Regulation adopted under Articles 60 and 301 TEC[34] with Community competence and action justified in a similar manner as to the adoption of Regulation 337/2000.[35] The measures continued the Community sanctions regime established by reference to Security Council sanctions. The system was renewed, with some changes, at the implementation of Resolution 1390 (2002). A Council Common Position was again adopted under Article 15 TEU.[36] However,

---

[27] Preamble, recital 2.

[28] Art 1.

[29] Art 2.

[30] Council Regulation (EC) No 337/2000 of 14 February 2000 concerning a flight ban and a freeze of funds and other financial resources in respect of the Taliban of Afghanistan [2000] OJ L43/1.

[31] Preamble, recital 3.

[32] Art 3.

[33] Council Common Position of 26 February 2001 concerning additional restrictive measures against the Taliban and amending Common Position 96/746/CFSP (2001/154/CFSP) [2001] OJ L57/1.

[34] Council Regulation (EC) No 467/2001 of 6 March 2001 prohibiting the export of certain goods and services to Afghanistan, strengthening the flight ban and extending the freeze of funds and other financial resources in respect of the Taliban of Afghanistan and repealing Regulation (EC) No 337/2000 [2001] OJ L67/1.

[35] According to recital 3, Resolution 1333 (as with its predecessor 1267) fell under the scope of the Treaty and, therefore, notably with a view to avoiding distortion of competition, Community legislation was necessary to implement the relevant decisions of the Security Council, as far as the territory of the Community is concerned.

[36] Council Common Position of 27 May 2002 concerning restrictive measures against Usama bin Laden, members of the Al-Qaida organisation and the Taliban and other individuals, groups, undertakings and entities associated with them and repealing Common Positions 96/746/CFSP, 1999/727/CFSP, 2001/154/CFSP and 2001/771/CFSP (2002/402/CFSP) [2002] OJ L139/4.

the legal basis of the parallel first pillar Regulation was extended to include, along with Articles 60 and 301 TEC, Article 308 TEC.[37] The addition of Article 308 to the legal basis of Regulation 881/2002 has been attributed to the need to take account of political developments taking place at the time. By January 2002 the Taliban regime in Afghanistan had fallen and so at the time the Regulation was adopted, the persons and entities listed did not have a direct connection with the territory or governing regime of a third country. The initial choice of legal bases of Articles 60 and 301 TEC, which was based on the principle that the individuals and entities listed were in effective control of the territory of a third country, or were associated with those in effective control and provided them with financial support, was thus deemed no longer adequate to address the situation in Afghanistan.[38] Under this technique, sanctions against individuals not linked with the government or the control of a country now fall clearly under the scope of Community law,[39] with Regulation 881/2002 consolidating and expanding the sanctions regime in the light of developments in the Security Council.[40] Parallel second and first pillar measures were adopted subsequently under the same legal bases, including measures implementing the exceptions to the sanctions regime introduced by Resolution 1452(2002),[41] while the list of individuals or entities subject to the Union sanctions regime is being regularly updated by Commission Regulations introducing the amendments in the lists made by the Sanctions Committee into the Union legal order.

A slightly different strategy was followed to implement Resolution 1373 in the Community and Union legal order. The contents of Resolution 1373 were split into two separate Council Common Positions: one concerning the general requirement for states to take action at the level of criminalisation, prevention

---

[37] Council Regulation (EC) No 881/2002 of 27 May 2002 imposing certain specific restrictive measures directed against certain persons and entities associated with Usama bin Laden, the Al-Qaida network and the Taliban, and repealing Council Regulation (EC) No 467/2001 [2002] OJ L139/9. As with the earlier Regulations, the avoidance of the distortion of competition was evoked as necessitating Community implementation of the relevant Security Council measures (Preamble, recital 4).

[38] See M Cremona, 'EC Competence, "Smart Sanctions" and the *Kadi* Case' 28 *Yearbook of European Law* 2009 559, 569. Cremona explains in detail the evolution of the interpretation of Arts 60(1) and 301 EC in Community legislation prior to the adoption of the Regulations in question. She notes that although neither of these provisions expressly mentions individuals, referring rather to 'economic relations with one or more third countries' the concept has been broadly interpreted, in the first place to allow for targeted sanctions against natural and legal persons who are connected to a government or regime—the aim being to put pressure on a third state by taking measures against those people or entities who are either part of the government or closely connected with it (at 567–68).

[39] It is noteworthy that the Preamble to Council Regulation (EC) No 881/2002 also contains references to Resolution 1373, which extends the scope of economic sanctions beyond the Taliban (recital 3).

[40] See in particular, Arts 2, 4 and 6 of the Regulation.

[41] Council Common Position 2003/140/CFSP of 27 February 2003 concerning exceptions to the restrictive measures imposed by Common Position 2002/402/CFSP [2003] OJ L53/62; Council Regulation (EC) No 561/2003 of 27 March 2003 amending, as regards exceptions to the freezing of funds and economic resources, Regulation (EC) No 881/2002 [2003] OJ L82/1.

and prosecution;[42] and one specifically concerning sanctions against individuals.[43] Adopted as emergency measures a few weeks after 9/11 (and the adoption of Resolution 1373), the Common Positions were adopted under a joint second and third pillar legal basis (Articles 15 and 34 TEU). The first, 'general' Common Position contains both provisions on freezing and provisions related to general obligations of criminalisation and prevention, ordinarily covered at the time by the third pillar. The second, 'sanctions' Common Position included both provisions on sanctions, and a general provision on cooperation and assistance between Member States (Article 4), also deemed to fall under the then third pillar. This Common Position was again accompanied by a first pillar Regulation adopted under Articles 60, 301 and 308 TEC.[44] According to the Preamble to the Regulation, Community action was necessary in order to implement the Common Foreign and Security Policy aspects of Common Position 2001/931/CFSP.[45] The absence of a reference to the necessity of Community action to prevent distortion of competition (a model followed in the Regulations implementing the other Security Council sanctions Resolutions described above) is noteworthy in this context. Community action was here justified in order to implement the second pillar elements of the parallel Common Position. In this manner, an autonomous system of Union sanctions has been established, complementing the system where UN sanctions are copied by the Community described above.[46] The legality of the choices of the EU legislator to enable the Union to implement the UN Security Council sanctions regime before Lisbon has been upheld by the Court of Justice in its ruling in *Kadi I*.[47] After the entry into force of the Treaty of Lisbon, which includes two separate but express legal bases for the adoption of terrorist sanctions

---

[42] Council Common Position of 27 December 2001 on combating terrorism (2001/930/CFSP) [2001] OJ L344/90. Along with general provisions on the freezing of funds and refraining from making funds available for terrorism, the Common Position calls, inter alia, for the criminalisation of terrorist finance (Art 1, elements of the definition being copied from Resolution 1373), the suppression of support for terrorism (Art 4), prevention (Art 5) and bringing persons who participate in the financing, planning, preparation or perpetration of terrorist acts to justice (Art 8). The Common Position further calls upon Member States to become parties as soon as possible to the relevant international conventions and protocols relating to terrorism listed in the annex to the Common Position (including the 1999 Terrorist Finance Convention—Art 14).

[43] Council Common Position of 27 December 2001 on the application of specific measures to combat terrorism (2001/931/CFSP) [2001] OJ L344/93.

[44] Council Regulation (EC) No 2580/2001 of 27 December 2001 on specific restrictive measures directed against certain persons and entities with a view to combating terrorism [2001] OJ L344/70.

[45] Recital 3.

[46] For a categorisation and overview of the various strands of the Community sanctions regime, see C Eckes, *EU Counter-Terrorist Policies and Fundamental Rights. The Case of Individual Sanctions* (Oxford, Oxford University Press, 2009).

[47] Joined Cases C-402/05 P and C-415/05 *Kadi and Al Barakaat International Foundation v Council and Commission* [2008] ECR I-6351. On the substantive outcome of *Kadi I*, see section IV below. For a critical analysis of the Court's ruling on the legality of EU action in the field pre-Lisbon and the extent to which the Community and Union had competence to implement the UN Security Council Resolutions on terrorist sanctions, see V Mitsilegas, 'The European Union and the Globalisation of Criminal Law' (2010) 12 *Cambridge Yearbook of European Legal Studies* 337–407.

in Article 75 and 215(2) TFEU,[48] EU Regulations were adopted and the relevant sanctions lists are updated on a regular basis.[49]

IV. Judicial Review of the EU Implementation of UN Security Council Resolutions: *Kadi I*

The relationship between Union law and the emergence of 'global administrative law' on counter-terrorism has been tested extensively in litigation in Luxembourg involving challenges to the EC/EU implementation of UN Security Council Resolutions. The seminal, pre-Lisbon, *Kadi I* litigation involved rulings by both the Court of First Instance (CFI)[50] and, on appeal, the Court of Justice.[51] Along with the constitutionality of the Union legislator's choice of legal basis to implement UN Security Council Resolution 1267, which the Court managed to accommodate,[52] the main issue at stake was the request by the applicants for the annulment of Regulation 467/2001—which, along with Common Position 2001/154/CFSP, implemented Security Council Resolution 1333(2000)—on the ground of the breach of their fundamental rights.[53] The assertion of Community competence for the adoption of economic sanctions against individuals rendered the answer to the other main claim of the applicants, namely that the measures in question were in breach of fundamental rights, central in determining the relationship between Security Council norms, and Union law and the position of the individual therein. At the heart of this issue is the question of the extent to which measures implementing Security Council Resolutions could be reviewed in the light of Community law. The Court of First Instance took a very narrow view, essentially ruling that it could only review the lawfulness of the norms in question with regard to *jus cogens*.[54] This ruling was rightly criticised for disregarding the autonomy of the Community legal order and for limiting the avenues for review on the grounds of fundamental rights.[55] In this context, the CFI ruling was marked

---

[48] For further details see Chapter 2 of this volume.

[49] For an up-to-date list of measures in force see: eeas.europa.eu/cfsp/sanctions/docs/measures_en.pdf.

[50] Case T-315/01 *Yassin Abdullah Kadi v Council and Commission* [2005] ECR II-3649; Case T-306/01 *Ahmed Ali Yusuf and Al Barakaat International Foundation v Council and Commission* [2005] ECR II-3533.

[51] Joined Cases C-402/05P and C-415/05P *Yassin Abdullah Kadi and Al Barakaat International Foundation v Council and Commission* [2008] ECR I-6351.

[52] For details, see Mitsilegas, 'The European Union and the Globalisation of Criminal Law', n 47 above.

[53] For a background to the legal framework of the case, see paras 11–45 of the *Kadi* ECJ ruling, n 51 above.

[54] *Kadi*, above n 50, paras 226 *et seq; Yusuf and Al Barakaat*, above n 50, paras 277 *et seq.*

[55] See, in particular, P Eeckhout, 'Community Terrorism Listings, Fundamental Rights, and UN Security Council Resolutions. In Search of the Right Fit' (2007) 3 *European Constitutional Law Review* 183.

by an uncritical deference to the security logic underpinning executive counter-terrorism action as embodied in this context by the Security Council measures.[56]

On appeal however, the Court of Justice responded with a remarkable departure from the CFI reasoning and outcome, in a judgment linking the importance of respect for fundamental rights and the rule of law with the autonomy of the Community legal order. The Court began by stressing unequivocally that the Community is based on the rule of law,[57] adding that fundamental rights form an integral part of the general principles of law the observance of which the Court ensures,[58] that respect for human rights is a condition for the lawfulness of Community acts, and that measures incompatible with respect for human rights are not acceptable in the Community.[59] At the same time, the Court stressed the *autonomy* of the Community legal order, by stating that an international agreement could not affect the allocation of powers fixed by the Treaties or, consequently, the autonomy of the Community legal system,[60] adding that the obligations imposed by an international agreement could not have the effect of prejudicing the constitutional principles of the EC Treaty.[61] In this context, the Court noted that the primacy of international agreements in Community law would not extend to primary law, in particular to the general principles of which fundamental rights form part.[62] In this light, the review by the Court of the validity of any Community measure in the light of fundamental rights had to be considered the expression, in a community based on the rule of law, of a constitutional guarantee stemming from the EC Treaty as an autonomous legal system which is not to be prejudiced by an international agreement.[63]

The Court combined these two lines of reasoning to assert its power to review the measures in question. In this context, the Court was careful to specify that 'the review of lawfulness … to be ensured by the Community judicature applies to the *Community* act intended to give effect to the international agreement at issue, and not to the latter as such' (emphasis added).[64] The Court thus attempted to draw a distinction between review of Community measures (which it had the power

---

[56] See, in this context, J Murkens, 'Countering Anti-Constitutional Argument: The Reasons for the European Court of Justice's Decision in Kadi and Al Barakaat' (2009) 11 *Cambridge Yearbook of European Legal Studies* 15.

[57] *Kadi*, above n 51, para 281.

[58] Para 283. The Court noted the special significance of the ECHR in this context, referring to its ruling on the compatibility of the second Money Laundering Directive with fundamental rights—see above 'Judicial Review of the EU Implementation of UN Security Council Resolutions—*Kadi I*'.

[59] Para 284. The Court also stressed that the wording of Treaty Articles such as 297 and 307 TEC cannot be understood as derogating from or challenging the principles of liberty, democracy and respect for human rights and fundamental freedoms enshrined in 6(1) TEU as a foundation of the Union, see paras 303–4.

[60] Para 282.

[61] Para 285.

[62] Para 308.

[63] Para 316.

[64] Para 286.

to conduct), and review of UN measures (which fell outside its jurisdiction, even under *jus cogens*).[65] According to the Court, while for the purposes of the interpretation of the contested Regulation, account had to be taken of the wording of Resolution 1390 (2002),[66] the UN Charter did not impose the choice of a particular model of the implementation of resolutions.[67] Moreover, the Regulation in question was not directly attributable to the UN.[68] The Court thus asserted its power for the full review, in principle, of the lawfulness of all Community acts in the light of fundamental rights.[69] It therefore found that the CFI had erred in law in this context.[70]

The Court then reviewed the Regulation and annulled it (setting aside the CFI judgment) finding that the rights of the defence, in particular the right to be heard, and the right to effective judicial review of those rights, were patently not respected,[71] and that the measures entailed an unjustified restriction of Mr Kadi's right to property.[72] However, the Court also ruled that the freezing of funds could not per se be regarded as inappropriate or disproportionate 'with reference to an objective of general interest as fundamental to the international community as the fight by all means against the threats to international peace posed by acts of terrorism'.[73]

In *Kadi*, the Court sent a strong signal about the autonomy of the Community legal order in external relations in general and the emergence of the Union as a global actor in security matters in particular.[74] The assertion of the autonomy of the Community legal order was based on what the Court deemed fundamental principles of the Community constitutional order, namely the rule of law and the respect of fundamental rights. The focus on these principles further enabled the Court to embark on a hierarchisation exercise, asserting the primacy of what it called 'a higher rule of law in the Community legal order' over international agreements. The determination of the Court to stress the autonomy and primacy of the

---

[65] Para 287. The Court further noted that 'any judgment given by the Community judicature deciding that a Community measure intended to give effect to such a resolution is contrary to a *higher rule of law in the Community legal order* would not entail any challenge to the primacy of that resolution *in international law*', see para 288 (emphasis added).

[66] Para 297.

[67] Para 298.

[68] Para 314.

[69] Para 326.

[70] Para 327.

[71] Para 334.

[72] Para 370.

[73] Para 363.

[74] As Halberstam and Stein have noted, 'until *Kadi*, the story of European constitutionalism has focused largely on establishing the Community's legal order as autonomous from those of the Member States. With few exceptions, the constitutional gaze has been inward looking, that is, setting off the Union's legal order from, and integrating it with, those of the Member States'. D Halberstam and E Stein, 'The United Nations, the European Union, and the King of Sweden: Economic Sanctions and Individual Rights in a Plural World Order' (2009) 46 *Common Market Law Review* 13, 62.

Community legal order was criticised by certain commentators in that it showed an unwillingness to engage in a dialogue with the UN Security Council,[75] while others viewed it rightly as a move of empowerment for the EU.[76] A key factor in the Court's interpretative choice was the nature of the measures under review: rather than being norms of general application, these were sanctions addressed to and directly affecting individuals.[77] The focus on the individual rendered imperative the articulation of a reasoning based on the protection of fundamental rights in a legal order based on the rule of law. In this context, it is significant that the Court had to translate the position of the individual from the international to the Union legal order. Under international law (whose logic is premised primarily upon the state as a referent object), the individual is sidelined.[78] By contrast, in the European Union legal order based on the rule of law and fundamental rights, the position of the individual is central. The differences between the international and the Community legal orders, and the special features of the Community legal order in this context left the Court with little choice but to focus on the individual when interpreting the relationship between Union law and Security Council norms.

These features of the Court's ruling in *Kadi* should not, however, be seen as signifying a complete dichotomy between Security Council norms on sanctions and Union law implementing these sanctions. The Court reiterated in *Kadi* its finding that when interpreting the Regulation account should be taken of the Security Council Resolution which the Regulation was designed to implement.[79] Moreover, a closer look at the relationship between European Union and Security Council norms and its interpretation by the Court demonstrates that the Court's stance on the autonomy of the Union legal order, in particular as regards the respect of fundamental rights and the rule of law, is rather nuanced. Notwithstanding the Court's assertion that the Community legislator had leeway as to the method of implementation of the Security Council Resolution in question, and that the Regulation in question was not directly attributable to the UN, the fact remained that the mechanism used by the Community consists of directly importing listings by the Sanctions Committee in the Community legal order without the opportunity for the Community to modify them. The Court thus accepted the verdict of a UN body operating beyond the scrutiny mechanisms of Union law, resulting in highly invasive measures against individuals.

---

[75] G de Búrca, 'The European Court of Justice and the International Legal Order after *Kadi*' (2009) NYU School of Law Jean Monnet Working Paper 01/2009, 36 available at: www.jeanmonnetprogram. org/papers/09/090101.html.

[76] T Tridimas, 'Terrorism and the ECJ: Empowerment and Democracy in the EC Legal Order' (2009) 34 *European Law Review* 103.

[77] ibid at 113.

[78] See, in this context, the criticism of the CFI ruling by Guild, who points out that the structure of politics and law at the international level leaves the individual without a voice or visibility, E Guild, *EU Counter-Terrorism Action. A Fault Line Between Law and Politics?* (Brussels, CEPS, 2010) 9–10.

[79] *Kadi*, above n 51, para 297.

It could, of course, be observed in this context that the Court's intervention in *Kadi* emphasised the need for procedural standards in the listing procedure. It could, therefore, be viewed as part of a process linked with improvements in Security Council norms and practice as regards procedural rights.[80] However, while the Court was prepared to review the compatibility with fundamental rights of both procedural and certain substantive aspects of the Community sanctions regime implementing Security Council Resolutions, it did not question the legitimacy, binding character or method of adoption of these Resolutions by a body such as the Security Council.[81] This reluctance may be understandable in the light of the Court's choice to assert jurisdiction with regard to measures which could be considered to be executive and thus outside judicial review. However, the fact remains that the Court did not question the fundamental choice by the Community to follow the security logic of the Security Council and copy the latter's system of far-reaching sanctions against individuals as a counter-terrorism tool.[82] As far as the EU is concerned, the imposition of UN-led individual sanctions as such remained a central plank of the Union's security policy.

V. Judicial Review of the EU Implementation of UN Security Council Resolutions: *Kadi II*

The Court of Justice was invited post-Lisbon to revisit its case law following the lodging of a request by Mr Kadi for annulment of a revised EU asset freezing Regulation which continued to list him therein notwithstanding the Court's ruling in *Kadi I*.[83] In the *Kadi II* litigation, the Court had to take into account a number of key developments which took place following the Court's ruling in *Kadi I* including, most notably, a series of revisions to the UN Security Council system of listing individuals whose assets should be frozen under Resolution 1267. It has been argued that the introduction of these revisions is evidence of the power of the Court's ruling in *Kadi I*.[84] UN Security Council Resolution 1822 (2008)

---

[80] For an analysis of subsequent revisions of Security Council Resolutions in this light, in particular by Resolution 1822 (2008), see M Scheinin, 'Is the ECJ Ruling in *Kadi* Incompatible with International Law?' 28 *Yearbook of European Law* 2009 637, 648–50.

[81] Indeed, the language of the Court in *Kadi* stressed the relationship of Community law with international agreements.

[82] See also, in this context, the criticism by Scheinin, who advocates the repeal of Resolution 1267 and its replacement with national or EU level terrorist listing pursuant to Resolution 1373, 'Is the ECJ Ruling in *Kadi* Incompatible with International Law?', above n 80.

[83] Regulation EC No 1190/2008 amending for the 101st time Regulation No 881/2001 [2008] OJ L322/25.

[84] LJ van den Herik, 'Peripheral Hegemony in the Quest to Ensure Security Council Accountability for its Individualized UN Sanctions Regimes' (2014) 19 *Journal of Conflict and Security Law* 427 at 441–44.

introduced the requirement for listing proposals to identify those parts of the statement of case that may be publicly released, including for use by the Sanctions Committee for development of the summary described below or 'for the purpose of notifying or informing the listed individual or entity, and those parts which may be released upon request to interested States'.[85] The Resolution also provides that the Sanctions Committee, when it adds a name to its Consolidated List, is to make accessible on its website 'a narrative summary of reasons for listing' and that it is to make accessible on the same site, 'narrative summaries of reasons for listing' the names on that list before the adoption of Resolution 1822/2008.[86] A further Security Council Resolution, 1904/2009, established an 'Office of the Ombudsperson', whose task is to assist the Sanctions Committee in the consideration of de-listing requests. The person appointed to be the Ombudsperson must be an individual of high moral character, impartiality and integrity with high qualifications and experience in relevant fields, including law, human rights, counter-terrorism and sanctions.[87] A subsequent Resolution, 1989 (2011), arguably passed in response to the critical ruling of the General Court at first instance in the *Kadi II* litigation,[88] extended the mandate and support of the Ombudsperson and included detailed provisions on listing and de-listing procedures.[89] The Security Council continues to have the ultimate decision-making power on de-listing and is not obliged to follow a de-listing recommendation by the Ombudsperson.[90]

Improvements in the listing procedure under Resolution 1822/2008 have been reflected in the EU legal order in EU Regulation 1286/2009.[91] According to the Regulation, the Commission will take a decision to list a natural or legal person for the first time only once a statement of reasons is provided by the Sanctions Committee.[92] Once the listing decision has been taken, the Commission must communicate without delay the statement of reasons to the affected parties, providing an opportunity to express their views on the matter.[93] The Commission must review its listing decision following the submission of observations which must be forwarded to the Sanctions Committee.[94] A similar process may apply for those listed before 3 September 2008.[95] Improvements in the UN listing system

---

[85] UNSC Resolution 1822/2008, para 12.

[86] ibid para 13.

[87] Para 20.

[88] See I Cameron, 'EU Anti-terrorist Sanctions' in V Mitsilegas, M Bergström and T Konstadinides (eds), *Research Handbook on EU Criminal Law* (Cheltenham, Edward Elgar, forthcoming).

[89] UNSC Resolution, 1989/2011, paras 12–35. Case T-85/09 *Yassin Abdullah Kadi v Commission* [2010] ECR II-5177 (*Kadi II*) General Court, 30 September 2010.

[90] ibid para 23.

[91] Council Regulation 1286/2009 amending Regulation No 881/2002 imposing certain specific restrictive measures directed against certain persons and entities associated with Usama bin Laden, the Al-Qaida network and the Taliban [2009] OJ L346/42.

[92] Art 7a(1).

[93] Art 7a(2).

[94] Art 7a(3).

[95] Art 7c.

have led to hopes that the differences between UN Security Council practice and EU constitutional law as demonstrated in *Kadi I* could be bridged.[96] However, further academic analyses have highlighted the persistent rule of law and human rights shortcomings of the UN Security Council sanctions system and the limits to the mandate and powers of the Ombudsperson.[97]

In deciding on the *Kadi II* appeal, the CJEU was faced with the markedly different approaches adopted by the General Court and the Advocate General in their examination of the case. The General Court applied, albeit reluctantly, the reasoning of the Court of Justice in *Kadi I* and advocated the full review of not only the apparent merits of the contested measure but also the evidence and information on which the findings made in that measure were based.[98] The General Court reiterated the CJEU emphasis in *Kadi I* on the need, in principle, for the full review of the contested Regulation in the light of fundamental rights[99] and went on to advocate extensive judicial review. The General Court highlighted the limits in judicial protection offered by improvements in the Security Council listing system.[100] It advocated the application in this case—as regards the extent and intensity of judicial review—of the principles set out by the General Court with respect to the scrutiny of the autonomous EU sanctions regime in its *OMPI* case law.[101] In particular, judicial review would include the review of the interpretation of the relevant facts made by the competent Union institutions: EU Courts

> must not only establish whether the evidence relied on is factually accurate, reliable and consistent, but must also ascertain whether that evidence contains all the relevant information to be taken into account in order to assess the situation and whether it is capable of substantiating the conclusions drawn from it.[102]

Secrecy is not compatible with the requirements of such level of judicial review: the General Court reiterated its findings in *PMOI II*[103] that the Council is not entitled to base its decision to freeze funds on information or material in the file communicated by a Member State, if the said Member State is not willing to authorise

---

[96] See J Kokott and C Sobotta, 'The *Kadi* Case—Constitutional Core Values and International Law—Finding the Balance?' (2012) 23 *European Journal of International Law* 1015.

[97] G Sullivan and M de Goede, 'Between Law and the Exception: the UN 1267 Ombudsperson as a Hybrid Model of Legal Expertise' (2013) 26 *Leiden Journal of International Law* 833; G Sullivan, 'Transnational Legal Assemblages and Global Security Law: Topologies and Temporalities of the List' (2014) 15 *Transnational Legal Theory* 81–127; C Eckes, 'EU Restrictive Measures against Natural and Legal Persons: From Counterterrorist to Third Country Sanctions' (2014) 51 *Common Market Law Review* 869–906.

[98] Case T-85/09 *Kadi v Commission* [2010] ECR II-5177. For a commentary, see C Eckes, 'Controlling the Most Dangerous Branch From Afar: Multilayered Counter-Terrorist Policies and the European Judiciary' (2011) Amsterdam Law School Legal Studies Research Paper No 2011-08, 12–13, available at: papers.ssrn.com/so13/papers.cfm?abstract_id=1865785.

[99] *Kadi II*, n 98 above, para 126.

[100] Para 128.

[101] Para 139.

[102] Para 142.

[103] Case T-256/07 *People's Mojahedin Organization of Iran v Council (PMOI II)* [2008] ECR II-3019.

its communication to the Union Courts whose task is to review the lawfulness of that decision; more importantly, the refusal by the Member State and the Council to communicate, even to the Court alone, certain information on which the contested measure was based, had the consequence that the Court was unable to review the lawfulness of the contested decision.[104] The General Court supported these arguments further by emphasising the draconian nature of freezing orders in respect of the applicant which had been in place for a long period of time[105] and putting forward the view that the measures in question are not temporary or precautionary, but actually of a criminal nature. In a passage worth highlighting at length, the General Court noted that:

> It might even be asked whether—given that now nearly 10 years have passed since the applicant's funds were originally frozen—it is not now time to call into question the finding of this Court, at paragraph 248 of its judgment in *Kadi*, and reiterated in substance by the Court of Justice at paragraph 358 of its own judgment in *Kadi*, according to which the freezing of funds is a temporary precautionary measure which, unlike confiscation, does not affect the very substance of the right of the persons concerned to property in their financial assets but only the use thereof. The same is true of the statement of the Security Council, repeated on a number of occasions, in particular in Resolution 1822 (2008), that the measures in question 'are preventative in nature and are not reliant upon criminal standards set out under national law'. In the scale of a human life, 10 years in fact represent a substantial period of time and the question of the classification of the measures in question as preventative or punitive, protective or confiscatory, civil or criminal seems now to be an open one.[106]

According to the General Court, the principle of full and rigorous judicial review of such measures is all the more justified given that such measures have a marked and long-lasting effect on the fundamental rights of the persons concerned.[107] In applying this standard of review, the General Court found that the rights of defence and effective judicial protection of Mr Kadi had been breached[108] and that the contested Regulation also entailed a breach of the principle of proportionality by infringing Mr Kadi's right to respect for property.[109]

In his Opinion on the appeal, Advocate General Bot advocated a much narrower scope of judicial review.[110] He argued that freezing is merely a precautionary measure and does not constitute a criminal sanction nor does it imply an

---

[104] *Kadi II*, n 98 above, para 145.

[105] Para 149.

[106] Para 150. The General Court also refers to the opinion of the United Nations High Commissioner for Human Rights (para 150) and to the interpretative notes to 'Special Recommendation II on Terrorist Financing' which recognises that the objectives of the recommended asset freezing measures are not only preventative but also punitive (para 163).

[107] Para 151.

[108] Paras 171–78

[109] Paras 192–95.

[110] Opinion of Advocate General Bot (delivered on 19 March 2013) Joined Cases C-584/10 P, C-593/10 P and C-595/10 P *European Commission, Council and United Kingdom v Kadi (Kadi II)*.

accusation of a criminal nature.[111] He then stressed that listing at EU level is based on the decision of the United Nations and that

> such a decision is based on a summary of reasons drawn up by the Sanctions Committee on the basis of information or evidence which is provided to it by the State(s) which made the listing request, in most cases in confidence, and which is not intended to be made available to the EU institutions.[112]

This deference to decision-making at UN level is coupled by the Advocate General's view that listings are 'part of a political process which goes beyond any individual case' and that

> the political dimension of this process in which the Union has decided to participate calls for moderation in the performance of the judicial review by the EU judicature, that is to say, it must not, in principle, substitute its own assessment for that of the competent political authorities.[113]

In this manner, the Advocate General downplays the impact of the listing process on the affected individuals and treats listing as a political, rather than a legal, issue which merits limited judicial scrutiny. In addition to these arguments, the Advocate General cites the improvements in the procedure before the Sanctions Committee since 2008, which also militate in favour of a limited review of the internal lawfulness of the contested Regulation by the EU judicature.[114] This view is in line with the arguments of the Commission, the UK and intervening Member States in the appeals before the Court of Justice.[115] According to the Advocate General,

> an effective global fight against terrorism requires confidence and collaboration between the participating international, regional and national institutions, rather than mistrust. The mutual confidence which must exist between the EU and the United Nations is justified by the fact that the values concerning respect for fundamental rights are shared by those two organisations.[116]

The assertion of such mutual trust enables the Advocate General to accept that the listing and de-listing procedures within the Sanctions Committee provide sufficient guarantees for the EU institutions to be able to presume that the decisions taken by that body are justified.[117] This mutual trust and the presumption of the compliance of Sanctions Committee procedures with EU law, along with the emphasis on the need to privilege the choices of states operating within the

---

[111] ibid, para 68.
[112] Para 75.
[113] Para 80.
[114] Para 81.
[115] Paras 82–84.
[116] Para 85.
[117] Para 87.

UN sanctions system led the Advocate General to limit considerably the scope of judicial scrutiny by concluding that

> the review performed by the EU judicature of the internal lawfulness of EU acts giving effect to decisions taken by the Sanctions Committee must not, in principle, call into question the merits of the listing, except in cases where the implementation procedure for that listing within the EU has highlighted a flagrant error in the factual finding made, in the legal classification of the facts or in the assessment of the proportionality of the measure.[118]

The Court of Justice adopted a more extensive model of judicial review than the one proposed by the Advocate General.[119] It concurred with the General Court and the Advocate General in refusing to afford the contested Regulation immunity from jurisdiction.[120] The Court then made express reference to the need for the European judiciary to ensure the (in principle) full review of the lawfulness of all Union acts in the light of fundamental rights[121] and mentioned in particular the respect for the rights of the defence and the right to effective judicial protection as enshrined in Articles 41(2) and 47 of the Charter respectively.[122] Respect for these rights entails a number of obligations related to the provision of reasons to the EU listing authority.[123] As regards the extent of judicial review, the Court found that the EU judiciary must determine whether the competent EU authority has complied with the procedural safeguards, including the obligation to state reasons mentioned above.[124] Moreover, effective judicial review requires that, as part of the review of the lawfulness of the grounds which are the basis of the decision to list or to maintain the listing of a given person, the Courts of the EU are to ensure that that decision is taken on a sufficiently solid factual basis. Judicial review cannot be restricted to an assessment of the cogency in the abstract of the reasons relied on, but must concern whether those reasons, or, at the very least, one of those reasons, deemed sufficient in itself to support that decision, is in fact substantiated.[125] To that end, it is for the Courts of the EU, in order to carry out that examination, to request the competent EU authority, when necessary, to produce information or evidence, confidential or not, relevant to such an examination.[126] The Court thus advocated a standard of evidence-based, detailed, substantive judicial review *in concreto* and not *in abstracto*.[127]

---

[118] Para 110.
[119] Joined Cases C-584/10 P, C-593/10 P and C-595/10 P, *European Commission v Kadi (Kadi II)* (CJEU, 18 July 2013).
[120] ibid, paras 65–68.
[121] Para 97.
[122] Paras 98–100.
[123] Paras 111–16.
[124] Para 118.
[125] Para 119.
[126] Para 120.
[127] For further details, see paras 121–24.

The Court of Justice thus put forward a standard of judicial review which consists of the substantive review of the listing, based on evidence and information submitted to the European judiciary. The Court attempted to accommodate to some extent security arguments related to secrecy.[128] In order

> to strike a balance between the requirements attached to the right to effective judicial protection ... and those flowing from the security of the EU or its Member States or the conduct of their international relations ... it is legitimate to consider possibilities such as the disclosure of a summary outlining the information's content or that of the evidence in question. [However], [i]rrespective of whether such possibilities are taken, *it is for the Courts of the European Union to assess* whether and to what the extent the failure to disclose confidential information or evidence to the person concerned and his consequential inability to submit his observations on them are such as to affect the probative value of the confidential evidence (emphasis added).[129]

> Having regard to the preventive nature of the restrictive measures at issue, if, in the course of its review of the lawfulness of the contested decision ... the Courts of the European Union consider that, at the very least, one of the reasons mentioned in the summary provided by the Sanctions Committee is sufficiently detailed and specific, that it is substantiated and that it constitutes in itself sufficient basis to support that decision, the fact that the same cannot be said of other such reasons cannot justify the annulment of that decision. In the absence of one such reason, the Courts of the European Union will annul the contested decision.[130]

While attempting to accommodate to some extent security considerations, the Court of Justice has adopted in *Kadi II* a rigorous, substantive test of judicial review of listing decisions by the European judiciary. The Court reiterated that

> such a judicial review is indispensable to ensure a fair balance between the maintenance of international peace and security and the protection of the fundamental rights and freedoms of the person concerned ... *those being shared values of the UN and the European Union* (emphasis added).[131]

While the emphasis on shared values may have been included to diffuse potential tensions with regard to the conflict between EU law and UN Security Council measures, the Court did not hesitate to emphasise the need to protect human rights in the face of a UN framework providing limited safeguards. The Court reiterated the substantial negative impact of sanctions upon the affected individuals[132] and, in a marked departure from the reasoning of Attorney General Bot, went on to say that the improvements at UN level with regard to listing do not provide the guarantee of effective judicial protection to the affected individual.[133] In an example

---

[128] See paras 125–27.
[129] Paras 128–29.
[130] Para 130.
[131] Para 131.
[132] Para 132.
[133] Para 133.

of judicial cross-fertilisation and dialogue, the Court of Justice based this finding on the ruling of the European Court of Human Rights in *Nada*.[134] The Court of Justice went on to define the essence of effective judicial protection, which is

> that it should enable the person concerned to obtain a declaration from a court, by means of a judgment ordering annulment whereby the contested measure is retroactively erased from the legal order and is deemed never to have existed, that the listing of his name, or the continued listing of his name, on the list concerned was vitiated by illegality, the recognition of which may re-establish the reputation of that person or constitute for him a form of reparation for the non-material harm he has suffered.[135]

The Court found that, while errors of law were made by the General Court,[136]

> it is necessary to determine whether, notwithstanding those errors, the operative part of the judgment under appeal can be seen to be well founded on legal grounds other than those maintained by the General Court, in which event an appeal must be dismissed.[137]

The Court then went on to review the substance of the allegations against Mr Kadi[138] and, dismissing the appeals, concluded that

> none of the allegations presented against Mr Kadi in the summary provided by the Sanctions Committee are such as to justify the adoption, at European Union level, of restrictive measures against him, either because the statement of reasons is insufficient, or because information or evidence which might substantiate the reason concerned, in the face of detailed rebuttals submitted by the party concerned, is lacking.[139]

The Court of Justice thus confirmed again, as in *Kadi I*, the autonomy of the EU legal order based on respect for the rule of law and fundamental rights. While the Court's ruling in *Kadi I* has had a noticeable impact in improving listing procedures at the UN level, the Court of Justice in *Kadi II* sent a clear message that such improvements can by no means equate to effective judicial protection. While the ruling has been criticised on the grounds that it disregards improvements at UN Security Council level,[140] the Court of Justice was right to continue to remind the international community that it is the individual who should be the focus of authorities in the invasive process of imposing restrictive sanctions. At the same time, the Court of Justice in *Kadi II* sent a clear message with regard to the relationship between the executive and the judiciary: the executive cannot use secrecy and confidentiality to evade judicial scrutiny, especially when the protection of fundamental rights is at stake. However, the Court of Justice did not appear to be as protective with regard to substantive fundamental rights, including the right to

---

[134] *Nada v Switzerland* (Application no 10593/08) [2012] ECHR 1691.
[135] *Kadi II* (CJEU), para 134.
[136] See, in particular, para 138.
[137] Para 150.
[138] Paras 151–62.
[139] Para 163.
[140] See in particular van den Herik, above n 84.

property. While the Court highlighted the far-reaching and adverse impact that restrictive measures have on the affected individuals, it fell short of endorsing the General Court's strongly worded statement that restrictive measures can be considered to be in essence *criminal* sanctions. The Court of Justice seemed to accept the preventive nature of sanctions, and did not engage with the argument of the General Court that procedural defects lead to a disproportionate impact on the affected individuals' right to property—with the logic and essence of restrictive measures remaining largely unquestioned. In this light, *Kadi II* should be viewed as another (albeit qualified) victory for procedural justice, perhaps at the expense of the protection of substantive fundamental rights including the right to property.

VI. Extending the Preventive Justice Framework in the Field of Counter-Terrorism: The Case of Measures on 'Foreign Fighters'

While the *Kadi* litigation can be seen as contributing to inserting some fundamental rights safeguards into the UN Security Council-led global terrorist sanctions regime, fresh concerns on the impact of preventive justice measures used for counter-terrorism purposes have emerged recently in the context of calls to regulate the phenomenon of the so-called 'foreign fighters'. Acting again as a norm producer in yet another example of 'global administrative law' actorness, the UN Security Council has adopted a Resolution calling for the adoption of a wide range of measures on 'foreign fighters'. In Resolution 2178 (2014), the UN Security Council, inter alia, has noted that it:

> Decides that Member States shall, consistent with international human rights law, international refugee law, and international humanitarian law, prevent and suppress the recruiting, organizing, transporting or equipping of individuals who travel to a State other than their States of residence or nationality for the purpose of the perpetration, planning, or preparation of, or participation in, terrorist acts or the providing or receiving of terrorist training, and the financing of their travel and of their activities;

> Recalls its decision, in resolution 1373 (2001), that all Member States shall ensure that any person who participates in the financing, planning, preparation or perpetration of terrorist acts or in supporting terrorist acts is brought to justice, and decides that all States shall ensure that their domestic laws and regulations establish serious criminal offenses sufficient to provide the ability to prosecute and to penalize in a manner duly reflecting the seriousness of the offense:

> (a) their nationals who travel or attempt to travel to a State other than their States of residence or nationality, and other individuals who travel or attempt to travel from their territories to a State other than their States of residence or nationality, for the purpose of the perpetration, planning, or preparation of, or participation in, terrorist acts, or the providing or receiving of terrorist training;

(b) the wilful provision or collection, by any means, directly or indirectly, of funds by their nationals or in their territories with the intention that the funds should be used, or in the knowledge that they are to be used, in order to finance the travel of individuals who travel to a State other than their States of residence or nationality for the purpose of the perpetration, planning, or preparation of, or participation in, terrorist acts or the providing or receiving of terrorist training; and

(c) the wilful organization, or other facilitation, including acts of recruitment, by their nationals or in their territories, of the travel of individuals who travel to a State other than their States of residence or nationality for the purpose of the perpetration, planning, or preparation of, or participation in, terrorist acts or the providing or receiving of terrorist training;

Expresses its strong determination to consider listing pursuant to resolution 2161 (2014) individuals, groups, undertakings and entities associated with Al-Qaida who are financing, arming, planning, or recruiting for them, or otherwise supporting their acts or activities, including through information and communications technologies, such as the internet, social media, or any other means;

Decides that, without prejudice to entry or transit necessary in the furtherance of a judicial process, including in furtherance of such a process related to arrest or detention of a foreign terrorist fighter, Member States shall prevent the entry into or transit through their territories of any individual about whom that State has credible information that provides reasonable grounds to believe that he or she is seeking entry into or transit through their territory for the purpose of participating in the acts described in paragraph 6, including any acts or activities indicating that an individual, group, undertaking or entity is associated with Al-Qaida, as set out in paragraph 2 of resolution 2161 (2014), provided that nothing in this paragraph shall oblige any State to deny entry or require the departure from its territories of its own nationals or permanent residents.[141]

It is worth quoting Security Council Resolution 2178 at length, as it is a clear demonstration of the re-emergence of a paradigm of preventive justice in the field of terrorist sanctions at the global level via 'global administrative law'. The Resolution focuses clearly on prevention: along with the preventive measures it advocates, the criminalisation that it calls for is also inextricably linked to prevention. The Resolution introduces a new dimension to the global regime of preventive justice. In addition to preparatory offences such as terrorist recruitment and funding, which raise fundamental challenges to freedom of expression, non-discrimination and the respect of political rights,[142] the focus is placed here primarily on the criminalisation of mobility and travel. As demonstrated in the case of *Nada* discussed above, restrictions on mobility are likely to contravene European human rights norms,

---

[141] UNSC Resolution 2178/2014, paragraphs 5–8.

[142] Scheinin has argued that paragraph 6 of the Resolution will provide a handy tool for oppressive regimes that choose to stigmatise as 'terrorism' what they do not like, including political opposition, trade unions, religious movements and minority and indigenous groups—M Scheinin, 'Back to post-9/11 panic? Security Council resolution on foreign terrorist fighters': www.justsecurity.org/15407/post-911-panic-security-council-resolution-foreign-terrorist-fighters-scheinin/.

including the right to leave. A broad criminalisation of mobility also challenges the principle of legality in criminal offences and sanctions, as it is not clear exactly what is criminalised and why. More broadly, the criminalisation of the mobility of the so-called 'foreign fighters' poses fundamental challenges to the relationship of trust between citizens and the state and blurs the distinction between citizens and foreigners on the one hand and immigration and criminal law on the other. Here, immigration-type measures (albeit in a more serious, criminal law form) are used to regulate the conduct of citizens; and, conversely, criminal law measures are used to regulate mobility, a conduct which has been traditionally the domain of immigration law.[143] By blurring these boundaries, the emergence of a preventive justice regime focusing on mobility results in over-criminalisation.

These challenges arise prominently in the recent incarnation of the provisions of UN Security Council Resolution 2178 in the Additional Protocol to the Council of Europe Convention on the Prevention of Terrorism, adopted by the Council of Europe.[144] In addition to widening the categories preparatory offences[145] the Protocol introduces a series of provisions expressly criminalising mobility and travel. States are called on 'to adopt such measures as may be necessary to establish travelling abroad for the purpose of terrorism … *from its territory or by its nationals*, when committed unlawfully and intentionally, as a criminal offence under its domestic law' (emphasis added).[146] Attempt is also criminalised.[147] Travelling abroad for the purpose of terrorism is defined as 'travelling to a State, which is not that of the traveller's nationality or residence, for the purpose of the commission of, contribution to, or participation in, a terrorist offence, or the providing or receiving of training for terrorism'.[148] The Protocol also criminalises funding travelling abroad for the purpose of terrorism[149] and organising or

---

[143] On the blurring of boundaries between counter-terrorism and immigration law in the context of the surveillance of mobility at the global level see V Mitsilegas, 'Immigration Control in an Era of Globalisation: Deflecting Foreigners, Weakening Citizens, Strengthening the State' (2012) 19 *Indiana Journal of Global Legal Studies* 3–60; and for an analysis focusing specifically on EU law, see V Mitsilegas, 'The Borders Paradox. The Surveillance of Movement in a Union without Internal Frontiers' in H Lindahl (ed), *A Right to Inclusion and Exclusion? Normative Faultlines of the EU's Area of Freedom, Security and Justice* (Oxford, Hart Publishing, 2009) 33–64.

[144] For a background to the Protocol see N Piacente, 'The Contribution of the Council of Europe to the Fight against Foreign Terrorist Fighters' (2015) *Eucrim* 12–15.

[145] Additional Protocol to the Council of Europe Convention on the Prevention of Terrorism. See the provisions on criminalizing the participation in an association or group for the purpose of terrorism (Article 2) and receiving training for terrorism (Article 3).

[146] Article 4(2).

[147] Article 4(3).

[148] Article 4(1).

[149] Article 5. '"Funding travelling abroad for the purpose of terrorism" means providing or collecting, by any means, directly or indirectly, funds fully or partially enabling any person to travel abroad for the purpose of terrorism, as defined in Article 4, paragraph 1, of the Protocol, knowing that the funds are fully or partially intended to be used for this purpose' (Article 5(1)).

otherwise facilitating travelling abroad for the purpose of terrorism.[150] The crimi-nalisation of this conduct is extremely problematic. In addition to the concerns expressed above, it must be stressed that the Council of Europe Protocol expressly grants legally binding force to UNSC Resolution 2178 and introduces extremely broad and difficult-to-define criminal offences including in particular travelling abroad for the purpose of terrorism from a state's territory or by its nationals, or the attempt to do so. The provision is problematic in five main respects: it a clear example of over-criminalisation, in criminalising attempt of an offence which is not clearly defined in the first place; it extends criminalisation extraterritorially in covering travelling 'abroad' by states' nationals even if the latter are not located in their state of nationality; it does not meet the threshold of what is required to uphold the principle of legality in criminal offences, as the offences are defined in a very broad manner; it is not in compliance with a number of fundamental rights, including the right to leave; and it undermines the relationship of trust between the citizen and the state by effectively creating different classes and categories of citizens—with citizens here becoming foreigners, or rather 'foreign fighters'. These challenges become more acute at the level of the European Union constitutional order, which is based upon the fundamental principle of free movement. The European Union is at the time of writing in the process of signing the Coun-cil of Europe Additional Protocol,[151] a development which may also lead to the adoption of internal EU law on the criminalisation of 'foreign fighters', probably by amending the existing EU substantive criminal provisions on terrorism. These developments will pose significant challenges to EU constitutional law, including upholding the provisions of the EU Charter of Fundamental Rights, and their incorporation in the EU legal order will most likely lead to a new round of *Kadi*-type litigation.

VII. Conclusion: Preventive Justice and the Limits of Procedural Justice

The post-9/11 introduction by the UN Security Council of a paradigm of preventive justice based on the establishment of systems of sanctions against

---

[150] Article 6. "'Organising or otherwise facilitating travelling abroad for the purpose of terrorism" means any act of organisation or facilitation that assists any person in travelling abroad for the purpose of terrorism, as defined in Article 4, paragraph 1, of the Protocol, knowing that the assistance thus rendered is for the purpose of terrorism' (Article 6(1)).

[151] European Commission, Proposal for a Council Decision on the signing, on behalf of the European Union, the Additional Protocol to the Council of Europe Convention on the Prevention of Terrorism (CETS No 196), COM (2015) 291 final, Brussels, 15 June 2015.

individuals and organisations suspected of being associated with terrorism has posed significant challenges to the European Union legal order. Although the EU legislator was willing to implement—without asking any questions—the Security Council paradigm in the Union legal order, the operation of the systems of terrorist sanctions has thrown a number of fundamental constitutional questions to the judiciary. Courts—and in particular the EU judiciary—were faced with two separate, but inextricably related questions: how to determine the relationship between EU law and UN Security Council action; and how to rule on the compatibility of EU law implementing the UN Security Council Resolutions with EU constitutional law, and in particular the protection of fundamental rights. Underlying these questions was a third, but key, question: how to determine the relationship between the executive and the judiciary in the preventive justice model consisting in the imposition of targeted terrorist sanctions. The prevailing view among commentators is that the *Kadi* litigation has confirmed the autonomy of the European Union legal order while upholding the protection of fundamental rights as a key value of the EU. While there is certainly a degree of accuracy in this assessment, this chapter has aimed to provide an alternative reading of *Kadi*: rather than affirming the primacy of EU law over UN Security Council measures, what the Court of Justice really wanted to do was to rebalance the relationship between the executive and the judiciary, by asserting the judiciary's powers of review of executive decisions. The emphasis of the Court in the *sine qua non* necessity of judicial review was evident in *Kadi I*, but also perhaps most notably in *Kadi II*. There, Advocate General Bot advocated limited judicial scrutiny by espousing a model of uncritical mutual trust between the European Union and the UN Security Council—which can be seen as the externalisation of the uncritical mutual trust paradigm which has been advocated by Member States, and largely justified by the Court of Justice, which applies internally in EU criminal law under the principle of mutual recognition in criminal matters.[152] However, in *Kadi II* the Court did not follow the Advocate General's analysis on mutual trust, as this would amount to a blind acceptance of mutual trust, inter alia, *between executives*. Upholding the rule of law means that the judiciary must be involved in reviewing the substance of terrorist listings.

The Court's rejection of the dominance of the executive in the paradigm of preventive terrorist sanctions has led to rulings emphasising the requirement to uphold fundamental rights. However, here again the Court's response has been more nuanced than it would seem at first sight in two respects. First, the Court placed great emphasis on procedural justice and the requirement of judicial review. However, in doing so, and in particular in *Kadi II*, the Court introduced limitations to openness and transparency in judicial review by accepting claims by the executive on the need to maintain secrecy. The Court here had to grapple with the interplay between evidence and intelligence: as Sullivan has noted,

---

[152] For an analysis see Chapter 5 of this volume.

'by bringing intelligence and evidence (and their different temporal ordering qualities) together into an uneasy relation at the interface with EU institutions, the listing assemblage is producing new recombinant mechanisms and practices that were not possible before and that in some ways exit existing normative frameworks'.[153] However, the balance between guaranteeing a fair trial and upholding secrecy may prove increasingly difficult to strike in this context. Secondly, the Court's emphasis on upholding fundamental rights has thus far been limited to upholding a model of procedural justice. The *Kadi* litigation privileged fair trial and judicial protection rights over the protection of substantive rights such as the right to property. This approach fits in well with the Court's willingness to assert its role in the review of terrorist sanctions, but is not satisfactory in terms of fundamental rights protection. The time has come for the Court of Justice to engage fully with the question of whether the preventive sanctions imposed by the EU implementing the UN Security Council Resolutions constitute in effect criminal sanctions as understood by the case-law of the Strasbourg Court and by the Charter of Fundamental Rights. The relationship between preventive justice and criminal law—and the safeguards that the latter may provide—needs to be addressed as a matter of urgency. The re-emergence of a preventive justice model in the form of the criminalisation of activities of 'foreign fighters' by the Security Council, and the legitimisation of this paradigm by the Council of Europe and the European Union will lead to renewed litigation in Luxembourg. The 'foreign fighters' initiatives pose similar, if not graver, challenges to fundamental rights in relation to the post-9/11 terrorist sanctions. It is only a matter of time before the European judiciary is called to address the relationship between preventive justice, criminal law and the protection of fundamental rights in a holistic manner.

---

[153] Sullivan, 'Transnational Legal Assemblages and Global Security Law', n 97 above, 109.

10

Conclusion. Placing the Individual at the Heart of European Criminal Justice

The entry into force of the Lisbon Treaty has introduced a number of changes of fundamental importance for the development of European integration in criminal matters at the institutional, constitutional and substantive levels. At the institutional level, a major change has been the normalisation of European Union criminal law, with the end of the old third pillar (which had to wait for five years after the entry into force of the Treaty to honour the deadline imposed by the Transitional Provisions Protocol) meaning that EU institutions have now assumed their full powers over both third pillar and post-Lisbon criminal law. At the broader constitutional level, and along with the full applicability of general and constitutional principles of EU law such as primacy and direct effect in the field of EU criminal law, a major development has been the constitutionalisation by the Lisbon Treaty of the EU Charter of Fundamental Rights, which has already had a marked impact on the evolution of EU criminal law after Lisbon. At the substantive level—and linked with constitutional developments relating to the articulation of EU competence in the field of criminal law—the entry into force of the Lisbon Treaty has been significant in empowering the European Union to legislate on a wide range of areas covering criminal justice as a whole, from criminalisation to judicial cooperation to prosecution. Key provisions in this context are: Article 83 TFEU, which provides express legal bases for both securitised and functional criminalisation; Article 82 TFEU, which constitutionalises mutual recognition in criminal matters while at the same time recognising that mutual recognition must be accompanied by minimum harmonisation in the field of criminal procedure, with the Treaty granting for the first time to the European Union express competence to legislate in areas of criminal procedure including defence rights (Article 82(2) TFEU); and Article 86 TFEU, which grants for the first time to the European Union powers to adopt legislation establishing a European Public Prosecutor's Office, which will have significant impact on the reconfiguration of the relationship between European Union and national law in the field of criminal justice. The constitutionalisation of EU criminal law and the expansion of EU powers to legislate in the field raise fundamental questions about the transformation of criminal justice after Lisbon. Key questions in this context, as mentioned

in the Introduction, are the questions of 'what kind of justice?' and 'whose justice?'
By drawing from the analysis in this book and synthesising key findings from its
chapters, this conclusion will aim to address these questions by focusing on two
broad themes: the impact of the Lisbon Treaty on national legal diversity; and
the impact of the Treaty on the reconfiguration of the relationship between the
individual and the state. The conclusion—and the book—will conclude by putting forward a model of justice focused on the priority of protecting fundamental
rights, placing the individual at the heart of European criminal justice.

A. The Impact of the Lisbon Treaty on National Legal Diversity—From Cooperation and Mutual Recognition to Interdependence and Harmonisation

Before the entry into force of the Treaty of Lisbon, European integration in criminal matters had evolved mainly on the basis of the application of the principle of
mutual recognition in criminal matters. Rather than pursuing actively harmonisation in the field of criminal law, this model of integration focused on establishing
a system of quasi-automatic inter-state cooperation, privileging the law enforcement objectives of Member States in an area without internal frontiers. Mutual
recognition was attractive to Member States concerned about the perceived
adverse impact of harmonisation on state sovereignty and national legal diversity,
and was applied—most prominently via the emblematic Framework Decision on
the European Arrest Warrant—to enforce security across the EU. The entry into
force of the Lisbon Treaty did not put an end to the prominent role of mutual
recognition in EU criminal law. Article 82(1) TFEU includes for the first time
an express reference to the principle of mutual recognition. Mutual recognition
has also been upheld consistently by the Court of Justice of the European Union,
which in a line of cases emphasised the need to comply with the requests of the
issuing Member State and, in Opinion 2/13, stressed the centrality of uncritical
mutual trust and the fact that Member States should not have expectations from
their counterparts to provide a level of fundamental rights protection equivalent
to their own if this level is higher than the EU level of human rights protection.
The implications of this approach for national criminal justice systems are noteworthy: the justice demands of the issuing Member State take primacy (which
is inextricably linked with the primacy of EU law, as expressed by the Court in
Melloni) over the perceptions of justice and the constitutional framework of
the executing Member State. In this manner, mutual recognition based on blind
mutual trust does in fact have profound implications for the receiving national
criminal justice systems, which have to adjust their domestic standards in order to
achieve the effectiveness of EU law as dictated by the Court. A similar far-reaching
impact can be seen in cases involving the intersection between substantive criminal law and criminal procedure, where—as seen in the important ruling of the
Court in *Taricco*—the quest for effectiveness has led to the granting by the Court

of direct effect to a Treaty provision (Article 325 TFEU), which was in turn converted to primacy and led to the disapplication of national law. The Court decided thus in a case which did not involve directly the implementation of a specific piece of secondary EU law in a Member State, in a ruling which will have a profound impact on the internal coherence of the national criminal justice system affected by it and whose implications are still being fully assessed at the time of writing. These examples are key in demonstrating that the entry into force of the Treaty of Lisbon—and the constitutionalisation of EU criminal law it has entailed—has confirmed the far-reaching impact that EU criminal law has in reconfiguring the balance of justice in national legal orders, even in cases where there is no, or not a high level of, EU harmonisation.

In addition to the effect that the constitutionalisation of EU criminal law has had on national criminal justice systems, a seminal development brought about by the Lisbon Treaty has been the gradual, but decisive, move from mutual recognition to harmonisation. The key provision in this context is Article 82(2) TFEU, which grants the Union legislator the power to harmonise—albeit via minimum rules— national rules in the field of criminal procedure. The insertion of Article 82(2) in the Treaty on the Functioning of the European Union is a game-changer: it confirms that mutual recognition in the field of criminal law is not effective if it is not accompanied by a series of harmonisation measures aimed at creating a level playing-field across the European Union. EU legislation under Article 82(2) TFEU can, as will be seen in the next section, have a transformative effect in enhancing decisively the protection of fundamental rights in Europe's area of criminal justice. Article 82(2) TFEU also affirms the substantial impact that EU criminal law can have on the criminal justice systems of Member States. As seen in the chapter on defence rights in particular (Chapter six), it is already evident by the measures adopted thus far and by the case-law of the Court of Justice that the minimum rules mentioned in the Treaty are in fact rules which are fully binding on Member States and whose effectiveness is required to be ensured by national authorities. In addition to its harmonising impact, Article 82(2) TFEU is also significant in that it affirms the trend in the Lisbon Treaty to ensure the interdependence of the various areas of EU criminal law, signifying thus a move towards greater coherence in European criminal justice. Examples of interdependence can be found throughout the Treaty criminal justice provisions: according to Article 82(2) TFEU, the Union has competence to legislate on criminal procedure if such legislation is necessary to facilitate mutual recognition; competence to harmonise substantive criminal law is granted to the Union not only to counter serious areas of cross-border crime (Article 83(1) TFEU), but also if harmonisation ('approximation' according to the Treaty) proves essential to ensure the effective implementation of a Union policy (Article 83(2) TFEU); and a European Public Prosecutor's Office will be established 'from Eurojust' (Article 86(1) TFEU). Moreover, it is clear from post-Lisbon judicial and legislative developments that in areas such as the fight against fraud on the EU budget, a number of Treaty legal bases may be applicable for different elements of the policy (Articles 83, 86 and 325 TFEU), creating an increasingly inter-linked legal framework. Negotiations on the European Public Prosecutor's Office have also demonstrated that even attempts to achieve vertical integration in Europe's area of criminal justice cannot happen without establishing avenues of interdependence between EU law and national procedural rules. The significance of this interdependence for national criminal justice systems should not be underestimated. Compliance by Member States with EU criminal law will increasingly be assessed by reference not only to isolated, individual provisions of secondary law, but also by reference to the EU system as a whole and its general objectives. Moreover, the growing interdependence of EU criminal justice policies renders Member States' selective participation in Europe's area of criminal justice increasingly untenable. This book has used the example of the United Kingdom to demonstrate the limits of integration à-la-carte in this context: in an increasingly interdependent area, how can the United Kingdom participate in the European Arrest Warrant system without participating in Directives on defence rights such as the Directive on access to a lawyer, which have been adopted under Article 82(2) TFEU because they are deemed necessary to facilitate the operation of the principle of mutual recognition, which the European Arrest Warrant embodies? And how is it possible for the United Kingdom to give full effect to its obligations stemming from Article 325 TFEU when it participates neither in the Regulation establishing a European Public Prosecutor's Office, nor in EU legislation on substantive criminal law on fraud (the third pillar fraud Convention and the currently negotiated fraud Directive)? Answers to these questions are far from straightforward and will need to be reassessed as European integration evolves in the following years.

B. The Impact of the Lisbon Treaty on the Relationship Between the Individual and the State—The Growing Importance of Fundamental Rights and the Rule of Law

The evolution of EU criminal law before the entry into force of the Treaty of Lisbon was characterised by a strong emphasis on promoting the security interests of the state at the expense of the protection of the individual. As I explained in the conclusion to *EU Criminal Law,*

> even a cursory examination of the content of the EU legislative production in criminal matters thus far would lead to the following conclusions: that EU criminal law focuses predominantly on enforcement, with limited space for the protection of fundamental rights; and that a great part of EU criminal law is 'emergency law', its adoption speeded up and justified as a response to terrorism.[1]

Seven years after this assessment, a key question is whether the same can be said of EU criminal law after Lisbon. In order to provide an answer to this question, EU

[1] V Mitsilegas, *EU Criminal Law* (Oxford, Hart Publishing, 2009) 323.

criminal law after Lisbon needs to be assessed from both a rule of law and a fundamental rights perspective. In terms of defining the rule of law for the purposes of this analysis, a useful typology is provided by Tamanaha.[2] Tamanaha distinguishes between formal and substantive versions of the rule of law. Moving from thinner to thicker categories, formal rule of law versions start with rule-by-law (law as the instrument of government action), moving to formal legality (law is general, prospective, clear, certain) and then to rule of law as democracy and legality (consent determines content of law). Substantive versions of the rule of law focus on the protection of individual rights, moving to the right of dignity and to justice, and ultimately to social welfare.[3] Tamanaha stresses the importance of 'rule of law, not man', as man is arbitrary.[4] Key elements in Tamanaha's typology are reflected in the theorisation of the rule of law by the late Lord Bingham.[5] According to Lord Bingham, the core of the rule of law principle is that 'all persons and authorities within the state, whether public or private, should be bound by and entitled to the benefit of laws publicly made, taking effect (generally) in the future and publicly administered in the courts'.[6] Bingham's understanding of the rule of law is based primarily on procedural aspects, including the accessibility of the law,[7] the requirement for law and not discretion,[8] limits to the exercise of public power,[9] the provision of means enabling dispute resolution without prohibitive cost or inordinate delay[10] and compliance by the state with its obligations in international law as in national law.[11] However, rule of law also includes substantive aspects, including equality before the law,[12] and the protection of human rights,[13] including the right to a fair trial.[14] In the context of the law of the European Union, where the rule of law is recognised as a key value of the Union,[15] an attempt towards conceptualising the rule of law has been made by the European Commission.[16] According to the Commission, the rule of law is based on a non-exhaustive list of principles, including: legality, which implies a transparent, accountable, democratic and pluralistic process for enacting laws; legal certainty; prohibition of arbitrariness

---

[2] BZ Tamanaha, *On the Rule of Law. History, Politics, Theory* (Cambridge, Cambridge University Press, 2004).
[3] ibid, 91.
[4] ibid, 122.
[5] T Bingham, *The Rule of Law* (London, Allen Lane, 2010).
[6] ibid, 8.
[7] ibid, chapter 3.
[8] Chapter 4.
[9] Chapter 6.
[10] Chapter 8.
[11] Chapter 10.
[12] Chapter 5.
[13] Chapter 7.
[14] Chapter 9.
[15] Article 2 TEU.
[16] European Commission, *Communication from the Commission to the European Parliament and the Council, A New EU Framework to Strengthen the Rule of Law*, COM(2014) 158 final, Brussels, 11.3.2014.

of the executive powers; independent and impartial courts; effective judicial review, including respect for fundamental rights; and equality before the law.[17] The Commission perceives the rule of law as a constitutional principle with both formal and substantive components, meaning that respect for the rule of law is intrinsically linked to respect for democracy and for fundamental rights.[18] From these different but related conceptions of the rule of law, a further categorisation emerges: *rule of law ex ante*, which relates to principles which are applicable in the law-making process (including legality, transparency and democracy); and *rule of law ex post*, which includes principles which are applicable after the enactment of legislation (including legal certainty, prohibition of arbitrariness and effective judicial protection including the protection of human rights).[19] The assessment here will focus on largely formal and procedural aspects of the rule of law, including all the elements of the rule of law ex ante, and the procedural justice components of rule of law ex post. The impact of the Lisbon Treaty on the protection of fundamental rights will be examined in its own right.

In terms of the rule of law in relation to EU criminal law, the entry into force of the Lisbon Treaty has introduced a number of significant improvements. Key developments in this context have been the normalisation of the powers of the European Parliament (which is now, with few exceptions, co-legislator in EU criminal law) and the application of the full jurisdiction of the Court of Justice in the field of EU criminal law. At the same time, the drafters of the Lisbon Treaty have made great efforts to achieve a high degree of legal certainty with regard to the articulation of the existence and extent of EU competence in criminal matters. However, even after these developments have taken place, a number of challenges related to the rule of law remain post-Lisbon. Unsurprisingly, these challenges continue to arise most prominently in the context of EU counter-terrorism law. Legality challenges have arisen in the context of the nexus between internal and external security in EU law. The Court of Justice has confirmed that, notwithstanding the existence of an express Title V legal basis for the adoption of EU law on terrorist sanctions, such legislation is primarily a Common Foreign and Security Policy measure and thus validly adopted under a legal basis which excludes the involvement of the European Parliament as co-legislator. The treatment of terrorist sanctions as a foreign and security policy, and not as a criminal justice matter, is not convincing and, if applied in other areas of Union external activity, will have the effect of marginalising democratic scrutiny in this sensitive field. The Court has attempted to compensate for this choice by calling for greater transparency in relation to the Parliament's right to be informed under the Treaty but this may not

---

[17] ibid, p 4.
[18] ibid.
[19] V Mitsilegas, 'Theorising Internal Security from the Perspective of the Rule of Law' in M Rhinard and D Bossong (eds), *Theorising European Internal Security* (Oxford, Oxford University Press, forthcoming).

be enough to address fully legality concerns. Rule of law challenges in the context of the separation of powers have arisen again post-Lisbon in the *Kadi II* litigation. There, the Court of Justice confirmed the requirement of judicial control of the executive. As it has been argued in Chapter nine of this book, the *Kadi* litigation and *Kadi II* can thus be read as not only affirming the autonomy of EU law in relation to the UN Security Council, but also as affirming the rule of law safeguard of the judicial control of executive acts.

The *Kadi II* litigation has also raised a number of important questions in relation to the protection of fundamental rights. The Court has reiterated (with a number of caveats regarding secret evidence) its commitment to procedural justice and the right to an effective remedy as a key rule of law element. However, its findings on substantive rights, and in particular the right to property, leave much to be desired, with the Court declining to challenge the model of preventive justice introduced by the UN Security Council post-9/11 and adopted uncritically by the EU legislator. A similar prioritisation of security considerations can be discerned in the case-law of the Court in other areas of EU criminal law post-Lisbon. The Court has upheld repeatedly the enforcement objectives of the European Arrest Warrant system leaving very limited scope for the consideration of fundamental rights claims by the national judiciary. The culmination of this approach was Opinion 2/13, where the Court effectively subordinated the effective protection of fundamental rights to a concept of mutual trust which was elevated by the Court—notwithstanding its inherently subjective nature—into a fundamental principle of EU law. On other occasions, the Court has been demonstrating considerable deference to national concepts of justice and security. Key examples of this trend have been cases such as *P.I.*, where the Court limited protection under EU citizenship rights in order to accommodate national perceptions of severity of criminal conduct via the use of Article 83(1) TFEU, and recent *ne bis in idem* case-law such as *Spasic*, where the Court limited fundamental rights protection in order to take into account the mistrust of the authorities of one Member State towards the efficiency of the authorities in another Member State. At the same time, the long overdue attention to the position of the defendant in criminal proceedings may be diluted by the parallel emphasis on victims' rights.

These examples, all arising in the recent past, demonstrate that the struggle between the effective protection of fundamental rights on the one hand, and the precedence of EU and national priorities in the field of security and national perceptions of justice on the other is far from over. However, these examples should not detract from the seminal contribution that the entry into force of the Lisbon Treaty has made towards the strengthening of the protection of fundamental rights in Europe's area of criminal justice. For the first time, the European Union has legislated for human rights in EU criminal law. The adoption of a series of Directives on the rights of the defendant is a seminal development, which will lead to the development of a substantial body of EU law in the field and will exert pressure upon EU Member States to provide a high level of effective protection of fundamental rights at national level. EU defence rights law is a decisive step towards reconfiguring the relationship between the individual and the state in Europe's area of criminal justice. The transformative potential of EU secondary law in the field is enhanced by another development of paramount importance— the constitutionalisation of the EU Charter of Fundamental Rights. The Charter is of fundamental importance, as EU criminal law and its implementation by the Member States must be in conformity with its provisions. Importantly, the Court of Justice has defined in a series of rulings from *Fransson* to *Siragusa* the scope of application of the Charter in a broad manner, including in cases which do not involve the direct implementation by a Member State of a specific provision of an EU instrument. This approach is significant for the evolution of EU criminal law, as it places Member States under the obligation of complying with the Charter in areas of national law which, while they do not implement directly, have a sufficient level of connection with EU criminal law. In the field of the operation of the European Arrest Warrant in relation to the measures on defence rights, this means that the Charter will apply to national law and practice relating to matters including pre-trial detention and the length of the criminal process. Member States will face enhanced institutional scrutiny, not only by the Court of Justice, but also by the European Commission which has assumed its full powers as 'guardian of the treaties' after Lisbon. In its scrutiny of national implementation of EU criminal law, the Commission is under the obligation to examine the compliance of national systems with the Charter along the lines analysed above. This means that the Treaty of Lisbon signifies a move towards a more systemic scrutiny of national criminal justice systems in order to ensure full compliance with fundamental rights.

C. The Promise of Rights—The Individual at the Heart of European Criminal Justice

Where does the above analysis leave us in relation to the question of the impact of the entry into force of the Lisbon Treaty on justice in the European Union? The examination of the meaning of justice (rather than the more traditional focus on the relationship between security and human rights) in the context of the development of Europe's Area of Freedom, Security and Justice is a relatively new phenomenon. In this context, it has been noted that it may appear that 'justice' is used as an empty category but that the language of justice is used to legitimise institutional stability and the administration of security by the European Union.[20] It has also been noted that justice must be underpinned by rule of law

---

[20] S Roy, 'Justice and Europe's Signifier' in D Kochenov, G de Búrca and A Williams (eds), *Europe's Justice Deficit?* (Oxford, Hart Publishing, 2015) 79–96, 83.

safeguards.[21] This book has argued that the entry into force of the Lisbon Treaty is of fundamental importance because it offers the potential of reconfiguring the relationship between the individual and the state by focusing on the individual (and not the state) as the key beneficiary in Europe's area of criminal justice. This analysis takes on board the human rights-based paradigm of post-Lisbon justice put forward by Andrew Williams,[22] but expands the analysis further by highlighting concrete ways in which the entry into force of the Lisbon Treaty places obligations upon both European Union institutions and national authorities to provide full and effective protection of the fundamental rights of affected individuals. This is achieved in particular by including in the European Union's constitutional, legislative and policy framework concrete powers and obligations to legislate on fundamental rights. Fundamental rights assume thus a two-fold importance. First, they operate as limits to EU and state enforcement action, by placing obligations on EU and national authorities to examine fully the fundamental rights implications of enforcement action not only on paper but also on the ground, as epitomised by the European Court of Human Rights in *Tarakhel*. Secondly, they operate as self-standing provisions of secondary law, which Member States are under the duty to implement fully and effectively. In the second case, the Court of Justice has already demonstrated its willingness to ensure full effectiveness of this protective EU law. This approach may operate in parallel with the Court's restrictive approach in the context of mutual recognition, where the Court—especially after Opinion 2/13—seems to be seriously at odds with the approach of the Strasbourg Court on the scrutiny of human rights violations. Lisbon is important because it gives a clear promise of rights, and in doing so, has the potential to bring the individual into the centre of the landscape of justice in the European Union. It remains to be seen whether the clear obligations to comply with fundamental rights enshrined in the Treaty will eventually change legislative and judicial approaches towards the extent, importance and operation of mutual trust in Europe's area of criminal justice.

---

[21] S Douglas-Scott, 'The Problem of Justice in the European Union: Values, Pluralism, and Critical Legal Justice' in J Dickson and P Eleftheriadis (eds), *Philosophical Foundations of European Union Law* (Oxford, Oxford University Press, 2012) 412–48.

[22] A Williams, 'Promoting Justice after Lisbon: Groundwork for a New Philosophy of EU Law' (2010) 30 *Oxford Journal of Legal Studies* 663–93.

BIBLIOGRAPHY

Acosta Arcarazo, D and J Martire, 'Trapped in the lobby: Europe's revolving doors and the others as Xenos' (2014) 39 *European Law Review* 362–79.

Albrecht, P-A, 'La Politique Criminelle dans L'État de Prévention' (1997) 21 *Déviance et Société* 123–36.

Alegre, A and M Leaf, 'Mutual Recognition in European Judicial Co-operation: A Step Too Far Too Soon? Case Study—The European Arrest Warrant' (2004) 10 *European Law Journal* 200–217.

Alexandrova, V, 'Presentation of the Commission's Proposal on the Establishment of the European Public Prosecutor's Office' in LH Erkelens, AWH Meij and M Pawlik (eds), *The European Public Prosecutor's Office. An Extended Arm or a Two-Headed Dragon?* (The Hague, Asser Press/Springer, 2015) 11–20.

Alvarez, JE, 'Hegemonic International Law Revisited' (2003) 97 *American Journal of International Law* 873–88.

Amoore, L and M de Goede (eds), *Risk and the War on Terror* (Abingdon/New York, Routledge, 2008).

Anagnostaras, G, 'Case Comment—Enhanced protection of EU nationals against expulsion and the concept of internal public security: comment on the PI case' (2012) 37 *European Law Review* 627–40.

Anagnostopoulos, I, 'The Right of Access to a Lawyer in Europe: A Long Road Ahead?' (2014) 4 *European Criminal Law Review* 3–18.

Ashworth, A and L Zedner, *Preventive Justice* (Oxford, Oxford University Press, 2014).

Asp, P, *The Substantive Criminal Law Competence of the EU*, Skrifter Utgivna av Juridiska Fakulteten vid Stockholms Universitet Nr 79, 2013.

——, 'Jeopardy on European Level: What is the Question to which the Answer is the EPPO?' in P Asp (ed), *The European Public Prosecutor's Office- Legal and Criminal Policy Perspectives*, Stifelsen Skrifter Utgivna av Juridiska Fakulteten vid Stockholms Universitet, 2015, pp 51–68.

Azoulai, L, 'Introduction: The Question of Competence' in L Azoulai (ed), *The Question of Competence in the European Union* (Oxford, Oxford University Press, 2014) 1–18.

Azoulai, L and S Coutts, 'Restricting Union citizens' residence rights on grounds of public security. Where Union citizenship and the AFSJ meet: *P.I.* Case C-348/09, *P.I. v Oberbürgermeisterin der Stadt Remscheid*, judgment of the Court of Justice (Grand Chamber) of 22 May 2012' (2013) 50 *Common Market Law Review* 553–70.

Bang Fugslang Madsen, H and T Elholm, 'EPPO and the Principle of Subsidiarity' in P Asp (ed), *The European Public Prosecutor's Office—Legal and Criminal Policy Perspectives*, Stifelsen Skrifter Utgivna av Juridiska Fakulteten vid Stockholms Universitet, 2015, pp 31–50.

Besselink, LFM, 'The Parameters of Constitutional Conflict after Melloni' (2014) 39 *European Law Review* 531–52.

Bingham, T, *The Rule of Law* (London, Allen Lane, 2010).

Caeiro, P, 'Jurisdiction in Criminal Matters in the EU: Negative and Positive Conflicts, and Beyond' (2010) 93 *Kritische Vierteljahresschrift für Gesetzgebung und Rechtswissenschaft* 366–79.

_____, 'Introduction (or: Every Criminal Procedure Starts with a Bill of Rights)' in P Caeiro, *The European Union Agenda on Procedural Safeguards for Suspects or Accused Persons: the 'second wave' and its predictable impact on Portuguese law* (Instituto Juridico, Faculdade de Direito, Universidade de Coimbra, 2015) 13–18.

Cameron, I, 'EU Anti-terrorist Sanctions' in V Mitsilegas, M Bergström and T Konstadinides (eds), *Research Handbook on EU Criminal Law* (Cheltenham, Edward Elgar, March 2016).

Cape, E, J Hodgson, T Prakken and T Spronken (eds), *Suspects in Europe. Procedural Rights at the Investigation Stage of the Criminal Process in the EU* (Antwerp, Intersentia, 2007).

Cole, D, 'The Difference Prevention Makes: Regulating Preventive Justice' (2015) 9 *Criminal Law and Philosophy* 501–19: papers.ssrn.com/sol3/papers.cfm?abstract_id=2459976.

Coninsx, M, 'The European Commission's Legislative Proposal: An overview of its Main Characteristics' in LH Erkelens, AWH Meij and M Pawlik (eds), *The European Public Prosecutor's Office. An Extended Arm or a Two-Headed Dragon?* (The Hague, Asser Press/ Springer, 2015) 21–40.

_____, 'Eurojust' in V Mitsilegas, M Bergström and T Konstadinides (eds), *Research Handbook on EU Criminal Law* (Cheltenham, Edward Elgar, March 2016).

Costello, C and M Mouzourakis, 'Reflections on Reading *Tarakhel:* Is "How Bad is Bad Enough" Good Enough?' (2014) 10 *Asiel & Migrantenrecht* 404–11.

Cotterrell, R, *Law's Community. Legal Theory in Sociological Perspective* (Oxford, Clarendon Press, 1995).

_____, 'Comparative Law and Legal Culture' in M Reimann and R Zimmermann (eds), *The Oxford Handbook of Comparative Law* (Oxford, Oxford University Press, 2008) 709–37.

Coutts, S, 'Union Citizenship as Probationary Citizenship: *Onuekwere*' (2015) 52 *Common Market Law Review* 531–46.

Covolo, V, 'The Legal Framework of OLAF Investigations. What Lessons for the European Penal Area?' (2011) 2 *New Journal of European Criminal Law* 201–19.

Craig, P, *The Lisbon Treaty. Law, Politics, and Treaty Reform* (Oxford, Oxford University Press, 2010).

_____, *EU Administrative Law*, 2nd edn (Oxford, Oxford University Press, 2012).

Cras, S, 'The Directive on the Right of Access to a Lawyer in Criminal Proceedings and in European Arrest Warrant Proceedings, [2014] 1 *Eucrim* 32–44.

Cremona, M, 'EC Competence, 'Smart Sanctions' and the *Kadi* Case', 28 *Yearbook of European Law 2009* 559–92.

De Baere, G, 'From "Don't Mention the *Titanium Dioxide* Judgment" to "I Mentioned it Once, But I Think I Got Away with it All Right": Reflections on the Choice of Legal Basis in EU External Relations after the *Legal Basis for Restrictive Measures* Judgment' (2013) 15 *Cambridge Yearbook of European Legal Studies* 537–62.

de Biolley and A Weyembergh, 'L'Espace Pénal Européen et les Droits des Victimes' (2005) 31 *Revue de la Faculté de Droit, Université Libre de Bruxelles* 93–122.

Deboyser, C, 'European Public Prosecutor's Office and Eurojust: "Love Match or Arranged Marriage"?' in LH Erkelens, AWH Meij and M Pawlik (eds), *The European Public Prosecutor's Office. An Extended Arm or a Two-Headed Dragon?* (The Hague, Asser Press/ Springer, 2015) 79–100.

de Búrca, G, 'The European Court of Justice and the International Legal Order after *Kadi*', NYU School of Law Jean Monnet Working Paper 01/2009 (2009), available at: www. jeanmonnetprogram.org/papers/09/090101.html.

Delmas-Marty, M, 'Guest Editorial: Combatting Fraud—Necessity, Legitimacy and Feasibility of the *Corpus Juris*' (2000) 37 *Common Market Law Review* 247–56.

de Witte, B, 'Article 53' in S Peers, T Hervey, J Kenner and A Ward, *The EU Charter of Fundamental Rights. A Commentary* (Oxford, Hart Publishing, 2014) 1523–38.

Dougan, M, 'Minimum Harmonization and the Internal Market' (2000) 37 *Common Market Law Review* 853–85.

_____, 'The Treaty of Lisbon 2007: Winning Minds, Not Hearts' (2008) 45 *Common Market Law Review* 617–703.

Douglas-Scott, S, 'The Problem of Justice in the European Union: Values, Pluralism, and Critical Legal Justice' in J Dickson and P Eleftheriadis (eds), *Philosophical Foundations of European Union Law* (Oxford, Oxford University Press, 2012) 412–48.

Durdevic, Z, 'Judicial Control in Pre-Trial Criminal Procedure Conducted by the European Public Prosecutor's Office' in K Ligeti, *Towards a Prosecutor for the European Union* (Oxford, Hart Publishing, 2013) 986–1010.

Eckes, C, *EU Counter-Terrorist Policies and Fundamental Rights. The Case of Individual Sanctions* (Oxford, Oxford University Press, 2009).

_____, 'Controlling the Most Dangerous Branch From Afar: Multilayered Counter-Terrorist Policies and the European Judiciary' Amsterdam Law School Legal Studies Research Paper No 2011-08 (2011), available at: papers.ssrn.com/so13/papers. cfm?abstract_id=1865785.

_____, 'EU Restrictive Measures against Natural and Legal Persons: From Counterterrorist to Third Country Sanctions' (2014) 51 *Common Market Law Review* 869–906.

Eeckhout, P, 'Community Terrorism Listings, Fundamental Rights, and UN Security Council Resolutions. In Search of the Right Fit' (2007) 3 *European Constitutional Law Review* 183–206.

_____, *EU External Relations Law*, 2nd edn (Oxford, Oxford University Press, 2011).

_____, 'Opinion 2/13 on EU Accession to the ECHR and Judicial Dialogue—Autonomy or Autarchy?', Jean Monnet Working paper 01/15.

European Commission, Monitoring Report on the state of preparedness for EU membership of Bulgaria and Romania, COM(2006) 549 final, 26.9.2006.

_____, Report to the European Parliament and the Council on the application of Directive 2004/38 on the rights of citizens of the Union and their family members to move and reside freely within the territory of the Member States, COM(2008) 840 final, 10.12.2008.

_____, Communication from the Commission to the European Parliament and the Council on guidance for better transposition and application of Directive 2004/38/EC on the right of citizens of the Union and their family members to move and reside freely within the territory of the Member States, COM(2009) 313 final, 2.7.2009.

_____, Report from the Commission to the European Parliament and the Council on the implementation since 2007 of the Council Framework Decision of 13 June 2002 on the European Arrest Warrant and the surrender procedures between Member States, COM(2011) 175 final, 11.4.2011.

_____, Communication from the Commission to the European Parliament, the Council, the Economic and Social Committee and the Committee of the Regions—Strengthening victims' rights in the EU, COM(2011) 274 final, 18.5.2011.

_____, Green Paper—Strengthening mutual trust in the European judicial area—A Green Paper on the application of EU criminal justice legislation in the field of detention, COM(2011) 327 final, 14.6.2011.

_____, Communication from the Commission to the European Parliament, the Council, the European Economic and Social Committee and the Committee of the Regions, 'Towards an EU Criminal Policy: ensuring the effective implementation of EU policies through criminal law', COM(2011) 573 final, 20.9.2011.

_____, Report from the Commission to the European Parliament and the Council. On Progress in Bulgaria under the Co-operation and Verification Mechanism, COM(2012) 411 final, 18.7.2012.

_____, Communication from the Commission to the European Parliament, the Council, the European Economic and Social Committee and the Committee of the Regions, 'Improving OLAF's governance and reinforcing procedural safeguards in investigations: A step-by-step approach to accompany the establishment of the European Public Prosecutor's Office', COM(2013) 533 final, 17.7.2013.

_____, Communication from the Commission to the European Parliament, the Council and the National Parliaments on the review of the proposal for a Council Regulation on the establishment of the European Public Prosecutor's Office with regard to the principle of subsidiarity, in accordance with Protocol No 2, COM(2013) 851 final, 27.11.2013.

_____, Commission Recommendation of 27 November 2013 on the right to legal aid for suspects or accused persons in criminal proceedings, [2013] OJ C378/11, 24.12.2013.

_____, Commission Recommendation of 27 November 2013 on procedural safeguards for vulnerable persons suspected or accused in criminal proceedings, [2013] OJ C378/8, 24.12.2013.

_____, Report from the Commission to the European Parliament and the Council on Progress in Bulgaria under the Co-operation and Verification mechanism, COM(2014) 36 final, 22.1.2014.

_____, Report from the Commission to the European Parliament and the Council on the implementation by the Member States of the Framework Decisions 2008/909/JHA, 2008/947/JHA and 2009/829/JHA on the mutual recognition of judicial decisions on custodial sentences or measures involving deprivation of liberty, on probation decisions and alternative sanctions and on supervision measures as an alternative to provisional detention, COM(2014) 57 final, Brussels, 5.2.2014.

_____, Communication from the Commission to the European Parliament, the Council, the European Economic and Social Committee and the Committee of the Regions: An open and secure Europe: making it happen, Brussels, COM(2014) 154 final, 11.3.2014.

_____, Communication from the Commission to the European Parliament and the Council. A New EU Framework to strengthen the Rule of Law, COM(2014) 158 final, 11.3.2014.

_____, Report from the Commission to the European Parliament and the Council on the implementation by the Member States of Framework Decision 2009/948/JHA of 30 November 2009 on prevention and settlement of conflicts of exercise of jurisdiction in criminal proceedings COM(2014) 313 final, 2.6.2014.

_____, Report on Progress in Romania under the Co-operation and Verification Mechanism, COM(2015) 35 final, Brussels, 28.1.2015.

_____, Report on Progress in Bulgaria under the Co-operation and Verification Mechanism, COM(2015) 36 final, Brussels, 28.1.2015.

European Ombudsman, *Special Report to the European Parliament following the draft recommendation to the European Anti-Fraud Office in complaint 2485/2004/GG*, Strasbourg, 12 May 2005, at: ombudsman.europa.eu/special/pdf/en/042485.pdf.

European Parliament, Report on an EU approach on criminal law A7-0144/2012, 24 April 2012.

———, Resolution of 27 February 2014 with recommendations to the Commission on the review of the European Arrest Warrant, P7_TA-PROV (2014)0174.

———, Motion for a Resolution on the mid-term review of the Stockholm Programme, 2013/2024 (INI), 4 March 2014.

———, Resolution of 12 March 2014 on the proposal for a Council Regulation on the establishment of the EPPO, P7_TA (2014) 0234.

Flore, D, 'Garantie Judiciaire et Droit Applicable: Quelques Éléments de Réflexion' in G Giudicelli-Delage, S Manacorda and J Tricot (eds), *Le Contrôle Judiciaire du Parquet Européen. Nécessité, Modèles, Enjeux*, Collection de l'UMR de Droit Comparé de Paris (Université Paris 1), vol 37 (Société de Législation Comparée, 2015) 299–310.

Fontanelli, F, '*Hic Sunt Nationes:* The Elusive Limits of the EU Charter and the German Constitutional Watchdog' (2013) 9 *European Constitutional Law Review* 315–34.

———, 'Implementation of EU Law through Domestic Measures after Fransson: the Court of Justice Buys Time and "Non-Preclusion" Troubles Loom Large' (2014) 39 *European Law Review* 682–700.

'Füle: Bulgaria and Romania's accession questioned the credibility of EU enlargement', *EurActiv*, 26 June 2014.

Fundamental Rights Agency, *Opinion of the European Union Agency for Fundamental Rights on a proposal to establish a European Public Prosecutor's Office*, FRA Opinion 1/2014, Vienna, 4 February 2014.

Garland, D, *The Culture of Control. Crime and Social Order in Contemporary Society* (Oxford, Oxford University Press, 2001).

Göhler, J, 'To Continue or Not: Who Shall Be in Control of the European Public Prosecutor's Dismissal Decisions?' (2015) 6 *New Journal of European Criminal Law* 102–25.

Grimm, D, 'Comments on the German Constitutional Court's Decision on the Lisbon Treaty. Defending Sovereign Statehood against Transforming the European Union into a State' (2009) 5 *European Constitutional Law Review* 353–73.

Groussot, X and S Bogojevic, 'Subsidiarity as a Procedural Safeguard of Federalism' in L Azoulai (ed), *The Question of Competence in the European Union* (Oxford, Oxford University Press, 2014) 234–52.

Guild, E, 'Seeking Asylum: Storm Clouds between International Commitments and EU Legislative Measures' (2004) 29 *European Law Review* 198–218.

———, *EU Counter-Terrorism Action. A Fault Line Between Law and Politics?* (Brussels, CEPS, 2010).

Halberstam, D, '"It's the Autonomy, Stupid!" A Modest Defense of Opinion 2/13 on EU Accession to the ECHR, and the Way Forward', Michigan Law School, Public Law and Legal Theory Research Paper Series, Paper No 432, February 2015.

Halberstam, D and C Möllers, 'The German Constitutional Court says "*Ja zu Deutschland!*"' (2009) 10 *German Law Journal* 1241–57.

Halberstam, D and E Stein, 'The United Nations, the European Union, and the King of Sweden: Economic Sanctions and Individual Rights in a Plural World Order' (2009) 46 *Common Market Law Review* 13–72.

Harding, C and JB Banach-Gutierrez, 'The Emergent EU Criminal Policy: Identifying the Species' (2012) 37 *European Law Review* 758–71.

Harman, L and E Szabova, 'European Public Prosecutor's Office—*Cui Bono?*' (2013) 4 *New Journal of European Criminal Law* 40–58.

Henderson, LN, 'The Wrongs of Victim's Rights' (1985) 37 *Stanford Law Review* 937–1021.

Herlin-Karnell, E, *The Constitutional Dimension of European Criminal Law* (Oxford, Hart Publishing, 2012).

Hillion, C, 'The European Union is Dead. Long Live the European Union: A Commentary on the Treaty of Accession 2003' (2004) 29 *European Law Review* 583–612.

Hinarejos, A, JR Spencer and S Peers, *Opting out of EU Criminal Law: What Is Actually Involved?*, CELS Working Paper, New Series, vol 1, University of Cambridge Faculty of Law, September 2012.

HM Government, *Review of the Balance of Competences between the United Kingdom and the European Union. Police and Criminal Justice*, December 2014.

Hodgson, J, 'Criminal Procedure in Europe's Area of Freedom, Security and Justice: the Rights of the Suspect' in V Mitsilegas, M Bergström and T Konstadinides (eds), *Research Handbook on European Criminal Law* (Cheltenham, Edward Elgar, March 2016).

House of Lords European Union Committee (then Select Committee on the European Union), *The Future of Europe: National Parliaments and Subsidiarity- the Proposed Protocols*, 11th Report, session 2002–03, HL Paper 70.

———, *Breaking the Deadlock: What Future for EU Procedural Rights?*, 2nd Report, session 2006–07, HL Paper 20.

———, *The Treaty of Lisbon: An Impact Assessment*, 10th Report, session 2007–08, HL Papers 62-I and 62-II.

———, *The European Union's Policy on Criminal Procedure*, 30th Report, session 2010–12, HL Paper 288.

———, *EU Police and Justice Measures: the UK's 2014 Opt-Out Decision*, 13th Report, session 2012–13, HL Paper 159.

———, *Subsidiarity Assessment: the European Public Prosecutor's Office*, 3rd Report, session 2013–14, HL Paper 65.

———, *The Impact of the European Public Prosecutor's Office on the United Kingdom*, 4th Report, session 2014–15, HL Paper 53.

———, *The UK's Opt-In Protocol: Implications of the Government's Approach*, 9th Report, Session 2014–15, HL Paper 136.

Husak, D, *Overcriminalisation. The Limits of the Criminal Law* (Oxford, Oxford University Press, 2008).

Iglesias Sanchez, S, 'The Court and the Charter: The Impact of the Entry into Force of the Lisbon Treaty on the ECJ's Approach to Fundamental Rights' (2012) 49 *Common Market Law Review* 1565–612.

Inghelram, JFH, 'Fundamental Rights, the European Anti-Fraud Office (OLAF) and a European Public Prosecutor's Office (EPPO): Some Selected Issues' (2012) 95 *Kritische Vierteljahresschrift für Gesetzgebung und Rechtswissenschaft* 67–81.

Jackson, J, 'Cultural Barriers on the Road to providing Suspects with Access to Lawyer' in R Colson and S Field (eds), *EU Criminal Justice and the Challenges of Legal Diversity. Towards A Socio-Legal Approach to EU Criminal Policy* (Cambridge, Cambridge University Press, forthcoming).

Jakobs, G, 'Bürgerstrafrecht und Feindstrafrecht' (2004) *Höchstrichterliche Rechtsprechung zum Strafrecht* 88–95.

Jimeno-Bulnes, M, 'The Proposal for a Council Framework Decision on Certain Procedural Rights in Criminal Proceedings throughout the European Union' in E Guild and F Geyer (eds), *Scurity versus Justice? Police and Judicial Cooperation in the European Union* (Aldershot, Ashgate, 2008) 171–202.

Johnstone, I, 'Legislation and Adjudication in the UN Security Council: Bringing Down the Deliberative Deficit' (2008) 102 *American Journal of International Law* 275–308.

Joint Committee on Human Rights, *The Human Rights Implications of UK Extradition Policy*, Fifteenth Report, session 2010–12.

Kaiafa-Gbandi, M, 'The Importance of Core Principles of Substantive Criminal Law for a European Criminal Policy Respecting Fundamental Rights and the Rule of Law' (2011) 1 *European Criminal Law Review* 7–34.

Kingsbury, B, 'The Concept of 'Law in Global Administrative Law' (2009) 20 *European Journal of International Law* 23–57.

Kingsbury, B, N Krisch and RB Stewart, 'The Emergence of Global Administrative Law' (2005) 68 *Law and Contemporary Problems* 15–62.

Klip, A, *European Criminal Law* (Oxford/Portland, Intersentia, 2009).

———, *European Criminal Law*, 2nd edn (Cambridge/Mortsel, Intersentia, 2012).

Kochenov, D, 'AG Bot in *P.I.* (Case C-348/09): Committing a crime disqualifies EU Citizens from permanent residence': europeanlawblog.eu/?p=281 (13.3.2012).

Kochenov, D and B Pirker, 'Deporting the EU citizens within the European Union: A counter-intuitive trend in Case C-348/09, *P.I. v Oberbürgermeisterin der Stadt Remscheid*' (2013) 19 *Columbia Journal of European Law* 369–91.

Kokott, J and C Sobotta, 'The *Kadi* Case—Constitutional Core Values and International Law—Finding the Balance?' (2012) 23 *European Journal of International Law* 1015–24.

Kostakopoulou, D, 'When EU Citizens become Foreigners' (2014) 20 *European Law Journal* 447–63.

Kostakopoulou, D and N Ferreira, 'Testing Liberal Norms: The Public Policy and Public Security Derogations and the Cracks in European Union Citizenship', Legal Studies Research Paper No 2013-18, University of Warwick, School of Law.

Krisch, N, *Beyond Constitutionalism. The Pluralist Structure of Postnational Law* (Oxford, Oxford University Press, 2010).

Labayle, H, 'Droit d'Asile et Confiance Mutuelle: Regards Croisés de la Jurisprudence Européenne' (2014) 50 *Cahiers de Droit Européen* 501–34.

Labayle, M and HG Nilsson, 'The Role and Organisation of Eurojust: Added Value for Judicial Cooperation in Criminal Matters' in J Monar (ed), *The Institutional Dimension of the European Union's Area of Freedom, Security and Justice* (College of Europe Studies, Peter Lang, 2010) 195–216.

Lazowski, A, 'And Then They Were Twenty-Seven … A Legal Appraisal of the Sixth Accession Treaty' (2007) 44 *Common Market Law Review* 401–30.

———, 'EU Criminal Law and Enlargement' in V Mitsilegas, M Bergström and T Konstadinides (eds), *Research Handbook on European Criminal Law* (Cheltenham, Edward Elgar, March 2016).

Lenaerts, K, 'Exploring the Limits of the EU Charter of Fundamental Rights' (2012) 8 *European Constitutional Law Review* 375–403.

Lenaerts, K, I Maselis, K Gutman, *EU Procedural Law* (Oxford, Oxford University Press, 2014).

Lenaerts, K and J Gutiérrez-Fons, 'The European Court of Justice and Fundamental Rights in the Field of Criminal Law' in V Mitsilegas, M Bergström and T Konstadinides (eds), *Research Handbook of European Criminal Law* (Cheltenham, Edward Elgar, March 2016).

Letschert, R and C Rijken, 'Rights of Victims of Crime: Tensions Between an Integrated Approach and a Limited Legal Basis for Harmonisation' (2013) 4 *New Journal of European Criminal Law* 226–55.

Ligeti, K, 'The European Public Prosecutor's Office' in V Mitsilegas, M Bergström and T Konstadinides (eds), *Research Handbook on EU Criminal Law* (Cheltenham, Edward Elgar, March 2016).

Ligeti, K and M Simonato, 'The European Public Prosecutor's Office: Towards a Truly European Prosecution Service?' (2013) 4 *New Journal of European Criminal Law* 7–21.

Ligeti, K and A Weyembergh, 'The European Public Prosecutor's Office: Certain Constitutional Issues' in LH Erkelens, AWH Meij and M Pawlik (eds), *The European Public Prosecutor's Office. An Extended Arm or a Two-Headed Dragon?* (The Hague, Asser Press/Springer, 2015) 53–78.

Loughlin, M, 'What is Constitutionalisation?' in P Dobner and M Loughlin (eds), *The Twilight of Constitutionalism?* (Oxford, Oxford University Press, 2010) 47–72.

Luchtman, M, 'Choice of Forum and the Prosecution of Cross-Border Crime in the European Union—What Role for the Legality Principle?' in M Luchtman (ed), *Choice of Forum in Cooperation Against EU Financial Crime. Freedom, Security and Justice and the Protection of Specific EU Interests* (The Hague, Eleven International Publishing, 2013) 3–60.

Manacorda, S, 'La Localisation de la Garantie Jurisdictionnelle du Parquet Européen' in G Giudicelli-Delage, S Manacorda and J Tricot (eds), *Le Contrôle Judiciaire du Parquet Européen. Nécessité, Modèles, Enjeux*, Collection de l'UMR de Droit Comparé de Paris (Université Paris 1), vol 37 (Société de Législation Comparée, 2015) 255–74.

Mancano, L, 'Criminal conduct and lack of integration into the society under EU citizenship: this marriage is not to be performed' (2015) 6 *New Journal of European Criminal Law* 53–77.

Marin, L, '"A Spectre Is Haunting Europe": European Citizenship in the Area of Freedom, Security and Justice' (2011) 17 *European Public Law* 705–28.

Matravers, M, 'The Victim, the State and Civil Society' in A Bottoms and JV Roberts (eds), *Hearing the Victim. Adversarial Justice, Crime Victims and the State* (Cullompton, Willan, 2010) 1–16.

Ministry of Justice and Home Office, *Fifth Annual Report to Parliament on the Application of Protocols 19 and 21 to the Treaty on the European Union (TEU) and the Treaty on the Functioning of the European Union (TFEU) ('the Treaties') in Relation to EU Justice and Home Affairs (JHA) matters (1 December 2013–30 November 2014)* (Cm 9006, 2015).

Mitsilegas, V, 'Defining Organised Crime in the European Union: The Limits of European Criminal Law in an Area of Freedom, Security and Justice' (2001) 26 *European Law Review* 565–81.

——, 'Countering the Chameleon Threat of Dirty Money: "Hard" and "Soft" Law in the Emergence of a Global Regime against Money Laundering and Terrorist Finance' in A Edwards and P Gill (eds), *Transnational Organised Crime: Perspectives on Global Security* (London, Routledge, 2003) 195–211.

——, *Money Laundering Counter-Measures in the European Union: A New Paradigm of Security Governance versus Fundamental Legal Principles* (The Hague, Kluwer Law International, 2003).

_____, 'Trust-building Measures in the European Judicial Area in Criminal Matters: Issues of Competence, Legitimacy and Inter-institutional Balance' in S Carrera and T Balzacq, *Security versus Freedom? A Challenge for Europe's Future* (Aldershot/Burlington VT, Ashgate, 2006) 279–89.

_____, 'The Constitutional Implications of Mutual Recognition in Criminal Matters in the EU' (2006) 43 *Common Market Law Review* 1277–311.

_____, 'Constitutional Principles of the European Community and European Criminal Law' (2006) 8 *European Journal of Law Reform* 301–24.

_____, 'The Transformation of Criminal Law in the Area of Freedom, Security and Justice', 26 *Yearbook of European Law 2007* 1–32.

_____, *EU Criminal Law* (Oxford, Hart Publishing, 2009).

_____, 'The Borders Paradox. The Surveillance of Movement in a Union without Internal Frontiers' in H Lindahl (ed), *A Right to Inclusion and Exclusion? Normative Faultlines of the EU's Area of Freedom, Security and Justice* (Oxford, Hart Publishing, 2009) 33–64.

_____, 'The Third Wave of Third Pillar Law: Which Direction for EU Criminal Justice?' (2009) 34 *European Law Review* 523–60.

_____, 'European Criminal Law and Resistance to Communautarisation Post-Lisbon' (2010) 1 *New Journal of European Criminal Law* 458–80.

_____, 'The European Union and the Globalisation of Criminal Law' (2010) 12 *Cambridge Yearbook of European Legal Studies* 337–407.

_____, 'The EU and the Rest of the World: Criminal Law and Policy Interconnections' in M Evans and P Koutrakos (eds), *Beyond the Established Orders. Policy Interconnections between the EU and the Rest of the World* (Oxford, Hart Publishing, 2011) 149–78.

_____, 'The Area of Freedom, Security and Justice from Amsterdam to Lisbon: Challenges of Implementation, Constitutionality and Fundamental Rights' in Julia Laffranque (ed), *The Area of Freedom, Security and Justice, Including Information Society Issues, Reports of the XXV FIDE Congress*, Tallinn (2012), vol 3.

_____, 'Security versus Justice: The Individualisation of Security and the Erosion of Citizenship and Fundamental Rights' in S Ugelvik and B Hudson (eds), *Justice and Security in the 21st Century. Risks, Rights and the Rule of Law* (Abingdon, Routledge, 2012) 199–216.

_____, 'The Changing Landscape of the Criminalisation of Migration in Europe. The Protective Function of European Union Law' in M Guia, M Van der Woude and J Van der Leun (eds), *Social Control and Justice. Crimmigration in an Age of Fear* (The Hague, Eleven International Publishing, 2012) 87–114.

_____, 'The Limits of Mutual Trust in Europe's Area of Freedom, Security and Justice. From Automatic Inter-state Cooperation to the Slow Emergence of the Individual', 31 *Yearbook of European Law 2012* 319–72.

_____, 'Immigration Control in an Era of Globalisation: Deflecting Foreigners, Weakening Citizens, Strengthening the State' (2012) 19 *Indiana Journal of Global Legal Studies* 3–60;

_____, 'Article 49 (the Principles of Legality and Proportionality of Criminal Offences and Penalties)' in S Peers et al (eds), *The EU Charter of Fundamental Rights. A Commentary* (Oxford, Hart Publishing/Beck, 2014) 1351–73.

_____, 'The European Union and the Global Governance of Crime' in V Mitsilegas, P Alldridge and L Cheliotis (eds), *Globalisation, Criminal Law and Criminal Justice. Theoretical, Comparative and Transnational Perspectives* (Oxford, Hart Publishing, 2014) 153–98.

_____, 'From Overcriminalisation to Decriminalisation. The Many Faces of Effectiveness in European Criminal Law' (2014) 5 *New Journal of European Criminal Law* 415–24.

_____, 'Solidarity and Trust in the Common European Asylum System' (2014) 2 *Comparative Migration Studies* 231–53.

_____, *The Criminalisation of Migration in Europe. Challenges for Human Rights and the Rule of Law* (London, Springer, 2015).

_____, 'The European Public Prosecutor before the Court of Justice. The Challenge of Effective Judicial Protection' in G Giudicelli-Delage, S Manacorda and J Tricot (eds), *Le Contrôle Judiciaire du Parquet Européen. Nécessité, Modèles, Enjeux*, Collection de l'UMR de Droit Comparé de Paris (Université Paris 1), vol 37 (Société de Législation Comparée, 2015) 67–87.

_____, 'Managing Legal Diversity in Europe's Area of Criminal Justice: The Role of Autonomous Concepts' in R Colson and S Field (eds), *EU Criminal Justice and the Challenges of Legal Diversity. Towards A Socio-Legal Approach to EU Criminal Policy* (Cambridge, Cambridge University Press, forthcoming).

_____, 'Theorising Internal Security from the Perspective of the Rule of Law' in M Rhinard and D Bossong (eds), *Theorising European Internal Security* (Oxford, Oxford University Press, forthcoming).

Mitsilegas, V, J Monar and W Rees, *The European Union and Internal Security: Guardian of the People?* (Basingstoke, Palgrave/Macmillan, 2003).

Mitsilegas, V, S Carrera and K Eisele, *The End of the Transitional Period for Police and Criminal Justice Measures Adopted before the Lisbon Treaty. Who Monitors Trust in the European Justice Area?*, CEPS Paper in Liberty and Security in Europe, no 74, Centre for European Policy Studies, Brussels, December 2014.

Mitsilegas, V and N Vavoula, 'Criminal Law: Institutional Rebalancing and Judicialisation as Drivers of Policy Change' in F Trauner and A Ripoll Servent (eds), *Policy Change in the Area of Freedom, Security and Justice: How EU Institutions Matter* (Abingdon/New York, Routledge, 2015) 133–51.

Monar, J, 'The Institutional Framework of the AFSJ: Specific Challenges and Dynamics for Change' in J Monar (ed), *The Institutional Dimension of the European Union's Area of Freedom, Security and Justice* (Brussels, Peter Lang, 2010) 21–52.

Monjean-Decaudin, S, 'L'Union Européenne Consacre le Droit à l'Assistance Linguistique dans les Procédures Pénales. Commentaire de la Directive Relative aux Droits à l'interprétation et à la traduction dans les procedures pénales' (2011) 47 *Revue Trimestrielle du Droit Européen* 763–81.

Moreno-Lax, V, 'Dismantling the Dublin System: *M.S.S. v Belgium and Greece*' (2012) 14 *European Journal of Migration and Law* 1–31.

Morgan, C. 'Proposal for a Framework Decision on procedural safeguards for suspects and defendants in criminal proceedings throughout the European Union' (2003) 4 *ERA Forum* 91–99.

Murkens, J, 'Countering Anti-Constitutional Argument: The Reasons for the European Court of Justice's Decision in Kadi and Al Barakaat' (2009) 11 *Cambridge Yearbook of European Legal Studies* 15–51.

Neframi, E, 'L'aspect externe de l'espace de liberté, de sécurité et de justice: quel respect des principes et objectifs de l'action extérieure de l'Union?' in C Flaesch-Mougin and LS Rossi, *La Dimension Extérieure de l'Espace de Liberté, de Sécurité et de Justice de l'Union Européenne après le Traité de Lisbonne* (Brussels, Bruylant, 2013) 509–32.

Nelken, D, 'Using Legal Culture: Purposes and Problems' in D Nelken (ed), *Using Legal Culture* (London, Wildy, Simmonds and Hill, 2012) 1–51.

Nic Shuibhne, N, 'Limits Rising, Duties Ascending: The Changing Legal Shape of Union Citizenship' (2015) 52 *Common Market Law Review* 889–938.

Nicolaidis, K, 'Trusting the Poles? Constructing Europe through Mutual Recognition' (2007) 14 *Journal of European Public Policy* 682–98.

Nicolaidis, K and G Shaffer, 'Transnational Mutual Recognition Regimes: Governance without Global Government' (2005) 68 *Law and Contemporary Problems* 263–317.

Nilsson, H, 'How to Combine Minimum Rules with Maximum Legal Certainty?' (2011) 4 *Europaraettslig Tidskrift* 665–77.

Nowell-Smith, H, 'Behind the Scenes in the Negotiation of EU Criminal Justice Legislation' (2012) 3 *New Journal of European Criminal Law* 381–93.

Öberg, J, 'Union Regulatory Criminal Law Competence after the Lisbon Treaty' (2011) 19 *European Journal of Crime, Criminal Law and Criminal Justice* 289–318.

Ostropolski, T, 'The Principle of Proportionality under the European Arrest Warrant—with an Excursus on Poland' (2014) 5 *New Journal of European Criminal Law* 167–91.

Panzavolta, M, 'Choice of Forum and the Lawful Judge Concept' in M Luchtman (ed), *Choice of Forum in Cooperation Against EU Financial Crime. Freedom, Security and Justice and the Protection of Specific EU Interests* (The Hague, Eleven International Publishing, 2013) 143–66.

Parizot, R, 'Les Interactions en Procédure Pénale: La Victime, Vecteur Symbolique de la Circulation du Jurisprudence' in G Giudicelli-Delage and S Manacorda (eds), *Cour de Justice et Justice Pénale en Europe* (Paris, Société de Législation Comparée, 2010) 177–202.

Peers, S, *EU Justice and Home Affairs Law*, 3rd edn (Oxford, Oxford University Press, 2011).

Piacente, N, 'The Contribution of the Council of Europe to the Fight against Foreign Terrorist Fighters' [2015] 1 *Eucrim* 12–15.

Piris, J-C, *The Lisbon Treaty. A Legal and Political Analysis* (Cambridge, Cambridge University Press, 2010).

Roth, R, '*Non bis in idem* transnational: vers de nouveaux paradigmes?' in S Braum and A Weyembergh (eds), *Le Controle Juridictionnel dans l'Espace Pénal Européen* (Brussels, Editions de l'Université de Bruxelles, 2009) 121–41.

Roy, S, 'Justice and Europe's Signifier' in D Kochenov, G de Búrca and A Williams (eds), *Europe's Justice Deficit?* (Oxford, Hart Publishing, 2015) 79–96.

Sarmiento, D, 'Who's Afraid of the Charter? The Court of Justice, National Courts and the New Framework of Fundamental Rights Protection in Europe' (2013) 50 *Common Market Law Review* 1267–304.

Satzger, H, *International and European Criminal Law* (Oxford, Beck/Hart/Nomos, 2012).

Sayers, D, 'Protecting Fair Trial Rights in Criminal Cases in the European Union: Where does the Roadmap take Us?' (2014) 14 *Human Rights Law Review* 733–60.

Scheinin, M, 'Is the ECJ Ruling in *Kadi* Incompatible with International Law?', 28 *Yearbook of European Law 2009* 637–53.

_____, 'Back to post-9/11 panic? Security Council resolution on foreign terrorist fighters': www.justsecurity.org/15407/post-9-11-panic-security-council-resolution-foreign-terrorist-fighters-scheinin/.

Schiff Berman, P, *Global Legal Pluralism. A Jurisprudence of Law Beyond Borders* (Cambridge, Cambridge University Press, 2012).

Schutte, JJE, 'Establishing Enhanced Cooperation Under Article 86 TFEU' in LH Erkelens, AWH Meij and M Pawlik (eds), *The European Public Prosecutor's Office. An Extended Arm or a Two-Headed Dragon?* (The Hague, Asser Press/Springer, 2015) 195–208.

Schütze, R, *From Dual to Cooperative Federalism. The Changing Structure of European Law* (Oxford, Oxford University Press, 2009).

Sicurella, R, 'Some Reflections on the Need for a General Theory of the Competence of the European Union in Criminal Law' in A Klip (ed), *Substantive Criminal Law of the European Union* (Antwerp, Maklu, 2011) 233–49.

Smulders, B, 'Is the Commission Proposal for a European Public Prosecutor's Office Based on a Harmonious Interpretation of Articles 85 and 86 TFEU?' in LH Erkelens, AWH Meij and M Pawlik (eds), *The European Public Prosecutor's Office. An Extended Arm or a Two-Headed Dragon?* (The Hague, Asser Press/Springer, 2015) 41–52.

Somek, A, 'The Concept of 'Law' in Global Administrative Law: A Reply to Benedict Kingsbury' (2009) 20 *European Journal of International Law* 985–95.

Spencer, JR, 'The UK and EU Criminal Law: Should we be Leading, Following or Abstaining?' in V Mitsilegas, P Alldridge and L Cheliotis (eds), *Globalisation, Criminal Law and Criminal Justice. Theoretical, Comparative and Transnational Perspectives* (Oxford, Hart Publishing, 2015) 135–52.

Steinbach, A, 'The Lisbon Judgment of the German Federal Constitutional Court—New Guidance on the Limits of European Integration?' (2010) 11 *German Law Journal* 367–90.

Sullivan, G, 'Transnational Legal Assemblages and Global Security Law: Topologies and Temporalities of the List' (2014) 15 *Transnational Legal Theory* 81–127.

Sullivan, G and M de Goede, 'Between Law and the Exception: the UN 1267 Ombudsperson as a Hybrid Model of Legal Expertise' (2013) 26 *Leiden Journal of International Law* 833–54.

Suominen, A, 'The Past, Present and the Future of Eurojust' (2008) 15 *Maastricht Journal of European and Comparative Law* 217–34.

Szasz, PC, 'The Security Council Starts Legislating' (2002) 96 *American Journal of International Law* 901–5.

Talmon, S, 'The Security Council as World Legislature' (2005) 99 *American Journal of International Law* 175–93.

Tamanaha, BZ, *On the Rule of Law. History, Politics, Theory* (Cambridge, Cambridge University Press, 2004).

Thwaites, N, 'Eurojust autre brique dans l'édifice de la coopération judiciaire en matière pénale ou solide mortier?' (2003) *Revue de science criminelle et de droit pénal comparé* 45–61.

Tonry, M, '"Rebalancing the Criminal Justice System in favour of the Victim": the Costly Consequences of Populist Rhetoric' in A Bottoms and JV Roberts (eds), *Hearing the Victim. Adversarial Justice, Crime Victims and the State* (Cullompton, Willan, 2010) 72–103.

Torres Pérez, A, '*Melloni* in Three Acts: From Dialogue to Monologue' (2014) 10 *European Constitutional Law Review* 308–31.

Tricot, J, 'Observations Critiques sur la Proposition de Règlement portant Création du Parquet Européen' in G Giudicelli-Delage, S Manacorda and J Tricot (eds), *Le Contrôle Judiciaire du Parquet Européen. Nécessité, Modèles, Enjeux*, Collection de l'UMR de Droit Comparé de Paris (Université Paris 1), vol 37 (Société de Législation Comparée, 2015) 155–74.

Tridimas, T, *The General Principles of EU Law*, 2nd edn (Oxford, Oxford University Press, 2006).

_____, 'Terrorism and the ECJ: Empowerment and Democracy in the EC Legal Order' (2009) 34 *European Law Review* 103–26.

Van Bockel, B, *The Ne Bis In Idem Principle in EU Law* (Alphen aan den Rijn, Kluwer Law International, 2010).

van den Herik, LJ, 'Peripheral Hegemony in the Quest to Ensure Security Council Accountability for its Individualized UN Sanctions Regimes' (2014) 19 *Journal of Conflict and Security Law* 427–49.

van den Wyngaert, C and G Stessens, 'The International *Non Bis In Idem* Principle: Resolving Some of the Unanswered Questions' (1999) 48 *International and Comparative Law Quarterly* 779–804.

van der Aa, S and J Ouwerkerk, 'The European Protection Order: No Time to Waste or a Waste of Time?' (2011) 19 *European Journal of Crime, Criminal Law and Criminal Justice* 267–87.

Van Elsuwege, P, 'The Adoption of "Targeted Sanctions" and the Potential for Inter-institutional Litigation after Lisbon' (2011) 7 *Journal of Contemporary European Research* 488–99.

van Tiggelen, G, A Weyembergh and L Surano (eds), *The Future of Mutual Recognition in Criminal Matters* (Bruxelles, Éditions de l'Université de Bruxelles, 2009).

Vergés Bausili, A, *Rethinking the Methods of Dividing and Exercising Powers in the EU: Reforming Subsidiarity and National Parliaments*, Jean Monnet Working Paper 9/02, NYU School of Law.

Vervaele, J, 'European Territoriality and Jurisdiction: The Protection of the EU's Financial Interests in Its Horizontal and Vertical (EPPO) Dimension' in M Luchtman (ed), *Choice of Forum in Cooperation Against EU Financial Crime* (The Hague, Eleven International Publishing, 2013) 167–84.

_____, '*Ne Bis In Idem*: Towards a Transnational Constitutional Principle in the EU?' (2013) 9 *Utrecht Law Review* 211–29.

Vogel, J, 'Introduction to the Ruling of the Higher Regional Court of Stuttgart of 25 February 2010—The Proportionality of a European Arrest Warrant' (2010) 1, *New Journal of European Criminal Law* 145–52.

_____ and J Spencer, 'Proportionality and the European Arrest Warrant' [2010] *Criminal Law Review* 474–82.

von Bogdandy, A and M Ioannidis, 'Systemic Deficiency in the Rule of Law: What it is, what has been done, what can be done' (2014) 51 *Common Market Law Review* 59–96.

Walker, N, 'The Problem of Trust in an Enlarged Area of Freedom, Security and Justice: A Conceptual Analysis' in M Anderson and J Apap (eds), *Police and Justice Co-operation and the New European Borders* (The Hague, Kluwer Law International, 2002) 19–34.

Wasmeier, M, '*Ne bis in idem* and the Enforcement Condition: Balancing Freedom, Security and Justice?' (2014) 4 *New Journal of European Criminal Law* 534–55.

_____, 'The Choice of Forum by the European Public Prosecutor' in LH Erkelens, AWH Meij and M Pawlik (eds), *The European Public Prosecutor's Office. An Extended Arm or a Two-Headed Dragon?* (The Hague, Asser Press/Springer, 2015) 139–64.

Weyembergh, A, 'An Overall Analysis of the Proposal for a Regulation on Eurojust' [2013] 4 *Eucrim* 127–31.

_____ and I Armada, 'The Principle of ne bis in idem in Europe's Area of Freedom, Security and Justice' in V Mitsilegas, M Bergström and T Konstadinides (eds), *Research Handbook on EU Criminal Law* (Cheltenham, Edward Elgar, March 2016).

White, S, 'Towards a *Decentralised* European Public Prosecutor's Office?' (2013) 4 *New Journal of European Criminal Law* 22–39.

Williams, A, 'Promoting Justice after Lisbon: Groundwork for a New Philosophy of EU Law' (2010) 30 *Oxford Journal of Legal Studies* 663–93.

Zimmermann, F, 'Choice of Forum and Choice of Law under the Future Regulation on the Establishment of a European Public Prosecutor's Office' in P Asp (ed), *The European Public Prosecutor's Office—Legal and Criminal Policy Perspectives* (Stifelsen Skrifter Utgivna av Juridiska Fakulteten vid Stockholms Universitet, 2015) 156–77.

INDEX

www.ingramcontent.com/pod-product-compliance
Lightning Source LLC
Chambersburg PA
CBHW060144280326
41932CB00012B/1632